BENEATH DARKENING CLOUDS

A novel

Copyright © Juliane Weber 2022

All rights reserved. This book or any portion thereof may not be reproduced or used in any manner whatsoever without the express written permission of the publisher, except for the use of brief quotations in a book review.

Portions of this book are works of fiction. Any references to historical events, real people, or real places are used fictitiously. Other names, characters, places and events are products of the author's imagination, and any resemblances to actual events or places or persons, living or dead, are entirely coincidental.

ISBN 979-8-8483-0982-9

Cover design by White Rabbit Arts

www.julianeweber.com

For my children, who think the world of me.

Ireland
Spring 1845

Prologue

"ALANNAH."

I turned toward my brother, echoing the smile I heard in Kieran's voice as I held my freezing hand behind my back. A white missile flew in my direction, but I nimbly ducked out of the way. With a grin I released my own snowball, hitting Kieran high in the chest, making a surprised expression appear on his face as snow spattered his collar and sprinkled his curly brown hair. I laughed but stopped suddenly as Kieran slumped down onto his knees, raising his hands to his throat, a look of horror blooming on his face.

With the slow certainty of death, blood started pouring out between his fingers, dripping down his hands onto the snow, puckering the pristine white surface with red blotches.

Kieran toppled backwards and I screamed. I tried to run away but couldn't move, a heavy weight keeping me locked in place as my eyes returned over and over again to Kieran's lifeless form. My feet scrabbled on the floor, and I screamed again, trying to push against the force that was keeping me pinned to the ground.

"Scream all you want, lassie, nobody will hear you."

The beady eyes above me bored into mine, black above a rat-like nose, the man's breath hot on my cheek as he pressed me down under him.

"Doyle." The single word escaped my trembling lips.

"Never seen a ghost before, have you?" he asked with a nasty laugh as he ran a sweaty palm up my leg, trying to push my skirt up above my hips.

I thrashed and kicked, trying to dislodge his unwelcome embrace, but froze as one hand rose slowly to my neck, pressing the naked blade of a knife against my throat.

I opened my eyes with a jerk, my heart pounding wildly as I kicked off the blankets that had become tangled around my legs. Staring unseeing at the ceiling, the memory of the nightmare at last started to recede, although the reality of its impact remained unchanged.

I swallowed heavily and clenched my hands into fists.

Slowly, very slowly, I felt my fear drain away, fear of the man I had thought safely dead, who had come upon me unawares and been only moments away from taking my life—as he'd taken my brother's not too long before.

I turned on my pillow, breathing heavily. Across from me, Quin was breathing heavily, too, his face suffused in the blissful contentment of a deep and untroubled sleep. I frowned, feeling momentarily irritated that my husband hadn't noticed I was experiencing no such contentment. As if in response to this uncharitable thought, a vision of Quin flashed across my mind—face contorted with rage as he lifted Doyle off his feet and slammed him against the wall, one hand closing around his throat in an inexorable grip of vengeful death.

I reached my own hand slowly toward Quin and stroked his cheek. His eyes opened briefly, a flash of green in the dawning light, and he gave me a dreamy smile, stretching out an arm and gathering me to him.

I snuggled closer to his comforting warmth and at last drifted off to sleep once more.

1.

"WELCOME TO GLASLEARG, Mr Dunne."

"Thank you, Mr Williams...sir," came the soft response from the slight, mouse-like man who stood in front of Quin. He gave a brief bow, his weather-beaten, bewhiskered face looking solemn.

"I'm glad to have you here at last."

The man threw him a startled glance and Quin could have kicked himself. Dunne had been hired as Glaslearg's new overseer—a role he'd meant to take on more than a year earlier, not long after Quin had come to Ireland from England to manage the estate himself.

"I hope you will find everything to your satisfaction," Quin said quickly to cover up his embarrassment. For the reason Dunne had not appeared for his duties all those months ago was that he'd managed to get himself arrested instead—an intriguing occurrence, no doubt, but not one that should necessarily be discussed on the man's very first day of employment.

Dunne straightened his shoulders and inclined his head. "I'm sure I will, sir." He looked at Quin expectantly, like a small dog eager to please its master. His round eyes and small nose enhanced the effect, reminding Quin of the man's unannounced arrival on his doorstep a few months ago, begging to be hired despite his previous misadventures.

Quin smiled, making Dunne give him a shy smile in return. Rather taken by Dunne's contrite manner, Quin had agreed, quite sure the man would indeed show up at the estate the second time round. Nevertheless, he'd breathed a sigh of relief when Dunne's arrival was announced by Denis, the elderly butler, a little earlier.

"I have had a room prepared for your use, as promised," he said to his new employee.

"Thank you, sir, that's most kind of you."

Quin waved away his thanks. "As overseer of the estate, you'll need a place to live.—I shall have a cottage built on the grounds for your use as soon as I'm able, but in the meantime, please consider the manor house your home."

Dunne inclined his head toward Quin in thanks, looking to be at a loss for words. The gesture quite surprised Quin and he wondered what conditions had been like for the man at his previous place of work for him to appear so grateful for the simple welcome he'd received at Glaslearg. Then again, Dunne *had* felt the need to lay into his former employer with his fists, which had resulted in the timid-looking overseer being arrested and imprisoned for drunken assault.

"I shall ask some of my staff to assist you in bringing your belongings into the house," Quin continued as a host of unanswered questions about the incident swirled through his head. "Once you have settled into your new lodgings, you may feel free to join Mrs Williams and myself in the dining room for supper." Seeing the look of bewilderment that started blooming on Dunne's face at the suggestion, Quin added, "Or you may take your supper in the kitchen, as you please."

"Thank you, sir." Dunne's ears were turning slightly pink—in embarrassment or pleasure, Quin wasn't entirely sure—as he bobbed a brief bow. Waiting for Quin's nod of approval, the man scuttled into the entrance hall and through the front door, likely heading toward the stable to start unloading his things.

Quin smiled after him for a moment before leaving the reception room himself. In the entrance hall, he caught sight of Finnian as he disappeared in the direction of the kitchen. Although the youth was referred to as the hall boy, Glaslearg hardly had enough staff to merit such a position—the estate having been substantially understaffed and otherwise neglected upon Quin's arrival. Finnian did, however, usually end up doing the most menial of tasks and so the name had stuck.

Quin followed him into the steamy confines of the kitchen, sniffing appreciatively at the smells emanating from the hearth. He raised his brows in surprise, though, when he saw that Finnian was seated on one of the benches and being tended to by Mrs O'Sullivan, the cook, for what looked like the beginnings of a black eye, with the maid Mary Murphy hovering anxiously around the two of them.

"And what's happened to you then?" Quin asked bluntly, before remembering his manners and greeting the women a little more pleasantly. Finnian glanced up at him with one half-swollen eye before looking back down at his knobbly knees while chewing industriously on whatever Mrs O'Sullivan had given him as a restorative.

"Naught but a wee accident, sir," the cook said, shaking her head. "Boys..." She shrugged, making her ample bosom heave.

"I see." Quin wondered at what age boys were considered men. Finnian must be about eighteen by now, he reckoned, giving the youngster a studious look.

Unable to come to his own defence with his full mouth, Finnian looked at Quin uncomfortably while his cheeks blazed brightly, long gangly arms fidgeting in front of him as he continued to chew energetically. "Um, Finnian," Quin addressed him as he finally swallowed the mouthful of food, his Adam's apple bobbing along his skinny throat, "please be kind enough to assist Mr Dunne in taking his things up to his room. Ask John for his help if you need it," Quin added, referring to the younger of the estate's two grooms.

"Yes, sir." Finnian nodded as he scrambled up from the bench and hurried out of the room.

Quin followed more leisurely behind him, chuckling to himself as he inclined his head toward Mary and Mrs O'Sullivan as he left. He made his way across the entrance hall to the study, where he spent the rest of the afternoon bringing his record books up to date, including making a note to follow up on the building materials he'd ordered for Mr Dunne's house.

All of Glaslearg's previous overseers had stayed in the manor itself, as Quin's father, The Baron Williams of Wadlow, who had bought the estate almost twenty years before, had lived in England without any intention of coming to Ireland himself; however, the estate now belonged to Quin, and he and Alannah were living in the house, with every intention of staying there. Quin had thus thought it better to provide Mr Dunne with separate lodging. Although the overseer's house would be a little larger, as befitted his position on the estate, it would be built in essentially the same style as Glaslearg's tenants' new homes. Over the past two years or so Quin had been in Ireland, he had organised and overseen the building of almost fifty sturdy stone cottages to replace the tenants' ghastly mud hovels—gloomy one-roomed constructions with straw-covered earthen floors without the benefit of even a single window or chimney to make them more habitable.

"Hmph," Quin grumbled, pleased that his tenants at least were better off than the thousands upon thousands of peasants across Ireland who continued to live in squalor, struggling to make ends meet under the miserable circumstances they had been born to. It was hardly a wonder the land continued to be plagued with unrest, considering the ever-increasing contrast between the rich few and the plentiful poor—a fact that could no doubt be laid at the feet of the English, Quin mused. Centuries of oppression and poor land management by their English conquerors had left Irish commoners with little to call their own, and even less chance of improvement.

Engrossed in his work and his wandering thoughts, Quin was alerted to the hour some time later by the chiming of the longcase clock in the drawing room across the hall. Startled to find it was already suppertime, Quin closed the book in front of him and replaced it on the shelf, realising suddenly he was quite hungry indeed as he made his way through the study door.

"Ooof," he exclaimed in some startlement, having collided with his valet, Rupert, who had travelled with him to Ireland from London. At the moment, Rupert seemed to be in a great hurry to get somewhere, and Quin grabbed him by the arms to stop him from falling.

"I'm so sorry sir!" Rupert cried, in evident distress as he righted himself.

Quin brushed off his apology. "And where are you off to in such a hurry?"

"I'm just…aahh…I mean…um."

"Are you not hungry?" Quin interrupted Rupert's stammering. Whatever his valet was up to, it didn't seem to be something he wished to share with his employer.

"Oh, no, sir. I've already eaten."

"Of course you have." Quin smiled, aware of Rupert's ravenous appetite.

The staff usually ate amongst themselves in the kitchen—the cosy confines of which at times appealed to Alannah and Quin as much as to the servants. Today though, they would be eating in the dining room. Rupert glanced toward the dining room door, as if waiting for Quin to finally make his way there so he could go about his business. He looked back at Quin expectantly, round eyes blinking above his round cheeks. Glancing at Quin's shirt, though, he started brushing energetically at the sleave, evidently to remove an imagined smudge of dirt.

Quin was quite sure there was nothing amiss with his wardrobe, but he let his valet do as he liked. Catching sight of Rupert's hand, he saw that the knuckles looked a little red and swollen. Seeing the direction of Quin's gaze, Rupert stopped his ministrations and dropped his hands, hiding the bruised one behind the other, making Quin cock his head in interest.

"Will you be needing me, sir?" Rupert asked, his cheeks going pink. Clearly, he had no intention of telling Quin what had happened to his hand.

Quin shrugged. It was none of his business. Although he was his employer, Quin tried to give his valet as much freedom as he might, hoping the young man would come to him if he got himself into any trouble—and that he had enough sense to avoid it in the first place.

"No, thank you, Rupert. You go ahead and have yourself a pleasant evening."

"Thank you, sir." Rupert gave Quin a brief bow before rushing off.

Quin shook his head slowly as he looked after his valet, before turning toward the dining room once more. Before he'd taken another step, Alannah appeared at the top of the staircase, smiling as she came down to join him. He offered her his arm, which she took with a twinkle in her deep blue eyes. He smiled appreciatively in return, letting his gaze caress her sleek black hair and ivory skin, counting himself very lucky to have such a beautiful wife.

Reaching the dining room, Quin saw that Mrs O'Sullivan had included a place for Mr Dunne and had already laid the food out for them. Dunne himself, though, was nowhere in sight. Nonetheless, Quin settled down to his meal. He'd done his best to make the man feel welcome, the rest would be up to Dunne himself.

Chewing contentedly a few minutes later, a gentle throat-clearing at the door caught his attention. Quin looked up from his plate and his eyes fell on his new overseer, who was hovering at the threshold, looking a little uncertain.

"Mr Dunne," Quin greeted him warmly after he'd hastily swallowed the food in his mouth. "Do come join us." He nodded his head, inviting the slight man into the room as Alannah smiled at him in greeting.

"Thank you, sir." Dunne gave a small bow and strode into the room. "Ma'am." He inclined his head toward Alannah before holding it up stiffly as he made his way to the place prepared for him. His eyes seemed to dart back and forth a little uncertainly, Quin noticed.

"Please." Quin waved his hand toward the laden table. "Do help yourself to anything you might like."

"Thank you," Dunne said once more, reaching tentatively toward one of the platters.

"Wine, sir?"

Dunne turned in some startlement toward Margaret the maid, who'd appeared behind him, looking a little flustered herself.

"Oh…no…no, thank you." Dunne shook his head, making Alannah give him a curious look.

Margaret inclined her head toward Dunne before leaving the room, a small frown on her face.

"Have you settled into your new apartments, Mr Dunne?" Quin asked pleasantly.

"I have, sir," Dunne answered between mouthfuls. "Your welcome of me has been most kind…"

Quin waved away his thanks. "Not at all, Mr Dunne. It's important to me to see my staff and tenants well taken care of." He paused briefly as a small smile grew on his lips. "My mother used to say that happy workers are more likely to give freely of their time and efforts. So, you see, I'm really being entirely selfish in my actions."

Dunne gave a startled laugh at Quin's jest, before looking from him to Alannah in some uncertainty at its meaning. Seeing the two of them smiling, the overseer visibly relaxed, letting his features slide into a more natural expression of contentment as he continued with his meal. He remained largely silent throughout, though, answering direct questions readily enough but offering very little in the way of conversation himself.

Quin shrugged. The man would likely start to feel more comfortable around them with time.

2.

"OUCH!"

"Oh, I'm so sorry mistress, I truly am!"

I waved my hand at Margaret's apology. She was assisting me in adjusting one of my gowns and had stabbed me rather painfully in my side with a pin.

"It's nothing, Margaret." I smiled at the small woman, who was looking rather anxious.

She smiled weakly in return before continuing with her work, neatly—and a little violently, I noted—jabbing the pin through the fabric. As she reached for another pin her hand knocked against the box of sewing paraphernalia, throwing it to the floor, sending ribbons, spools of thread and buttons flying across the floor.

"Oh dear," I said, watching a spool of yarn unravel itself all the way to the door.

"What have I done?" Margaret wailed, throwing her hands up into the air, before dropping down to her knees and attempting to scrape the mess into a pile.

"Ouch!" she cried suddenly, sitting back on her heels and lifting her hand, where I could see a straight silver pin neatly embedded in the tip of her index finger. She pulled it out, making a little blood swell to the surface of the small puncture wound.

"Oh no," she exclaimed and burst into tears.

I blinked, rather surprised at her reaction. Although I knew Margaret to be a sensitive woman, I didn't think the current situation merited quite such hysterics.

"There, there," I said soothingly to the top of her capped head, patting the little maid on her narrow back with one hand while reaching for a handkerchief with the other. I handed it to her, and she used it to dab her eyes. I looked around and found a scrap of fabric that I wound around her bleeding finger before coaxing her off the floor and onto the side of the bed.

"It's only a little mess, Margaret, no reason to be upset." I squeezed her hand in reassurance, but she shook her head, her face wet with tears.

"No, no," she moaned as a fresh flood escaped her reddening eyes. "It's more than a little mess."

"Now, now, we'll have this cleaned up in no time," I said confidently, attempting to get up from next to her. She clung to my hand, though, making me sit back down on the coverlet.

I narrowed my eyes at her, feeling some concern. There was definitely more bothering her than a few scattered sewing implements.

"What is it, Margaret?" I asked softly, turning to face her, laying a hand on her arm.

She looked down, sniffing repeatedly while wringing her hands.

"I...I'm..." She paused, her lower lip wobbling slightly as a fresh onslaught of tears threatened. "I'm...I'm with child, mistress," she finally whispered, not looking at me as the tears overflowed and ran down her cheeks.

My heart gave a sudden, solid thump. "Oh," I managed, mechanically patting her arm as I attempted to push aside my own feelings. I looked more closely at her. Although Margaret had worked for my family for many years, she was about my own age, in her mid-twenties. From what she'd told me it was clear she was far from celibate, so this was hardly unexpected. Nevertheless, it came as a bit of a shock—not least of all because her unwanted pregnancy reminded me rather painfully of the fact that I was not pregnant myself.

"Oh, Aoife is going to kill me," she cried, cutting in on my thoughts, rocking slowly back and forth as she hugged herself. She'd pronounced the name Ee-fa, and I knew she was referring to Mrs O'Sullivan, our cook and head staff member.

"Nonsense," I countered immediately. Although Mrs O'Sullivan could be a little stern and expected a degree of professionalism from the other servants, I had never known her to be unfeeling. And while some reservations naturally existed between employees and their employer, I would have hoped for her to realise Margaret was in no danger of being mistreated by us, least of all by me, who'd known her for much of my life and thought of her as a friend.

Margaret shook her head miserably as her tears continued to flow, her face looking blotchy and her eyes looking swollen.

"Oh...what will I do?"

"Get married, of course," I answered practically.

"Married?" She seemed shocked at the suggestion.

"Of course!" I gave her a stern look. "Why not?"

"Because...because...well because I don't love him," she sputtered, looking dejectedly down at her lap.

"That hardly seems important right now, does it?" I wrinkled my brow, starting to feel just a little bit annoyed.

"Well...well I suppose not." She was silent for a moment before turning her red-rimmed eyes toward me once more. "Oh, mistress, I truly am sorry."

"You needn't apologise to me," I countered, shaking my head.

"But...you see...I tried...I mean...I wanted to..." Margaret gave up and looked pointedly down at my abdomen.

I froze, understanding immediately what she meant.

For the fact that I had no children of my own and was not currently pregnant myself was not due to a lack of trying on my part—or on Quin's—but rather because I had as yet been unable to *stay* pregnant. I had experienced a miscarriage over a year ago, shortly after my brother had been murdered. Among all the horrors surrounding that dreadful event, I hadn't been entirely sure what was happening to me then. Unfortunately, I was more familiar with the process now, having had the same thing happen again not too long before.

And with each week that passed without new life stirring within me it felt like little parts of my soul were being ripped out of my body instead.

I took a deep breath. "I see," I said, attempting a neutral tone. "Clearly it didn't work." I paused for a moment, unsure what to say. "Um...How far along are you?" I finally asked, deciding I didn't need to know the details of how she'd tried to rid herself of the child.

Margaret looked down, patting her stomach. "Almost four months."

"Four months?" I exclaimed in surprise, looking at her more closely. It was hard to tell under the layers of skirts and petticoats and with the apron tied around her waist, but was there a small swelling visible? I looked at her face. Her cheeks did appear a little more rounded but still, I would have expected something more obvious after four months.

Then again, what did I know about such things?

I cleared my throat and turned toward Margaret once more. "So what are you going to do?" I asked, trying for casualness. Before she could answer, though, I blurted, "Who's the father?"—having suddenly thought of the question and wondering why it had taken me so long.

"Oh," Margaret responded in some surprise. "It's…um…it's John."

I raised my brows. "John, the groom?"

"Yes." Margaret nodded and looked back down at her lap.

"I see." We were both quiet for a moment. "Then I guess you'll have to marry John," I finally said with a shrug. Although he tended to be fairly quiet, the groom seemed to be a nice enough man. I thought he was rather a lot older than Margaret but at least he was not already married to someone else—besides, she'd found him appealing enough to get herself into this predicament in the first place so I presumed she would eventually resign herself to her fate. "Does he know?" I asked abruptly, turning toward Margaret and looking down at her midsection.

She shook her head, looking rather dejected.

"Oh dear." I patted her hand. "Then this will all come as rather a shock to poor John." Unbeknownst to him he would soon be encumbered with a wife and baby to take care of. I laughed softly, feeling a little sorry for the man.

Margaret gave me a brief smile in return, looking somewhat relieved at last. She took a deep breath. "Are you going to tell him, mistress, or should I?" she asked, with a glint of humour flashing across her tear-streaked face.

I smiled back at her. They would be alright, I thought, taking Margaret's hand and giving it a gentle squeeze.

AFTER MARGARET HAD left to tell her unsuspecting soon-to-be husband of his luck I went down to the study. Thinking about Margaret and her predicament made me contemplate Glaslearg's servants and tenants. Although Quin and I did our best to make our employees and the other families who lived on the estate feel comfortable, I wondered if perhaps there was more that we could do.

What more, exactly, I wasn't sure.

We provided assistance where we could and tried to be fair in all our dealings with those who depended on us, taking an active interest in everyone's welfare. And while there naturally remained a certain distance, a degree of friendship had developed as we went about our daily lives on the estate, working closely together—so much so that Quin and I had invited the servants and tenants to our wedding feast, to the utter horror of other members of the gentry.

I smiled at the memory, knowing I wouldn't have wanted it any other way.

I had grown up on a small estate with few staff members, who had always been an integral part of my life. It was natural for me to care for those around me. And despite his aristocratic roots, Quin felt much the same. His mother had always concerned herself with the less fortunate—a trait that had rubbed off on her son. In fact, Quin's concern for the Irish people was one of the things that had endeared him to me from the start.

Without question, the two of us belonged to the dismally small group of Irish landowners who thought of their tenants as people—not just the income they generated by paying their rent. And yet, despite all our efforts, even the tenants on Glaslearg remained stuck in a cycle of poverty their children were likely to inherit.

While oppressive, the thought suddenly gave me pause. For perhaps, there *was* something else we could do to help—or rather, that *I* could do. I looked outside the window as the idea took shape. The sky was grey and brooding, but the view did nothing to impair my growing excitement.

I could teach them, I thought with conviction, nodding to myself. I could teach them to read and write, not to mention to speak English.

Although most Irish people could understand and speak some English—their English conquerors having gone to considerable trouble over several centuries to civilise the barbaric Gaelic-speaking natives—many still had only a minimal grasp of the language. Particularly among a large number of Ireland's poor peasants, Gaelic was still the preferred tongue, some speaking it exclusively.

English was the language of the future, though, and if the tenants wanted a better life for themselves and their children, they had to learn English.

I could teach them that, I decided, determining to give lessons to anyone who was interested. I'd already been teaching Mary Murphy, a tenant who was now working in the manor house as a maid, and a few other women who'd shown an interest based on her success.

But I needed to teach the children, I thought.

Although there were numerous schools to be found across Ireland, including some that also taught girls, such education was mostly aimed at the middle classes. Upper class children were often tutored privately at home—as my brother and I had been—or were sent to expensive boarding schools in continental Europe.

There were no provisions for the children of the poor.

"I will teach them," I said out loud, lifting my head in conviction lest anyone dare to stop me.

"Teach whom?"

I turned toward Quin, who'd stuck his head through the study door, which I tended to leave ajar while working there.

"The tenants' children," I responded proudly as he came into the room.

He cocked his head.

"If they are to have a better life than their parents, they need to be educated," I insisted.

Quin wrinkled his brow. "It will still be exceedingly difficult for any of them to break out of this cycle of poverty." He moved his head contemplatively from side to side. Despite the fact that I'd just been thinking the same thing, I narrowed my eyes at him. "But of course, a good basic education won't hurt their chances," he said quickly.

I smoothed out my brow, accepting this dubious statement as support—I was far too excited about my idea to let anyone spoil it. "Perhaps I can teach them up here in the drawing room.—Or do you think they'd feel more comfortable in one of their own cottages?" I looked questioningly toward Quin.

"Why don't you just ask them?" he suggested. "And find out how many would send their children to you in the first place."

"Hm...I hadn't thought anyone might object."

"It's only because to you the benefits of an education are obvious. These people here though..." he trailed off, spreading his hands.

"I suppose..." I agreed slowly.

Ireland's peasants worked mostly to see their families fed. Material possessions were few and the means of acquiring any wealth even fewer. They probably could not envisage a much brighter future, even for their own children, because what they were living was all they knew. While they no doubt wished for their lives to be easier, they were more likely to see the benefits of leaving Ireland altogether and starting anew elsewhere—as indeed many people were doing—rather than grasping the hypothetical benefits of learning to read and write or learn a different language.

"Well, all I can do is try." I shrugged, determining to stick to my resolve, convinced—as my father had been—that an education was never wasted.

"I think it's a wonderful idea," Quin said with a smile.

I smiled back at him before asking, "What are you doing here?" It was not yet noon and Quin had told me he and our new overseer would likely be out all day, intending to assist with the last of the spring planting.

"I came to fetch ink and paper to make a list of the conacre leasings," he explained, reaching for the necessary implements. "In our haste this morning, neither Mr Dunne nor I thought to pack them."

"I see."

"It's mostly the same people as last year but I do like to keep proper records of everything."

"Of course," I agreed, remembering the mess that had greeted Quin upon his arrival at the estate almost two years before. He had discovered that the steward who'd meant to run the estate according to his father's wishes had charged poor peasants exorbitant prices to lease conacre land—tiny patches of farmland labourers used to grow potatoes, their staple diet—without telling Quin or his father about it or handing over the money thus earned.

It had required considerable effort to find out any more than that, though, as the overseer had kept no record of who had actually leased which patch, nor which peasants had already paid the rent by the time Quin came to take over the estate. Although neither Quin nor I entirely approved of the conacre system—it being open to exploitation—thousands of landless labourers across

Ireland depended upon it for their survival, and those who'd rented conacre on Quin's land before had come back again this season. We could hardly send them away. The best we could do was to offer them a fair price and hope the land yielded a decent crop.

"Alright, I'm off again." Quin stuffed the writing material into a satchel. He grinned at me, before leaning down and briefly kissing my forehead. I looked after him as he made his way out of the study to return to his business with Mr Dunne.

The overseer had been at Glaslearg for about a week now. Our newest employee had thrown himself into his duties with alacrity since his arrival, showing no signs of his previous trouble with the law. In the short time he'd been at Glaslearg, Dunne had trudged from one end of the estate to the other, had visited the tenants on their small plots of land, and had conversed extensively with Quin and me.

I smiled, thinking about how startled Dunne had seemed when he'd first realised he'd be expected to discuss the estate's business with a woman. He'd looked at me with big eyes when Quin had asked me to join the two of them in the study. But just as I'd been about to utter a stern word or two, he'd blinked and shaken his head, before turning toward me with features that seemed entirely attentive. He'd listened respectfully to all I'd had to say, and nothing in his behaviour since had suggested an attitude that was anything to the contrary. And so, I had come to accept his acceptance of me.

The favourable impression I'd had of him when I'd met Dunne for the first time the previous year had grown into a genuine liking for the man. While he tended to be rather quiet, I'd come to find that his comments were honest in their simplicity. He didn't embellish anything to his advantage or fill moments of silence with trivial nonsense for the pleasure of hearing his own voice. Instead, he listened when spoken to and answered simply and truthfully when asked a question, characteristics I found compelling, even if he gave little of himself away in the process.

I knew he must have a story to tell about his past but respected his reluctance to talk about it. It was none of my business, after all, and he was under no obligation to tell me anything if he didn't want to. He did seem to enjoy the company Quin and I offered, though, having joined us regularly for his meals after his first cautious foray to our dining table. Quin had even managed to coax him into accompanying us to the drawing room after supper once or twice, there to let the last of the day's tensions fade away.

As it turned out several hours later, this particular day had evidently been filled to bursting with such tensions. Not only did the overseer join us again for supper after he and Quin had arrived at the estate looking exhausted, but he immediately agreed to Quin's invitation to retire to the drawing room thereafter. Quin himself headed straight toward the whiskey decanter as soon as we got there. I raised one brow in his direction, but he shrugged good-naturedly. Although they were tired, they were evidently pleased with the progress they'd made that day.

Quin handed me a glass containing a generous portion of amber liquid before turning toward Dunne with the filled tumbler he held in his other hand. I looked at Quin in some surprise. To my knowledge, Dunne had consumed no alcohol since he'd come to Glaslearg, declining all offers of wine and other spirits at the dinner table and beyond.

Knowing what I did about his past, I wondered about the reasons for his abstinence. Might he be worried about repeating the drunken behaviour that had seen him arrested?

I leaned forward inconspicuously to watch his reaction. Dunne looked a little surprised himself at Quin's offer—his demeanour reminding me once more of the startled mouse he so resembled—but after a slight moment's hesitation he took the proffered drink with a nod of thanks, sipping slowly as he settled into his chair. He seemed entirely in control of himself at present but, perhaps, once he'd had a few more sips...

I would watch him closely, I decided, for any signs of a violent outburst.

I glanced toward Quin and was startled to find he was watching me with a look of amusement on his face. I narrowed my eyes at him suspiciously, making him break into a wide smile. I darted a quick glance toward Dunne and his tumbler of whiskey, raising both brows emphatically when I looked back at Quin. He only shrugged, though, the smile still on his face. I exhaled rather forcefully through my nose, making Dunne look up at me in some surprise, while Quin emitted a short laugh.

"Ah, Mr Dunne," I said to cover up my embarrassment. I could feel my cheeks start to blaze but ignored them as I turned toward the overseer, who was looking slightly alarmed at my peculiar behaviour. "Have you found everything at Glaslearg to be to your liking thus far?" The question was more for the purposes of having something to say rather than any particular concerns for his wellbeing—he had expressed himself more than content on numerous occasions, after all.

Dunne, though, appeared to take the question seriously. "Oh, yes, ma'am," he answered solemnly, his face taking on an anxious expression as he looked at me. "Mr Williams and yourself have been most kind to me, ma'am, most kind." He nodded vigorously as he leaned toward me in his chair, his brows knitted together above beseeching brown eyes.

"That's good, Mr Dunne," I said with some gravity, suppressing a laugh at his overly earnest expression but allowing myself to smile at him. "Please do let us know if you require anything else, though."

"Thank you for the kind offer, ma'am, but I'm sure I won't be needing anything else." He shook his head slowly back and forth, swirling his remaining whiskey absently around his glass. "Glaslearg is already more home to me than Thompson's ever was," he added softly, his face taking on a faraway look.

I widened my eyes slightly in surprise at this statement. Although he'd never mentioned it in my hearing before, I knew Dunne was referring to the estate he'd been working on before his arrest, with the owner of said estate—Mr Thompson, I presumed—being the man Dunne had assaulted in a drunken rage. I glanced quickly at Quin, who raised his brows and cocked his head in response to my curious look. Turning his attention back to Dunne, Quin watched him for a moment longer, before leaning toward the overseer with a solemn expression on his face.

"Was the man so unpleasant then?" he asked in a gentle voice.

Dunne raised his head in some startlement, looking at Quin in confusion at his question. I wondered if the man even realised he'd spoken aloud a few minutes before.

There was a long pause.

"He…" Dunne finally started in some hesitation. "Yes," he said shortly. "Yes, he was."

He looked back down at his whiskey glass for a moment, as if assessing it, before lifting it to his mouth in sudden determination and draining the remaining contents in a single gulp. Coming up for air, he started coughing explosively, his eyes watering with the effort as he sputtered helplessly for a minute or two. When he had at last recovered, he placed the empty tumbler on the tabletop with a dull thump, shaking his head as he did so.

"I'm not in the habit of drinking such strong spirits," he croaked through his raw throat as he wiped his eyes.

"Oh?" I exclaimed without thinking, lifting my brows in surprise, before suddenly realising my outburst had been anything but tactful. "I'm sorry, Mr Dunne," I murmured, aghast. "I didn't mean to imply..." My cheeks were burning, and I swallowed heavily in embarrassment but the overseer himself came to my rescue.

He waved away my attempted apology. "It's hardly surprising for you to think so...considering..."

"Ah..." I stammered, not sure how to respond. I cleared my throat and glanced at Quin, who appeared to be finding my discomfort vastly entertaining. I scowled at him, making him grin at me. "Even so, Mr Dunne"—I turned back toward the man—"I had no right to pass judgement on your personal affairs. I do apologise."

He shrugged a little uncomfortably at my close scrutiny but inclined his head toward me in acceptance. Quickly, though, he dropped his eyes, making me do the same as an awkward silence descended on the room.

"So you're not in the habit of drinking strong spirits, Mr Dunne?"

My head snapped up at Quin's voice and I gaped at him in disbelief at what he'd asked. He raised his brows and lifted one shoulder as if to suggest his question had been entirely appropriate. I felt heat rising in my cheeks once more, this time in embarrassment for Quin, not myself.

"Um..." Dunne stuttered, making me cringe in discomfort for him. I turned to Quin once more, narrowing my eyes at him in irritation. He ignored me, though, looking at Dunne with interest.

"I am not," the man said shortly, not looking at either of us. He paused for a moment, compressing his lips briefly. "I find that spirits...alter the senses," he continued slowly. "An effect I find, for the most part, unnecessary to enjoy life's pleasures…and unable to erase its disappointments." He inhaled strongly through his nose before going on. "Generally, I drink only when very much troubled…or when I need to forget." He'd added the last phrase in a breathy voice suffused with such sadness that I wanted to reach out to him and lay a hand on his arm in comfort.

I made no move to do so, though, only watching him to see what he would say or do next. After a long moment, he lifted his head, looking up with slightly glazed eyes—an effect of the whiskey, I thought, or the memories that haunted him, perhaps.

"The last time I touched a drop of alcohol was the first time I ever really got drunk," he said slowly, his eyes unfocused as he looked at Quin. "And the blow that saw me arrested was the first time I've ever hit another person in my life." He blinked a few times before rubbing a hand tiredly over his face, his palm rasping over the short brown beard sprouting like soft fur on his cheeks. "So you see," he continued suddenly, as if a thought had just occurred to him, "my own experience has proved my own belief.—If I hadn't resorted to the fleeting relief to be found at the bottom of a whiskey bottle, I would never have been arrested." He compressed his lips briefly in a tight line before giving a dismissive shrug. "But it is done now.—And I must move on." He swallowed heavily, making an obvious effort to keep his features under control.

When he looked up again, his face was suffused with sadness. He got up slowly from his chair and inclined his head, first toward Quin and then toward me. "I wish you a good night, sir…ma'am." The corners of his mouth lifted briefly in a reluctant smile before he turned away and walked out of the room, teetering only slightly.

I looked after him in some concern, hoping he would make it up the stairs to his room. When I heard no sounds of distress, though, I rounded on Quin in some annoyance. "Why did you have to ask him about his drinking habits?" I demanded.

"I wasn't the one who brought it up," he countered with a small shake of the head, giving me a wry look. I flushed, remembering my own social blunder in response to Dunne's comment. "I think the man needs somebody to talk to," he continued before I could say anything, making me lift my brows. "Talking about your troubles can help you deal with them.—Isn't that so?" He looked at me expectantly.

"It is," I agreed. "But that doesn't mean we should be allowed to pry into other people's business!" I cocked my head in defiance.

"You're right." He nodded slowly before shrugging his shoulders. "But I do think he simply needs somebody who will listen to him."

"You're good at listening," I said softly, laying my hand on Quin's arm, a sudden feeling of tenderness welling up inside me as I looked at him.

He narrowed his eyes, peering suspiciously at me from underneath dark brows. "Is that your way of telling me I should rather keep my mouth shut?"

I burst out laughing. "You can take it as you like, I'm only telling the truth." Quin lifted one brow, trying to look stern, but one corner of his mouth turned up in amusement. "Mr Dunne will be able to count himself lucky if he can confide in you," I added more seriously. "But perhaps you should wait for him to come to you.—Just give it time."

3.

"AH, THAT'S BETTER!" Quin said, straightening up from brushing down his horse. His spine gave a few pleasant pops and he sighed. Although he had two grooms at his disposal, Quin enjoyed seeing to his horse himself whenever he could, finding it relaxing at the end of the day. This day had been a long one of riding, and both horse and rider were looking forward to their rest. Quin slapped Gambit affectionately on the rump in farewell before making his way out of the stable.

Stepping outside, he thought he heard a noise coming from the side of the building. Curiously, he turned into the narrow passage that lay between the stable and the neighbouring outbuilding. Although it was dim, he could see the sound he'd heard was that of a scuffle.

"What is this?" Quin asked in a raised voice, stepping briskly toward the mass of limbs flailing on the dirt floor, fists thudding rhythmically into sensitive body parts. He recognised the lanky form of Finnian and yanked him off his adversary. Finnian yelped in sudden alarm as he was pulled up by the back of his shirt, turning around in annoyance, having clearly not heard Quin come up behind him. The young man's eyes went wide, though, when he saw who'd interrupted him, turning on his heel and attempting to escape. Quin grabbed him by the arm and pulled him roughly back around.

"Stay!" he commanded, making Finnian stop and lower his face as he carefully ran his tongue along a split lip. Quin narrowed his eyes at him before turning to the second figure that was slowly getting up off the ground. It was Rupert, his valet, looking dishevelled, with his shirt torn and blood trickling down his face from a cut above the eye.

Quin made no attempt to assist him.

"What is the meaning of this?" he demanded, glaring at the two young men, who were now skulking against the stable wall, studiously avoiding looking at each other—or at Quin.

"Well?" His tone was icy as he looked from one to the other.

Finnian was fidgeting with his gangly arms but showed no desire to want to answer Quin, while Rupert was staring unmoving at his shoes—which were dirty and scuffed, a state of affairs that must have been deeply upsetting to the normally fastidious valet.

"One of you had better tell me what's going on here," Quin said in a menacing voice, which at least had the effect of Rupert looking up at him, shamefaced, followed by a brief glance from Finnian.

Quin growled deep in his throat as he glared at the two delinquents.

"It's his fault, sir!" Rupert finally answered explosively.

"No, it isn't!" Finnian retorted immediately, turning angrily toward Rupert.

"I wanted to..."

"He said..."

"Stop it!" Quin thundered, leaning forward. "You are going to tell me in a civilised fashion exactly what's going on here or by God you can go to bed without your supper!" This seemed like a ridiculous threat to Quin as soon as it had crossed his lips—he was dealing with young men after all, not children—but quite to his surprise it seemed to be working.

"I thought..."

"She told me..."

"I saw her first!"

"No, you didn't!"

"Am I to understand," Quin interrupted brutally, "that this is about a girl?"

Finnian and Rupert nodded in unison, both staring solemnly down at their feet, looking so ridiculous that Quin almost laughed out loud.

"I see," he managed instead. "And has either of you lain with her?" he demanded, making Finnian hunch his shoulders while a bright red blush sprouted on Rupert's round cheeks.

"No, sir, we just...ah...well, we only..."

"We didn't...not really...I mean...hmph..."

"I see," Quin repeated, not wanting to hear the sordid details. "And does either of you want to marry her?"

The two young men glanced at each other before both shaking their heads, avoiding looking at Quin. He narrowed his eyes at them and blew out forcefully through his nose.

"In that case," he finally hissed, "you'd do well to keep your pricks in your trousers!" Rupert drew in his breath in shock at his employer's unaccustomed use of such language, while Finnian's eyes grew large and round. "Otherwise, one of you will find yourself with a wife—whether you want to marry her or not!" He glared at them, making them visibly squirm.

"Speaking of which…go mend your clothes and get yourselves cleaned up. We've got a wedding to attend in the morning."

MARGARET AND JOHN were married on a damp and cloudy day, the bride looking shy but radiant, blooming with life. The bridegroom on the other hand wore a rather startled expression as he stood awkwardly by her side, evidently contemplating how he'd gotten himself into the situation.

The reason for the haste was still barely apparent for those who weren't aware of it, Margaret's pregnancy manifesting as no more than a small swelling of her abdomen that could just as well have been caused by her eating a Sunday roast. While this had at first seemed strange to me, Mrs O'Sullivan had assured me in her wisdom that it was nothing unusual, with some women showing little more than a rounded belly as they brought forth new life, while others expanded majestically in all directions, like the dough that rose every morning to make our fresh bread.

Remembering her picturesque description as I watched the proceedings, I wondered how I might look one day if I were ever to fall pregnant and stay so. I glanced at Quin, who gave me a fleeting smile. I haven't given up hope yet, I thought determinedly, as I looked back toward the parish priest who was performing the marriage ceremony. Margaret and John were Catholic, as was the vast majority of Ireland's common folk, and so it was a Catholic ceremony we were attending.

Margaret was reciting her vows in a soft voice, the small maid smiling a little nervously up at the man who would soon be her husband, who towered above her even though he was not particularly tall himself. When it was John's turn, he straightened his shoulders and looked down at Margaret solemnly, seeming determined to make the best of it. Although their marriage would not be one based on love, I thought there was a good chance they would find happiness, nonetheless.

The ceremony was concluded with a shy kiss between the new husband and wife, greeted by cheers from the congregation, who soon turned their attention to the celebrations to come. Before long, these were well under way up at the big house. To everyone's delight, even the weather participated, with a pale sunshine seeping through the thin layer of clouds, portending at least a brief respite from the general dampness of the season.

Ale flowed by the barrelful and vast quantities of food disappeared into hungry mouths, the festivities as much a celebration of the estate's abundance as Margaret and John's wedding.

"How are you feeling?" I asked Margaret during a quiet moment when no one was around to hear.

"Oh, very well ma'am, I thank you." She patted her abdomen fondly. "*A muirnín* is giving me no trouble at all."

"There you are Mrs Mullen."

I had been about to ask something else but turned toward John, who'd just arrived, looking quite smug at the use of Margaret's newly acquired married name. It sounded rather strange to my ears—Margaret had always just been Margaret to me—but I smiled as a soft blush crept into her cheeks and she looked fondly, although somewhat shyly, at her new husband. Behind John was a group of men, who now came forward and made a big show of offering their congratulations to the bride, who laughed at all the attention.

"And you'll soon have a babe in the cradle as well," one of the men commented light-heartedly, making John and Margaret blush. They both turned crimson as the next man piped up, elbowing John knowingly in the ribs, "Even sooner than you thought, ey?" The man laughed uproariously, showing several missing teeth.

I felt a blush break out on my own cheeks—clearly, there hadn't been much need for me to converse with Margaret in secret after all.

"*Ní haon ábhar gáire é.*"

A prickling sensation crept over my scalp at the sound of the cracked old voice emanating from the crowd. I hadn't seen her between the men, but a small, ancient-looking woman now hobbled forward, her wrinkly eyes intent on Margaret, who shied away from the apparition before her. The men had gone silent, a few shuffling their feet and looking down, others peeking at the old woman from beneath lowered brows, clearly feeling—as I was—that there'd been something ominous in the tone of her voice as she admonished the men for laughing.

A gnarled hand emerged from underneath the aged shawl that covered the old woman's stooped shoulders, reaching up slowly and touching Margaret lightly on her cheek. Margaret stood stock-still, one corner of her mouth lifting reluctantly. The attempted smile froze on her lips, though, as the old woman uttered a cry and dropped her hand, pointing briefly at Margaret's midsection.

"*Anbhás ag teacht,*" she murmured in a shaking voice, suddenly gripping Margaret's upper arms. "*Anbhás ag teacht.*" She looked searchingly into her face as Margaret tried to pull away, struggling against the old woman's surprisingly firm grasp.

"*Mamó!*" I turned toward a young man who was hurrying in our direction, a look of concern on his face. "*Mamó,*" he repeated as he came up alongside Margaret and the old woman. "*Tar liom,*" he urged her, pulling her gently by the arm. "*Tar liom.*" Finally, the old woman's grip loosened, and she allowed herself to be towed away by her grandson.

"I...sorry," the young man murmured in heavily accented English as he led her away. He wasn't someone I knew, and I assumed he and his grandmother had come from one of the neighbouring estates to attend the wedding. I looked back at Margaret whose face was drawn, her lips compressed into a tight line.

"Crazy old woman," one of the men said into the awkward silence. A few others guffawed in welcome release.

"Like mother of my wife," another man piped up, clarifying what he meant by drawing a circle with his finger next to his temple. Soon enough, the men were cheerful once more as they compared anecdotes on their colourful relatives.

"She didn't know what she was saying," I said softly to Margaret, laying a hand on her shoulder.

"No…no, of course not…" She nodded, seeming to want to convince herself. She shook herself lightly and put on a forced smile.

"Come dance!" John had come up next to us and wrapped one arm around Margaret, whose eyes lit up at sight of him. "Hm?" He cocked his head at his new wife, who nodded and let herself be towed away.

I followed along slowly behind them, trying to shake off the sense of unease that still clung to me.

"*Anbhás ag teacht*," the old woman had said as she'd looked at Margaret in horror.

Death is coming.

"SHE WAS OLD and senile. She didn't know what she was saying."

"Yes, no doubt you're right." I nodded, willing myself to agree with Quin—I had tried to convince Margaret of the same thing after all. After the old woman's ominous warning had been laughed off, the celebrations had gone on merrily into the night, but her words kept coming back to me, scuttling darkly down my spine.

"Perhaps she was remembering someone else. Someone she once knew, who bore a resemblance to Margaret." Quin shrugged and climbed into bed next to me. "Perhaps a daughter who died in childbed." He gathered me to his chest. "It's common enough."

"It is," I agreed, feeling suddenly sad for the old woman, who'd undoubtedly lived a hard life. "At least we don't have to worry about that." If there was one benefit to not being able to stay pregnant it was being in no danger of dying during childbirth.

I sighed, not sure if I was willing to give up on my hope of having a child even so.

Quin kissed me on the forehead. "Everything will work itself out," he murmured into the top of my head as he gathered me close once more, wrapping himself around me.

I felt him drift off to sleep but found myself lying awake well into the night, my thoughts not letting me rest, pattering around my brain like tiny feet that crawled their way down into my heart, until I at last joined them in slumber.

4.

THE DAY AFTER the wedding dawned warm and sunny, with only a few wisps of cloud scattered across a piercingly blue sky. With a sense of celebration still hovering in the air, Quin suggested we go for a ride along the riverbank after breakfast. I quickly agreed and changed into a riding habit.

Ambling slowly away from the manor house we talked of this and that, enjoying each other's company. We crossed the small wooden bridge that led over the stream and followed the water along the northern bank. Insects flitted around us, and birds filled the air with their melodic song, the small creatures enjoying the fine weather as much as we were.

By mutual consent, we dismounted when we reached a favourite spot by a bend in the river, where a grassy slope faced a towering oak tree on the opposite bank. As Quin hobbled the horses I sat back on my elbows on the soft, springy grass, lifting my face to the warm sunshine, letting the light dance behind my closed eyes. I felt Quin sit down next to me, and suddenly his lips were on mine, making me reach out a hand to caress the nape of his neck. When he finally pulled away, he flopped down on the grass beside me. I followed suit, lying on my back and staring up at the sky, sighing in contentment. My hand found his and our fingers entwined as we lay silently side by side.

I closed my eyes again and started feeling drowsy in the sun's comforting embrace. I was just dozing off when Quin sat up quite suddenly, making me open one eye lazily in curiosity.

"I'm going for a swim," he announced and jumped up.

I gaped at him in some surprise, and he laughed as he yanked his shirt out of his waistband. He quirked an eyebrow at me and pulled it off over his head, unencumbered by cravat or waistcoat on this most casual of outings. I enjoyed the play of his muscles across his chest as he continued disrobing, until at last he stood in front of me, bare as the day he was born and grinning from ear to ear.

"Will you join me?" he asked suggestively and offered me his hand.

"Um..." I stammered. While I certainly enjoyed the feeling of Quin's naked body next to mine, I wasn't quite so sure about immersing myself in the stream. It was barely the beginning of summer and a wet and cool season it had thus far been. The water was sure to be icy.

"Suit yourself." Quin's voice broke in on my thoughts and I laughed at the sight of his bare white buttocks as he headed away from me, making his way around the bend in the river to a small eddy pool behind a jumble of obstructing rocks. I watched him wade through the shallower streambed before disappearing around the bend.

Shrugging, I got up.

Wriggling my way out of my clothes—which would no doubt have been easier had I let Quin assist me—I left my stockings and garters in a puddle behind me and headed toward the water's edge. I felt not a little daring, unclothed and out in the open for anyone to see. There was no one else here, though, and so it was also quite invigorating to follow Quin to the eddy pool with nothing but a soft breeze caressing my bare flesh. As I came around the bend, I could see that Quin had by now immersed himself in the deeper water of the pool.

He caught sight of me, and his eyes beckoned to me above an approving smile.

I found the look on his face quite gratifying and held his gaze intently as I made my way slowly to the water's edge, swaying my hips ever so slightly before dipping the toes of one foot elegantly into the water. I squeaked and jumped back—the water was as cold as I had feared. Quin laughed and I smiled back sheepishly, hovering on the streambed, unsure how to proceed.

"You won't notice the cold once you're in," he assured me, no doubt attempting to sound encouraging.

I lifted one brow sceptically. "It's the getting in part that's the difficulty." This statement made him laugh once more but suddenly, he lunged toward me and grabbed me around the waist. I yelped as he pulled me into the pool and dunked me in up to my neck. I gasped, standing up quicky, shivering in reaction in the cold water that still came up to my navel.

Quin grinned at me, but I narrowed my eyes at him, feeling a little annoyed. "Are your legs still cold?" he asked casually.

"Well...no," I admitted. It was, in fact, starting to feel quite pleasant, standing in the cool water with the sunshine on my back, a few tendrils of damp hair snaking down my breasts.

Quin reached out an arm and pulled me slowly toward him, until he had me pressed firmly against his chest, which was comfortably warm from the sun. He let his hands slowly caress my back, sliding them down over my buttocks. "Not so bad, is it?" His warm breath tickled my ear.

"No." I let my own hands glide across his broad shoulders, enjoying the novel sensation of his bare skin against mine under an open sky, with the water lapping around us. I lifted my face to his and pulled him down for a lingering kiss, noticing with some satisfaction that he was enjoying this experience very much himself, if his physical reaction was anything to go by. Coming away grinning, he suddenly disentangled himself from me.

"First, a swim!" he informed me, before diving briskly under the water.

There was hardly space to do much in the way of swimming in the small eddy pool and so I had high hopes that we'd soon be able to continue with our earlier pursuits. I laughed and decided I'd go for a dip myself. I started cautiously submerging myself in the cool water inch by inch, before thinking better of it, taking a deep breath and letting myself drop to the riverbed in one swift motion. I came up spluttering, wiping my wet hair out of my face as I gasped for breath. Despite the shock of it, the cold water was quite refreshing, and I lowered myself into it once more, swimming the few strokes to the bank and back again until I reached the pile of rocks.

After a few minutes I began to feel a little cold and climbed out onto the bank. Quin was submerged in the water, evidently trying to see how long he could hold his breath, like a little boy. I laughed and started heading back toward our things. With a few clothes spread out beneath me I lay down on the spongy grass and let the sun warm me, closing my eyes and wriggling my toes in delight.

"You look very appealing in the sunshine."

I lifted myself onto my elbows, nodding appreciatively at the sight of Quin standing wet and naked in front of me, adorned only with the smattering of scars that marred his otherwise-smooth skin. I lifted one brow as my gaze drifted down the length of his body. "I see," I said, a smile forming on my lips.

He grinned and lay down next to me, placing a large hand on my belly. I drew in my breath sharply at the unaccustomed coldness of his touch.

"You'll be warm soon enough," he said softly and rolled on top of me, making me squirm. "Shhh." He cut off my complaints with a kiss, stroking my cheek, before tracing his hand slowly down the side of my breast and along the outside of my leg. After a moment, his fingers snaked their way between us, caressing me lightly. I returned the favour and he murmured appreciatively in my ear.

I was suddenly feeling very warm indeed. Just as I thought I could bear it no longer, he removed his hand, replacing it with something even more satisfying.

I gasped at the suddenness of the intrusion but pressed him closer with one hand on his lower back, the other urging his mouth to mine, locking us together from head to foot. When he broke away from the kiss, trembling and breathing heavily, I opened my eyes to the blue sky above us, cradling Quin's head next to mine. And suddenly, I felt as light as the birds that flew overhead, floating on the current that swept over me, carrying me higher and higher into the heavens as I left my bodily form behind.

5.

ONCE THE EXCITEMENT of Margaret and John's wedding had abated, I turned my attention toward realising my dream of teaching the children who lived on the estate. A number of the tenants had immediately expressed their enthusiasm for the idea, while others had seemed rather sceptical, not least of all because they worried the teaching would take their children away from their duties at home. I had ensured the parents I would instil in the children the importance of both learning and familial responsibilities and had agreed we'd start with only two mornings a week. And so, to my delight, a small but eager group of children had shown up a few days ago for the first lesson, which had been held in the Connell's cottage.

Hearing of my intentions, Mr Connell—who'd become something of a spokesperson for the tenants—had graciously offered to let me use his home for the teaching, thinking the manor house would be a little too grand for the purpose. After some consideration I had agreed, thinking it would also be easier for me to ride to the tenants' cottages than it would be for the children to make their way to the manor house on foot. And while we didn't have any benches or desks, nor yet any school supplies, the children were more than willing to learn.

"Settle down, everyone," I said in Gaelic to the shuffling bodies that sat in front of me now, preparing to start my second lesson. The children did settle down to a degree—at least until the door suddenly flew open and little Alfie Garvey shot in, panting and looking rather dishevelled.

I waved the boy to an open spot near me, where he plopped down onto the stone floor. "Now that we're all here, let's begin. In our first lesson we spoke about…"

"There's pig shit on your face!"

This unexpected exclamation caused the room to erupt into hoots of laughter, while the unfortunate recipient of the accolade turned bright red.

"No, there isn't!" little Alfie yelled with a scowl, nevertheless running one hand gingerly over his face, which did in fact sport several unsightly streaks.

"There is, there is, there is!" Cormac Fitzgerald countered, nodding madly and pointing a finger at poor Alfie.

"There isn't!"

"There is!"

"No, there isn't!"

"Yes, there is!"

"Enough!" I said sternly, having to raise my voice to be heard above the ruckus. Cormac shut his mouth, swallowing whatever remark he'd been about to make, while the other children threw me guilty looks as they quietened down. "That's not a very nice thing to say, Cormac.—Even should it be true," I added, seeing Alfie wrinkle his nose as he passed his fingers under it. Without comment, I gave him my handkerchief, which he rubbed vigorously over his face and hands.

"Keep it," I said, seeing him contemplate whether he should give it back to me. I looked around the room, catching an eye here and there. "If there is one thing in this world that doesn't cost a thing, then that is kindness.—Above all else, we should always try to be kind."

"Yes, ma'am," came the chorus of responses from the children. Cormac was looking down into his lap but grudgingly grumbled his agreement, which made Alfie raise his nose in a rather self-satisfied way.

"Now, Alfie, were you perhaps helping your parents tend the fields earlier this morning?"

"I was, ma'am. I was helping them spread the...um...well the..." He glanced at Cormac, who opened his mouth—doubtless to point out that Alfie had just proven his own guilt—but closed it quickly when I narrowed my eyes at him.

"The manure, I presume," I said with a nod. "And can any of you tell me why we do that?" Although I had primarily intended to teach the children English, and to read and write, I decided there could be no harm in providing a wider learning experience when the opportunity arose.

"To make the potatoes grow," a girl at the back replied eagerly, making her braids swing.

"You're quite right, Bridget, but do try to remember to raise your hand when you wish to say something." I smiled at her, making her smile shily back as she nodded.

"But how does that work? Ah…" The little boy who'd asked the question belatedly stuck his hand into the air, his ears turning pink.

"Well, you see, Jacob, just like you need food to grow and to run and play—and help your parents around the house—so does a potato plant need food to grow and produce potatoes."

"And it eats pig shit?" Jacob burst out, before clapping his hands over his mouth, his whole face now crimson.

The other children sniggered, and I pressed my lips together so as not to laugh out loud myself. "In a way.—You see, manure contains nutrients, which are tiny particles all living things need. And it's these that the plant eats, as it were." The children were looking at me in fascination. "All of which makes pigs quite useful in many ways, doesn't it?"

Jacob's twin brother Samuel was bouncing up on his haunches, one hand stuck out high above his head.

"Yes, Samuel?"

"Our pigs also pay the rents," he informed me with some pride.

"You're quite right," I said, and smiled. "Most of your families will have one or two pigs at home, which are raised for the rent money. And while the pigs grow big and fat on the potatoes they share with you and your parents and your brothers and sisters, their manure helps to feed your crops—so that you'll have a bountiful new potato harvest in the autumn."

Most of the heads nodded in understanding—it was a way of life they were all familiar with. What they were less familiar with was the English language, and it was a topic I wanted to return to in the short time we had for our lessons.

"Now," I said, lightly clapping my hands together to get their attention once more, "who knows the English word for pig?"

"I DON'T RECALL pig excrement ever being a topic of study while I was growing up."

I laughed, snuggling closer to Quin. "Neither do I."

We had gone to bed, but neither of us was quite ready for sleep yet and so instead, we'd been telling each other about our day.

"And are you enjoying yourself in your new role?" Quin asked, leaning back a little so he could look into my face.

"Well it's only been two lessons and it's not so many children as yet, but yes, so far I am." I smiled, picturing the eager faces and the pride that radiated off the children when something newly taught was understood, or correctly recalled. "There's something terribly rewarding about teaching—a sense of accomplishment. And..."

"Yes?" Quin coaxed.

"I feel...or rather I hope...that the little I'm doing will help these children have a better future." Quin found my hand with his and squeezed it lightly. "I wish...for them to have choices—choices their parents never had."

I compressed my lips, remembering the feeling of having my future decided for me against my will. And I had grown up in luxury, whereas the tenants were stuck in a pauper's trap likely to ensnare their children—but if I could give those children a little hope, the belief that they just may be able to improve their lot in life, then that was worth something.

"Do you ever wonder," I said, staring unseeing at the ceiling, "why you were born the son of a baron, while countless others are born into a life of poverty and misery?"

Quin took a deep breath before answering. "I do. Or rather, I did.—I found it's not a very productive line of thought." He gave a humourless laugh. "I would either feel terribly guilty for my own good luck or terribly pompous at the thought that my privileged destiny was somehow divinely intended."

"That is what many of the nobility believe, no doubt."

"The divine right of kings and such?" He shrugged. "I don't believe in all that, although I'm sure there are still plenty who do. As for my own good fortune—however I may have come by it, I believe it bears the responsibility to assist those who are less fortunate than I."

"You're certainly doing that," I said, stroking his cheek.

He smiled at me and gave me a gentle kiss. "I do what I can."

"And how are you getting on with our new overseer?" I asked, having to blink away the tiredness that was starting to creep over me.

"Very well." He nodded enthusiastically. "While he may look unassuming, he is very competent, and we work well together. I'm glad I hired him."

"That's good."

"He does seem rather a shy fellow, though, who doesn't much talk about himself."

"I told you, just give it time," I said, patting Quin's arm before being overcome by a jaw-cracking yawn I tried unsuccessfully to stifle.

Quin chuckled. "Perhaps you ought to sleep now."

"Perhaps," I agreed as my eyes started to close.

He gathered me into his chest, and I started drifting off as his heartbeat thumped steadily beneath my ear.

6.

GIVE IT TIME, Alannah had said.

When it came to Mr Dunne, Quin agreed.

He smiled encouragingly at the man sitting at the desk across from him. As Alannah had predicted, Dunne had started warming up to Quin over the last few weeks, revealing a little more about himself each day while they went about their business on the estate. They'd just been discussing some accounts when he'd casually mentioned that his father had been the schoolmaster of the school for boys at Ballygawley, the town where he was born.

"He was a very passionate man," Dunne said when Quin showed his interest. "Poetry and literature were ever close to his heart. And he did much to improve the school."

"And you clearly benefited from a good education yourself." Quin closed the ledger in front of him, folding his hands over it.

Dunne nodded. "So I did, both at school and at home—there were no set school hours for me." He gave Quin a wry look. "But I didn't mind. My father soon recognised my aptitude for numbers and administrative tasks and found a place for me in the household of his elderly uncle who was quite well off. In the end, I took over the management of the estate during his dying years."

"I see. And he was clearly very pleased with your work for you to have done as well for yourself as you have."

Dunne shrugged self-consciously at the compliment but inclined his head in acknowledgment, nonetheless. "He was very kind with his praises, and so I was quickly able to find a new position after his passing."

"And have you worked on many different estates over the years?" Quin asked.

Dunne shook his head. "Not that many. After my great-uncle's death I was employed at the Johnson estate for almost ten years. When old Sir Johnson died, I moved around a little, finding work here and there, until I heard of a landowner in need of an overseer...after the previous one had fallen drunken into the estate's creek and drowned." Dunne frowned and compressed his lips, a far-away look appearing on his face.

Based on Dunne's expression Quin assumed the landowner in question to be the infamous Mr Thompson. He wondered just how dreadful the man must be for his overseers to have been driven to such inebriated misadventures. He didn't ask, though, remembering Alannah's advice to let Dunne come to him—a tactic he was finding to be successful.

"I see," he said instead. Murmuring words of encouragement and asking the occasional unobtrusive question seemed quite effective at coaxing Dunne into opening up about himself.

The overseer shook his head briefly, his features clearing. "And now I find myself here," he ended his account, spreading his hands as his lips twitched into a smile.

"And we are happy to have you," Quin assured him.

The longcase clock in the drawing room across the hall chimed suddenly, making both men look toward the door.

"But I am keeping you with my ramblings, sir." Dunne made as if to get up, looking a little anxious.

Quin waved an arm, suppressing a laugh. He had discovered that the overseer possessed a distinct sense of decency—detaining his employer for half an hour while he talked about himself may very well be considered the height of selfishness by the man. And while such a characteristic might have been considered at odds with Mr Dunne having committed drunken assault, Quin strongly suspected there was far more to the tale than a disgruntled manager taking out his frustrations on his employer in a moment of intoxicated idiocy.

"Not at all, Mr Dunne," he said, wondering if the overseer would ever reveal what happened that day, "I've quite enjoyed our talk. But right now, I believe our supper awaits."

THEIR PLEASANT CONVERSATION continued into the dining room, with Dunne telling Quin and Alannah a bit about his early life in Ballygawley. Alannah looked rather distracted, remaining largely silent, and so it was mostly the men who did the talking.

When Quin cautiously asked the overseer about his more recent past, Dunne made a brief remark about some kind of romantic disappointment. Quin wondered whether that had anything to do with the man's drunken state at the time of his arrest. Despite the overseer remaining tight-lipped about the affair, it had quite piqued Quin's curiosity.

Getting ready for bed at the end of the evening, Quin grinned at his reflection in the dressing table mirror at the thought of the stoic Mr Dunne locked in a passionate embrace with a wispy lass.

He pulled his shirt over his head and flexed his shoulders. His eyes fell on the long scar that ran across his abdomen and he suddenly felt the smile slide off his lips. Unable to prevent the scowl that formed instead—and the dark mood that immediately accompanied it—he vigorously splashed cold water from the ewer onto his face.

Giving Mr Dunne time to reveal more about himself was all very well and good; not so was having to wait around for answers to another question much occupying his mind—the question of who had set Martin Doyle free after he'd been imprisoned in Omagh gaol and condemned to death.

Murderer, traitor and all-round violent felon, Doyle had been convicted of his crimes and supposedly been hanged, only to show up at Glaslearg very much alive, murder Alannah's brother—who'd previously plotted with Doyle to overthrow the English in Ireland but had broken all ties with him and testified against him—and attempt to rape and murder Alannah. As always, Quin's scalp prickled when he thought about the sight of Alannah's bruised and bleeding body as he pulled the vile Doyle off her, feeling no shame at the distinct satisfaction he'd experienced as he ended the man's life with his bare hands.

He rubbed a towel vigorously over his face and chest to dispel the haunting images.

And yet, someone had orchestrated Doyle's supposed hanging and his escape from gaol, resulting in all the dreadful events that had followed. Quin could not rest until he'd found the culprit. He was feeling more than a little impatient with his lack of progress. Over a year had passed since Doyle's reappearance, and Quin was no closer to having any idea who had planned his escape and the ruse of his execution, or why.

Breathing out heavily through his nose as he glowered at his reflection, Quin scoffed at the fact that nobody appeared to have seen or heard anything suspicious when a presumably innocent man had been hanged in Doyle's stead. Even if the spectators at the hanging had been too preoccupied with their own bloodlust to realise anything was amiss, the hangman or the guards on duty that day should surely have noticed something peculiar about the condemned man's behaviour. But the guard who'd fetched the false Doyle from his cell and led him to the gallows was nowhere to be found, while the other guard had only gone as far as admitting to Quin that the prisoner had indeed decried his own innocence before his death. The hangman had thus far had nothing useful to say at all, having evidently paid the prisoner the barest of mind, despite his pivotal role in the fellow's demise.

Quin wasn't completely convinced, though, that the second guard and the hangman were being entirely truthful with their version of events.

He threw the damp towel aside, suddenly determined to visit Omagh gaol yet again. Perhaps this time, he might be able to persuade one or both of the men to reveal something more, when all his previous attempts had failed. What more there might be to reveal, Quin didn't know. If it was simply a matter of the two men trying to avoid trouble for having ignored the condemned man's pleas, they likely would have little more to tell. However, Quin had started to wonder whether the guard and the hangman may have had their instructions—to keep quiet about anything suspicious, perhaps?

He turned toward the bed, where Alannah was busy removing the coverlet, a distant look on her face.

"I'll be going to Omagh tomorrow," he announced without preliminaries. "I shall speak to the guard and the hangman once more."

Alannah's eyes went wide, and her hands stopped moving. She looked at him for a long moment, her gaze skimming down his bare torso before coming to rest for a moment on the thin scar Quin himself had just been contemplating. She compressed her lips and turned away from him in silence.

Quin frowned at her back, watching her slowly fold the comforter into a neat rectangle. He knew she had reservations about him trying to find whoever had freed Martin Doyle—the man who'd given him that scar—as she feared he would place himself in danger while living in the past. But she had promised to support him even so, and her discontented expression now was making him feel decidedly irritable. After all, his efforts were as much for her benefit as they were to still his own curiosity. Until they knew who had planned Doyle's escape and why, they couldn't be sure they themselves weren't in any more danger. Although the events had happened many months before, he would be foolish to wholly discount the possibility.

"They must know something!" Quin insisted as Alannah placed the folded coverlet onto the chaise longue.

She paused in the act of lifting the sheets. Her eyes flitted toward him, and she gave the briefest of nods. "Good night," she said shortly, sliding into bed and turning onto her side away from him.

"Good night," Quin responded through clenched teeth. Scowling, he yanked off his trousers and changed into his nightshirt before getting into bed himself, facing the opposite direction.

Although she'd barely said a thing, Alannah's dissatisfaction with his actions was clear. Suppressing a sigh, he rolled onto his back and stared at the ceiling. Despite her obvious displeasure, Quin had every intention of following through with his plans. Irritably, he rolled back onto his side, going through the brief exchange once more. He may have been a little brash with his announcement, he admitted to himself, thinking he might have eased his way into the conversation instead of springing the idea of another visit to Omagh on her. Nevertheless, he'd hoped for a different reaction.

She hadn't said he shouldn't go, though, instead assenting with a curt and unenthusiastic nod. Finally deciding that did in fact constitute her grudging support, he managed to drift off to sleep.

QUIN SET OUT early the following morning to make the fifteen-mile trip to Omagh. Ignoring the wind and rain that accompanied him, he found himself thinking again about Alannah's distinct lack of enthusiasm for what he was doing. Feeling suddenly annoyed, he spurred on Gambit to greater speed. He leaned over the horse's sturdy neck as it thundered along the road, drops of water flying, dispersed by its hooves.

Quin's thoughts continued to wander between Alannah and what he might find in Omagh as he gave the horse its head. He had grown up virtually on horseback and had no difficulty keeping his seat, no matter the weather, nor when his mind was otherwise occupied. He slowed down a little, though, as he approached a rickety wagon making its sluggish way along the path, drawn by a very elderly looking, dripping mule and bearing a farmer who didn't look in much better shape himself. Leading Gambit smoothly around the obstruction, Quin made an effort to suppress all thoughts of Alannah's objections, instead turning his attention back to what had made him make this trip in the first place.

He was sure the missing guard was the key to finding out what had happened the night before Doyle was supposed to have been executed. According to the warden, the man had started working at Omagh goal about a month before the hanging, only to give up his post shortly thereafter. If that fact alone wasn't suspicious enough, the man seemed now to have completely disappeared, Quin being unable to find even the slightest trace of him since he'd left the gaol, nor anything before he arrived. It was almost as if he'd never existed, which made Quin think the guard himself or someone else had arranged his presence at the gaol for the sole purpose of seeing Doyle escape.

As to who the instigator of the entire affair might have been and who the hanged man himself might have been, Quin was none the wiser.

Ignoring the raindrops that ran down his neck, he loosened Gambit's reins and leaned forward once more, pounding on toward Omagh, hoping to get a little closer to the truth.

QUIN SHRUGGED OUT of his damp coat and stepped out of his muddy boots, sighing in relief as he wiped his sweat-soaked hair away from his brow.

"Master Williams."

"Denis." Quin looked across the entrance hall to the door to the drawing room, where the elderly butler was making his slow way toward him. Quin took a few steps further into the house to meet him halfway.

"Has all been well in my absence?" Quin asked with a smile, not expecting to hear an answer to the contrary.

"Yes, sir." Denis gave him a grave nod. "You...need me, sir?" The old man raised his bushy grey brows enquiringly.

"No, thank you, Denis. You can go about your business. I'll go join Mrs Williams." He cocked his head toward the drawing room, thinking Alannah might be in there. While it was only mid-morning, she didn't appear to be in the study—the door was closed, and Alannah had gotten into the habit of keeping it ajar when she worked there.

Denis shook his head, though. "Not there." He raised one arm and pointed to the ceiling with his index finger. "Up," he added by way of an explanation for his gesture.

"Oh," Quin said in some surprise but shrugged a moment later, thanking Denis before making his way upstairs.

He found Alannah in the bedroom, reclining on the chaise longue with a book. She didn't appear to be reading, though, her eyes clearly not focused on what was in front of her. Quin watched her for a minute through the open door of the sitting room, wondering what she was thinking about. There was a look of sadness about her that he'd become all too familiar with over the past months. Although she seemed to be coping well enough for the most part, he knew Kieran's death still weighed heavily on her mind—how could it not?

He clenched his jaws, his heart suddenly heavy, hoping his presence might give her comfort, even if some of his actions might not.

He cleared his throat to announce himself as he entered the room, making Alannah look up in some startlement.

"Quin," she said with a small smile as he came toward her.

He dropped a kiss on her forehead as she moved her legs to the side so he could sit down next to her. He was about to ask how she was feeling when she spoke up before him.

"Um..." she started a little uncertainly, making him cock one brow expectantly, "what did you find out?"

Quin looked at her for a moment before answering, weighing his words. "The guard and the hangman were bribed," he said at last, deciding to be as straightforward as she had been herself—there was little point in giving the topic the run-around, after all.

"Oh." Quin thought she looked rather defeated at his revelation.

He took her hand and leaned toward her. "It was the guard who's disappeared, the one who took the prisoner to the gallows on the day of the hanging. He told them to...ignore anything peculiar about the condemned man." Quin compressed his lips angrily, feeling no joy in the fact that his suspicions had been confirmed—that Kieran's life had been sold for a few measly coins.

"I see," Alannah said softly, looking down.

"The second guard swore to me that he thought his colleague was only referring to the prisoner's appearance, as Doyle—or the man everyone thought to be Doyle—had evidently been beaten before the execution. The second guard thought the other must have done the beating, and so he went along with the coverup, as much because he wanted the money as because he would have liked to have beaten Doyle himself, or so he admitted." Quin snorted. "Doyle was not the most popular of prisoners, it seems," he added with some irony, wondering whether any prisoners were ever popular with their captors.

Quin glanced at Alannah to gauge her reaction. She was quiet, looking into her lap, a small frown on her face. When she didn't say anything, Quin continued, "The hangman corroborated the guard's tale. He did also say, though, that the condemned man seemed strangely incoherent, even for one about to meet his death, his mouth working incessantly but to little apparent effect." Alannah looked curiously up at Quin, clearly not understanding what he meant. "Most of what the man muttered made no sense, the hangman said, a mixture of unintelligible sounds and jumbled words.—Although he did admit he heard the man cry 'not me' or some such once or twice before he died, just as the other guard said that he had heard him profess his innocence."

"And the missing guard?" Alannah asked softly.

Quin shook his head. "The second guard and the hangman swear they know nothing of the man's whereabouts. And in this, at least, I believe them."

"So you're no further than you were before," she said with a sigh, looking down once more.

Quin frowned at Alannah's comment. He may not have solved the mystery of Doyle's escape, but he felt he'd made some progress at last.

"We know more than we knew before," he countered, leaning toward her intently.

"Perhaps." She shrugged, making Quin scowl in annoyance at the top of her head. He hadn't spent two days in Omagh for nothing, he fumed. At least they now knew for certain that Doyle's escape had been a carefully orchestrated plan, involving bribery and deception, and no doubt a good number of other crooked tactics. Besides, he thought irritably, any small bit of information helped, drawing him slowly toward the answers he sought.

"What will you do now?" Alannah asked.

Did he detect a hint of derision in her tone? Scorn at his supposedly pitiful attempts to get to the truth, perhaps, or anger at his very pursuit of it?

"I'm going to locate the missing guard," he declared with some heat, lifting his chin defiantly. The effect was largely lost on Alannah, who was staring past him with a vacant expression in her eyes. "First, though," he went on angrily as he forcefully pushed himself up from the chaise longue, "I'm going to wash."

WALKING TOWARD THE drawing room that evening Quin reflected on the day's events. After his irksome return to Glaslearg the day had progressed along a reasonably normal course. Alannah had disappeared downstairs while he'd gone about his ablutions, after which he'd spent the afternoon ensconced in the study, there mulling over the information he had come by in Omagh and trying to figure out how best to go about trying to locate the missing guard.

Besides making inquiries himself and calling on the Irish Constabulary Police Force to help him in his quest, he knew he could count on Archie, Ham and Ollie in Dublin to lend their assistance. Close friends of Quin since their time together at officers' training in the British Army, the three soldiers would be happy to help in any way they could. Quin didn't know, though, how much help they could actually provide. Dublin was some way from Omagh, and so it was unlikely they would be able to find out much of any particular use where they were. But he would certainly ask them, nonetheless—perhaps an acquaintance of theirs would know something.

Quin stopped at the door to the drawing room, looking around. Alannah usually joined him there in the evenings but today she was nowhere to be seen. Nor was Mr Dunne anywhere to be seen, having retired to his bed after supper, citing exhaustion. Quin thought it likely that Dunne's hasty retreat had less to do with any exhaustion on his part than the awkward silence that had pervaded the dining room during supper. He and Alannah had hardly spoken to each other since his arrival that morning—Alannah acting distant and withdrawn—and she had spent most of the day in the library.

Avoiding him, perhaps? He wondered with some irritation.

He scowled at the empty room, tempted to simply settle into one of the comfortable chairs by himself and leave his irascible wife to her own devices.

"That likely won't solve anything," he grumbled.

After a little more thought he turned on his heel and walked purposefully to the library, which adjoined the drawing room. It wasn't quite as majestic as the name would suggest, but Glaslearg's reading room did boast a modest collection of books, gleaned mostly from Alannah's family home, supplemented with his own small selection. As he had suspected, he found Alannah seated in one of the armchairs that stood in front of the fireplace, a book open on her lap but a faraway look on her face.

Quin took a deep breath before entering the room. "Are you alright?" he managed to ask as she glanced up at him.

She nodded in response, holding his eyes briefly, but all too quickly she looked back down at her book. Quin frowned but didn't comment.

"May I?" He waved a hand toward one of the empty chairs.

"Of course," Alannah responded with a slightly quizzical expression. He compressed his lips in response to her apparent obliviousness to his annoyance but selected something to read at random and settled down next to her, hoping their close proximity might do something to improve their current relations.

He opened the volume he held and paged through it absently, taking no notice of the contents. His eyes wandered toward Alannah, who seemed similarly disinterested in reading, staring into the empty fireplace instead, a small frown on her face. She made no move to talk to him, though, and eventually turned her attention back to her book. Quin scowled, feeling hard done by but vowing not to be the one to break the silence—she was the one who was being unreasonable, after all, he told himself. Despite her misgivings she'd said she would support him in his search for the person who'd set Doyle free and yet her actions didn't suggest any such thing.

Quin gave the crown of her head a long look as the silence around them deepened.

Feeling thoroughly irritated, Quin looked back down at his own reading material, more to distract himself than anything else. He was surprised to see, though, that the book he thought he'd been holding turned out not to be a book at all but rather one of Alannah's medical journals, which she must have received from her former tutor from London. Mr Henderson sent her such items whenever he could, aware of his former student's penchant for all things scholastic in nature. Interested despite himself, Quin paged slowly through the journal, his eyes catching unfamiliar terms and peculiar descriptions of diseases and their treatments, or their possible ramifications.

He cocked his head in some surprise as he came across a paragraph entitled AN UNTOWARD RESULT OF DRUNKENNESS. He wasn't sure whether drunkenness was necessarily a disease but found the description entertaining, nonetheless.

"The museum of the Royal College of Surgeons, in Dublin," he read, further intrigued by the observation that the reported drunkenness had occurred here in Ireland, "contains the picture of a man whose face was eaten away by a pig, while he was lying in a state of intoxication. The entire nose, both cheeks, and parts of both ears, in fact, all the most eatable parts of his face, were chewed off by the animal." Quin shook his head in disbelief, thinking the man must have been very drunk indeed not to have noticed such voraciousness aimed at his own flesh. According to the report, though, "...the wounds all healed, and he recovered..." although not without the "disabilities of enunciation, chewing and swallowing" such damage would naturally entail.

Quin blinked rapidly a few times as he envisaged what the man must look like now—assuming he'd survived the few years that had passed since his fateful porcine encounter, which seemed dubious at best—but suppressed an unexpected laugh at the observation that the man's main regret, or so it was reported, was his inability to use his pipe following the incident.

Quin gave a further astonished shake of the head, glancing at Alannah as he did so. She was looking down at her book, her face slightly turned away from him so he couldn't see her expression. He frowned at her for a moment, before lowering his eyes back to his own reading material, searching for further entertaining medical anecdotes to take his mind off his marital woes. Having found nothing that quite compared with the efforts of the pig—and having struggled through the unfamiliar terminology of the remaining medical lore—he closed the journal several minutes later, intending to replace it on the shelf and select something more to his tastes as the silence in the room dragged on.

"What's the point of it all?"

Quin turned toward Alannah in surprise. Having hardly spoken to him all day, she had now spoken so softly he'd barely heard her—and he wasn't even sure whether she'd meant him to. She was looking into the empty hearth, showing no signs of having addressed him.

"Do you ever wonder?" she spoke again, quietly, still facing the cold fireplace.

He frowned in some confusion at her question but made an inquisitive sound, assuming she was aiming her comments at him after all.

"Life," she said slowly, making the word sound like a sigh—a sigh that cut through Quin's heart with the sharp note of desolation it bore on its wings. "It's fraught with hardships and injustice," she went on softly, "anger and hatred...with bigotry and violence riddling our existence like a disease." She shook her head slowly before turning toward him at last. "What's the point of it all?" She lifted one shoulder as she looked at him.

Quin's throat constricted at the sight of her downtrodden expression, his earlier irritation forgotten. But he eyed her for a moment before answering, drawing his brows together in thought as he placed the medical journal on the small table next to his chair.

"I've often wondered the same thing," he said finally in a soft voice, "obsessively so for a time, when I was younger." He paused. "I came to realise that...life is there for the living." He gave a small laugh, thinking how ridiculous and simplistic the notion sounded when spoken out loud. "All we ever have is this moment," he continued quietly, leaning forward and taking Alannah's hand. "There will always be obstacles, circumstances beyond our control, but we can't let them consume us. We have to find what joy there is in the little things...and embrace what happiness life offers to the full."

Alannah's eyes softened for a moment but all too soon, she dropped her gaze again and turned back toward the fireplace. With a suppressed sigh, Quin leaned back in his chair, letting his eyes wander aimlessly around the room.

"Did he ever know true happiness, I wonder?" Alannah's low voice made Quin turn back toward her, cocking his head enquiringly. "Kieran," she said softly, looking down at her lap.

Quin's heart gave a painful thump at hearing her murdered brother's name, and he reached for her hand once more, making her turn toward him and look up at him. He was filled with sadness to see that her deep blue eyes were shiny with tears.

"Today," she started slowly, "is...would have been...his twenty-sixth birthday."

Quin's heart sank as he watched her compress her trembling lips, suddenly seeing the day's events in an entirely different light. He had thought she was being selfish, but he'd been the one who had been blind, too involved in his own affairs to see her sorrow.

"Alannah, I'm so sorry." He dropped to his knees in front of her chair, his heart heavy with his own regret as much as his sadness for her. "I didn't realise," he murmured, wondering how he could have missed the date. He pulled her gently into his arms, wishing he'd insisted on speaking with her earlier, that he hadn't jumped to conclusions when she hadn't reacted the way he'd thought she should.

She lifted one shoulder in a shrug. "It's alright," she whispered as he cradled her head in one hand, while stroking her back with the other, wanting to take away her pain.

"You were so distant the whole day," he said softly as he held her. "I thought...I thought you were angry with me for going to Omagh."

She turned her head so she could look at him, an expression of surprise on her face. "But I said I would support you."

"I know," Quin stammered, feeling foolish for doubting her words. "It's just..."

"I don't like it, Quin." She shrugged. "It's difficult to pretend otherwise. But I won't stand in your way...and I do hope you find what you're looking for."

Quin could hear the sincerity in her voice and pulled her into a tight embrace once more, his throat constricting as he did so. He held her for several minutes, without speaking, feeling her heart thumping next to his as she leaned trustingly into him. After some time, he drew slowly away from her but took both of her hands in his and looked intently into her face.

"For what it's worth," he said gently, holding her eyes. "I think Kieran was happy...in the end."

Alannah's eyes filled with tears at his words. She took a deep breath, letting it out slowly through her mouth as a few tears overflowed and rolled down her cheeks.

"I think you're right," she whispered before having to sniff repeatedly as her nose began to run.

Quin handed her the handkerchief from his pocket, which she used to dab her eyes and blow her nose. She made as if to give the handkerchief back to him but changed her mind just as he was reaching for it, making them jostle momentarily over the damp piece of fabric. Their eyes met and they both laughed suddenly, a welcome release from the day's emotions. Quin took firm hold of the handkerchief and pulled it out of Alannah's grasp before stuffing it resolutely back into his pocket.

"I'm here for you, Alannah," he said determinedly, "...mucus and all." He grinned at her, getting a weak smile in response. He pulled her back toward him, wrapping her in his arms. "I don't ever want you to feel like you can't talk to me about something," he murmured into her hair. "I want to know what's on your heart...so that I can help you bear your burdens."

"You do, more than you know." Abruptly, she tightened her arms around him, with such force that he grunted in surprise. He was about to make a humorous comment about her having to loosen her grip to allow him to breathe when she spoke again, so softly he could barely hear her. "I couldn't bear to lose you too."

His heart contracted painfully at her words and his throat felt tight.

"I'm not going anywhere," he whispered as he tightened his arms around her. He closed his eyes and swallowed heavily, wishing he could halt the inevitable, that there was some way to hold off the separation that would eventually come to them all.

7.

A WEEK OR so later Quin was sitting at the breakfast table when Alannah came through the door to join him.

"We've been invited to Dublin," he announced.

"Dublin?" Alannah looked at him as she sat down.

"Yes! I've received a letter from my friend from the army." He patted the folded sheet of paper that lay next to his plate. "It looks like our shy Oliver Penhale has managed to find himself a bride—none other than the buxom lass whom he's been mooning over for more than a year."

"Oh," Alannah said with some surprise, "and now they are to be married?"

"Indeed they are, and we are invited to celebrate their betrothal." Quin opened the letter once more and scanned the single page. "I for one am highly curious to find out how this happy circumstance came about! Last I heard, Ollie hadn't so much as worked up the courage to speak to her." He grinned, imagining his slight friend in the ample grasp of a well-rounded lass.

"Then we must go, of course!" Alannah replied, smiling. "And I would very much like to meet your other friends!" Although she'd met the formidable Archibald Bellinger when they'd last been to Dublin—and seen him again when he'd shown up unannounced at their wedding—she had yet to make the acquaintance of Oliver Penhale and Hamilton Wolstenholme.

"Excellent!" Quin rubbed his hands together in anticipation, feeling ridiculously excited at the prospect of seeing his friends again. "Then we'll go, just the two of us."

"What, travel without servants?" Alannah asked in feigned shock, a hand to her chest.

"I think we'll manage, and I dare say they'll enjoy their time off!" A slow grin started spreading along his lips. "Although what we'll do with all that time alone, I don't know."

Alannah smiled mischievously, holding Quin's eyes with her own. "We'll think of something, no doubt."

"No doubt!" Quin leaned toward her and kissed her firmly on the lips.

"That's settled then," Alannah murmured against his mouth. "I'm looking forward to the trip!"

A gentle throat-clearing at the door caused Alannah to move away from Quin, throwing a sideways glance toward the entryway in some embarrassment. Quin had no such qualms, though—he was in his own house, after all, with his lawfully wedded wife—and pulled her back toward him by the nape of her neck, enjoying the feeling of her lips against his for a little longer. Finally, he turned nonchalantly toward the door, where a pink-cheeked Mr Dunne was just coming in.

"Good morning, Mr Dunne," Quin greeted the overseer cheerfully. "Ready for the big day, are you?"

The last phase of the building work on Dunne's house was to begin that day, to be completed in good time before the summer harvesting of the wheat and oats. Quin glanced outside the window. The building was likely to be a damp business, judging by the soft drizzle that had been their companion for what seemed like an innumerable number of days. Quin shrugged, turning back toward the table.

"Oh, yes, sir," the overseer was saying, his cheeks still pink, now presumably in excitement at the prospect of soon having his own home.

"Very good." Quin nodded at the slight man as he took his seat, looking a little startled at Quin's jovial mood. "I'll have another task for you soon," Quin continued as he handed Dunne the basket of bread.

"Sir?" Dunne puffed out his chest at being so addressed. Although he'd been on the estate for some time now, he hadn't yet been called upon to perform a task of any size on his own.

"You shall be in charge of the preparations for the harvesting of the summer crops," Quin told him.

"Of course, sir." The man gave a curt nod, his face taking on a serious expression.

"Mrs Williams and I shall be visiting Dublin," Quin explained, although no explanation was necessary. Dunne had been hired to perform exactly such duties. Still, Quin felt having a more personal relationship with one's staff never hurt and, indeed, he preferred it that way. "We shall be away for about two weeks or so, during which time I shall depend on you to oversee the running of the estate."

"Yes, sir," Dunne responded gravely, squaring his narrow shoulders as he set himself for the task ahead.

Quin smiled at the sight. He had every faith that Dunne would fulfil his duties admirably and was pleased the trip to Dublin would give the overseer a chance to prove himself as he took the reins in their absence.

"Oh," Alannah exclaimed suddenly, making Quin turn toward her.

"What is it?"

"I've only just thought...what about the children?" Quin gave her a blank look. "The children I've been teaching," she clarified with a slight frown at his ignorance.

"Ah."

"I could teach them in your absence."

Quin looked at Mr Dunne in some surprise.

"Would you?" Alannah asked the overseer eagerly. "I really wouldn't want them to miss any lessons while I'm away, they've been getting on so well. And a few more joined us just last week."

"It's no trouble, Mrs Williams," Dunne said. "No trouble at all.—My father was a schoolmaster, you see."

"Of course."

"And it won't interfere with any of my other duties," he hastily assured Quin. "I'll simply rearrange my time a little to have two mornings a week off."

"Well, that's settled then," Quin said with a smile. "Now, shall we eat?"

QUIN FROWNED AT the folded sheet of paper before stuffing it back into the envelope as the rain continued to spatter against the window.

Aside from the letter from Olli announcing his betrothal, several others had arrived at the estate that morning. But in the excitement of planning their trip to Dublin—and the numerous practicalities daily farm life entailed—Quin had only gotten around to opening the other letters in the late afternoon. Receiving any sort of mail was something of an irregular event, one that usually filled Quin with equal parts eagerness and annoyance in anticipation. Although he very much enjoyed reading the letters that arrived from his friends in Dublin, he was far less enthusiastic about those that made their way to Glaslearg from his father's house in London. Not to disappoint, today's store had included the expected brief note from Quin's father, The Right Honourable The Lord Williams, The Baron Williams of Wadlow, third of that name. Having numerous names and titles at his disposal, Wilfred Ernest Cecil Williams was nevertheless thrifty with his word use, as he was in nearly all areas of his life, including the spending of money, the dispensing of compliments and the showering of affection upon his only son. In fact, the baron was so practiced in his thriftiness that he managed, despite the economical word use in his meagre note, to convey his discontent, both with life in general and his son in particular.

Today, though, it was not the baron's miserable correspondence that had soured Quin's mood—Quin being quite used to his father's disgruntlement by now—but rather an unexpected message from an entirely unexpected source.

The guard at Omagh gaol.

Quin exhaled in irritation, remembering his last trip to the town.

Every time he'd gone there, Quin had asked everyone who would speak to him to inform him if they remembered anything at all peculiar about the days leading up to Doyle's hanging, no matter how trivial it may seem. His continued badgering had finally yielded sufficient information for him to conclude that the guard and the hangman had been bribed, allowing another man to be hanged in Doyle's place and Doyle himself to escape—although he was no closer to identifying the how and the why of it.

Now, though, it appeared the guard had remembered something else, perhaps emerging from his paid stupor at last. Having previously bent the truth in favour of monetary recompense, the guard now appeared to be trying to make up for his shortcomings.

According to his letter, a carriage had arrived at the gaol at sunset on the day before the hanging. As it passed the guard, the driver had informed him with a snigger that it was a visitor for the warden, the man evidently being in the habit of entertaining a variety of women in his quarters. The guard hadn't thought much of it at the time—or so he made Quin believe—but had lately remembered the incident when he'd noticed another lady of the night visiting the warden a few days before.

Unlike his erstwhile guest, this woman had snuck into the keep well after sunset, using her own two feet for transport and attempting to keep herself concealed—no doubt as per her client's instructions. Quin scowled, having learnt on one of his visits that the warden had a wife and several children who resided on a homestead some way out of town. While this secretive behaviour was undoubtedly aimed at keeping the warden's wife in the dark, it had at least done something to illuminate the appearance of the carriage in the guard's mind.

The man now questioned the truthfulness of the driver's account—an observation that made Quin snort at the irony—and wondered whether the carriage had in fact held a female visitor at all. The carriage curtains had been drawn and so he'd been unable to see the occupant, but he now doubted whether any woman of the streets would have made her entrance in such a fashion. And while it might have been possible that the warden had caught the eye of someone better off, who would have been able to procure a carriage to take her to her clandestine rendezvous, one particular factor made that possibility unlikely.

Upon its arrival the carriage had been greeted by the guard who was now missing.

Quin dropped the letter into one of the desk drawers, his brows knitted together in thought. Knowing the same guard who'd disappeared soon after taking the false Doyle to be hanged had also met the mysterious carriage the evening before the execution was suspicious indeed—a suspicion that led Quin to concur that the carriage likely *hadn't* held a woman visiting the warden as the driver had made out.

Quin tapped a finger slowly on his chin as he stared unseeing at the desk and its open drawer. It was far more likely, he thought, that the carriage had held whoever had been hanged in Doyle's stead. The man must have come from somewhere, after all, since nobody at the gaol had been reported missing after the hanging.

But who was this unknown man? Where had he come from? And who had gone to the trouble of bringing him to Omagh to hang in a murderer's stead?

And why?

A shout from the kitchen across the hall broke in on Quin's thoughts. By the sounds of the crash that accompanied the exclamation, whatever vessel had hit the floor was beyond repair.

Quin's eye fell once more on the desk drawer and the letter it contained. Some of the things that had happened after Doyle's escape were also beyond repair—events that had shattered their lives into a thousand little pieces, like so many pieces of smashed pottery.

Quin stared at the letter for a moment longer. "I shall find the answers I seek," he growled under his breath before slamming the drawer shut.

8.

QUIN SIGHED. "IT'S ghastly, isn't it?"

"It is," Alannah agreed quietly from next to him on the wagon seat.

They had departed Glaslearg early in the morning the day before and would soon be arriving in Dublin. Thinking they would pick up supplies in the city, they'd decided to travel by wagon instead of taking the more comfortable carriage. While Quin's father would be horrified to see his son so much as glance at a wagon, even driving it himself didn't bother Quin in the slightest— particularly not in light of the poverty and misery that had greeted them along the way.

They had come across numerous villages and clusters of cottages, most no better than the mud huts Glaslearg's tenants had lived in upon Quin's arrival on the estate two years before. Having seen his tenants' old cottages close-up, he knew just how appalling they were; single-roomed, gloomy structures without the benefit of windows or a chimney, inhabited not only by numerous people but also by their animals, with pigs, chickens, dogs and even cows crammed into the miserable interior. After the briefest of looks at these constructions, Quin had determined to build the families on his land proper houses, made of stone and with windows and a chimney to boot, feeling that no human ought to live like that.

But while his own tenants could now live more comfortably, not least of all because Quin and Alannah also made their wellbeing a priority, there were many more in Ireland who were not so lucky. Living in their horrendous mud huts on the estates of upper-class landowners—many of whom simply didn't care—countless people were struggling to survive. Over the past two days, he and Alannah had encountered numerous poor peasants begging on the street, or just milling about the town square with nothing but misery and dejection on their faces. With so many people occupying the same space, there was simply not enough work for all of them to earn a living, and with ever-increasing prices and few possessions or opportunities to begin with, Ireland's commoners were sliding deeper and deeper into poverty.

Alannah echoed his sigh and Quin shifted the reins, reaching out to take her hand.

"How can they go on like this?" she asked, lifting her shoulders in a dejected shrug.

"I suppose they have no choice," Quin answered in resignation.

"It makes me feel so helpless...seeing all those people who have nothing, who have been reduced to begging for their daily bread, dressed in rags. And guilty...for all we have ourselves."

Quin gently squeezed her hand. "We are helping where we can."

"I know. It's just that....handing out a few pennies or crusts of bread? It never seems enough!"

"I know."

They lapsed into silence.

"I had read about the misery of the Irish populace, of course," Quin said a few minutes later, "although most of England doesn't seem to care one bit about Ireland or her problems." He glanced at Alannah to see her reaction. She only shrugged, though, aware of England's general disinterest—it was obvious enough to see, after all. She turned toward him, pressing herself deeper into the wagon seat to avoid the raindrops dripping down the overhanging roof. Quin was grateful he'd had the foresight to have the wagon covered—with the wet summer they were having, it would have been quite unpleasant to drive for two days in the rain.

"Having decided to come here," he continued, "I thought I'd prepare myself." He gave a humourless laugh. "Not that anything I'd read in London could have prepared me for what awaited me here. I had thought the descriptions I'd found must have been exaggerated, that things couldn't possibly be so much worse than in England.—I was wrong. And I haven't even been to the western or southern parts of Ireland, where things are reportedly worse."

He had read of a town on the western coast that had once flourished under the linen trade, only for it to be reduced to squalor as mechanised linen manufacturing decimated local industry, with the inhabitants of the town forced to travel halfway across the island to find work for minimal pay during harvesttime to afford their rent. But with poor farming conditions in large parts of Ireland and an already overrun agricultural sector, more and more people were struggling to find any work at all.

Quin exhaled strongly through his nose, recalling another article he'd come across. It had described in vivid detail how hundreds of men, women and children had congregated on their village street and quay to beg their priest for food, in desperate need of help.

"Will it ever change, do you think?"

Quin shook himself at Alannah's question. "I don't know," he responded slowly. Ireland was continuously fraught with unrest, and he couldn't see how her plentiful problems might be easily solved. Centuries of oppression had left their mark. "O'Connell is certainly a popular figure with some influence but..."

"Even if he were to achieve a repeal of the Act of Union, it's difficult to say whether ordinary people's lives would improve."

Alannah's thoughts mirrored Quin's own, and he compressed his lips into a tight line. The lawyer Daniel O'Connell had been campaigning for years for Ireland to be given back its own parliament after it had been merged with that of Great Britain at the turn of the century. While he hadn't yet achieved this goal, he *had* been influential in the emancipation of Ireland's Catholics some years before, allowing Catholics to hold civil and military offices, sit in parliament and perform various other duties long prohibited under Protestant English rule. But while this reform was considered a victory by some, it held no benefit for the general Catholic population, who continued to live in poverty— much as they were likely to do with a repeal of the Act of Union.

"They do seem to love him, though," Alannah said, making Quin nod.

"I've read that O'Connell's an excellent orator who's very ably combined his own ideas with the commoners' concerns." He paused briefly as he navigated the wagon over a washed-out portion of road. "By campaigning about widespread changes including land reform and other local grievances, he's got the ears of the poor."

"Oh, he most certainly does! I've heard that some of his meetings have attracted over a hundred thousand people."

Quin raised his brows, although he could well believe it. With the vast number of desperate people in Ireland, many of them would inevitably flock to someone they thought was taking their complaints to heart.

"Although I suppose there are those whose sole purpose in attending O'Connell's meetings is to defy their landlord." Alannah lifted one shoulder, catching Quin's eye.

"No doubt," he said, aware that many landowners were adopting the approach of letting things take their course, hardly lifting a finger to help those in need. How anyone could be so heartless was beyond comprehension to Quin. He thought about the people who lived on his own land and knew he could never ignore their needs. They were not his kin, but he'd come to care a great deal about them and couldn't possibly let any of them suffer while he lived in luxury.

"I wonder if things will be better in Dublin," Alannah said, turning her head in the direction of the group of beggars they'd just passed.

"Hmph," Quin responded noncommittally, having not much more to offer. They had visited Dublin about two years earlier and had come across a number of desperate people then. How much worse it might have become in the meantime, he had no idea.

"Do you still have connections in Dublin?" he asked, as the thought suddenly occurred to him. "You were born there after all. You've never mentioned anyone but..."

"No, not really."

"Oh, I see. And you have no relations there at all, not even distant ones?"

"No. My mother's family came from Dublin as you know, but her own mother died in childbed long before I was born"—she raised her voice a little to be heard above the rain drumming on the canvas roof—"and her father shortly before she died herself. My aunt, my mother's younger sister, married into money and was living in a grand house in Dublin until she herself died in childbed several years ago. There's nobody else."

"Hm." Quin frowned. "Childbearing seems to be a frightfully dangerous business." His heart gave a painful thump at the thought. It had already proved difficult for Alannah to so much as fall pregnant, not to mention stay pregnant past the first few weeks—what other horrors might still be awaiting them?

"It is, I suppose." Alannah shrugged. "Still, it's all worth it in the end, isn't it?" She smiled at Quin, her eyes shining, clearly imagining holding their own child one day.

"I'm not so sure," Quin grumbled, remembering how devastated she had been just a few weeks ago when another early pregnancy had ended in heartache. And things could end even worse. His heart clenched like a fist at the thought of Alannah dying in agony during childbirth. Perhaps they'd never have any children, Quin thought almost elatedly, wanting only to keep Alannah safe. They had been married for almost two years now, after all, and it hadn't happened yet.

He glanced across at her, feeling guilty for having such thoughts.

He decided it would be safer to change the subject. "Um...and you never went to Dublin with your parents as a child?" he managed to ask.

Alannah shook her head, seeming unaware of his misgivings. "We moved to Niall when I was two, of course," she said, making Quin nod, forcing himself to focus. Alannah had told him about her father moving with his wife and two young children from Dublin to the countryside to take over the family farm—which was called Talamh na Niall, or Niall for short—after Alannah's uncle had died unexpectedly. Said farm adjoined Quin's own land, which was how he'd come to meet Alannah in the first place. Much to Alannah's anger and sorrow, her brother had lost the farm not long before his own death, having been blackmailed into giving it up for fear of otherwise being condemned as a traitor alongside his erstwhile accomplice Martin Doyle.

"The first time I went to Dublin after that was with my father when I was seventeen," Alannah was saying, making Quin shake himself back to attention.

"I see." He made an effort to close his mind to thoughts of Doyle, Alannah's brother Kieran and all that had happened before. "Did your mother not visit her father and her sister then, or her friends?" he asked, curious. "Surely, she would still have had connections there, even a few years after she left."

"She did," Alannah said slowly. "In fact, she went to Dublin for one month every year she lived at Niall until she died when I was thirteen. But she only ever took along her maid and her coachman."

"I see." Quin was silent for a moment, not sure how to respond.

"I think...that she wanted that time to herself. Whenever she returned from one of her trips, Kieran and I would pester her until she told us all about her time in Dublin. I often found myself imagining her life there based on her stories...going to dinner parties and grand balls, mingling with aristocrats and feeling like she belonged there." Alannah shrugged. "She did belong there...once. After she died, I started wondering, though, whether her stories were true, or whether it was something of an act she put on out of spite, to remind my father she was unhappy with her lot in life.—Not that anyone needed any reminding," she added under her breath.

Alannah had told Quin her mother had not been happy with her husband's decision to leave Dublin, that she'd felt cheated of the grand life she'd envisioned for them in the city—finding herself living the life of a farmer's wife instead.

"And she had no difficulty leaving her children for a month each year?" Quin asked. "Even when you were little?"

"Not really." Alannah paused briefly before going on. "I don't want to say she was a bad mother or that she didn't love us but...she was happy to have the nursemaid deal with our day-to-day care, interacting with us mostly when it suited her.—It's not entirely unusual, is it?"

Quin made a noncommittal sound in his throat. He was fully aware that many upper-class women left most of the childrearing to their staff, but it was not a situation he'd been familiar with himself. His own mother had been most attentive to his needs when he was growing up, rarely relying on outside assistance for his care. Quin doubted she even would have considered going anywhere without him for an extended period of time while he was young.

"She did dote on Kieran, though, in her own way," Alannah continued, "fussing over him at every opportunity, telling him he was too good for the cruel world he found himself in." Quin glanced at her and saw she had compressed her lips at the memory. Suddenly, though, she laughed. "As he got older, I think he started enjoying the time she spent away from us in Dublin as much as she did." Quin laughed with her until her amusement faded and she sighed. "My mother found it difficult to find joy in life," she said softly. "She couldn't see past the obstacles...both real and imagined. I promised myself long ago I wouldn't do the same."

"You haven't," Quin said gently, reaching for Alannah's hand once more. He looked across at her, but she dropped her eyes. "We all have moments where our circumstances can seem a little overwhelming." He gave her hand a gentle squeeze. "It's what we do *after* those moments that's important."

She looked up at him and gave him a small smile. He smiled back at her before placing his arm around her shoulders and drawing her close beside him. Shifting in his seat and adjusting his hold on the reigns until he found a comfortable position, he turned his eyes back toward the road ahead as the drizzle abated at last.

9.

"LIFE AS YOU know it is over, lieutenant!"

The group of men burst into laughter as the lieutenant's homely face took on a pained expression at having to endure yet another joke at his expense.

"Yes, sir," Oliver Penhale responded meekly to his superior, clearly wishing himself to be someplace else.

"She's a looker, though, Penhale," Captain Fletcher continued in slightly slurred tones, "I'll give you that." The older man lifted his chin toward the other side of the room, where a buxom redheaded woman was surrounded by several others, all of them chittering animatedly among themselves.

Quin suppressed a grin. Although the woman in question did tend to catch a man's eye, said eye was disposed to settle on her lower, well-rounded endowments rather than being captured by the attractiveness of her face—this being rather plain in comparison to what other physical enticements she had to offer.

"Uh…thank you, sir." Ollie's cheeks turned pink, making Quin bite his lip to keep from laughing out loud.

A less likely pairing than Lieutenant Oliver Penhale and Miss Anne Cartwright could scarcely be imagined—he being slight of stature and rather reserved in temperament, she being ample in proportions and possessed of an exceedingly boisterous character. But the heart wants what it may, and Ollie had fallen in love, their differences notwithstanding. To Ollie's own evident astonishment, the object of his affections had returned his feelings and after months and months of pining heartache, the two of them were finally to be wed.

Quin chuckled briefly. He had of course been delighted to read of Ollie's good fortune in the letter announcing his betrothal but had also been exceedingly curious about the circumstances surrounding it. The last Quin had heard, Ollie had been sick with heartache, thinking he stood no chance of winning over the one he desired, even were he able to work up the courage to so much as approach her—which, by all accounts, he was not.

Much had happened in the months between then and now, though, it seemed.

"It all started with a pair of gloves," the bear-like Archibald Bellinger had informed Quin and Alannah on the evening of their arrival in Dublin, he, Ollie and Ham having joined the two of them in the taproom of the inn they were staying at.

"A pair of gloves?" Quin asked, turning toward Ollie. "Did you throw them at her feet in challenge for her affection?"

Archie guffawed and Ham sniggered, while Ollie himself shook his head.

"I did not," he said shortly. "I simply went to buy some. Or rather, to collect a pair I'd ordered."

"Whereupon the sight of your elegantly begloved hands caught your beloved's adoring eye?" Quin suggested with a raised brow.

Ollie rolled his eyes before darting a quick glance at Alannah, evidently unsure how she would react to the men's tongue-in-cheek exchange. Seeing her smiling, though, he turned back to Quin.

"Very funny," he responded drily. "If you'd let me speak, you'd arrive at the conclusion of the tale all the sooner."

Quin spread his hands apologetically and motioned to Ollie to continue.

"As I said, I had gone to the glover to collect a pair I'd ordered the week before. Having received my wares and paid, I headed to the door. Just at that moment, though, Miss Ca...ah...my betrothed," he amended with flushed cheeks, "happened to enter."

"She ran right into him," Ham added, leaning forward enthusiastically, steepling his hands under his prominent nose—the only marring feature in his otherwise handsome face.

"We collided, yes," Ollie went on with gravity. "I caught her by the elbow before she should fall but she dropped her basket, and I dropped my hat and newly purchased gloves."

"How awful," Alannah put in with a straight face, making Archie laugh out loud, his wide shoulders heaving with mirth.

Ollie flushed and cleared his throat. "Um, yes." He wrinkled his brows in some seriousness. "Miss Cartwright—Anne—was most apologetic, feeling herself responsible for the incident, insisting she'd barged into the shop without proper care. I of course assured her that no blame at all lay upon her, as I had been the impatient one in my hasty exit."

Watching Ollie retell the encounter made Quin smile. If ever anyone had fallen head over heels in love with anyone, it was Oliver Penhale. Glancing over at Alannah, though, Quin's smile grew. And he himself, he amended. Alannah'd had a very similar effect on him, after all.

"And so, out of remorse for the regrettable role she played in their fateful meeting, Miss Cartwright grudgingly agreed to marry Ollie here," Archie concluded the tale with a grin.

"Um, not quite," Ollie said, his ears turning pink.

"Picking up the spilled contents of her basket did, however, give Ollie the opportunity to talk to her," Ham pointed out. "Something he'd been wanting to do for months on end."

"Ever since he first saw her." Archie groaned, making Ollie look a little uncomfortable. "Oh, you should have seen him," Archie continued with a long-suffering air and a shake of the head on his sizeable shoulders. "Wallowing in misery at the thought of his unrequited love—when he hadn't so much as spoken a word to her!"

"Yes...well, women are..." Ollie snapped his mouth shut abruptly and glanced sideways at Alannah.

"Terrifying?" Quin suggested.

Ollie cleared his throat and shrugged. "A little," he admitted, avoiding Alannah's eye.

"In any case, you spoke to her..." Quin said encouragingly.

"I did."

"Well, your words seem to have had an effect."

Ollie's cheeks reddened once more at Quin's statement, and Quin could picture all too well the awkwardness that must have pervaded that first encounter. While Ollie was an intelligent man who could take on all manner of difficulties, his confidence—and his wits—tended to desert him when attempting to converse with members of the fairer sex, leaving him stranded in dim silence. Quin could only imagine how much worse it must have been when the woman in question was someone for whom Ollie had developed amorous feelings, which—to Quin's knowledge—wasn't something that had happened before. Fortunately, Ollie's faculties appeared to have returned to him in the end, as evidenced by the impending wedding.

"I suppose they did." Ollie put on a show of confidence. "In either case, having collected the scattered items and left the glover's, we walked a way together along High Street until we reached her waiting coach."

"At which point she invited him to call on her the following afternoon!" Ham jumped in, his eyes wide above his sizeable nose as he leaned toward Quin.

Quin raised his brows, in equal parts impressed and surprised. Unprepossessing Ollie must have left quite an impression on her.

"She did," Ollie agreed with a nod.

"And you accepted the invitation of course."

"I did."

"And that was that," Archie said, spreading his large hands in conclusion. "They were betrothed a short time later." He sounded both pleased and amazed at the telling, evidently startled at the speed at which Ollie's dalliance was hurtling toward the altar, but happy for his friend, nonetheless.

Quin looked fondly at Alannah. Their own relationship had progressed much faster than some might consider proper, but Quin wouldn't have wanted it any other way—he'd known from the moment he saw her there could never be another for him.

"I'm happy for you," he said to Ollie, leaning toward him and clapping a hand on his shoulder. "I wish the two of you a lifetime of joy."

Quin smiled to himself now in remembrance, picturing the delighted—yet slightly bewildered—look adorning Ollie's face that evening as he'd described the circumstances which had led to tonight's celebration. Clearly, he was quite unable to believe his own luck.

"Your woman's easy on the eyes, too, isn't she, Lieutenant Williams?"

Captain Fletcher's elbow in his ribs brought Quin back to the present.

"*Mr* Williams," Quin corrected absently. Although he'd served in the British Army in combat, he'd resigned his commission some years before. He turned in the direction of the captain's look, toward the far side of the room where

Alannah had joined the other ladies. She looked radiant in her green gown, with her black hair gathered loosely at the side of her slender neck so it cascaded forward over one shoulder in a thick tail. As he looked at her, she lifted her eyes, catching his, a slow smile spreading across her lips.

"She's far more than that," Quin said softly, holding her eyes.

"I daresay." The captain turned his head curiously back to Quin and again to Alannah, teetering slightly as he did so. "Can't complain about the shaking of the sheets, either, ey?" The captain elbowed Quin in the ribs once more and laughed at his own witticism, a waft of whiskey fumes drifting from his open mouth.

Quin snorted as he looked back at Captain Fletcher, cocking his head knowingly as he did so, unable to deny the fundamentals of the man's euphemistic observation.

The captain roared with laughter at Quin's unmistakable expression. "Lucky man you are, sir," he said once he'd recovered, giving Alannah an appreciative nod. "Lucky man you are." He thumped Quin on the back before staggering off.

Quin laughed after him before turning back toward the other men, who had continued their friendly banter while Quin had been lost in thought.

"Now be sure to locate your target before you snuff out the light," one red-nosed man was saying to Ollie, who rolled his eyes at the military jargon.

"Right you are, Wentworth!" another fellow jumped in eagerly. "No good going off with a loaded gun if you don't know where to aim it!"

The assembly erupted raucously, their great whoops of delight making the rest of the party throw curious glances in their direction.

"If you're not sure what you're looking for," a helpful sort added once the hilarity had subsided, leaning confidentially toward Ollie, "just lay her on her back and..."

"I'm sure our Oliver will have no trouble whatsoever on his wedding night," Quin cut in before the man could complete what would no doubt have been a vulgar remark, "nor any other night he'll be lucky enough to spend with his bride."

Quin lay his arm companionably over Ollie's shoulder, making the newly betrothed look relieved, self-assured and embarrassed all at the same time. A rare feat indeed, Quin thought wryly.

"Subjecting you to the inquisition, are they?"

Quin turned his head to where Archie had made his way toward them, followed by the shorter form of Ham.

"If you mean torturing me with an endless supply of lecherous comments, then yes, they are," Ollie responded drily, looking after the other men as they started drifting away, the jesting temporarily at an end. Looking back at Archie, Ham and Quin, he grinned. "Not that I'm complaining."

"I'd be surprised if you did!" Ham said. "After months of self-inflicted agony, this must feel like a picnic."

Ollie laughed sheepishly.

"Come, you'll miss the dancing!"

An arm shot out and grabbed Ollie by the hand, turning him toward the doorway on the far side of the room, through which the sounds of fiddle and flute were drifting. Quin chuckled at Ollie's surprised expression at the sudden appearance of his affianced but threw an appreciative glance at Miss Cartwright's curvaceous form. She caught his eye and smiled mischievously at him, her green eyes sparkling amidst the light dusting of freckles that bedecked her face. Quin smiled back at her, giving her a slight bow.

"Miss Cartwright," he greeted her formally, suddenly understanding exactly what had attracted Ollie to his future bride. She was a very fetching woman indeed, using her God-given assets to best advantage. Ollie himself was completely taken by her charms, following in her wake like an obedient puppy as she led him across the floor.

Quin grinned after them, his smile widening as he spotted Ham and Archie, who'd followed the pair and were now hard at work trying to entice a couple of lone ladies to join the two of them on the dancefloor.

"Enjoying yourself?"

"I am," he said, turning toward Alannah, who had come up beside him. His heart gave a pleasant thump at the sight of her.

While there might be others who held a passing attraction, she was the only one he wanted.

"You?" He cocked his head as he reached out a hand to brush back a lock of her glossy hair, his fingers grazing her skin in a whisper of touch that teetered on the edge of social boundaries.

"I am," she responded, holding his eyes. "Would you like to dance?" She raised her dark brows enquiringly.

"I would."

Quin offered her his arm, leading her into the adjoining room and spinning her onto the dancefloor in an elegant pirouette. Buoyed by the joyous atmosphere he pulled her back toward him, holding her as close as the dance allowed before reluctantly letting her go once more. She laughed as she spun away from him, his eyes following her as she glided across the room.

They danced and danced as the music went on, the sound thumping through Quin's veins in a lively staccato that matched his jubilant mood. Alannah's cheeks started turning pink with exertion but still they danced on, until at last they had to take a breath.

"Any regrets?" Quin asked as they sat down, catching hold of Alannah's left hand with his right. He ran his thumb over the ring he'd placed on her finger almost two years before, stroking the fine filigree pattern—two hands bound with an endless knot, clasping a crown-topped heart.

Alannah shook her head. "None.—This is only the beginning, a lifetime with you will not be enough."

"There are many more years to come." Quin leaned toward her and gave her hand a gentle squeeze. "Would you care to make your way back to the inn?"

"I would."

As soon as the words crossed her lips Quin jumped up and pulled her from her seat, making her laugh as she took his arm. Grinning, he led her past the remaining revellers, bidding farewell to those they wouldn't see again for some time. They had been in Dublin for the past six days and would only be staying for one more. In some ways Quin didn't want to go back, wanting to hold onto the sense of freedom that came with being away from one's duties.

Alannah, too, had enjoyed being away from the estate, wandering through the busy city streets at Quin's side, the two of them talking and laughing, rekindling the closeness that had bound them from the start. Quin was loathe to give it up once more, but he could feel the pull of responsibility tugging at his heart and his head, the need of the people who depended on him. And he knew she felt it too.

They bid Archie, Ham and Ollie a fond goodbye, Quin thumping Ollie on the back in congratulations once more. Quin promised he and Alannah would be back for the wedding, but that was still some way off—a time spent away from friends who'd become closer than family, whose existence transmuted into words on paper in the interim; words that might never find their way to their intended recipient, as letters were misplaced or lost in transit, disappearing forever.

But what news there was would reach them one way or another, Quin thought to himself with a smile, even if a little slowly. Knowing his friends were there was the important thing. He waved to Ham and Archie, who were making their way back to the barracks, having decided to join Quin and Alannah in their leave-taking. Ollie would follow some time later once he'd dispatched the last of the night's celebrants. As much as he may want to stay with Miss Cartwright at her family's home, he would have to wait until the wedding to spend the night with her under the same roof.

Fortunately for Quin, such formalities were already out of the way for him. He pulled Alannah a little closer, enjoying the feel of her next to him, even through the layers of fabric separating them. Once back in the privacy of their room at the inn, he had every intention of removing those layers of fabric, letting her garments slide slowly to the floor one by one, until she at last stood bare before him, her naked skin beckoning his touch.

His fingertips tingled at the thought while his heart started thumping steadily.

There were some hours left to the night yet, Quin thought as he quickened his step, hours that needn't be wasted on sleep.

10.

WHEN I WOKE up the next morning it was very late indeed, as I could tell by the angle of the light coming in through the window. The light itself quite surprised me, as I couldn't remember when I'd last seen the sun. For what felt like weeks on end, it had been dreary and wet, with almost incessant rainfall dripping from the seemingly endless, low-hanging grey clouds.

I stretched languorously, enjoying the rare sunlight.

I hadn't slept so soundly in months and felt truly refreshed for the first time in a long time. The last few days had given me a spring in my step, spending time alone with Quin and meeting his friends. Archie, Ham and Ollie had accepted me into their circle with little hesitation, making me feel entirely at ease with them despite our short acquaintance. Archie had greeted me like an old friend and expressed his regret at the news of Kieran's passing, with a sincerity that was plain to see and touched me with its obvious depth of feeling. I sighed briefly at the memory but smiled to myself thinking about shy Ollie and his imminent wedding—a wedding I was very much looking forward to attending.

Finally getting out of bed, I looked around the room and espied a piece of paper on the dresser. It was a note from Quin, informing me that he'd gone to run some errands and would be back in the afternoon.

Estimating it to be mid-morning already—and possibly closer to noon—I hurriedly got dressed before making my way downstairs. The taproom was empty, except for Mr Kelly, the innkeeper, who was sitting at one of the tables. Seeing me, he got up and came toward me.

"Mrs Williams," he greeted me with a jovial smile, his round cheeks bobbing like plump red apples. "I trust you've had a good rest?" He blinked his button eyes at me expectantly.

"I have, thank you, Mr Kelly." I nodded at him and smiled. I was about to ask if there was anything in the way of breakfast to be had, feeling suddenly ravenously hungry, when he spoke again.

"I'll just be off to get you a bite to eat." Without asking for my agreement, he turned on his heel and was off, his round form making its surprisingly rapid way across the room toward the adjoining kitchen.

I laughed and started heading to a comfortable-looking seat when the sound of the inn door opening caught my attention. I turned toward it in anticipation, thinking Quin might have returned early. It wasn't Quin who had opened the door, though, and the smile froze on my lips when I saw who had.

He was dressed in a fine pair of cream trousers and a waistcoat in a darker shade to match, along with an extravagantly tied cravat and cutaway morning coat. The points of his greying moustache were styled just so, and the set of his shoulders and the cock of his head declared him to be a man confident in his own appearance, and his own importance.

The door swung shut and he turned into the room, holding his walking stick and his hat in one hand. Catching sight of me standing at the bottom of the staircase, gaping at him, he lifted one brow in my direction but showed no other signs of being surprised at my presence at the inn. Without looking, he handed his hat and walking stick to the burly man who'd come through the door after him, a slow smile blooming on his lips as he eyed me.

"Mrs Williams," Herbert Andrews said in a delighted voice as he came toward me, making me stiffen as disjointed images flashed across my mind's eye.

Despite my distinct lack of enthusiasm, I had once been meant to marry Andrews—or at least my brother Kieran and his repugnant acquaintance Martin Doyle had hoped for such a thing to occur, in return for a sizeable chunk of Andrew's large fortune, with which they'd hoped to finance a rebellion against the English crown. Instead, Kieran and Doyle had been arrested as they'd attempted to take me to Andrews against my will. In a surprising turn of events, Andrews had declared himself a British spy and testified against Doyle at the trial following the arrest and—even more surprisingly—exonerated Kieran from any traitorous intentions. This behaviour had by no means been indicative of Andrews' benevolent disposition, though, as he'd subsequently threatened to testify against Kieran after all, managing thus to blackmail him into giving up his family farm, our beloved Talamh na Niall.

Returning to the present, I narrowed my eyes at Herbert Andrews, realising suddenly that he'd addressed me using my married name. I wondered how he knew Quin and I were wed—Andrews and I were hardly in the habit of keeping in touch.

"How wonderful to find you in my establishment," he said, giving me a broad smile that showed off his clean-cut features, which were still handsome despite his middle years.

"*Your* establishment?" I asked, startled.

"Why, yes." Andrews seemed surprised at my ignorance. "The Huntsman's Inn belongs to me, as do several others. Mr Kelly simply runs it for me."

"I see," I said shortly, thinking Quin and I would be leaving that very day if I had anything to say about it.

"Huntsman was my mother's maiden name," Andrews went on, oblivious to my hostility. He sighed nostalgically and was silent for a moment before turning toward me with an amused look on his face. "You didn't think my fortune was made solely from farming, did you?"

"I didn't think about your fortune at all," I responded coldly.

Andrews gave a short laugh, seeming not the least bit affected by my discourtesy. He waved an arm casually at one of the tables in the taproom, beckoning me toward a chair with a lift of his chin.

"Come." He reached out a hand toward me. "Let us sit together while we talk."

I pulled my arm away before he could touch me and took a step back, making him blink once or twice as he looked at me.

"I have no intention of sitting with you, or of talking to you!"

"Oh?" Andrews cocked his head in some surprise.

Out of the corner of my eye I caught sight of Mr Kelly, who had emerged from the door to the kitchen holding a laden plate—which was presumably meant for me—but was now hovering indecisively at the threshold as he observed Andrews and me. His eyes flitted back and forth between the two of us, until at last, with a final frightened-looking glance at Andrews, he scuttled back into the kitchen.

I scowled, turning my attention back to the man myself.

"How could you possibly think I would have anything to do with you?" I hissed, making his eyes go round in astonishment. "After what you did to my brother?"

"Your brother?" Andrews looked quizzically at me as he slowly rubbed his chin.

"Kieran O'Neill," I said, emphasising each syllable as it crossed my lips.

He looked at me thoughtfully for a moment longer before his features finally cleared. "Ah...yes, Mr O'Neill. Now I recall." He nodded slowly. "But I'd heard he'd met with an accident," he said suddenly, a look of concern blooming on his attractive face. "How very regrettable." He shook his head and sighed. Abruptly, his eyes widened, and he put a hand to his chest. "You can't think *I* had anything to do with that, can you?"

I took a deep breath and swallowed heavily before responding. "You took away his land," I said in a shaky but controlled voice, ignoring Andrews' reference to Kieran's death, "his home, his birthright."

Andrews looked at me for a moment, his head cocked to one side. Slowly, he smoothed out his moustache with the fingers of one hand, before lifting one shoulder indifferently.

"Under the circumstances I believe I was quite...generous."

"Generous?" I sputtered in disbelief.

Andrews spread his hands in a magnanimous gesture. "I let him keep the furniture after all...and the servants." He gave me a pointed look, as if he knew said furniture and servants had made their way to Glaslearg when he'd taken the farm from Kieran. "It worked out for the best, didn't it?" he said, making me feel a sudden need to launch myself at his throat. "I must admit, though," he continued, unperturbed by my reaction, "I *am* rather surprised he acquainted you with the details of our transaction. I was quite sure he would be far too embarrassed to admit his failings as a man, even to his sister."

I clenched my jaws, waiting to speak until I thought I had myself under control again. "What interest could you possibly have had in Talamh na Niall?" I managed to ask at last. "It's a small farm with no commercial value. All it ever did was sustain the people who lived there. You couldn't possibly have thought it would make you any money!"

"Oh, but it has. The tenants are paying a very handsome amount in rent.—The benefits of limited real estate, you see."

"You wanted my brother's farm so that you could lease it to someone else and collect the rent?" I was quite unable to hide the incredulity in my voice.

"Why not?" Andrews gave me a look of feigned surprise.

I glared at him, not fooled by his act.

He gave an ungentlemanly snort at my persistence and shook his head. "No, I did not," he admitted, "…at least not originally." He looked at me for a moment, as if trying to decide how much to tell me. At last, he shrugged. "It would have been a convenient location for my mill."

"Your what?"

"My flax mill. I had started dabbling in the linen trade, you see, turning over large tracts of my land to the growth of flax.—A profitable industry, you know." He looked down his nose at me, as if he were trying to educate a senseless child.

I stuck out my chin, which made him snigger with unconcealed mirth.

"I already had several flax fields in Ulster province," he went on, "and I thought to myself, why not build my own flax mill, along with all the processing machinery necessary to prepare linen for export on site, using the best and most advanced equipment that money could buy?—Just think, milling, bleaching and finishing all in one place, not to mention one of the first wet spinning factories in Ulster province…nay, in all of Ireland!" He smiled euphorically, his eyes shining in evident pride at the thought of such an undertaking.

I, on the other hand, wasn't nearly so enthralled by the idea—nor by the man himself—and continued to eye him askance.

"I thought I would acquire an additional plot of land, one that would be used predominantly for the mill, which I had hoped would become a profitable venture in itself."

"Why do you need a whole farm for that?" I blurted out, suddenly unspeakably annoyed at having to listen to him prattle on about flax. "Surely, you could simply build your mill on some of your existing land."

"It has to do with the location!" he snapped, glaring at me. "The farm contains a convenient waterway, which is essential for the running of the mill itself. And it lies within easy access of a number of thoroughfares to a variety of destinations, which is, of course, a boon for easy trade. Besides," he went on impatiently, "I had envisaged something far grander than the primitive mill huts found on every hill." He compressed his lips in distaste. "And for such a largescale factory as I intended to build, I simply needed more space than was readily available on my existing land."

"A largescale factory to ruin countless people's livelihoods, no doubt." I let my breath out in disgust, aware that the advent of mechanised linen production had been disastrous for its rural counterpart, with thousands of peasants who had been dependent on income generated by the linen industry becoming largely destitute as the work of their hands became redundant.

"Should I not have built it out of concern for a few commoners?" Andrews asked in tones of disbelief, evidently having very little concern for anyone but himself. "Their days as linen producers were numbered anyway. One can hardly halt progress! Peasants fiddling about in mud huts in competition with heavy machinery? They never stood a chance!"

The fact that he was probably right did nothing to improve my mood. "So to build this grand factory of yours, you thought you would blackmail my brother into giving up his land?" I demanded, choosing to ignore for the moment the question of whether or not industrial progress should—or could—be halted for the sake of people's livelihoods.

Andrews gave me a long look. "The estate I had been eyeing for the purpose would have provided ample space for the mill and its workings, as well as numerous additional fields. Unfortunately, though, it was snapped up from under my nose." He scowled at the audacity of someone daring to thwart his plans.

I paused in sudden interest. I had heard of no recent changes in ownership of estates in the vicinity of Niall—besides Niall itself.

"With no other land readily available," Andrews continued, "I looked around for other opportunities. It was thus that my eye fell on your family's farm. Although it wouldn't provide much in the way of additional flax acreage, being substantially smaller in size compared to its more desirable neighbour, it was nevertheless equally well suited as far as its location was concerned. To my delight, I was informed it had acquired an unexpected, and supposedly reluctant, new proprietor not too long before, one who might be persuaded to take his young family back to a more urban setting should an enticing monetary compensation be agreed upon.—Or so I was led to believe."

I gave a start, realising that Andrews couldn't be talking about my brother. A recently arrived, new proprietor with a young family? That was hardly a description that would fit Kieran. It did, however, fit my father. If so, the events Andrews was describing must have occurred almost two decades ago, probably no more than a few years after my father had arrived at Niall to take over the running of the farm following my uncle's death. And if that was the case, the neighbouring estate Andrews had initially wanted to acquire must have been Glaslearg, with Quin's father being the one who'd bought it out from under him.

Andrews hadn't noticed my sudden discomposure and went on without pause, confirming my supposition with his next statement. "I was quite sure your father would accept my more than generous offer and return to Dublin with glee...but alas..." He spread out his hands, clearly baffled by my father's choice to stay at Niall.

"The farm was worth far more than money to my father," I said through clenched teeth as I tried to control my rising anger, which was threatening to overwhelm me.

"Evidently." Andrews pressed his lips together in irritation. "Still, it was most regrettable...for both of us."

"Do you mean to say...that you plotted your revenge over all these years?"

"Oh no, my dear, of course not." Andrews put a hand to his chest. "I had already built my mill elsewhere and had quite forgotten the entire affair. I hadn't seen your father for at least a dozen years when your brother happened to cross my path."

"That's a lie," I hissed. "My father came to see you in Dublin only a few years ago, to invest some money. I was with him."

"Oh...how right you are," Andrews responded mildly, not at all bothered at having been caught out. Suddenly, he chuckled. "And what an entertaining interaction that was too. I dare say, your father wasn't much pleased at the thought of dealing with me. He knew, though, that I was likely the best person to help him with his investment. And so I was, of course...despite our previous differences regarding his land.—Nevertheless, an opportunity presented itself some years later."

"The opportunity to marry me to gain a farm you didn't need anymore?"

"Why...yes."

"But..." I started as a horrible suspicion came over me, "Kieran was the owner of the farm, not me. If you wanted Niall..."

"An accident might have happened," he said with a shrug, "it is a dangerous world after all." He gave me a dark look that made the hairs on the back of my neck stand up. "And with you as sole remaining heir..."

Quite suddenly, my heart started pounding violently, hammering painfully in my chest as a thought struck me with such force I could barely breathe. I closed my eyes briefly as dark spots appeared in my field of vision. When I opened them, I stared at Andrews, a flurry of emotions flooding my mind.

"It was you," I finally whispered, realising as I said the words that I'd known it all along. "You...you set Doyle free."

Andrews' eyes blazed abruptly as he looked at me, his face contorted in a grimace of fury and his hands clenched into fists. He took a quick step toward me, and I took an automatic step back, heart caught in my throat as he glared down at me.

But just as suddenly, his features calmed and he unclenched his fists, resuming an expression of casual indifference.

"Why?" I asked quietly.

He lifted one shoulder. "Because I could. Your father should have sold me his farm when he had the chance. When your brother appeared on my doorstep unexpectedly..." He sniggered. "It was the easiest thing in the world to convince the two of them to hand you over in exchange for the money.—You didn't think your brother cared quite so little about you, did you?" He gave me a pitying glance and I felt angry heat rise in my cheeks. "Doyle was so desperate for the money...he didn't even hesitate. And your brother went along with it without complaint. And when they were arrested..." He sniffed in contempt. "It saved me the trouble of having to arrange it myself after we were wed."

"You were never a spy."

"Of course not, my dear. I may keep my ears to the ground...but a spy? No. I simply needed a story the judge would believe." He waved a hand flippantly. He had been believed.

"But...Doyle."

"A thug to do the dirty work, no more."

"And the hanged man?" I demanded as the question occurred to me. "Who was he?"

His lips compressed briefly, and he narrowed his eyes, but then he shrugged. "A nobody."

"But...but...why?"

He stared at me for a long moment, making my skin prickle.

"You knew," I whispered. "You knew Doyle would come after us."

"Don't be ridiculous," he responded with a soft laugh. "It was only a bit of fun."

I shook my head, unable to speak. I realised then that it had probably all been something of a game to him. A test, perhaps, to see how far-reaching his powers might be. A bit of fun, as he had called it, for a man who'd lived a long life acquiring all the wealth he could possibly want, and the privileges said wealth bought. Fuelled by spite for my father's refusal to abide by his wishes, Andrews had ruined Kieran's life; not because he still had any particular interest in his property but simply—as he had so eloquently put it—because he could. Kieran had set himself up to be exploited, and Andrews had taken full advantage.

"Ah, Mrs Williams," he said nostalgically as he evidently saw comprehension dawn on my face, "your circumstances may have been far beneath my own, but you really should have married me. Your fine intellect would have made an excellent match for mine." He smiled at me, his handsome features suffused with a look of regret that his plan had been thwarted. "Don't you see, my dear?" he continued, ignoring my expression as I gaped at him in a mixture of astonishment and disgust. "Money rules the world. And why should I care about those who haven't got any?"

He looked at me thoughtfully for a moment longer, a regretful smile lingering on his lips. Then, abruptly, he gave me a curt bow, turned on his heel and strode purposefully toward one of the doors that opened out of the taproom on the ground floor, where he disappeared without a backward glance, followed by his muscular guard like a loyal dog.

I stared at the spot where he had vanished, my mind a complete blank.

"It's his private study, ma'am. He uses it once in a while."

I turned toward the voice of Mr Kelly, the innkeeper, who had come up behind me. He threw a quick glance at the closed study door before looking back at me.

"He's not a bad man to work for," he said, sounding rather nervous. "Just as long as his wishes are met." His eyes flitted toward the study once more, darting back and forth as if he were afraid of being overheard.

I nodded vaguely and gave him a weak smile, unsure how to respond.

"Might I interest you in your breakfast?" he asked cautiously, blinking rapidly.

"Ah..." I started, contemplating whether I still had an appetite.

Just then, the inn door opened, causing both of us to turn startled toward it. The patron who'd entered gave us a surprised look before nodding in greeting and making his way toward one of the tables. As he sat down, several more men entered the taproom from the street, their cheerful conversation filling the air.

"Or perhaps you'd prefer your dinner?" Mr Kelly grinned at me, making his round cheeks look even rounder.

I gave a short laugh and nodded. "Thank you, Mr Kelly, I would. Although"— the smile I'd pasted to my face was rapidly replaced with a frown as I glanced at the door through which Herbert Andrews had disappeared—"I believe I should like to eat in the privacy of my room."

"IT WAS ALL a game to him," Alannah said that afternoon as she sat down on the bed in their room.

She had told Quin about Andrews' revelations when he'd returned to the inn not long before. Thoroughly agitated and fuming with rage, she'd paced restlessly around the room during the telling, until she'd finally calmed down sufficiently to take a seat. Quin's eyes had grown ever wider, and his own anger had risen as she'd replayed her conversation with the man.

"He's heartless...and ruthless," he agreed, sitting down next to her and taking her hand in his. She had wanted to leave the inn the instant he'd arrived but had finally agreed to stay one more night—it was already mid-afternoon, and they would be leaving in the morning in any case, to return to Glaslearg.

"He didn't care about me, much less about Kieran or Doyle or any rebellion they might have started. He only wanted to manipulate them."

"I suppose it made him feel powerful," Quin said, gathering her close. He had his own reasons for convincing her to stay another night, wanting to have a word or two with the man himself before they departed. "I doubt he cares much about anyone except himself...or anything except his wealth and influence. From what I've heard he has a finger in every pie, probably looking for opportunities to reap his personal benefits, wherever he might find them."

"That does at least explain why Doyle thought he was a rebel and the courts found it easy to believe he was a spy."

"He tells people what they want to hear...all the while looking to use them."

"He would have done the same even if I'd married him," Alannah said slowly while she absently ran her thumb over Quin's hand.

He nodded. "Only waited until the legalities were complete. He probably promised Doyle he would give him the money after the wedding but would have turned him over to the police before the ink was dried on the contract."

"And he would have said I consented to the marriage...or said nothing at all. There would have been no need to explain anything once the paperwork was signed. And any accusations from Doyle would have simply been brushed off...just as they were at the trial."

They were silent for a moment.

"I still find it difficult to believe, though," Alannah finally went on, "that he would have orchestrated Doyle's escape. His own testimony saw the man convicted—it was the very reason we dismissed the possibility of Andrews' involvement in the first place, although it seemed likely even then." She looked up at Quin, searching his face, confusion plain in her features.

He clenched his jaws briefly before responding. "We thought whoever had released Doyle must have done it out of loyalty or a sense of duty, or for personal gain perhaps. We hadn't considered that any personal gain might have been quite so..." Quin paused, struggling to find a word to describe Andrews' actions.

"Vindictive?" Alannah suggested, making Quin shrug irritably. "But even so...surely, Andrews must have felt himself in danger of Doyle's vengeance. He knew he would come after *us*, I'm sure of it! That look he gave me"—Alannah shuddered—"he *knew*, I'm sure he knew! And surely, he also knew Doyle was likely to come after him too."

Quin shook his head and sighed. "Andrews is arrogant, greedy and narcissistic. Traits like that don't go hand in hand with feelings of vulnerability…or even logic. He's used to getting what he wants and people behaving the way he wants them to. Even if he'd felt himself a possible target, he wouldn't have thought himself in any real danger. He has a guard who follows him day and night, several sizeable mansions to hide in and enough money at his disposal to buy any other means of protection he may need. It wouldn't have occurred to him that a lowly being like Martin Doyle would have been able to do him any harm."

"And he was right."

Quin gently stroked Alannah's cheek, looking searchingly into her eyes. They were deep blue in the dimly lit room, shining like dark pools bathed in pale sunlight.

"I know regret doesn't help," she said quietly, "but…if it wasn't for him…" She clenched one hand into a fist and swallowed heavily before breathing in deeply and slowly unclenching her fist.

"I know." Quin pulled her into a tight embrace.

"We did learn something of value at least. We know now who was responsible for Doyle's escape…so you can stop looking." She lifted her face toward him, giving him a searching look.

Quin held her eyes only briefly before looking down, making a non-committal sound in his throat as he pulled her closer so she couldn't see his face.

"Can we do anything about it?" Alannah asked quietly, her breath tickling his neck. "Have him arrested?"

"On what grounds?" Quin put her away from him so he could look into her eyes once more. "You know I want to see the man punished as much as you do but…I have looked…and we have no proof of anything. And it would be our word against his."

"Nobody would believe us," Alannah whispered, looking down.

"I'm sorry." Quin swallowed the lump in his throat.

She was silent for a few minutes, evidently lost in thought.

"I think he did it all out of spite," she said finally, "because my father wouldn't sell him the farm all those years ago."

"You're probably right."

"He thinks my father acted against him, so he made my brother pay for it when he had the chance."

"The sins of the father…" Quin muttered with a humourless laugh. "He probably remembers every slight against him…real or imagined and feels it his right to retaliate against those who dare to defy him or use others to do so for him."

He could feel Alannah nod, but she didn't comment.

"Are you alright?" Quin asked softly, leaning back a little to look at her.

"Yes, I think so. It's a bit of a shock, of course, to find out just how devious the man actually is. And I am still terribly angry…to think he purposefully let a murderer go free, knowing, and possibly even wishing, that he would likely harm one of us…" She paused briefly, compressing her lips. "But"—she lifted her shoulders in a slight shrug—"compared to what I've had to endure already…this discovery seems to be rather mild in its effects."

She gave Quin an attempted smile, making him snort. "I suppose it would be," he muttered, tightening his arms around her once more.

"He's right, though," she said after a minute or two, making Quin look at her quizzically. "Money rules the world. Those who have it can buy their way out of anything."

"While those who have none face transportation for stealing a shilling to see themselves fed." Quin shook his head slowly and took a deep breath, letting it out in a sigh. "Rich or not, the man won't interfere in our lives again," he said finally, "I shall make sure of it!"

QUIN HURRIED DOWN the stairs, glancing briefly behind him in the direction of his room. He had told Alannah he was going in search of something to eat for their supper and he intended to do just that, but first…

He stopped at the bottom of the staircase and looked around. It was still early but the evening's customers had already begun flocking into the inn, and

Mr Kelly was in high demand. It wasn't the innkeeper Quin was in search of, though, nor the barmaid, who was being run off her feet by the thirsty clientele.

His eyes quickly scanned the walls of the taproom. In addition to the main entrance that opened onto the street, there were four doors leading out of the inn's main room. The large swinging door, he knew, led to the kitchen, leaving him with three possible options.

He picked the nearest one and knocked, expecting to have to repeat the process with the other two doors, if indeed he was to have any luck at all.

To his surprise, his knock was answered immediately, and Quin knew by the sound of the voice that he had found what he'd been looking for. He clenched his jaws briefly before going in.

Herbert Andrews was sitting alone at a spacious desk, some papers laid out before him, an expectant expression on his face as he looked toward the door. He blinked in momentary surprise when he caught sight of Quin but quickly smoothed out his features into ones of welcome as he rose from his seat.

"Mr Williams, I believe?" he said in a pleasant tone, reaching out a hand toward Quin.

"Mr Andrews." Quin gave the man a curt nod but didn't shake his hand.

Andrews shrugged and waved at Quin to take a seat on the other side of the desk, looking at him with slightly pursed lips.

"What can I do for you, Mr Williams?" he asked, spreading out his hands in invitation.

Quin wasn't fooled, though, and decided to get straight to the point, giving the man a cold stare. "I would appreciate it, Mr Andrews, if you would cease to interfere in my wife's affairs."

To Quin's extreme annoyance, Andrews started to laugh, shaking his head in mirth as he chuckled to himself. "Oh, Mr Williams, what *has* your wife been telling you?—Women are far too sensitive and emotional. Surely you know that? They simply cannot be expected to understand a man's business, isn't that so?"

Quin drew his brows together. "And what business would that be? The business of trying to force a woman into a marriage she doesn't want? Or perhaps the business of blackmailing a man out of his land?"

Andrews laughed again, looking briefly up at the ceiling before returning his eyes to Quin. "My dear fellow, your wife may have a fine intellect for a woman, but such things are beyond even her mind to understand."

"And what is there to understand about arranging the release of a convicted murderer? Knowing full well he was likely to exact his revenge on those he felt had betrayed him?"

Andrews shrugged. "I can hardly be held responsible for the actions of others."

Quin braced his hands on the desk, leaning over it to glare at Andrews. "Because of *your* actions, my wife's brother is dead...whether you choose to believe it or not. And I highly doubt Doyle's likely vengeance never even crossed your mind!"

Andrews looked at him haughtily, without the slightest hint of remorse on his features. Quin stared at the man for a moment longer before sitting back down, his hands clenched into futile fists.

Finally, Andrews sniffed and lifted one shoulder dismissively. "If she'd given it a bit more thought, she might have realised Mr Doyle had done her a favour."

"A favour?" Quin sputtered.

"Come, Mr Williams"—Andrews shook his head—"Mr O'Neill was hardly a model citizen...much less a devoted brother. Was he not more than willing to sell his sister to the highest bidder?" He snorted and emitted a humourless laugh. "And certainly, Mr O'Neill knew what he was getting himself into with Mr Doyle." He spread out his hands, indicating the inevitably of Kieran's fate. "It had nothing to do with *me*.—Women, of course," he went on earnestly before Quin had recovered sufficiently from his shock to respond, "can't be expected to understand such things. They are simply too soft...and too irrational. That's why they need a man to keep them in line...and make such choices for them."

"Is that so?" Quin growled, eying Andrews with extreme dislike.

Andrews, however, paid no attention to Quin whatsoever. "If you ask me," the vile man said, "most women are useful for precisely one thing." He slowly spread the thumb and index finger of one hand over his moustache, a lewd expression blooming on his face as he did so. "Ah," he sighed, his eyes taking on an unfocused, dreamy look, "but to have a young woman in your firm grasp, utterly at your mercy...it's one of man's greatest pleasures, is it not?" He looked across at Quin, one corner of his mouth turning up in a sneer. "And to have a succulent one such as your wife panting in your ear..."

"Mr Andrews," Quin hissed between clenched teeth as he got up from his chair, his nostrils flaring as he tried to suppress his rage, "I would advise you to desist from speaking upon the instant!" He enunciated each word as he glowered at Andrews across the desk from him.

Andrews raised his hands, a look of feigned surprise appearing on his features. "We're only making conversation, Mr Williams," he said casually. "Is it not the prerogative of men to discuss such topics?"

Quin drew himself up to his full height, before leaning over the desk toward the older man, who was still sitting down.

"You will not speak of my wife in this fashion, nor will you speak *to* her at all." Quin blew out his breath forcefully before going on. "Neither my wife nor I wish to have anything whatsoever to do with you! Nor do we invite your unsolicited interest in our private affairs!"

At this, Andrews started pushing away his chair to get up, but Quin leaned further over the desk and reached out a hand, grabbing the older man by the cravat before he could get up. "Do you understand me?" Quin's eyes bored into Andrews' as he tightened his grip on the closely wrapped fabric.

Andrews' dark eyes widened, and he gave an almost imperceptible nod, but Quin didn't let go of him just yet. "You may think you're untouchable," he said in a quietly menacing tone, "but I have a few influential connections of my own. It would behove you to remember that!"

Quin gave Andrews' cravat one last squeeze before letting go of it in disgust and turning on his heel. As he reached the door, to his surprise it opened, revealing an equally surprised-looking tall and muscular man, who was in the process of swallowing what appeared to be the last bite of his supper. The man sputtered as he choked on his food, glancing at Andrews in confusion as he tried to recover from his startlement.

Quin gave an amused snort, having only now taken conscious note of the peculiar fact that the guard—who this man must surely be—had been absent throughout his conversation with Andrews. With the guard hovering uncertainly in the doorway, still coughing intermittently, Quin turned back toward Andrews.

The man was still sitting at his desk, looking a little subdued at last.

"Even your guard must leave your side some time." Quin gave Andrews a final cold glare before turning his back on the man once more and striding resolutely out the door.

"WHAT TOOK YOU so long?" Alannah asked when Quin returned to their room some time later, laden with a platter of food, a bottle of wine and two glasses. She took the platter from him and deposited it on the small table that stood on one side of the room.

Quin shrugged as he placed the bottle and glasses beside the food. "The taproom is crowded," he said noncommittally, avoiding Alannah's eye. "Are you hungry?" he asked before she could say anything else, pulling out one of the two chairs for her.

"Only a little," she responded as she took a seat. "But there's far too much food for just the two of us, even if I were ravenous!" She looked down at the generous fare, which included a large loaf of freshly baked bread, several slices of cold meat and a sizeable chunk of cheese, as well as a dish of butter and even a selection of fruit.

Quin smiled as he sat down across from her. "I asked Mr Kelly if he might prepare a little something for us to eat that I could take up to our room. Either he's generous to a fault...or he thinks I eat like a horse."

Alannah laughed, cutting off a piece of bread and handing it to Quin before taking some for herself. Quin slathered his bread with butter and took a large bite, chewing contentedly as he poured them some wine.

"The wine isn't bad either," he said a moment later. "And the quality of the food is by no means obscured by its quantity." He took another bite of bread and reached for a slice of meat.

Alannah nodded but frowned. "If it wasn't for the owner of the place we might come here again. As it is..." She clenched her jaws briefly in anger before cutting herself a piece of cheese.

Quin made a sound of agreement but didn't say anything.

"Did you come across Andrews in the taproom?" Alannah cocked her head in Quin's direction, her brows drawn together as she looked at him.

Quin cleared his throat before studiously looking down at the platter and picking up what remained of the loaf of bread. "I didn't see Andrews in the taproom." He carefully focused his attention on the piece he was tearing off the loaf, not bothering with the knife. It wasn't a lie, he said to himself, he hadn't seen Andrews in the taproom after all—and she hadn't asked about the study.

He lifted his eyes cautiously, raising one brow as he offered her the piece of bread. She looked at him askance for a moment before shaking her head. "I've had my fill," she said.

"You've hardly eaten anything," he objected.

"I told you I wasn't very hungry." She picked up her wine glass and brought it to her lips.

They lapsed into silence, Alannah sipping demurely while Quin finished eating. Swallowing his last bite a few minutes later he leaned back with a contented sigh, closing his eyes for a moment. When he opened them, Alannah was looking at him with a strange expression on her face, one black brow raised above her penetrating blue gaze.

"What did you say to him?" she asked abruptly, giving Quin a frank look.

"Say?" He shook his head in feigned ignorance. "To whom?"

Alannah wasn't fooled, though, crossing her arms in front of her chest and blinking at him expectantly.

"Ah." Quin paused and coughed. "I...Well I told him to keep his nose out of our business, that's all," he finally muttered, scowling with remembered irritation. He looked at Alannah cautiously, trying to gauge her reaction.

To his surprise, she laughed.

"How did you know?"

"I know you better than you think." She gave him a wry look. "You got this speculative look in your eyes when I told you Andrews had disappeared into his study at the inn. I was quite sure you wanted to speak to him as soon as you tried to convince me to stay another night. And when you took the better part of an hour to return with a platter of cold food..." She lifted her shoulders.

"I see," Quin murmured, feeling more than a little sheepish.

"Why didn't you just tell me?"

Quin was silent for a moment, his throat feeling suddenly tight. "Because I want to protect you," he finally said, clasping both of her hands in his, "to shield you from those who mean you harm." He looked searchingly into her eyes. "After everything that's happened already"—he swallowed, trying to suppress the lingering guilt that crept up at him in unguarded moments—"I don't want to see you come to harm again. I only want to see you safe, Alannah!"

Alannah's features softened, a tender expression appearing on her face. "I know you do," she said quietly, holding his eyes and giving his hands a gentle squeeze. She paused briefly. "What will you do now?"

"What *can* I do? There's no proof of anything."

Alannah cocked her head in his direction, raising one brow and giving him a knowing look.

Quin didn't respond immediately, looking thoughtfully at her instead. "It seems you do know me better than I think." He gave a wry laugh before sobering up. "I could pretend I'm content at having discovered that Andrews was the one who arranged Doyle's escape...but I'm not. I said I wanted to see the person responsible for Doyle's release *punished*. And I still stand by that."

"You're going to look for proof." It wasn't a question.

Quin gave a curt nod. "I am." He held her eyes for a moment, looking for signs of reproach. There was only concern there, though, and a hint of fear. "Everything will be alright," he said softly, a small smile growing on his lips at the words.

Alannah didn't say anything but nodded slowly and took a deep breath, before getting up and taking a few steps toward him until she was facing his chair. She reached a hand toward him, and Quin let himself be pulled up from the seat. Once he was standing in front of her, she wrapped her arms around him and pulled him close.

"I trust you, Quin," she murmured into his chest, making Quin close his eyes as he tightened his arms around her.

11.

"I'LL BE GOING out for a bit."

"Out?" Alannah looked at Quin in confusion, before glancing out the window, where night was beginning to fall. "Where are you going?"

Quin cleared his throat, breaking eye contact. Alannah inhaled sharply. "Andrews." The single word hovered between them in the air. "What are you going to do?"

Quin shrugged. "Follow him." He risked a peek at Alannah. Her face was impassive, but her hands were clasped tightly in her lap. "I have to do something," he insisted, somehow feeling he needed to justify his actions.

"I see, but..."

"I only want to watch him, see if he gets up to anything tonight."

"And if you're caught?" she demanded with a long blue look.

He gave her a long look of his own. "Should I rather do nothing?—I have so many questions!" He started striding up and down the room. "What happened to the missing guard? Does he work for Andrews? Does he still live? And who was the hanged man?"

"I want to know those things too but..."

"You said Andrews called him a nobody," Quin went on, ignoring Alannah's objection, "but..."

She slowly shook her head. "I don't think he was just anybody. The look on Andrews' face when I asked who the hanged man was...I think it must have been someone he knew, someone he...was not overly fond of." She wrinkled her brow as she watched Quin's pacing.

"Someone he wanted to get rid of." Quin nodded to himself, avoiding looking at his wife. "But who was he?" he demanded suddenly, coming to a stop. "Another criminal like Doyle who had been doing Andrews' dirty work and become expendable? A business rival? Someone who had some dirt on Andrews and needed to be silenced?"

"I don't know."

"Well, I intend to find out!" Quin thumped a fist into his palm in determination. He threw on his jacket and stuffed several coins into his trouser pocket. He had no idea where the night would lead him and wanted to be prepared.

"He's been watching us, you know."

Alannah's soft voice made him turn back to face her, a prickling sensation creeping up his back.

"How else would he have known we were married? And how would he have known we were here? Mr Kelly himself said Andrews rarely comes to the inn and yet he wasn't the least bit surprised to see me. And he knew about Kieran's death…"

Alannah swallowed heavily and Quin clenched his jaws. "He may not be a spy for the British," he said slowly, kneeling down in front of Alannah as she sat motionless in her chair, "but that doesn't mean he hasn't got eyes everywhere.—Although he may simply have read about our marriage and about Kieran in the local paper and heard about our visit from Mr Kelly." Alannah gave him a doubtful look and pressed her lips together in a tight line.

Quin gently squeezed her hand and kissed her on the forehead. "I have to go," he said and started heading toward the door.

"Be careful!" she called after him, making him pause momentarily on the threshold. He gave her a curt nod, unable to promise anything else.

QUIN WATCHED THE group of men disappear around the corner and scowled.

Andrews wasn't among them.

He had left the inn with high hopes of not only following Andrews as he went about his crooked business, but also uncovering all his secrets. Unfortunately, though, Quin had as yet not even been able to locate the wretched man.

When he'd come down the stairs into the taproom, a maid was just locking up the study, Quin's first point of reference. Mr Kelly, the innkeeper, had been quite suspicious of Quin when he'd asked where he might find Andrews—no doubt remembering the confrontation earlier that day—but had at last admitted Andrews had numerous residences, although only one of these was in Dublin itself. Having eventually managed to persuade the innkeeper to tell him where this latter residence was, Quin had headed out onto the darkening streets of Dublin in search of his prey.

Arriving at his destination, though, he'd been disappointed again.

Lurking in the shadows on the opposite side of the street, Quin eyed Andrews' apartment. There was no light or movement discernible through the windows, and aside from the group of men who'd passed by Quin a few minutes ago, the street was dim and quiet.

"No doubt he's doing his plotting elsewhere," Quin said under his breath. Then again, he supposed it was quite possible the man was simply asleep in his bed. "I doubt that!" he muttered, shaking his head. Andrews didn't strike him as the type who would be peacefully snoring under the covers at this hour. Besides, if he were there—even tucked into bed—surely there would be servants about. The complete lack of activity suggested Andrews wasn't expected there anytime soon.

Which meant he could be absolutely anywhere.

Quin sniffed irritably as he looked up and down the empty street, trying to decide what to do. There was, of course, no reason to think Andrews would choose this particular night to reveal anything damning about himself—even were Quin able to find him in the first place. Still, he wouldn't have many opportunities to spy on the blasted man and he wasn't willing to give up just yet.

He finally decided to head toward the army barracks, thinking he might be able to confer with his friends. The barracks were situated on the western side of the city, on the northern banks of the Liffey. Quin was currently on the southeastern side of Dublin, where the city's more affluent inhabitants had their homes. As darkness descended in full, he started walking toward St Stephen's Green, thinking he might be able to hail a cab there to take him the rest of the way. Reaching the green, he took a quick drink from one of the public fountains that stood on each corner of the park, before making his way to the few remaining cabbies waiting for customers. At the juncture with Kildare Street, he heard someone call his name. He turned toward the voice, a broad smile growing on his face.

"Archie," he greeted his friend, who thumped him enthusiastically on the back.

"And here I thought I'd bid you farewell last night." Archie grinned at Quin, and they both laughed.

"You have a habit of running into me just when I need you," Quin said, making Archie lift his brows in surprise.

"Oh?"

"I was just looking to find a cab to take me to the barracks to see you."

"The wife tired of your advances, is she?" Archie dug Quin in the ribs with an elbow.

"Not quite," Quin responded tersely, before explaining to Archie that he was looking for Herbert Andrews.

"But I've just seen him," Archie exclaimed, waving a hand in the direction he'd come from.

"You have?"

"Why yes, at the Kildare Street Club. He's a member there."

Quin nodded. The Kildare Street Club was frequented by many Anglo-Irish gentlemen; it made sense for Andrews to be a member. "Is he still there?" he asked hopefully.

"He was five minutes ago, when I left. What do you want with him anyway?"

Quin compressed his lips angrily before telling Archie briefly about Alannah's encounter with the man and what she'd found out about him.

"That wretched old yob!" Archie scowled and turned toward Kildare Street. "To arrange the escape of a violent criminal? And a man of such social standing as he. I'm going to…"

Quin grabbed his friend by the arm before he could take another step.

"What?" Archie rounded on him, looking annoyed.

"I don't want to confront him," Quin said with a shake of his head.

"You don't?"

"No! I want to follow him, to see if I can find out something about all of this." He waved his hand vaguely, encompassing Herbert Andrews' numerous misdeeds—both known and suspected. Archie's confused expression began to clear.

"I see. A bit of clandestine work, is it?" His face split into a mischievous grin. "Then count me in!" He clapped Quin on the back, making him laugh.

"Weren't you just on your way to your bed?"

Archie flipped a dismissive wrist. "Pish posh. Now," he said in a low voice, placing a conspiratorial arm around Quin's shoulder. "I know exactly what we're going to do." He turned Quin and pointed a finger toward the street down which he'd just come. "There's an alleyway almost directly across the street from the club. We'll hide there until the lickspittle shows up…and then we'll follow him and see what he's up to."

"Assuming he's up to anything tonight," Quin said with a shrug.

Archie shook his head disparagingly. "Always the pessimist. Now let's go."

Quin grinned as Archie propelled him up Kildare Street. When they got close to the club, they stayed near the buildings on the other side of the street. Keeping an eye on the club's entrance, they managed to reach the alleyway without incident. There they squeezed into a deep doorway, from which they could observe the club.

"What will you do after tonight?" Archie asked.

"Depends on what I find out." Quin breathed in deeply and clenched one hand into a fist. "I want to know who the hanged man was!" he growled, feeling anger bubble up inside him yet again. "I do not for one minute believe Andrews orchestrated this entire affair just for sport, or even to send Doyle after us." Quin compressed his lips at the thought. "I'm sure there's more to it!"

"You're probably right." Quin could feel Archie nod next to him. He suddenly froze, though, pressing further back into the shadows and urging Quin to do the same with a hand on his arm. Quin complied, looking across at the club, where the door had just opened, spilling a jumble of men and the sounds of laughter out onto the street. He scanned the faces of the club's patrons but couldn't spot Andrews among them.

"Hmph," he grumbled, relaxing his stance once the men had disappeared in the direction of St Stephen's Green.

"He'll show up," Archie assured him with a nudge of the elbow and an annoyingly sprightly air.

"Hmph."

"You know, you really ought to consider returning to civilisation, Quinton Williams. This rustic living of yours is doing your vocabulary no good." Archie grinned, making Quin laugh.

"I thank you for your concern, Archibald Bellinger," Quin responded in his most pompous tone. "However, I can assure you that I remain entirely capable of eloquent speech. Even when conversing with the less than attentive livestock."

Archie snorted with mirth and Quin chuckled alongside his friend, feeling some of the day's tension lift in Archie's presence. Whatever happened, he had someone he could count on.

"There he is!" Archie's hissed exclamation and his sudden grip on Quin's arm made him look back toward the club's entrance, where an elderly gentleman and his burly companion had just emerged.

Quin breathed in heavily through his nose at the sight of Andrews, strolling so nonchalantly through the night. Walking slightly in front of his guard, the man moved briskly down the street, swinging his walking stick. Heading to the public carriages to find his bed, no doubt, Quin thought irritably.

"Come," Archie whispered in Quin's ear, having evidently judged the duo to be far enough away to be followed unnoticed.

Quin and Archie crept along the shadows once more, this time in the opposite direction. Having expected Andrews to head directly to St Stephen's Green, Quin was rather surprised when the man instead turned west, into one of the smaller roads leading off Kildare Street. He raised an eyebrow at Archie, who shrugged and picked up the pace, the two of them hurrying to keep Andrews in their sight. They reached the corner just in time to see the guard disappear down another smaller alleyway. Quin and Archie followed, always worrying they might lose Andrews and his guard as they made their way through the backroads of Dublin, but not daring to get too close.

Quin wondered what the man was up to. Clearly not expected at his residence this night, he could be heading anywhere—an inn, the home of a friend, a mistress or one of his particularly unsavoury acquaintances. Andrews was by now moving quite stealthily himself, making Quin hope for the latter as he crept around yet another corner the man had turned.

He stopped abruptly and grabbed Archie by the arm, preventing him from going any further. They had reached a dead end, which appeared to be situated behind some kind of warehouse. The city's gas lighting barely lit up the dark space and no light spilled from the surrounding buildings. If ever Quin had seen a place well suited to a surreptitious rendezvous, this was it. His heart gave a sudden lurch, thinking he may yet get some dirt on Andrews after all.

It gave another solid thump when a man Quin hadn't noticed before detached himself from the darker shadows next to one of the buildings. He glanced at Archie, who nodded his understanding, before following Quin as he crawled along the ground to a pile of discarded crates and other assorted rubbish to get a closer look.

"You forget yourself, Morrison." Quin recognised Andrews' voice, which was tight with anger. "I am never late."

"Of course not, sir." The other man's tone was dripping with sarcasm, which evidently didn't escape Andrews either. "Remember where your money comes from!" he snapped, his expression hidden in the shadows.

"Yes, sir. But…speaking of money…well…with everything I know…"

Before the man could utter another word, Andrews lifted his walking stick and jabbed it viciously into his midsection. "If you think you can blackmail me," he hissed, leaning over the unfortunate Morrison, who was bent over with his arms pressed to his middle, "think again!" He jerked his head toward the guard, who had been watching the confrontation from a distance. At his master's bidding, he positioned his bulk behind Morrison. With a swift motion he grabbed the smaller man by one arm, pinning it against his back, making Morrison squeal and struggle. Undisturbed, the guard started pushing the arm he gripped up by the elbow, until there was a distinct pop that made Quin grimace in disgust. Morrison cried out and dropped to the ground, as the guard disappeared back into the shadows.

"You wouldn't be the first to try such a thing," Andrews observed mildly, standing over Morrison's recumbent form. "The end result is always the same." Andrews made a sharp cutting motion with his hand through the air and Morrison scrambled a little further away on his knees. "Now," Andrews continued lightly, "can we return to our business?"

Morrison nodded, pushing himself off the ground with a groan. He stood swaying slightly before answering, gripping his arm by the elbow. "What do you need from me...sir?" he croaked at last.

"A matter of some...nuisance came to my attention today." Quin started at Andrews' words. Was he referring to Alannah and him?

"You need me to get rid of this nuisance?" Morrison's question made Quin clench his hands into fists.

"Tempting...very tempting, Morrison. But, alas, disposing of the heir to a barony would be rather onerous—although it would leave the delightful wife free for my amusement." Andrews chuckled and Quin growled deep in his throat. He was about to leap up and throw himself at the man, but Archie laid a restraining hand on his arm, pulling him back down into a crouch behind the crates.

"Who then?" Morrison asked, still cradling his arm. The fact that the man seemed quite certain he needed to get rid of someone—anyone—gave Quin a good idea of how Andrews conducted his business. While some of it was no doubt honest, he clearly had no qualms about using crooked tactics when he felt so inclined.

Quin suddenly wondered whether Morrison had been the one sent to inform Kieran that Andrews was confiscating his farm.

He pushed the thought aside to focus on the present. That Andrews had arranged tonight's meeting must surely mean the man hadn't been quite as unaffected by his earlier encounters with Alannah and Quin as they had thought.

His next statement confirmed as much.

"The proof, Morrison! We need to get rid of the proof! Without it they have nothing...but should the blasted man find Reid, he might get him to talk. And that could be...inconvenient."

"Oh, this has to do with the Doyle hanging." Quin could see Morrison nodding to himself in the darkness.

"Of course, it does," Andrews snapped. "What did you think we were talking about?" Morrison hunched his shoulders, making him whimper in pain. "Reid must be eliminated." Andrews' voice was cold as he enunciated each word, standing ramrod straight, declaring judgement.

"But he's well hidden," Morrison objected softly.

"He might still be found!" Andrews hissed, leaning toward the other man. "He was invaluable during the Doyle affair, but he has now become a liability." Quin's heart started pounding in excitement as he realised they were likely talking about the missing guard who had helped Andrews cover up his involvement in Doyle's escape. "I must look to my own interests," Andrews went on. "I'm sure even Reid himself would understand." He flipped his wrist and Quin suppressed a snort, doubting very much that the man would be in agreement with his own demise, even were he to understand the apparent need for it. "See to it!" Andrews commanded, thumping his walking stick on the ground for emphasis. "And see to that shoulder," he added with a jab of the stick to Morrison's dislocated shoulder, making the younger man cry out, "or your task may prove difficult."

Morrison nodded meekly and Andrews turned on his heel, the meeting clearly at an end. He started walking toward the alleyway behind Quin and Archie, and the two of them shrank back against the jumble of crates, holding their breaths in the darkness.

"We need to follow that Morrison fellow," Archie whispered as they listened to the receding footsteps.

Quin nodded and cautiously peeked out of their hiding place. He couldn't see anyone in front of the factory, but it was impossible to make out much in the shadows. He beckoned to Archie, and they slowly crept out into the open space. It seemed deserted.

"Let's head toward the alley," Quin said in a low voice.

When they reached the alleyway, there was no-one in sight. Quin cursed under his breath, not knowing which way Morrison might have gone. For no particular reason he decided to head in the opposite direction to the one from which they'd come. Archie shrugged and followed him, loping alongside Quin as he led them at random through the backstreets of Dublin.

Quin had just about given up ever seeing Morrison again when a movement ahead caught his eye. His heart lurched as he made out the shape of a man in the shaft of light spilling from an upper storey window. Was he walking awkwardly, with a hunched shoulder? Quin wasn't sure, but he sped up, wanting to get a closer look. He had almost reached the pool of light when there was a sudden sharp thud behind him, followed by a dull and heavy thump.

Quin spun around.

"Archie!" he exclaimed in horror. Archie was lying on the ground, blood running from the back of his head down his cheek and onto the cobblestones. Quin dropped to his knees, trying to feel for a pulse, while simultaneously looking around for impending threats.

He saw a shadow out of the corner of his eye. As he tried to turn away, he heard another sharp thud, this time accompanied by a sudden, intense pain on his temple. It was the last thing he took note of before darkness overcame him and he collapsed across the body of his friend.

WHEN HE CAME to, Quin was lying on his front with his head turned to the side. He felt something soggy under his cheek and tried to move away but stopped abruptly as pain seared through his skull. Wanting to lift his hands to his aching temple he found that they were tied behind his back.

Suddenly, his memory returned. "Archie," he moaned.

"Your friend is dead." Quin started at the voice coming from near his head. With a groan of pain, he turned onto his side to look at his assailant but could only make out a dark, hulking mass with an indistinct face. A smell of decay crept up his nose, making him feel vaguely ill. Clearly, he was no longer in the semi-lit, semi-clean alleyway he'd been in earlier. He couldn't have been moved far, though. As big as the man looming over him was, Quin was no featherweight himself, and he didn't think he had lost consciousness for very long.

"What do you know?" the man barked, a dull thwacking sound accompanying his words.

As Quin's mind cleared and his eyes adjusted to the darkness, he realised the man was holding some sort of club, which he was smacking rhythmically against his palm. He also realised he recognised the voice—it was Herbert Andrews' guard.

"I don't know anything," Quin said automatically, his brain flitting rapidly through his options while he tried to free his hands. He was clearly at a disadvantage, and nobody knew where he was. Was Archie really dead? Quin's heart contracted painfully at the thought. There had been an awful lot of blood, but he knew even minor head wounds could bleed tremendously, so he stubbornly held onto hope.

The man sniffed contemptuously. "Mr Andrews told me, didn't he? So, I ask again, what do you know?" The club landed on his palm with a meaty thud.

"I know no more than he admitted to himself." There was little point in denial, when the guard had himself been present during part of his encounter with Andrews and had seen Alannah confront him.

"I don't believe you," the man snarled, leaning menacingly over Quin, who in turn leaned a little further back—mostly to hide his hands as he worked on the rope that bound them. Fortunately, it was a fairly thin rope that seemed to have been tied in some haste, leaving Quin with just enough slack to give him a little hope.

"What did you overhear?" the man demanded suddenly.

"Ah...hear...?" If he could just move his wrists a bit more, he'd be able to get a grip on the blasted knot.

"I know you were at the factory." The hissed words were filled with disgust. "You're not nearly as clever as you think!"

Quin was starting to fear just that. It had become clear to him the instant he had recognised Andrews' guard that the man must have followed Archie and him when they'd attempted to pursue Morrison. Neither of them had actually seen Morrison or the guard leave, as they'd hidden themselves behind the crates to prevent detection and had only been able to follow the sound of the receding footsteps.

"I couldn't hear anything," Quin lied, trying to buy himself time, "I was too far away." His wrists were burning as the rough fibres cut into his skin, but he had at last managed to manoeuvre his hands into a position to be able to work on the knot.

"Liar!" the guard spat, hefting the club, making Quin redouble his efforts. "If I leave you 'ere it'll look like just another street killing. Nothin' Mr Andrews would object to..."

Quin's heart lurched but the fact that the man was hesitating gave him a little hope. "But you forget...I'm the heir to a barony." The knot was slackening ever so slightly as one end slowly, slowly came free.

The guard noisily sucked in his breath. "So you did hear!" he roared and lifted the club over his head, making Quin pull frantically on the rope. The knot loosened at last, and he yanked his hands apart, sending a searing pain through his wrists. The club came hurtling down toward his head and Quin got his arm up just in time. He cried out as the heavy weapon crashed onto his forearm with a bone-jarring thud.

With his eyes watering from the pain, Quin tried to roll away, instead landing in a rotting pile of rubbish. Slipping and sliding, he tried to get to his feet, hampered by his useless arm. He saw the dark outline of the club lifted over his head once more and raised his arms to cover his face. He closed his eyes and waited for the crunch of broken bones. When the thud came, he flinched, but felt no pain.

Did that mean he was dead?

He cautiously opened his eyes.

"Archie?" he sputtered in disbelief, taking in the sight of his friend as he stood over the crumpled form of the guard, who was lying in what looked like the splintered remains of a wooden crate. "Archie!" he repeated joyfully as he slowly pushed himself up with his good arm.

"Quinton, good to see you," Archie said mildly and thumped him on the back. He stopped suddenly, swaying slightly.

"I thought you were dead." Quin realised he couldn't yet stand and sat down abruptly, a groan escaping his lips as he jarred his arm.

"A knock on the head isn't going to do me in," Archie assured him as he slowly sat down next to him. "I've got the skull of an ox...oooh." He cradled his head in his hands. "Although I will admit that it does hurt."

Quin gave a relieved laugh, before glancing toward the guard. "Do you think he's...?"

Archie shrugged. Quin crawled awkwardly through the muck toward the fallen man and felt around for a pulse. He finally found one, slow but reasonably steady, he thought.

"How's the arm?" Archie asked, watching Quin curse under his breath as he sat back down.

Quin carefully slipped off his jacket and felt gingerly along the injured forearm. "No splintered bone ends sticking out, at least." He snorted, throwing the ruined jacket aside. "Hurts like hell, though. And I will admit I find it doubtful that I'll be able to walk any great distance tonight." He rubbed his temple, where a large bruise was forming, wondering how they would ever get out of the alleyway.

The guard moaned. Perhaps he was coming round.

"I have an idea." Quin turned back toward Archie. Although he couldn't see his face clearly in the dim light, he thought his friend seemed a little hesitant. "I have...some acquaintances," he went on cautiously. "If I've got my bearings right, I believe the...um...residence shouldn't be too far from here. We should be able to get a carriage from there."

The guard started twitching suddenly, clearly on the verge of waking up.

"Then let's go," Quin said, getting laboriously to his feet and giving Archie a hand. He heaved himself up with a groan, clinging to Quin for support. The two of them staggered out of the small, dark alley, and Archie led them a short distance through the deserted streets until they reached a moderate, plain-looking house. As they teetered up the steps to the back entrance, Quin wondered what sorts of acquaintances would receive them beaten and bloodied well past midnight.

To his surprise, Archie's brisk knock was answered promptly, by a rather fetching middle-aged woman whose welcoming smile turned to a look of horror when she saw who had landed on her doorstep.

"Lieutenant Bellinger!" she cried with a hand to her ample bosom. "What has happened?"

Seeing his friend in the light for the first time, Quin recoiled a little himself. One half of Archie's face was covered with dark, crusty blood, while the other side was smeared with assorted filth. His hair was plastered to the back of his head with more blood, revealing an egg-sized bump, with the rest sticking up wildly around the sides. As for his clothing...burning it was likely to be the best thing for it.

Looking down at himself, though, Quin realised he looked no better—and possibly worse.

The woman's loud exclamation had attracted the attention of the establishment's other inhabitants. For an establishment it most certainly was, one evidently dealing with matters of the flesh. Quin's eyes went wide as he took in the appearance of a dozen or so young women, all clad in silky garments that slithered around their nubile bodies. Starting to feel rather dazed, he stared at a red-haired beauty whose dark nipples peeked out from beneath a near-transparent costume as she descended the stairs. He tore his eyes away from the sight and looked toward Archie, blinking stupidly.

His friend grinned, which Quin rather wished he hadn't as it made him look even more ghastly. Before he could say anything, the madam—or so Quin believed her to be—clapped her hands and started issuing orders, which soon resulted in the two men being driven up the stairs by numerous scantily clad ladies of the night, as the others disappeared back into the surrounding doorways.

"Oh, you poor dears," one of them tutted, patting Quin on the shoulder.

"We'll have you right as rain in no time," another assured him as she led him into a room where a pair of maids was bustling about.

"Um…" Quin looked around for Archie, spotting him on the far side of the room. Before Quin could call out to him, he felt a hand tugging on his waistcoat. "What?" He looked down and swatted weakly at the intrusion, but soon felt another, this time on his waistband, while a third pair of hands swiftly undid his cravat. "Ah…" He tried to extricate himself from the roving fingers, but his objections went unheard. Before he knew it, they had undressed him to his skin and were ushering him into a large copper bathtub he hadn't noticed between the dozens of lanky limbs.

The steam coming off the water did in fact look extremely inviting and so—despite the general awkwardness of the situation—he carefully lowered himself into the tub, leaning against the backrest and stretching out his legs as far as he could. He sighed as the warm water caressed his skin but winced as the rope burns on his wrists began to burn. He closed his eyes briefly, waiting for the discomfort to ease, while also trying to ignore his pounding head and throbbing forearm, as well as the numerous half-naked women who continued to busy themselves around the room.

"I knew we wouldn't be turned away, but I hadn't quite expected a reception such as this."

Quin opened his eyes and looked at Archie, who was reclining in another copper tub, his knees sticking up into the air, as were Quin's.

"Luckily, a few of the girls were just preparing to bathe." Quin turned his head in the direction of the silky voice, which belonged to the red-head he had noticed earlier, who was rummaging through a basket on a stand. Having found the bar of soap she'd evidently been looking for, she sauntered over to Quin, swinging her hips, making her breasts sway hypnotically with every step. "Very fortunate for Lieutenant Bellinger and his...friend," she said and gave Quin a sultry look. Her gaze travelled slowly from his eyes down the length of his body, eventually resting somewhere in the depths of the tub.

Placing his hands as unobtrusively as possible between his legs, Quin felt a heat that had nothing to do with the water temperature rising in his cheeks. He was trying to think of something to say but realised that nothing he had thus far experienced in his life enabled him to make a comment suitable to his current situation. He closed his mouth with a snap as the red-head began pouring warm water over his head and gently washing his hair. As Quin lay there transfixed, she leaned over him so that her breasts bobbed in front of him beneath their translucent covering. He quickly closed his eyes. She chuckled, and washed his face with a soft touch, before turning her attention to his arms and legs. When she reached into the water to wash him elsewhere, he snatched her hand away, thanking her profusely and sending her on her way.

"*Anything* you want, sir," she murmured, one brow raised suggestively.

"Ah...yes...thank you." Quin cleared his throat, making her laugh. When she finally closed the door behind her, he leaned his head back in relief. After a moment he turned to Archie. "So, these are your acquaintances," he said, making his friend open one bloodshot eye.

Archie shrugged. "The heart wants what it wants."

"The *heart*, yes, I quite understand." Quin chuckled and started shaking his head, before stopping abruptly.

"Unlike you, I don't have a beautiful wife in my bed," Archie said with a grin. "The occasional rendezvous is quite...welcome."

"Yes, I suppose it would be." Quin wondered how his wife would react if she knew her husband currently found himself stark-naked in a whorehouse. He pushed the thought aside. It's not as if he'd wanted to come here—besides, he had no intention of doing anything other than bathe. He did fear she was worrying about him, though, and so he stood up gingerly, wanting to get back to the inn. He swayed a little, the bump on his head making itself felt.

The door opened and Quin clutched himself reflexively. The returning women giggled, exchanging whispered comments as they appraised him standing dripping in the bathtub with his hands across his crotch. To his immense relief, he was handed a large towel, which he used to dry himself clumsily with one hand, declining all offers of assistance. As quickly as he could, he donned the clean shirt and trousers provided, grateful to be clothed again at last, even if the items were a little small.

"I like you better without, but it does suit you," a petite blonde observed, surveying him appreciatively. "I'm free tonight, you know." She batted her eyelashes at him.

"Thank you, but no," he responded in what he hoped was a non-offensive tone. "I'm married."

The blonde pursed her lips. "They usually are." She smiled coquettishly and ran her hand slowly across Quin's chest before leaving the room.

"What about you, Lieutenant Bellinger?" Quin turned toward Archie, who was letting himself be dressed by a voluptuous brunette as the madam looked on. "Hm?" The madam raised a questioning brow at Archie, who seemed to be thoroughly enjoying the brunette's ministrations, based on the blissful look on his face as she tucked the shirt into his trousers.

"Eh?" Archie's eyes cleared and he looked down at the hands still busy with his waistband.

"Libby is available." With an outstretched arm the madam presented her offering, who dipped her hand a little lower, presumably giving Archie an idea of what he might expect should he choose to linger.

"Um..."

"Ahem," Quin interrupted. "You're welcome to stay if you wish, Archie, but I need to get back to the inn." He glanced outside the widow. It was still dark, but he was sure it must be close to dawn by now.

Archie sighed. "I'm afraid I must decline," he said regretfully, bowing to the two women. When he straightened up, he groaned and placed a hand to his head. "I suppose it's for the best anyway."

"Well do visit us again when you're feeling up to it." The madam's lips curled into a suggestive smile, making Archie grin.

"I certainly will!" Turning to Quin he said, "Now let's get you back to your wife."

12.

WHEN THE CARRIAGE finally arrived at the inn, the sun was just peeking over the horizon. Quin and Archie had thanked the madam profusely and given her what money they'd had with them. The woman had wrinkled her nose as they'd rummaged through their filthy clothing, but had graciously accepted the contents of their pockets, nonetheless.

With his temple throbbing incessantly, Quin had collapsed onto the carriage seat, wanting nothing so much as to close his eyes and sleep for a week. Archie had gotten in next to him, looking a little cross-eyed and cursing magnificently when the jolt of the carriage getting underway caused him to bump his bruised head against the padded backrest.

A short but unpleasant ride had seen Quin deposited on the doorstep of the inn. Archie was continuing on in the carriage, returning to the barracks. Quin sincerely hoped he could have himself excused from his duties for the day—if Archie felt anything like Quin himself, the day would be unpleasant enough, without the blast of cannon and gunfire that would be waiting for him on the training grounds.

Quin groaned at the very thought as he looked through the glass inset of the inn's main door. At that opportune moment, the rotund form of Mr Kelly, the innkeeper, came into view, fully dressed and aproned, ready to start the day.

"Why Mr Williams," the man exclaimed with a hand to his chest as Quin staggered into the taproom, "whatever happened?" The innkeeper shook his head at Quin's dishevelled appearance, his eyes lingering on his temple, which must look a right mess by now, before dropping down to the deep red rope burns on Quin's wrists.

"An accident, Mr Kelly," Quin said, trying to sound flippant. "Nothing to worry yourself over."

"But..." Mr Kelly waved vaguely at Quin's left arm, which he was supporting gingerly in his other hand.

"Mr Kelly, I appreciate your concern, but I would very much like my bed." Quin must have sounded desperate enough that he was rewarded with a reluctant nod.

Quin stumbled up the stairs, his head feeling like it might explode any minute. Trying the door cautiously, he was happy to find that it wasn't barred from the inside. He had barely opened it when he heard Alannah's voice.

"Quin?"

"It's me," he whispered, closing the door behind him and making his way toward the bed, exhaustion dragging at him as he crossed the room.

"Where have you been?" Alannah sat up in the bed as he collapsed onto it.

"It's a long story," he responded, patting her gently on the arm. "I'll tell you in the morning."

"But...what happened?" She lifted a hand gently to his head. "Are you alright?" she asked, concern wrinkling her forehead as she looked him up and down in the growing light.

"I'm fine." He drew her briefly toward him with his sound arm. "I'll tell you everything in the morning."

"It *is* morning. So you can tell me now!" She pulled away from him and scowled.

"Alannah, I'm tired..."

"And you think I'm not?" she interrupted him sharply. It was bright enough by now that he could see the dark circles under her eyes and the concern in their depths. "Do you think I haven't been lying awake this whole time? That I went right to sleep after you left?" She crossed her arms and glared at him.

"No...no, I didn't think that. It's just..."

"Just what?" She got up in a huff of bedclothes. "You leave at sundown, in search of a man we know to have few scruples, only to return at dawn looking like the two of you had a good go at it." Her eyes fell on his wrists, and she pursed her lips. "And that he got the better of you too.—Under the circumstances, I think I deserve an explanation!"

"And I think I deserve a little sympathy!" he responded grumpily, starting to feel a bit put out himself. He had been knocked unconscious, tied up and dragged through filth, threatened with his life and indecently propositioned by a horde of prostitutes. He was in no mood to also be scolded by his wife!

"Sympathy?" she hissed. "And did you even think about *me* at all when you decided to go after Andrews on your own? You knew you would be placing yourself in danger and yet you went anyway…despite my objections.—And look at you now!" She clenched her jaws as she looked down at him in anger, making Quin scowl at her in turn.

"As it happens, I wasn't alone."

"Oh?" She raised one brow, hands on her hips.

"Archie was with me."

"And what does *he* look like?" Alannah demanded, raising her chin.

"Not much better," Quin admitted, before breaking into a reluctant smile. He cocked his head and patted the bed. Alannah looked at him sceptically for a moment longer before sitting down next to him, muttering to herself, "If two trained soldiers come away from an encounter with an elderly man looking like *that*, then I worry about the state of the British Army!"

Quin laughed before groaning as pain shot through his head. He closed his eyes and lay back on the pillow. "If it makes you feel any better," he mumbled as exhaustion took hold of him once more, "it wasn't Andrews who did this."

"It was his guard." There was no question in Alannah's tone.

Quin nodded slowly. "Now please," he said with a sigh, cracking open one eye, "can I tell you more later?"

"Alright," Alannah agreed grudgingly. She placed a cool hand on his cheek. "Try to get some rest." She finally lay down, carefully wrapping herself around him as he drifted off to sleep.

QUIN MOANED, WAKING me for the dozenth time. Although he seemed to be asleep, he had been tossing and turning intermittently, clearly uncomfortable.

I gave up the pretence of sleep.

I had managed a few snatches, which was all I was likely to get. I propped myself up on my elbow to look down at my husband.

The bruise on his temple was a dark purple mass and his wrists were encircled by angry red welts. The sleeves of his shirt had not been fastened at the cuff and I could see part of his left forearm, which seemed to be blue from elbow to wrist. I clenched my jaws at the thought of what must have transpired the previous night—and wondered what might have happened had Archie not been with him. I wanted to shake Quin awake to get some answers but reluctantly let him sleep. He had clearly been exhausted—a state of affairs that was unusual enough.

My mind kept playing out possible scenarios, envisaging Quin and Archie being manhandled by Herbert Andrews' hulking guard and landing in Dublin's back alleys with their throats slit. I swallowed heavily, pushing away the thought. The latter clearly hadn't occurred—but something else most certainly had. Besides the bruising, Quin was not wearing his own shirt and trousers, which I had already noticed when he'd come in at dawn. And despite his adventures, he looked clean and smelled of soap. Where had he bathed and changed his clothing? And why had he gone somewhere else instead of heading straight back to the inn after whatever had befallen him?

I breathed out heavily. I supposed I would have to have a little more patience while I let him rest. Quite sure I would get no further rest myself, I quietly got out of bed and got dressed. I had just finished when Quin stirred behind me. He groaned, clutching his head. I sat down next to him on the bed, gently stroking his shoulder.

"I'll go and ask Mr Kelly if he has some willow bark, shall I?" I suggested, keeping my voice low.

Quin squinted up at me with bloodshot eyes. "That's a good idea," he responded slowly, still holding his head, "if we want to be on our way soon."

"You still want to leave today?" I stared at him, dumbfounded. How did he expect to travel all the way back to Glaslearg in his current state?

"You don't?"

I gave an unladylike snort. "Not if you can barely stand!"

He lifted his head to frown at me, making him suck in his breath sharply. "I suppose you have a point," he conceded, carefully lowering his head back onto the pillow.

I patted his arm and got up. "I'll be right back."

When I returned Quin was dozing again. I set the cup I'd brought upstairs to steep on the table—a stronger dose would probably do him good anyway. I swirled the bits of ground-up bark around with the spoon, remembering a letter from my former tutor Mr Henderson, in which he'd described how scientists had isolated the compound thought to be responsible for willow bark's pain-relieving properties and how they were trying to modify this compound to make an even more effective medicine. It was effective even now, though, and I hoped it would provide Quin with some relief.

My stomach growled suddenly, making me realise I hadn't thought to ask Mr Kelly for something to eat when I went in search of the willow bark. I shrugged, looking at the leftover bread from the night before. It was a little stale, but with some of the remaining butter and cheese it was quite edible.

When Quin opened his eyes again a short while later, I helped him lift his head so he could drink the cooled tea. He made a face at the bitter taste but obediently drank it all, before lying back down.

"You don't look too good," I observed.

He cracked open one eye, which flashed irritably at me. "You wouldn't look so good either after a night like yesterday."

"Speaking of which…" I raised one brow and cocked my head.

Quin sighed and pushed himself carefully up in bed. I helped him adjust the pillows, so he was propped up against the bedstead.

"I suppose I do owe you an explanation."

"Well how nice of you to realise that," I muttered, trying not to get annoyed but failing miserably. I took a deep breath. I would at least let him explain what had happened before admonishing him for putting himself in danger.

Quin scowled at me but began talking at last, explaining how he had run into Archie, how the two of them had followed Herbert Andrews through the streets of Dublin and what they had overheard.

"So Andrews wants to eliminate the guard from the gaol," I said, wrinkling my brow.

Quin lifted one shoulder in a shrug. "I'm surprised he didn't do it before. I had hoped to find the missing guard myself, of course, but there was always the possibility that he'd already been dealt with. I doubt there's much we can do about it now, either, with no way of knowing where this Morrison fellow may be, nor where the guard has been hiding."

"But Andrews is worried."

"He is," Quin responded with a slight nod. "We know about his involvement in Doyle's release. He can't have something like that become common knowledge."

"Do you think"—I swallowed heavily as my breath started coming a little short—"do you think that he'll..."

"Send someone after us?" Quin suggested, making my heart leap into my throat. I nodded. Quin reached for my hand, clasping it tightly. "I doubt it," he said, slowly shaking his head. I noticed, though, that he quickly looked away.

"But..." I began to object.

"Alannah, we're not as easy to get rid of as some thug he picked up off the street."

"Well, that makes me feel so much better." Quin chuckled but I wasn't appeased. "What about Kieran?" I asked, looking down.

"That was Doyle," Quin said gently, stroking the back of my hand with his thumb. "He didn't care who knew what sort of man he was. Andrews, though...he has a reputation, connections and business ventures to consider. He doesn't want to risk all that. As long as he knows we don't have any proof he'll leave us be."

"Is that so?" I gave Quin a sceptical look, letting my eyes settle on the numerous bruises adorning his body.

He flipped his wrist. "That only happened because I got caught."

"You really do have a way of making me feel right at ease," I grumbled. "And if you were to find some proof? What then? I know you won't stop looking..."

"We'll have to make sure he doesn't know about it until it's too late. Because even if we do find out something, he'll likely believe he can simply talk his way out of it. He's done it enough times before, after all. But if we have enough to see him arrested..."

"Then he'll come after you all the sooner."

Quin frowned but I raised my brows defiantly. We looked at each other for a long moment before I decided it might be better to change the subject. There wasn't much we could do about the previous night's events in any case—at best Andrews' guard might be arrested, but that would likely have little impact on Herbert Andrews' himself, besides making him angry. And although I worried about Quin, I did also want to see Andrews behind bars.

"Um…" Looking around for some sort of distraction, my eye fell on Quin's shirt. "Where did you get those clothes?" I asked, cocking my head.

"Ah…" To my surprise, a soft red hue started creeping from Quin's neck up to his forehead. "Well…" he began, avoiding my eye as he looked down at his lap. "Archie and I…well it was Archie's idea, it was, I had nothing to do with it…and…"

"What was Archie's idea?" I demanded to put a stop to his ramblings.

Quin cleared his throat and twiddled his thumbs, evidently contemplating what to say. I narrowed my eyes at him.

"We…well…you must understand we were both in a dreadful state. We needed to get to a carriage…and…well…" I exhaled forcefully, waiting impatiently for him to get to the point. "We went to a…" he mumbled a word I was sure I must have misunderstood.

"You went where?" I asked slowly, leaning toward him.

"A whorehouse." This time he enunciated each sound, making me blink stupidly. "Archie knew about the place…and…well…hmph…"

"I see."

"It was our only option. Both of us could barely walk, we'd never have made it back here on our own."

"And the…um…whores were kind enough to let you change your clothes?" Getting a whiff of his freshly washed hair, I added, "And to let you bathe as well."

"I would have been happy with the carriage!" he insisted. "But…well…before I knew it, they had…hmph…"

I looked at Quin for a moment as he sat there, propped up against the pillows with his ears and cheeks glowing bright red, looking like a schoolboy who had been caught at some mischief, and I suddenly had to laugh. I laughed and laughed, until tears were streaming down my face as I pictured Quin being bundled into a bathtub by an assortment of prostitutes.

"Were you able to defend your virtue, at least?" I finally managed to ask, wiping my eyes.

"I did, thank you," he answered shortly, looking at me grumpily, which just about set me off again. "I hadn't realised my virtue would be such a source of amusement for you."

"I take your virtue very seriously, I assure you."

"It's not as if I didn't have the opportunity, you know." He stuck out his chin and looked down his nose at me.

"I'm sure you did," I said soothingly, patting him on the hand.

"And that doesn't bother you?" he sputtered, which made me laugh again. After a moment I moved a little closer to him, holding his eyes.

"I know I can trust you, Quin," I said softly, stroking his cheek, "even in a room full of whores." I leaned toward him and gave him a gentle kiss. He put a hand on the nape of my neck to pull me closer, the pressure of his mouth increasing.

Coming away a few minutes later, he chuckled, murmuring into my ear, "I'll take you over any whore, Mrs Williams."

13.

WE STAYED IN Dublin for two more days to give Quin time to recover from his night-time adventures.

Mr Kelly revealed himself to be adept at healing and bustled in and out of the room between his usual duties, plying Quin with foul-tasting concoctions and odorous compresses, insisting that he stay in bed. Despite the fact that it made my skin crawl to think Herbert Andrews might be in the same building with us at any moment, I had to admit the rest had done Quin a world of good. By the time we were ready to go back home he no longer suffered from headache and was more or less back to his normal self—although the bruising on his temple and forearm was still apparent, and the rope marks were still clear to see.

I felt a sense of relief when we finally made our way into Glaslearg's courtyard after an extended return trip plagued by near constant rainfall, and I looked forward to a degree of normalcy after the excitement of our time in Dublin. Our arrival was greeted by the emergence of John and Bryan from the stable, followed in short order by the household staff, all of whom bustled about us, goggling at Quin's bruises with big eyes.

Quin brushed off their concerns, assuring them he was quite alright. Mrs O'Sullivan wrinkled her brow and gave him a sceptical look but said no more, instead rushing back into the house with promises of having a meal prepared for us in no time.

I smiled after her and caught Margaret's eye. She ran a hand over her growing belly before disappearing through the door. She must be about seven months along by now I thought as I followed the other women into the manor. Margaret seemed content with the way in which things had turned out and I was happy for her and looked forward to her baby's arrival—although I did still yearn for my own.

With a small sigh I made my way upstairs to freshen up, followed a few minutes later by Quin. When we went back down, delectable smells were emanating from the kitchen. Opening the door, I saw that Mrs O'Sullivan and Mary Murphy were hard at work, with the gangly form of Finnian hovering at the edge of the table. A long-fingered hand crept surreptitiously forward, snatching a morsel from one of the platters, only to be met with a sharp blow from the cook's wooden spoon.

Finnian yelped in alarm, making me laugh. He turned and looked at me with a guilty expression on his face, holding the affronted hand in the other.

"We'll have the dining table set up in a moment," Mrs O'Sullivan said, waving her spoon, which made Finnian take a quick step back.

"Oh, don't bother, Mrs O'Sullivan." I shook my head. "We're more than happy to eat here." I glanced at Quin, who nodded his agreement, while Mrs O'Sullivan pursed her lips in disapproval. Clearly, she preferred things to be done in a more proper fashion.

"Of course," Quin said, coming into the kitchen and looking approvingly at the generous spread. "I'll never understand how you manage to prepare a feast in the time it takes me to remove my boots." He smiled at the cook, who immediately looked appeased. She beamed back, her round cheeks going pink.

"Och, it's nothing, sir. But now come, come, no need to wait then. Ye must be starved."

I was in fact quite hungry after the long ride back and eagerly sat down, my mouth watering in anticipation of tasting Mrs O'Sullivan's excellent cooking.

"You may join us, Finnian," I said to the young man, who was eying the table with longing, licking his lips. He glanced briefly toward Mrs O'Sullivan for confirmation before sitting down on the bench opposite Quin and me as Mary placed another dish in front of us.

The door opened, making us all look up as Rupert came in, sniffing appreciatively. A brief scowl crossed Finnian's face at sight of the valet, but he smoothed out his features as Rupert sat down beside him, throwing Finnian a quick glance. Quin had told me the two youngsters had been having a go at one another about a girl.

Clearly, they hadn't quite resolved their differences.

Mrs O'Sullivan placed another dish on the table, paying no attention to the animosity between Finnian and Rupert. "Ye'll be a right sight at the festivities tomorrow, sir," she observed, eying Quin's temple with a wrinkled brow.

"Festivities?" He wrinkled his own brow, ignoring her comment.

"The festival of Lughnasa," Finnian piped up with a mouthful of food. Getting a stern look from Mrs O'Sullivan, he quickly swallowed, looking down at his plate.

"Oh." I nodded slowly. With our prolonged stay in Dublin and the longer than expected return trip I had quite lost track of time. Tomorrow was the last day of July, which meant the harvest season would soon begin, marked by the festival.

"What did you have planned?" I asked as I reached for one of the platters.

"Nothing grand," Mrs O'Sullivan replied with a wave of the hand, "just a small gathering with a few families. And since we didn't know when you'd return"—she glanced sideways at Quin—"we thought we'd hold the gathering down by the river."

"That seems fitting." My comment made Quin give me a curious look. "It's said that the Celts often celebrated Lughnasa with some kind of excursion," I explained, "to an ancient site, a mountain top or a river or lake. Back then there was also horse racing, ball games and the ficheall, and even great fairs." I paused as I realised everyone at the table was looking at me. "Um...of course, it's all done on a smaller scale today."

"How do you know all that?" Rupert asked, leaning toward me.

"It's called *reading*, Rupert." Quin winked at me before turning to his valet. "You ought to try it some time."

Rupert's round cheeks went pink, and he cleared his throat in embarrassment.

"It's also called having a grandmother who was fascinated with all things Celtic. She could spend hours contemplating the origins of every imaginable tradition, regaling me with stories when I was a child.—Did you know that the festival of Lughnasa is named after the Celtic god Lugh, who is said to have come up with many of the rituals that survive until this day?"

"So it's a *pagan* festival?" Rupert's eyes went wide.

"You're in *Ireland*, you dolt!" Finnian's voice was laced with scorn. "Haven't you noticed?"

Rupert glared at his age-mate and opened his mouth to respond but I forestalled him. "Many Irish traditions have Celtic origins, Rupert, although they've long since been mixed with Christian beliefs." I glanced at Quin, remembering similar conversations I'd had with him. "Even during Lughnasa, some people make pilgrimages to holy sites to pray to the saints, while others get priests to bless their fields before the harvest. But it all began with the Celts.—Lughnasa is even the Gaelic name for the month of August if you needed any more proof."

I smiled at Rupert, who nodded slowly, seeming reasonably impressed. Quin slapped him lightly on the shoulder.

"In any case," he addressed his valet with a grin, "it's bound to be a day well spent."

THE FOLLOWING DAY dawned bright and blue, and I was glad to see the clouds seemed to be staying away, making me look forward to the festivities all the more.

Quin and I spent the morning in the study, catching up on all that had passed in our absence—everything was in order, though, with Mr Dunne having had things well under control. After a light midday meal, we met Denis and Mrs O'Sullivan in the entrance hall mid-afternoon. The cook had prepared an enormous picnic basket, which Quin eyed appreciatively before hefting it up off the floor as Rupert clattered down the stairs. Outside, we met Mr Dunne, Bryan, Finnian, Margaret and John, and we headed off down the path with a festive air.

"Are you sure you don't want to take one of the horses?" I asked Margaret, who was walking beside me. "Or a wagon?"

Margaret patted her abdomen fondly. "Och, I thank you, mistress, but I'll be quite alright. I'll enjoy the walking while I can." She winked at me, splaying her feet as she pretended to waddle along with her arms extended beyond the small bulge that was all the evidence of her advancing pregnancy.

I laughed, thinking it unlikely that Margaret would ever extend to such proportions. "Well, if you're sure…"

She nodded and waved an arm. "Besides, we've hardly had a clear day like this all summer. Walking's the best way to enjoy it!"

I looked around and had to agree. We had come to the end of the path that ran past the outbuildings and reached the small stream. The soft sunlight glinted off the bubbling water, and the reeds and grasses on the bank swayed gently in the light breeze. On the other side of the stream, the golden fields of wheat and oats awaited the harvest, a plentiful bounty illuminated by the sun's gentle touch.

We ambled along the small river, the men taking turns to carry the heavy picnic basket. Hearing the sound of giggling up ahead I turned toward a clump of bushes, spotting several children collecting bilberries, mouths and hands stained with the dark blue juices. They squealed when they saw us, one girl stuffing a handful of berries into her mouth before disappearing on the other side of the shrubs.

I laughed, making the other children smile as they continued their foraging, a few of them greeting me shily. Before long we heard the sound of voices and found several people congregated on a relatively flat spot on the riverbank. I recognised Mary Murphy and her stern-looking husband, Robert, as well as several other tenants, who would have walked there from their cottages on the other side of the estate.

I felt a light tug on my hand and looked down to see Mary's oldest daughter smiling at me, beckoning. She was holding a small wreath of wildflowers and I removed my bonnet and bent toward her so she could place it on my head.

"Thank you, Bridget," I said, making her beam at me. She dropped into a brief curtsy before scampering off, heading toward a basket from which she removed another flower wreath. Looking around I noticed that several women wore flowers in their hair or bonnets, with wreaths or single flowers brightening the homespun clothing, while others had blooming garlands draped around their necks or nosegays pinned to their bodices.

A trampling of small feet behind me announced the return of the berry pickers, whose hands, pockets and aprons were stuffed with their prize, their clothes and faces marked with their efforts.

"You're looking very colourful yourself," I said to Quin, who had come up beside me.

He gave me a startled look and I pointed at his temple, which was still greenish blue, although there was no longer any swelling. He flipped his wrist dismissively, giving me a glimpse of the thin red line that remained from the rope burn.

"Then I'll fit right in with that lot," he said, nodding toward the blue-tinged children. "You, though"—his green eyes glinted in the sunlight—"you look beautiful." He extended a hand and pushed a wayward strand of hair behind my ear. "You should always wear flowers in your hair!"

"A bit impractical on a daily basis," I observed, making him give me long-suffering look. "But thank you," I added with a laugh.

"Mr and Mrs Williams!"

Quin and I turned toward the stocky, middle-aged Mr Connell, who had come up behind us alongside his wife and a few others. The men shook hands and the women greeted each other warmly, the tenants expressing their joy at our timely return while throwing furtive glances at Quin's bruised face. The conversation soon turned toward the afternoon's activities, though, and the women chattered happily about the picnic fare they'd brought along while the men contemplated the possibility of lighting a bonfire in the evening. Since there were few trees about from which to glean firewood, nor a convenient pile of turf stored around the riverbend, it seemed an unlikely prospect, but I let them be.

More tenants flocked to the grassy bank throughout the afternoon and spontaneous applause erupted when the O'Hagans arrived pulling a small handcart piled high with turf—it seemed we would have a bonfire after all, albeit a small one. Soon, small groups had formed, and food was being shared, with animated conversation and laughter filling the air. After a time, some of the young men decided to test their strength and skill in friendly wrestling matches and throwing and running contests.

With his feet bare and his sleeves rolled up to the elbows, revealing one mottled blue forearm, Quin was in the thick of it, pitting himself against the youngsters as the women cheered on their menfolk, clapping and slapping their thighs in encouragement. The children shrieked in delight at the vigorous activity, holding their own contests when the men paused, sweating freely and panting for breath.

"Not bad," I said to Quin, who was bent double beside me. "Stronger than most and faster than many."

He straightened up with a puff of air. "If I hadn't been recently injured, I'd have beaten all of them in all contests." He grinned self-righteously.

"False modesty clearly isn't one of your faults."

"Not at all!"

We laughed and he offered me his arm, leading me to the edge of the stream as a sudden racket announced another contest getting underway behind us. We had placed a few bottles of ale in the cool water and Quin gulped his greedily before sinking onto the soft grass, patting the ground beside him. I sat down, sipping the refreshing ale, watching a pair of finches flit about in a clump of bushes on the opposite bank. It was evening by now, with the sun sinking steadily down to the horizon, and some of the older men were busy piling up the turf on a large flat rock at the water's edge. I glanced at the sky, but it seemed the rain was staying away.

When the small bonfire was lit at dusk, one of the men brought out a bodhran and started thumping out a lively beat. The drum was soon joined by the melodious sounds of a flute, the two instruments weaving together into a spirited tune that had numerous people tapping their feet. Before long adults and children alike were dancing without care, their joyful anticipation of the impending harvest permeating their movements and the laughter that filled the night sky. Quin and I danced with the rest as the waxing moon rose slowly above us, casting the festivities into a soft light.

"I need a rest," I panted some time later, fanning my hot face with my hand.

Quin smiled at me, his own face flushed with exertion. Catching sight of Margaret's beckoning wave, he offered me his arm. Before we could take a step toward her, though, a scowling Rupert stormed past us, taking no notice of Quin or me. Surprised, I looked in the direction from which he'd come.

On the edge of the group of dancers, I spotted Finnian, who was mooning over a slender girl, who was leaning coquettishly toward him. As I watched, another youth stalked boldly toward the pair, catching the girl's attention and placing himself squarely in Finnian's way. Quite unbothered by the change of admirer, the girl ignored Finnian and batted her eyelashes at the newcomer, making Finnian take on the precise expression that Rupert had just displayed before storming off himself.

"Oh dear," I said, looking at Quin.

He grinned. "If that's the girl they're fighting over they may soon find themselves commiserating with each other instead."

I laughed, taking Quin's arm once more. He led me toward a group of people on the riverbank who were facing a grizzled old man sitting on a rock. I recognised Grandfather O'Reilly, whose old but strong voice was carrying over the crowd.

"He's telling stories," I said softly to Quin. We waved to Margaret in welcome before sitting down at the edge of the circle. "It's the story of Lugh." I felt some excitement listening to the Gaelic words, remembering my grandmother regaling me with similar tales when I was a child.

"And so it was that Lugh arrived at the court of Dagdha," I translated Grandfather O'Reilly's words for Quin. "Lugh is a Celtic god," I reminded him before continuing with the story the old man was telling. "He had learned many skills and had a great and powerful reach with his sword."

"That's why he's called Lugh of the Long Arm," a little boy interrupted excitedly, making the adults smile indulgently.

"Just so, Jacob," came Grandfather O'Reilly's kindly reply. "And because he had so many skills, he wanted to be in the company of the other gods at King Nuadhu's fort. But the gatekeeper did not want to grant Lugh this honour." The old man wrinkled his brow and shook his head. " 'But I am a skilled builder,' Lugh said to the gatekeeper. But the gatekeeper was not moved. 'We already have a builder,' he replied, barring Lugh's way. 'I am also a skilled poet,' Lugh said, but again the gatekeeper did not let him in. 'We already have a poet,' he said, shaking his head. And for every skill Lugh said he possessed the gatekeeper gave the same reply. The King did not need another smith, harper, magician or physician, nor did he need another champion or warrior, the gatekeeper insisted." Grandfather O'Reilly paused dramatically, young and old watching him eagerly, although most had probably heard the legend countless times before. "But Lugh did not give up. 'Do you have anyone who has mastered all the skills I have listed?' he asked. The gatekeeper fell silent, thinking about what

Lugh had said. Finally, he stepped aside. 'No Lugh, son of Cian and Ethniu, no-one here has mastered all the skills you possess. You may enter King Nuadhu's court and be welcome.' "

The onlookers gave a collective sigh at the conclusion of the story.

"Tell us more!" Jacob's twin brother Samuel demanded.

Grandfather O'Reilly chuckled. "Hm, let's see now. I could tell you how Lugh killed his grandfather Balor by striking him in his Evil Eye or how Lugh became the new King of the Tuatha De Danann.—But maybe you want to hear about Lugh's son, who became Ireland's most famous warrior?"

"Cú Chulainn, Cú Chulainn!" Mary Murphy's son Robert was squealing with excitement, bouncing up and down madly, causing several other children to be similarly affected.

I laughed and glanced at Quin, who was watching the scene with amusement. He held my eyes for a moment and squeezed my hand.

"Cú Chulainn," Grandfather O'Reilly said pensively, making me turn my attention back to him as several heads nodded enthusiastically. I dutifully continued translating. "The son of Lugh and an Ulster princess, Cú Chulainn was named Sétanta at birth. One day he killed the fierce guard dog of Culann the smith while trying to reach King Conchobar Mac Nessa. The smith was devastated by his hound's death and so Sétanta promised to guard Culann's house until a replacement hound could be reared. He was called the hound of Culann, or Cú Chulainn, after that."

"I already know that!"

A ripple of laughter spread through the crowd at small Robert's objection.

"You do, do you?" Grandfather O'Reilly raised thick, grey brows in mock surprise. "Then I'm sure you also know about Cú Chulainn's most famous battle, when he defeated the army of Queen Medb of Connacht single-handedly to defend Ulster from invasion during The Cattle Raid of Cooley?" Robert nodded vigorously. "Hm...and do you know that Cú Chulainn knocked down fifty boys who were bigger than him when he was only six years old?"

"I know that too!" Robert assured the old storyteller at high volume.

"Tell us the story of how he fought at Clochafarmore," a small girl called out, coming to sit down cross-legged in front of old Mr O'Reilly and looking up at him expectantly. Small Robert opened his mouth to say something but soon closed it and shrugged. He had probably heard all the stories before and would no doubt be happy to hear them again even so.

Grandfather O'Reilly smiled before turning toward the small girl. "Cú Chulainn had been a great hero, but even great heroes must one day pass to the other world. Cú Chulainn fought many battles. His last one was another against Queen Medb." The old man paused, looking around at the crowd of onlookers, who were watching him, transfixed. "Wanting to avenge her loss during the cattle raid, Queen Medb conspired with Cú Chulainn's enemies and sent a strong force against him. Cú Chulainn fought valiantly, cutting through Queen Medb's army again and again until finally, he was mortally wounded by his greatest foe, Lugaid." Some of the children gasped, clutching a parent's hand or hiding their faces. "But even close to death, Cú Chulainn would not admit defeat. With the help of his warriors, he tied himself to the big standing stone Clochafarmore and for three days, while his lifeblood pumped out of him, he continued to fight with his sword in one hand and his shield in the other, striking down any who came near. His enemies were afraid of this great warrior who refused to die and only when the raven of death landed on Cú Chulainn's shoulder did they dare to approach him."

"Was he dead?" a tiny boy whispered, his eyes big as saucers as he leaned forward in his mother's lap.

Grandfather O'Reilly nodded gravely. "He was. A great hero had fallen. But his death was avenged by another great warrior, Conall Cernach, who slew Lugaid.—And the story of Cú Chulainn lives on until today."

A hush descended on the onlookers at the conclusion of the story. One of the children yawned hugely, setting off several others. I put my hand in front of my mouth to stifle a yawn of my own as I felt tiredness come over me, too. Slowly, people started drifting away while Grandfather O'Reilly continued to sit on his rock, a faraway look on his face. I wondered what other stories he had to tell, about his own life and the hardships he'd had to endure in an Ireland so very different to that in the legends.

"It's past midnight." I turned toward Quin's soft voice and he squeezed my hand. "Shall we start heading back?"

I looked around the clearing. Here and there, small groups of people were still talking and laughing, while a few youngsters continued to dance. Some of the tenants were collecting their things, preparing for the walk back to their cottages, while several others looked to be spending the night on the streambank. As I stood up, a movement in front of some bushes caught my eye and I smiled at the children who were lying there, blissfully asleep.

"Goodnight, mistress." Mary Murphy had come up next to me, carrying her youngest, who was rubbing her eyes with her small fists.

"Goodnight, Mary," I responded softly, smiling at the little girl. I nodded toward Mary's husband, who was bidding farewell to Quin with the usual gruff expression on his face before leading his family away, holding a burning torch in his hand.

Quin and I started walking along the stream, pausing frequently to wish our tenants goodnight. Margaret and John joined us as we made our way back to the manor house, with Finnian and Rupert appearing suddenly from opposite directions, scowling briefly at each other before falling into step with the rest of the small party.

I looked for Mr Dunne, Bryan and Denis but shrugged when I didn't see them anywhere. Likely they had made their own way back already or had simply fallen asleep under a bush like so many others. Although it was not such a long walk to the manor, the festivities had made the day feel like a holiday and staying out in the open for the night would no doubt prolong that feeling—something many would be looking forward to. With the festival of Lughnasa came the beginning of August, and the harvest season was upon us. Soon, the men would collapse onto their pallets at night, exhausted from the long day's work.

I suddenly had the urge to turn back and lie down under a bush myself. Then again, I no longer felt tired. The night air was cool and fresh, and the soft light of the half-moon reflected off the scattered whisps of clouds. I felt invigorated walking on the spongy grass alongside the burbling water, even at this late hour, and with the promise of the impending harvest, it seemed like a world of possibilities had opened up before me.

I caught Quin's eye and he smiled at me, the flame of the torch he held flickering in the light breeze. I lifted one brow and cocked my head suggestively, making a slow grin appear on his face.

There were some advantages to heading to the privacy of one's bedroom after all. The thought made me emit a short laugh, which earned me a few curious glances from our fellow travellers before we all continued on in silence.

Quin and I walked close beside each other, exchanging frequent glances. I was acutely aware of him, as our arms would touch briefly, or the fabric of my skirt would brush against his leg. When he gave me his hand to lead me across the small bridge, my fingers tingled at his touch.

Reaching the manor house a short time later, we bade the others farewell before heading upstairs to our room. Alone at last, I turned eagerly into Quin's waiting arms, closing my eyes and pulling his head down to mine. He kissed me slowly and tenderly, but I pressed my hands against his back, urging him closer.

"I see you're in a sprightly mood," he murmured.

I smiled wryly. "Put your mouth to better use."

He chuckled, but obliged me, running his lips along my neck, up one side and down the other. I pushed his jacket off his shoulders and untied his cravat, before removing his waistcoat and shirt.

I reached for the top of his trousers, but Quin spun me around, his hands finding the row of buttons at the back of my dress. "My turn first." With practised ease he soon had me undressed to my undergarments, which put up little resistance in the face of his single-minded attentions. His trousers and smallclothes quickly joined the other items on the floor, leaving puddles of fabric scattered around the room.

I ran my hands up and down his bare skin as his fingertips slid along my back and thighs, making the blood thrum through my veins. Suddenly, he lifted me and carried me to the chaise longue, where he settled me on his lap with a contented sigh. He cupped the back of my head, urging my mouth to his, my breasts pressed against his chest as he guided my movements with his other hand on the small of my back. His breath was coming faster and faster, until he gave a cry that mingled with my own. His head fell against the backrest, and I collapsed onto his chest, his arms tight around me in our union as our joined heartbeats began to slow.

14.

"SLÁINTE."

"*Sláinte*," Alannah echoed the toast with a smile, lifting her glass to Quin before turning toward Mr Dunne.

"To your success," Quin added as he turned to the man himself.

The overseer cleared his throat and dropped his eyes as he raised his glass, his cheeks turning pink as they all took a sip. "I've only done my duty, sir." He shook his head diffidently.

"Now, Mr Dunne, don't be modest," Quin countered, smiling at the overseer. "Without your commendable efforts the crops would never have been collected so speedily."

"Oh, sir, it was nothing," Dunne insisted, shuffling his feet awkwardly.

Humility seemed to come naturally to the slight man, Quin thought with some amusement. Even so, Dunne had done an excellent job of overseeing the harvesting of the estate's oats and wheat, organising the tenants and a few additional labours to clear the fields in record time, and yielding a plentiful bounty.

"And the early potatoes have also been unearthed," Quin cheerfully continued his praises. "By the looks of the remaining crops we'll have an excellent potato harvest come the autumn."

"I'm glad to see not even weather like this can dampen your spirits." Alannah's comment made all of them look outside the drawing room window, where a steady drizzle was falling.

"What, a little rain?" Quin grinned at her.

"A little rain?" Alannah shook her head. "It's been raining almost incessantly since the beginning of summer. Always assuming that summer did in fact arrive at all...one would never know it, looking outside." This was undoubtedly true.

After the brief respite following their return from Dublin, the prevailingly wet conditions had once again set in.

"The year of our Lord, it was 1845," Mr Dunne suddenly intoned in a grave voice. The overseer looked seriously from Quin to Alannah and back again as he went on, "it was infinitely damp, and the sun did not shine. Forever we'll remember the year '45 as the year that the summer just never arrived. *In Éirinn, tá an aimsir claochlaitheach,*" he ended with a flourishing wave of the hand toward the window.

"Why, Mr Dunne," Alannah exclaimed in delight, breaking out into a wide smile, "I had no idea you were a poet!—The Gaelic part means the weather in Ireland is fickle," she added, turning toward Quin. Although he could understand a few words of Gaelic by now, to him the language still tended to sound like unintelligible rumbling for the most part.

Dunne cleared his throat, his cheeks going pink in obvious embarrassment. "I'm hardly a poet, Mrs Williams," he said gruffly, "although my father did hold that honour."

"He did?" Quin was intrigued. He'd known Dunne's father had been a schoolmaster but not that he'd been a poet.

"Oh, yes." Dunne's voice was filled with pride. "Descended from a long line of poets, he was."

"We have a long tradition of poets in Ireland," Alannah said enthusiastically.

"Yes," Dunne agreed, forgetting his usual reservedness around Alannah as he immersed himself in the topic. "Poetry has long been used to record the history of Ireland. Just think of the *Lebor Gabála* or *Acallam na Senórach.*"

"Think of what?" Quin looked from Dunne to Alannah, not understanding a word.

"The *Lebor Gabála,*" the overseer started explaining in a slow and patient voice, "is a famous collection of Gaelic poems that tells the story of the different peoples that occupied Ireland in days long gone—the followers of Cessair, Partholón and Nemed, the Fir Bolg and the treacherous Tuatha Dé Danann, who were finally conquered by the sons of Milesius."

"And the *Acallam na Senórach,*" Alannah took over, "tells the tale of the great hero Fionn mac Cumhaill and his band of warriors, the *fianna,* who guarded Ireland for the High King."

Mr Dunne nodded. "Irish poets were once highly respected and learned individuals, and it was a great honour to belong to the *filidh* and compose such songs and verse for nobles and kings. Alas, few descendants of the *filidh* remain, with most modern poets coming from the middling class, without the formal education for which Irish poets were once renowned."

"And your father?" Quin asked, fascinated.

Dunne's chest swelled with pride. "Although my father was only a schoolmaster, he could trace his ancestry all the way back to Lughaidh Ó Cléirigh, the famous Ulster poet."

Alannah's eyes widened. "Lughaidh Ó Cléirigh? Why, he wrote the *Beatha Aodha Ruaidh Uí Dhomhnaill*, the story of Red Hugh O'Donnell and his fight against the English with Hugh O'Neill, the Earl of Tyrone." She gave Quin a sideways glance.

"I am fully aware of Ireland's history with England," he assured her with a wave of the hand, as always experiencing mixed feelings when contemplating England's occupation of half the world. Although he was an Englishman and had served in the British Army, he could never quite agree with England's imperialistic practices, particularly where the oppression of other peoples was concerned. Turning to the overseer, though, his usual cheerfulness returned. "So Mr Dunne, will you be composing an epic poem about your time here at Glaslearg?"

Quin grinned, making Dunne laugh, something that he rarely did. "You never know, Mr Williams, you never know."

15.

"JESUS, GOD AND all the Saints!"

"Margaret, you mustn't blaspheme!" Mary Murphy turned toward me in some shock, her eyes wide at the sort of language cascading out of Margaret's mouth as she struggled through the delivery of her first child.

"I'm praying!" Margaret snapped, her face damp with sweat, strands of hair sticking to her forehead. "Did you recite poetry while pushing a flaming tree trunk out of your...? Arghhh!"

Margaret's conclusion was drowned out by another cry that emerged from her throat as her abdomen bunched up hard like an enormous fist.

"Push now!" the midwife commanded, completely focused on her job at the foot of the bed, ignoring everything else around her.

Margaret obeyed, the effort leaving her panting and her face crimson. "Oh God, oh God, oh God, I can't!" she wailed as her head flopped back onto the pillow.

"Yes, you can. You must!"

I gave a start at the midwife's tone. Was something wrong? My heart gave a sudden lurch as I remembered the ominous words the old woman had uttered at Margaret and John's wedding, pointing at her midsection with a gnarled hand.

"Push, Margaret, push!" the midwife repeated sternly.

No, I thought, as my heart started beating steadily once more, likely this was just the way it went. I had never attended a birth before but had of course heard stories. Screaming and swearing were evidently part of the process, as seemed to be the woman reaching a point where she thought she couldn't continue.

"I can't," Margaret moaned, her eyes squeezed tight shut.

"Push!" the midwife commanded once more. "Push now!"

Margaret lifted her head, straining to obey, the cords in her neck sticking out.

"That's it, that's it!" the midwife encouraged. "Just a little more."

Margaret gave a little more, her face going purple with the exertion, and all of a sudden, a tiny little body slithered out between her blood-streaked thighs, into the waiting arms of the midwife. The stout woman gathered the little bundle up as a healthy wail emerged from the tiny mouth.

"It's a boy," the midwife announced with a smile, giving the baby a brief inspection before wrapping him in a soft towel and laying him on Margaret's chest. Margaret was grinning from ear to ear, oblivious of the sweat, blood and slime that covered her, and to the further ministrations of the midwife, who was dealing with the afterbirth.

"He's perfect," she whispered as she looked adoringly at her son's face. "Just perfect." Her voice broke as she burst into tears, hugging the tiny body to her.

Mary and I looked at each other across the bed, both of us grinning like loons while tears streaked down our own cheeks. The three of us huddled together over Margaret's baby, and I marvelled at how such a tiny creature would one day become a full-grown man.

A knock at the door made me look up from contemplating a miniature ear a short time later.

"Yes?" Margaret asked, looking toward the door.

"Ah...um...it's me."

I recognised the voice of John, Glaslearg's groom and Margaret's husband. Margaret raised her brows as she glanced toward the midwife, who was packing up her things. She had inspected mother and baby thoroughly, finally announcing they were in good health. She would keep an eye on them over the next few days but showed no signs of concern.

"You may come in," the midwife called before turning back to Margaret. "I'll come see you in the morning."

The door opened, revealing a nervous-looking John, who was kneading his hat in his hands. Behind him I could see Quin, who had been waiting with John in the adjoining room.

"You have a son," the midwife told John with a smile as she walked past him.

"A son? I...I have a son?" he stammered as the midwife left and Quin popped his head into the room.

"Congratulations!" he said.

Margaret smiled briefly at him in thanks, but her attention was soon caught by John, who was walking toward the bed with big eyes. Seeing the tiny bundle asleep on Margaret's chest, his homely face split into a wide grin. "My son," he murmured with a thick voice, "my son."

I got up quickly, making space for him, and he kneeled next to the bed, planting a kiss on Margaret's forehead and running a finger gently over the baby's head. She beamed back up at him and I smiled at the peaceful scene, before making my way out of the room, followed by Mary.

She quietly closed the door behind us, and we turned back toward the manor house, Mary walking beside us. She would be staying the night with us, instead of having to walk all the way back to her own cottage at the other end of the estate.

As a wedding gift to Margaret and John, Quin had built them a small stone cottage not far from the manor grounds, near to Mr Dunne's new home. While the estate's servants usually slept in the manor's attic, Quin had wanted to give the newlyweds a little more privacy for their growing family. He had also wanted them to remain close by, though, as both Margaret and John would continue to work up at the main house—although I'd assured Margaret she could take all the time she needed to adjust to motherhood and that she'd be able to hand over some of her duties until she felt able to take them on once more.

Margaret and John seemed quite content with this arrangement and, indeed, their marriage. Although their relationship had evidently not been based on love, I thought they had gotten quite close over the last five months. Judging by the scene I'd just witnessed, there was definite affection between the two of them.

I smiled to myself but suddenly felt a selfish stab of jealousy as I thought about the tiny soft bundle Margaret and John could now call their own.

Quin offered me his arm and I pushed the thought aside.

I too had much to be thankful for, after all.

MARGARET AND HER son quickly recovered from the birth and the baby soon wormed its way into all of our hearts. The proud parents had decided to name their firstborn Quinton, much to my own Quinton's surprise, but unashamed delight. Within a few days the little boy was nicknamed Quinnie, being a tiny creature that seemed destined to remain so, much like his diminutive mother. But with his large, beguiling eyes, one couldn't help but be charmed by little Quinnie.

"Aren't you a darling?" I ran my finger along the soft skin of one cheek. Quinnie was lying on my lap, little fists waving in the air as he looked up at me with interest.

I caught Margaret's eye and she smiled at me. "He's even more of a darling when he sleeps at night," she said, stifling a yawn as she came to stand next to us. Looking down at her son her expression softened once more. "Och, but you're a good boy, you are. Still"—another stifled yawn made Margaret blink—"it would be grand to be able to sleep through the night again."

Quinnie's mouth quirked into a smile, making Margaret and me laugh.

"I think he knows he can get away with anything because he's so charming," I said, running a hand over the light dusting of soft hair on his miniature head.

"Babies can't really smile yet, my mother always said." Margaret nevertheless looked adoringly at him with a smile of her own. Quinnie's hands started waving a little more forcefully and he smacked his lips.

"He's getting hungry," Margaret observed, reaching to take the baby from my lap.

"Does he ever cry?" I had yet to hear him emit more than a few mewls when he wanted to nurse or needed a new clout.

"Only in the middle of the night." Margaret winked at me as she sat down, leaning against the chairback and placing Quinnie to her breast.

I watched in fascination as the small body moulded itself to its mother's breast, mouth clamped tightly around the nipple, little hands kneading the air. I wondered what it would feel like to hold my own child just so.

After a time Quinnie's mouth slackened, dropping open as his eyes closed in contentment. I watched his small chest rise and fall in peaceful rhythm and felt utterly at peace myself. Margaret lifted him gently to her shoulder and patted his back, eliciting a small belch that made us both smile. She placed him into his cradle, where he continued sleeping tranquilly, as Margaret and I stood shoulder to shoulder looking down at him.

Margaret squeezed my hand.

"You'll have one of your own one day," she said softly.

I squeezed back, my heart filling with hope.

16.

"SIR, SIR, COME quick!"

"What?" Startled, Quin looked up from the papers he'd been studying, to see a boy of about ten hovering at the door to the study, breathing heavily and red in the face. Evidently, he had run all the way to the manor house from the cottages at the other end of the estate.

"*Seo libh!*" the boy exclaimed, clearly distressed as he lapsed into Gaelic, practically vibrating with pent-up energy, his eyes flitting back and forth between the desk at which Quin sat and the doorway.

"What is it...Conor?" Quin drew the name out of the dozens stored in his head.

"Come quick, sir!" Conor repeated before his face fell. "*Prátaí.*" The single word came out in what was almost a wail, making Quin wrinkle his brows in concern. It was the Irish word for potatoes, he knew. He also knew the tenants had been preparing to harvest their potato crops, making him feel suddenly anxious about what had caused the boy to run all the way to the manor house in evident distress.

"What about them?" he demanded as he got up from his chair, sounding sterner than he'd intended. The boy hunched into himself and looked like he was about to cry.

"It's alright," Quin said soothingly, walking slowly toward the boy, commanding himself to remain calm. Whatever it was, they would deal with it and besides, it would do no good to shout at the poor child, who was clearly upset enough as it was. "Why don't you tell me what happened on our way to the stable?" Quin patted the boy's shoulder, feeling some of the tension go out of him. His cheeks were still red from the exertion, but he nodded willingly enough. He didn't say anything further, though, turning eagerly toward the door instead.

Quin hurried toward the stable, the boy running after him. He quickly saddled Gambit and indicated to Conor that he should ride in front of him. Wide round eyes greeted this statement, but Conor allowed himself to be lifted onto the horse's sturdy back, clinging to the mane as soon as he had taken a seat.

"Sir?"

Quin turned toward Bryan, the very elderly groom who had hobbled into the stable carrying a bucketful of water that was sloshing to and fro with his arthritic movements. One brow was raised questioningly as he glanced toward the saddled horse and its terrified-looking occupant.

"There seems to be some concern about the potato crop," Quin responded, trying to sound casual. Bryan's grey and sprouting brows rose up to his hairline. The potato crop was of infinite importance not only to Glaslearg's tenants, but also to most of Ireland's vast number of peasants. "I'm sure it's nothing serious," Quin added, attempting to ease the groom's worries.

"Yes...serious," Conor piped up from his mount, mouth turned down and a look of fear on his face—whether from the prospect of riding a horse or in memory of what he'd seen at his farmstead, Quin couldn't tell. "Black...rotten..." the boy managed, before pressing his lips together tightly.

Quin's heart gave a lurch at the description, recalling an article he'd read in the spring, about a potato blight that had devastated crops in the Americas. Had this horror made its way to Ireland? Surely not, he hoped fervently, while his thoughts started running wild. He knew potato seeds were regularly transported across the Atlantic in trade. Could the American blight have been imported along with the seeds? Quin felt as if a deep chasm were opening up beneath him as his mind flitted unbidden to the calamity such a thing would entail, with millions of people across Ireland solely dependent on the potato harvest for their survival.

"*Prátaí?*" Margaret's husband John, the younger of the two grooms, came into the stable carrying a bale of hay. He turned toward Quin in evident concern, having clearly heard some of the exchange.

"Let us not worry ourselves needlessly," Quin said, forcing himself to remain calm, trying to reassure his staff as well as himself. "I shall go with Conor here to inspect the crop myself and then we shall decide how to proceed.—A little spoilage is quite normal, isn't it?" He smiled at the two men and the boy, but Conor shook his head, looking dubious.

Quin took a deep breath before leading Gambit out of the stable and launching into the saddle behind Conor. He nodded toward Bryan and John as they set off, trying not to let his imagination get away from him. He had received no further reports about a blight, after all, he thought, trying to remain positive.

Then again, delivery of any such mail could be slow in coming, especially reports from other parts of the world.

He spurred on Gambit and the horse sped along the path past the outbuildings and toward the stream. Hooves thundered across the wooden bridge and along the track as it continued toward the edge of the estate, past the empty fields that had already yielded their healthy bounty. Nearing the tenants' land, Quin slowed his horse, seeing a large group of men, women and children gathered on one of the small plots, several faces marked with unease. Looking at the potato vines that grew there he could immediately see what had raised their concern, many of the normally vital-looking plants hanging limp, the leaves shrivelled and discoloured. The tenants had been talking animatedly among themselves but turned toward Quin as he dismounted and handed down the boy. Conor ran immediately to one of the women, who gathered him to herself and pressed him to her ample breast, her face marked with the tracks of tears.

Quin turned toward Conor's father, a scruffy looking fellow called McGuire, who had stepped forward from the crowd, lips pressed together in a tight line.

"Sir...I...." He faltered, waving an arm feebly across the field.

Looking more closely Quin could see that at least half of the potato vines were clearly ruined, rotting where they stood. What concerned him more, though, was the potatoes that had been strewn across the field, evidently dug up and discarded in an ever-increasing frenzy, with the vines dropped where they had grown. Normally plump and light brown in colour, these potatoes were shrunken and misshapen, covered in dark bruises and putrid patches, with some broken open to reveal a rotten centre, while others were reduced to little more than black sludge.

Quin swallowed heavily, wondering whether any potatoes could be salvaged from this field at all. He turned toward the McGuires, who were huddled together, Mrs McGuire crying silently while she stroked Conor's head over and over again, with Mr McGuire looking exceedingly grim.

Quin put a hand on Mr McGuire's shoulder and leaned down toward him. "Your family is not going to go hungry," he said sternly, shaking his head while looking the man in the eye.

McGuire nodded mechanically, a look of relief flashing over his scraggly face. "Thank you…sir…but…" He waved a hand toward the ruined field that had meant to bear the family's sustenance.

"We'll salvage what we can," Quin responded firmly before turning toward the other tenants. "How many more fields are affected?"

"The Fitzgeralds'," came a voice from the crowd. "The Garveys'," came another.

"The McAndrews'."

"The Fagans'."

"The Caseys'."

"The O'Hagans'."

Quin swallowed, his heart giving a painful thump at each name called. He was about to say something when he saw a horse and rider coming toward the gathered crowd. It was Alannah, he realised, turning toward her as she reached the edge of the field and dismounted, leading her horse the rest of the way.

"Have you heard?" she asked, just as he said, "Have you seen?"

Judging by her face, though, the answer was obvious. She nodded, looking at the rotten potato vines and their spoilt bounty. "I was teaching at the Connells' cottage when I heard a commotion outside and went to investigate." She shook her head sadly and he reached out and squeezed her hand.

"They had noticed some damage to the vines before," she continued, "but nobody expected *this*!"

"No." Quin shook his head. He had been told of a degree of crop damage in September, but the tenants hadn't been overly concerned, and he hadn't heard anything further since. It was now the second week of October and it looked as though whatever disease had taken root in the potato vines had spread, not only ruining the stalks and leaves but—more distressingly—also destroying the edible tubers the vines bore.

Quin turned back toward the assembled tenants. Several of them were looking distinctly uneasy, although a good number of faces showed no more than fatalistic acceptance—a bountiful harvest was never a certainty and any losses would be dealt with as they came, as had been done before. Many of the children, however, seemed to realise something was not quite right, huddling close to their elders, quietly observing the scene before them with big eyes.

Quin took a deep breath. "We shall gather what healthy potatoes there are," he said in a loud and clear voice that carried over the crowd. "And we'll do it quickly, before the sickness can spread further. Everyone will help."

A few grim-looking men and women nodded, seeming glad to be told what to do, while others looked grimmer still at his words, his plan of action clearly obvious. The potato harvest tended to be a community affair in any case, and none of the tenants were likely to abandon their neighbours to their fate if it could be helped.

Quin shrugged. "Sharing amongst yourselves will help those in need," he continued, perhaps stating another obvious point. "And I shall also make available a share of the estate's oats and wheat for those who need it. Do not be afraid to ask.—Nobody is going to go hungry!" he reiterated his earlier statement to the McGuires, which made even the grimmest of faces nod in approval. "Not one family is going to suffer unduly because of this misfortune. We shall all work together to see us through this poor harvest so we can look forward to next year's successful one."

When Quin said no more the tenants turned away, gathering their spades and returning to their fields.

"It's the same on the Connell's land," Alannah said, turning toward Quin, her eyes showing the worry she felt. "The rest of the tenants are gathered there."

Quin swung up onto his horse. "Then we must ride there at once."

"IT'S MUCH THE same everywhere," Quin said tiredly, rubbing a hand over his face.

In the chaotic days that had followed the discovery of the first rotten potato, he had trudged across the estate, helping the tenants with the harvest where he could—and providing comfort and reassurance where all help had come too late. Although the extent of the damage was less than Quin had initially feared, it was bad enough, nonetheless.

The McGuires' field had been the worst affected, with almost the entire potato crop ruined—bar one small pile of sorry looking brown globes that could hardly feed an entire family over the next twelve months. A few others had also been badly hit, with less than half of the harvest having survived. The damage on the other plots varied, with some having gotten away with only minimal spoilage, including a few that seemed miraculously untouched.

Having seen his tenants store what healthy potatoes there were, Quin had ridden out into the countryside to see how other farmers had fared.

"There are several fields that have been completely ruined," Quin murmured as he peeled off his filthy jacket. "When over the next hill others have been entirely spared."

"How?" Alannah asked, helping him shrug out of his damp shirt. A steady drizzle had been falling over most of the past week, doing nothing to improve anybody's mood.

Quin shrugged. "Mr Byrne mentioned they'd experienced an early frost.—He thought that might have stopped the rot from spreading." He reached for one of the large towels on the washstand and began vigorously rubbing his head to dry his damp hair.

"It'll be alright, won't it?" Alannah had spoken softly, her voice tinged with concern. "Some crop loss is normal, of course, but this…"

"No," Quin responded with a frown as he emerged from the towel, dropping it on the floor. "I don't think this is normal.—Whole fields destroyed and so many more affected? Such widespread damage surely isn't normal."

Alannah sighed. "At least this year's oat harvest was particularly bountiful. We'll be able to help the tenants with that."

Quin nodded absently. "One can only wonder what will happen to those who don't have anyone else to rely on…"

17.

THE NEWS WASN'T good.

Reports of damage to the potato harvest were flooding in from far and wide. With ever-increasing urgency, peasants across Ireland were digging up their rotting fields, desperate to salvage something to feed their families. Hundreds of frightened landowners and parish clerics had written to the Mansion House Committee in Dublin, raising their concerns. Now, the committee had decided to hold a public meeting to discuss these concerns.

Quin wrinkled his brow as he looked over the letter once more, wishing it bore better tidings.

A messenger carrying the letter had arrived from Dublin earlier in the afternoon. Quin's friend Archie had sent him—rather than waiting for the letter to be delivered by the much slower mail coach—knowing Quin would want to hear such news right away.

The public meeting was to be held on the 31st of October, which was in three days. Quin glanced out the window at the grey sky, but quickly made up his mind.

He would leave for Dublin first thing in the morning.

THE MUSIC HALL on Abbey Street was crowded. Presided over by The Right Honourable John Ladaveze Arabin, the Lord Mayor of the city of Dublin, the public meeting gave concerned citizens the opportunity to make their voices heard.

As Quin had already surmised from Archie's letter, every county in Ireland had been affected by the blight. Feeling ever more dejected, Quin listened to harrowing accounts from Kilkenny and Limerick, where huge losses of the potato crop had occurred. Similar reports came from other counties, either through letters sent to the committee or by messengers that had made the trip to Dublin, looking for help. Other areas seemed to have fared better, although no place in Ireland had been completely unaffected. Even in Ulster, where much less damage was reported, a considerable loss of the expected potato yield had nevertheless occurred, as Quin had seen on his own estate. And for the poor peasants who depended in large part—or entirely—on the potato crop for their survival, even a comparatively small loss could prove devastating.

The Lord Mayor, who'd been listening with a grim expression on his face, lips pressed into a tight line, now brought proceedings to an end.

"These alarming accounts of the failure of the potato crop must be dealt with." His loud and clear voice carried over the anxious-looking crowd. "We shall form a deputation," he declared after a short pause, "with the aim of presenting an address to His Excellency Baron Heytesbury, the Lord Lieutenant of Ireland, pressing upon him the need for the government to act immediately, and by all means necessary, to prevent the famine and pestilence this crop failure will otherwise give rise to."

A muted applause greeted this declaration. While many of Ireland's poor would likely depend on governmental assistance in the months to come, it remained to be seen how those in power would respond.

"ARCHIE!"

Quin folded up the newspaper he'd been reading and got up to greet his friends. He'd arranged to see them the day after the Mansion House meeting, hoping to find some distraction over the lunch hour at least.

"Quin!" Archie thumped him vigorously on the back.

"Ham, Ollie."

"It's good to see you Quin," Ollie said with a grin, "although I'm sorry about the circumstances of your visit." His smile faded as they all sat down around the table.

"As am I." Quin sighed and rubbed a hand tiredly over his face before waving at the newspaper. "I've discovered that the arrival of the blight in Ireland was recorded in the Dublin Evening Post on the ninth of September.—I suppose I should consider myself grateful for having had the pleasure of being blissfully ignorant for a few extra weeks."

"I'm sorry, Quin," Archie said with a frown. "I would have told you if I'd read about it then!"

"I know Archie. But it wouldn't have made a difference anyway. And I suspect all of the United Kingdom will know about it now."

They all lapsed into silence for a moment.

"I'm sure Glaslearg's tenants will fare well enough," Quin said at last, "but what about all the others?"

Ham shrugged. "I suppose it'll depend largely on how London reacts."

"And that's the big question, isn't it?" Quin compressed his lips briefly before shaking his head. "But let's not discuss this any further. It's all I've thought and talked about for days on end."

Archie nodded in understanding as the barmaid arrived bearing four tankards of dark and foamy Guinness beer. "I took the liberty of ordering before you arrived," Quin said with a grin, feeling his mood improve at last.

He lifted the mug to his lips, savouring the rich and creamy taste in his mouth. Placing the half-empty vessel back onto the tabletop a short while later, he turned toward Ollie. "And how is the future Mrs Penhale? I trust the wedding plans are proceeding smoothly?"

Ollie's ears went pink at the mention of his affianced. "She's very well, thank you. And all is proceeding according to plan."

"Meaning she hasn't yet changed her mind," Ham put in with a grin, earning himself a scowl from the intended bridegroom.

"Now, now, Ham, don't be jealous," Quin said, patting Ham on the shoulder. "You'll soon find someone yourself, I'm sure." This statement made Ham and Ollie exchange facial expressions, before they all started laughing good-naturedly.

Once the amusement had subsided, Archie gave Quin a speculative look. "I know you don't want to talk business," he began slowly.

"But?" Quin lifted a questioning brow.

"I have some information about Herbert Andrews."

"Andrews?" Quin's heart gave a sudden lurch.

Archie nodded, a frown on his face. "Ever since our night-time encounter I've been wanting to get back at the bastard."

"The guard?" Ham asked wryly.

Archie gave a short laugh. "Him too!—To get to *Andrews*, though," he continued, sobering up, "we need to dig up some dirt."

"And you've found some?" Ollie leaned across the table toward his friend.

"I have."

"And?" Quin pressed him.

"Well, I have several acquaintances as you know, and acquaintances of acquaintances and so on, some of whom are in a position to…"

"Archie!" Quin gave him an impatient look.

"All right, all right." Archie lifted his hands defensively. "In any case, through convoluted means I managed to find out a little about how our Herbert Andrews acquired the family business." He wiggled his eyebrows meaningfully.

"Was it not an inheritance?" Ham looked quizzically from one man to the other, his eyes flickering above his prominent nose.

"It was, yes," Archie agreed slowly, "however, the manner of his father's death was…suspicious."

"Oh?" Quin rubbed his chin.

Before Archie could elaborate, though, the barmaid arrived with their food. Quin absently started eating, paying little attention to what he was putting into his mouth. When they'd all settled back down after the barmaid had left, he turned back to Archie. "What was suspicious about the father's death?"

Archie swallowed a mouthful of stew before answering. "The man had apparently been in good health one day—and not particularly old either—only to fall ill quite suddenly and be dead the next."

Quin frowned. It wasn't unheard of for even robust individuals to be taken by a sudden fever or other illness. He compressed his lips as he thought of his mother, who had met a similar fate. "But…"

Archie put up a hand to silence him. "There was meant to be an inquest. You see, the coroner noted that while most of the symptoms pointed to an acute illness, there were others that were…highly unusual."

"So…his death was unnatural?" Ham lifted one aristocratic brow and Archie nodded.

"The father was murdered?" Quin blurted out, leaning forward intently. A few patrons at neighbouring tables looked curiously at him, making Quin clear his throat in some embarrassment before turning back to Archie.

"Quite possibly," his friend concurred, "only it was never proved. The coroner had wanted to conduct the Marsh Test, but before he could do so the body vanished."

"What?" Quin exclaimed while at the same time Ham asked, "What's the Marsh Test?"

"The Marsh Test," Ollie piped up, his homely face taking on a lecturing air as he pushed his empty plate away, "is a chemical test used for the detection of arsenic."

"Poison." Quin contemplated this new revelation. He tried to picture Herbert Andrews coercing a servant to slip something into his father's food and found he could imagine it all too well. He was quite sure Andrews would not have been content to wait around for his inheritance for several decades once he'd come of age.

"When was this?" Quin asked Archie, who was downing the rest of his beer.

"Ahh." With a contented sigh, Archie lowered the tankard and licked a line of foam off his upper lip. "1809," he said, stifling a belch. "Herbert Andrews had just turned twenty-one. He inherited everything."

"How convenient for him," Ham put in with a snort.

"And you say the body vanished?" Quin asked.

Archie nodded. "The night before the inquest. Andrews made a hue and cry about it, of course, but there was talk…"

"No doubt," Quin said, frowning. "Knowing what we know about him now, he probably had a man on the inside who helped him cover it all up."

"And he would have had no difficulty at all getting hold of the arsenic," Ham observed, making Ollie nod his agreement.

"An everyday poison, conveniently available at a store near you."

Quin snorted at Ollie's jest, realising at the same time, though, that his friend was right. Sold alongside simples such as flour and sugar, arsenic was available to young and old for myriad uses—the production of cheap tallow candles, the creation of bright green dyes, the preservation of bodies by doctors and taxidermists, and the elimination of rats, to name a few. And if someone were to use this easily available substance to rid himself of a pesky family member or hated rival, none would be the wiser.

"So what do we do with this information?" Ham's voice broke in on Quin's thoughts.

"Nothing...at least for now." Quin looked around the table at his friends, grateful for their help. "We keep looking, asking questions, waiting for him to make a mistake...or until we find some proof. And then..." He slammed one fist into his palm, thinking with relish of Herbert Andrews behind bars.

"I look forward to the day!" Archie declared with a grin before wrinkling his brow. "Have you found out any more about Doyle's supposed hanging?"

Quin shook his head. "Nothing. How about you?"

"No," Archie said with a sigh. "I've been scouring old newspapers from the days around the hanging, but I've found nothing more interesting than an Englishman leaving a Dublin inn without paying." He waved a hand dismissively. "Right now, though," he continued, looking grim, "I'm afraid duty calls." He dropped a few coins on the table and pushed back his chair. "Lieutenant Penhale, Lieutenant Wolstenholme."

Ollie rolled his eyes and Ham groaned dramatically before they both reluctantly got up. Quin laughed, standing up too to bid them goodbye.

After they had parted ways, Quin took a stroll through the streets of Dublin, enjoying the rare sunny day despite the distinct nip in the air. Mid-afternoon he turned away from the River Liffey and walked to a tavern in an upscale part of town, where several landowners had wanted to meet to discuss the failed potato harvest and its impact on their estates. Quin had wanted to attend the gathering, although he was unsure what to expect. While he and Alannah had decided immediately to assist the families on their own estate in any way possible, he was fairly certain there would be others who would see no need to do anything. After all, it was far from common for the upper classes to have the sort of relationship he and Alannah had with their servants and tenants—many simply would not even consider going out of their way to help the less fortunate living on their land.

"Hmph," he grumbled as he came up to the tavern door. Looking inside he saw that it was already packed. He made his way through the crowd, squeezing past groups of men in animated conversation, until he found a spot near the back where he had a little more room to breathe.

He heard the chime of the door opening as more people joined the meeting before an elderly gentleman called things to order. Once everyone had finally quietened down and the discussion got under way, it quickly became apparent that feelings were noticeably mixed.

As Quin had expected, several landowners seemed to be more concerned with their own interests than anything else, although there were a few others—to Quin's great relief—who recognised the need for immediate action. Quin nodded approvingly at the short and tubby fellow who had made his way to the front of the crowd to speak.

"The ports need to be opened immediately," the man was saying, "to allow for the import of grain. Further, the export of oats must be prohibited at once."

"A prohibition on export? Have you quite lost your mind?"

Quin turned with a frown in the direction of the speaker, sure he recognised the voice. Scanning the crowd, he was not surprised when his eyes fell on a handsome, middle-aged gentleman with greying hair and a pointy moustache, who stood ramrod straight, with an arrogant set to his shoulders. Quin scowled at Herbert Andrews as the man continued his objections to the proposed relief efforts. "How do you intend to offset the loss in income such foolhardiness would incur?"

"It's scarcely foolhardiness to provide thousands of people with something to eat," Quin interjected angrily, standing up straighter to look over the heads of the other men, a few of whom were nodding in agreement to what he'd said. Andrews' eyes widened when they fell on Quin, a look of distaste blooming on his face. "Making less profit on your grain is hardly the point, is it?" Quin went on, wondering why the blasted man kept cropping up everywhere he went—if not in person, then in unwelcome conversation with his friends. "Besides, all of *us* can surely survive a little loss in income.—Certainly more so than the peasants can survive a lack of food!"

Andrews opened his mouth to say something. Before he could speak, though, Quin said, "It is your Christian duty to help those in need, sir."

"My Christian duty, you say?" Andrews' voice was tinged with incredulity as he stared at Quin, oblivious to the murmurs among the crowd, who had become spectators to the duel of words between the two men. "Is this blight not a visitation from God Himself? Who are *we* to interfere?"

"That, Mr Andrews, is utterly preposterous, and you well know it!" Quin pointed a finger at Andrews, practically spitting with rage as exclamations erupted around the room—some in outrage, others clearly in agreement with the older man.

"Is it?" Andrews retorted, sticking his nose into the air. "Then perhaps, Mr Williams, you might explain to me why the peasants seem largely unbothered by their supposed plight, having done very little to save their precious harvest in the first place."

"And how exactly," Quin bellowed above the rising noise of the crowd, "do you propose the peasants should have saved their harvest?—Did you even see what the blight did to the potato crop?" He very much doubted Andrews had set foot on a single ruined field. "Clearly not," he growled before the man could respond, "for if you had, you would know there was precisely nothing that could have been done by anyone to save the affected potatoes."

"And perhaps it is the very dependence on the potato that is the problem in the first place. It is simply unnatural for so many to be reliant on a single crop, particularly one as lowly as the potato."

If there hadn't been several people standing between him and Andrews, Quin might have leapt at the man's throat. He breathed out heavily through his nose until he felt himself capable of responding to this latest ludicrousness. "They are dependent on the potato because of the limited land at their disposal, the farming conditions that exist in Ireland, the very theft of their land by their English conquerors in the first place..." Quin stopped speaking abruptly, trying to get himself under control. One or two men around him were nodding, while a far greater number was scowling at him in outrage at what he'd said, making him even angrier. "The potato," he continued through gritted teeth, ignoring his audience, "is the only crop that can sustain so many on so little land here."

"As I said, it's unnatural." Andrews waved a hand, ignoring everything Quin had said. "And God's interference in this year's potato crop is the evidence thereof. I say we need to let the situation run its course. We cannot be expected to suffer losses ourselves for the sake of those who cannot help themselves." Quin was about to object when Andrews continued, "I shall of course encourage those with surplus potatoes to share with others who have too few." Andrews looked around, clearly thinking himself magnanimous. "*That* is the Christian thing to do, Mr Williams."

This absurd statement made Quin emit a loud snort, but he said no more. It was clear the man could not be reasoned with. *Money rules the world. And why should I care about those who haven't got any?* That's what he'd said to Alannah and that was exactly the stand he and many others were taking now, not even willing to contemplate the idea of losing some of their own profit to help the less fortunate.

And at that moment, Quin realised with a sinking heart that the government's response was likely to be the same...

He took a deep breath, feeling dejected. Catching sight of Herbert Andrews once more, he glared at him. Then he remembered, though, what he'd learnt about the man earlier that day—how he may well have killed his own father to make himself wealthy. Quin clenched his fists, determining to somehow see Andrews punished for all his wrongdoings.

A small smile grew on his lips at the thought. Andrews was still looking at him, too, and he narrowed his eyes suspiciously, giving Quin a distinct feeling of satisfaction.

With a final smirk, he turned his attention away from Andrews and back to the crowded room, where the discussion was coming to an end. Before long, the men started to disperse, some throwing him disgusted glances as they passed. Quin shrugged it off but nevertheless sighed in relief when the tavern was nearly empty.

Making his own way outside, he was suddenly overcome with a desperate longing for Alannah, wishing fervently that she was waiting for him at the inn. What he wouldn't give to have her stroke his head and kiss his lips, making him forget, for a brief moment, the troubles around him.

Instead, he was returning to a cold room and an empty bed.

"You won't find what you're looking for."

Quin turned in startlement toward the voice coming from behind him. Herbert Andrews was lurking under the eaves of the adjoining building, his top hat on his head and walking stick in hand.

Quin lifted one brow, looking around surreptitiously until he spotted Andrews' guard a short distance away. "Oh?"

"It's too late." Andrews enunciated each word as he looked pointedly at him, making Quin's heart give a forceful thump.

"Leaving more bodies in your wake, I see." He assumed Andrews' statement referred to the missing guard from Omagh gaol, who presumably had by now been eliminated by one of his henchmen, thereby removing all proof of Andrews' involvement in Martin Doyle's escape.

"I'm sure I don't know what you mean," Andrews responded coolly, sticking his nose into the air.

"Is that so?" Quin gave Andrews a long look.

The older man's mouth compressed briefly in a tight line. Before long, though, he sniffed dismissively and turned on his heel. "Good day, Mr Williams," he called without looking at Quin as he walked away. Andrews' burly guard brushed past Quin as he followed his master, glaring at him and showing his crooked teeth in a sneer.

"Hmph." Quin looked after the receding pair with distaste. "You'll get what's coming to you, you bastard," he muttered under his breath as he watched Andrews' jauntily bobbing top hat disappear down the street.

Although it wasn't much, he finally had a bit of dirt on the man. And if he (or Archie) could discover that much, then there was probably more.

And one day, there would be enough to put him away.

18.

I HURRIED THROUGH the entrance hall, throwing my coat over my shoulders as I reached the door. I flung it open, only to stop suddenly at sight of an unexpected visitor, whose hand was lifted in the act of knocking.

The ragged boy who stood in front of me dropped his hand and hunched his shoulders. Big green eyes flashed briefly up at me before returning to the floor as he pulled his scruffy cap from his bedraggled red hair and awkwardly shifted his feet, which were encased in even scruffier looking shoes.

I estimated the boy to be about ten or eleven, although it was hard to tell through the grime on his face and hands. "Can I help you?" I forced myself to smile at him, despite the latest worry that had been brought to my attention just moments before.

"Um..."

"Are you hungry?" I asked gently. Looking at his skinny frame I doubted he'd been accustomed to regular mealtimes even before the poor potato harvest had further cut rations.

He nodded jerkily, not meeting my eyes.

I compressed my lips in sympathy, thinking he must have been quite desperate to have come to us. Most upper-class landowners would be less than thrilled at having such an urchin knock at their door—and he was likely to know that.

"Come in," I said, opening the door wide and inviting him into the house. He hesitated briefly on the threshold before following meekly behind me as I led him to the kitchen.

Mrs O'Sullivan looked up from her work at the kitchen table as we entered, wrinkling her brow at sight of our guest.

"Mrs O'Sullivan, this is..." I cocked my head at the boy.

"Benjamin," he murmured, glancing sideways at the cook.

"This is Benjamin. Please be kind enough to give him something to eat." Looking him up and down I added, "And see if we don't have some better clothes for him. Something that Finnian or Rupert have outgrown, perhaps?"

Just then, the door opened and Finnian himself entered the kitchen, having no doubt followed his nose to the enticing smells emanating from the hearth. Seeing the three of us he stopped, eying Benjamin with curiosity.

"Finnian, lad," Mrs O'Sullivan addressed the gangly youth, "show our guest here where he can have a wash." Turning toward Benjamin she smiled. "I've got a nice hunk o' bacon on the boil with some cabbage. That'll need a little while longer but I've a boxty ye can nibble on whilst ye wait."

Benjamin licked his lips, craning his neck toward the covered dishes on the tabletop.

"You have to wash first," Finnian reminded the boy self-importantly, beckoning him to follow.

Mrs O'Sullivan caught my eye and grinned. "You too, Finnian," she called after the retreating boys, making Finnian hunch his shoulders. "And don't forget to wash behind yer ears!"

I gave a brief laugh, but soon sobered up as I remembered where I'd been heading before Benjamin had arrived unexpectedly on our doorstep.

"I'll be at the McGuire's cottage," I said to Mrs O'Sullivan as she turned her attention back to her cooking.

She lifted an enquiring brow. "Is aught amiss?"

"I'm afraid so. Conor came up to the house.—He said the potatoes they'd stored are also spoiling."

"But they had hardly any to start with!" Mrs O'Sullivan's eyes were wide with shock. "What about the others? Are they all lost?"

"I don't know but I must go and find out." I took a deep breath before straightening up and turning toward the door. "Mr Dunne has gone to Ballygawley, and I promised Conor I would come."

"*Go ndéana Dia trócaire orainn.*"

I paused at Mrs O'Sullivan's heart-felt plea behind me, dreading what I might find.

God have mercy on us, indeed!

The poor harvest had already been a hard blow for the tenants, especially for families like the McGuires, who had lost a substantial portion of their crop. Was the little they'd been able to salvage doomed as well?

I swallowed heavily as I quickly made my way to the stable, wishing Quin were here beside me. While Mr Dunne was more than capable and Mrs O'Sullivan had the running of the household well under control, I dearly missed Quin's solid presence and the comfort of his arms around me—especially in times like these.

I pushed the thought aside as I reached John, who was waiting for me with Milly.

"I'm sorry to have kept you waiting," I said. Conor had been bristling with impatience to be underway and I had sent him ahead to tell the groom I would be needing my horse. Now that I was here, though, Conor was nowhere to be seen.

"He's already left," John told me before I could ask. "He didn't want to wait..."

"He's going all the way back on foot?"

John shrugged at my bafflement and handed me the reins.

"I suppose I'll catch him up," I muttered to myself, ignoring the small but distinct frown blooming on John's face as I mounted my horse.

Having had a rather unfortunate incident with my side saddle a few years earlier, I had taken to riding astride. While my husband tended to find this amusing, some men—and John was clearly one of these—found it deeply offensive. I sniffed in dismissal, having greater worries than what people might think about me and the sight of my scandalously exposed, bestockinged calves. Quin had asked me to at least restrict my unorthodox riding practices to my travels around the estate, to which I had grudgingly agreed, since we tended to use alternative modes of transport anyway when going anywhere further afield.

Once past the outbuildings, I led Milly along the path to the tenants' cottages at the other end of the estate. As I had suspected I soon caught up with Conor, who was loping along at a steady jog. I suggested he ride double with me, but he vehemently refused, declaring that a lady never ought to share her horse. Glancing at my legs with wide eyes he opened his mouth once more but quickly snapped it shut, evidently thinking better of whatever else he'd been about to say.

I shrugged. I didn't have time to argue with him or to accompany him at a walk—he'd have to make his own way back. Waving him goodbye I continued along the path, my stomach knotted in anxiety at what awaited me.

It was as bad as I had feared.

"They're all ruined."

Mrs McGuire's softly spoken Gaelic made me tear my eyes away from the storage pit and look at the older woman. She was staring into the pit with dry eyes, seeming unable to believe what she was seeing. The few unspoiled potatoes the McGuires had managed to salvage from their field had deteriorated into what was mostly black sludge.

"We stored them just like always, made sure to do it carefully because we had so few. And now…" She waved an arm feebly across the putrid tubers.

I took her hand and squeezed it firmly. "You shall have more of the estate's oats and wheat. This doesn't change a thing!" I looked into her eyes, seeing the lines that were etched deep into her skin, a sign of the hard life she had lived.

She nodded mechanically. "Thank you, mistress."

As she walked slowly back to her cottage, Conor ran panting up to her, his cheeks red with the day's exertions. She patted his head, still seeming in a daze, her shoulders drooping.

I looked after mother and son as they disappeared into their cottage, clenching my jaws. Finally, I mounted Milly and began to ride slowly around the neighbouring homesteads. I enquired after the tenants' welfare and urged them to inspect their stored potatoes for damage. It quickly became clear that the blight had not been stopped with the harvest—most families whose potato vines had been affected found that the stored potatoes were continuing to rot.

With a heavy heart, I instructed the tenants to get rid of every last potato that looked in any way damaged and to store the others carefully.

After that, all we could do was hope.

19.

I PULLED ON Milly's reins, and she whickered, tossing her head. I laughed and stroked the horse's sturdy neck.

"Today we're just riding for fun," I told her, making her ears twitch. She turned alongside the river willingly enough, strong muscles bunching beneath my thighs as she adjusted her gait to the change in terrain.

It was a beautiful sunny day, though cold, and I relished in the opportunity to take Milly for a ride—one that had no purpose other than the simple joy of it. Although I was happy to provide a sympathetic ear and a comforting hand to those in need, I had to get away from it all for just a while, to escape the clutching grasp of fear and uncertainty that had been my constant companion for weeks on end.

Milly's hooves sank into the soft earth as she picked her way along the riverbank. It had snowed a little the day before and the air was crisp and fresh. A few white clumps still lay scattered here and there, sparkling in the sunlight. There was a stark beauty to the dreary landscape, and I drank it in in large gulps.

We passed a shallow depression filled with heather, a gentle splash of pale colour amidst the surrounding browns and greys. I spotted movement on the far side and smiled at the sight of a large hare standing on its hind legs, watching us. Its white underbelly flashed briefly before it dropped back down onto all fours and sped away, its movements marked by the bobbing of its snowy tail through the faded grass.

I breathed in deeply, feeling content. After a while I closed my eyes to the swaying motion of the horse, letting Milly lead the way. We ambled along peacefully until clouds started billowing in the distance, and I decided to head back. With the sun obscured, I was grateful for my gloves and my thick cloak, pulling up the hood to cover my ears. The wind picked up and I urged Milly onwards, feeling invigorated as we raced home beneath the darkening clouds.

We had ridden further than I'd thought and by the time we arrived back at the stable, the brief storm had passed, leaving nothing but a few puddles in its wake. I shook my head, making droplets spray across Milly's back. Although we'd managed to avoid the worst of the storm, we hadn't gotten away entirely unscathed.

As I dismounted, John appeared, coming over to remove Milly's saddle.

He started leading the horse away, but I put out my hand to stop him. "I'll take it from here, thank you, John."

He shrugged and handed me the reins. "Old Bryan'll likely need me in the barn then."

With John and Bryan busy elsewhere the stable was empty of human occupants, and I paused a moment before going any further, avoiding looking at the bales of hay in the corner. It was there that Martin Doyle had accosted me a few years earlier. At times, the memory of the encounter was so vivid I could barely step foot inside the building. Now, though, with the sunlight breaking through the clouds once more, the stable felt welcoming, nothing like that dark and gloomy day.

I secured Milly with a slipknot and fetched the grooming implements, looking forward to the soothing motions of cleaning and brushing the horse. She whickered softly when I started drying her thick winter coat, resulting in a chorus of responses from the stable's other inhabitants. I laughed, inhaling the animals' heady scent as dust motes swirled in the shafts of sunlight coming through the narrow window slits below the roof.

I removed flecks of mud and bits of shrubbery clinging to Milly's coat, before brushing it to a gleaming shine with long, sweeping strokes, the swishing of the brush as much a comfort to me as to the horse. Turning my attention to her mane and tail, I was so engrossed that I barely heard the clopping of hooves outside, until it finally dawned on me that the sound likely meant we had a visitor.

Straightening up, I squinted against the light of the setting sun coming in through the open double door, which cast horse and rider into shadows.

But I would know him anywhere.

"Quin." I dropped the brush in my hand, flew down the length of the stable and flung myself into his arms.

"Alannah."

He caught me easily, lifting my feet off the ground and crushing me to him. We held each other without speaking as the world around us disappeared. After a while, he pressed his mouth hard against my cheek and cradled my head with one hand, his other arm still tight around my waist. I was suddenly overcome with emotions and gave a strangled sob as my throat constricted, trying to hold back the tears that had sprung to my eyes.

"It's alright," he whispered, "I'm home now."

I tightened my arms around him, and we clung to each other for what seemed like a long time—but wasn't nearly long enough. When at last he put me down, he cupped my head in both hands, smiling at me as he wiped away my tears with his thumbs. He tilted up my chin and kissed me on the mouth, his lips soft and welcoming, making me close my eyes, hardly able to believe he was there in front of me.

The strength of his kiss increased, and I pressed myself closer to him, a promise to each of us of more to come.

An exclamation of surprise at the stable door made us reluctantly break apart. Quin's arm stayed around my waist, though, as we turned toward John and Bryan, who were standing at the threshold carrying buckets of bran mash for the horses' supper.

"Mr Williams."

"Sir."

Both grooms smiled widely, inclining their heads, and Quin greeted them happily.

After a brief exchange of words, the two men turned their attention back to the horses. I asked Bryan to finish grooming Milly, while John placed his buckets on the floor and went to fetch Gambit. With his owner otherwise occupied, the horse had wandered into the corner and was nibbling contentedly on bits of hay.

As the grooms went about their business, I looked back up at Quin. He held my eyes, his mouth lifting at the corners as he offered me his arm. I took it gladly, my heart swelling with joy at having him beside me once more.

"IT'S GOOD TO be home!"

Quin sighed with satisfaction as he sank into the padded armchair in the drawing room. He'd been in Dublin for almost two months, a time filled with worry and doubt—he was more than happy to be surrounded by Glaslearg's comforting familiarity once more.

"It's good to have you back," Alannah said, reaching out a hand toward him. He clasped it firmly, running his thumb over her smooth skin. This was the longest Quin had been separated from Alannah since their wedding, and he was very much looking forward to greeting her properly in the privacy of their room a little later. A smile grew on his lips at the thought, making a soft blush break out on her cheeks.

"It is sir."

Margaret's shy voice reached Quin from a distance, and he made an effort to pull his attention away from his wife and smile at the maid. Feeling jovial after his homecoming, Quin had invited Margaret and John to join them in the drawing room after supper alongside Mr Dunne.

Little Quinnie squawked in Margaret's arms, making John reach for him. The groom's eyes filled with adoration as he picked up the small bundle, rocking him gently. Quinnie didn't seem interested in sleep, though, instead looking around the drawing room with big eyes. Quin had been amazed to see how much the baby had changed in the weeks he'd been away. Although he was still tiny, he was sturdy and alert, eagerly taking in his surroundings.

Quin smiled at the little boy, before catching Margaret's eye.

"Would you like to hold him, sir?"

"Hold him? *Me*?" Quin looked down at his sizeable hands, slightly terrified of holding something so fragile.

Margaret laughed but soon had Quinnie placed in Quin's arms, John looking on watchfully but with a smile on his homely face. Quin sat stiffly, unsure what to do. His namesake wasn't bothered by his reluctance, though, seeming entirely comfortable with Quin, babbling happily to himself and pumping tiny fists into the air. Quin carefully supported the baby with one hand, holding the other above him and wriggling his fingers. Quinnie grasped his index finger, making Quin's eyes widen, surprised at the strength of the tiny digits.

"You're going to grow big and strong, aren't you?" he asked, utterly charmed by the tiny human he was holding.

"It suits you, sir."

Quin smiled at Mr Dunne, whose cheeks were turning slightly pink as he glanced at Alannah. She was wearing a similarly doting expression as the others, although hers was tinged with longing. Quin's gaze met hers and they looked at each other for a long moment before he turned his attention back to the baby. Quinnie had let go of his finger and was reaching his hands toward his face. Quin leaned in closer and pudgy fingers lightly slapped his cheeks. A sudden yank on his nose made him laugh, eliciting a toothless smile and gurgle of delight in response. Soon, though, Quinnie started crinkling up his nose and rubbing small fists across his eyes.

"He'll be wanting his bed," Mrs O'Sullivan said, cooing at the baby before depositing a plate of biscuits on the table.

"Aye." Margaret reached for her son and Quin reluctantly gave him back, feeling something of a loss as the small weight was lifted off his arm.

"Here, sir." Rupert had materialised beside him, looking very self-important as he held out a tumbler of whiskey to Quin.

"Thank you, Rupert." He took the glass and lifted it in farewell to Margaret and John. As they left, Rupert poured whiskey for Alannah and Mr Dunne, the latter quirking an eyebrow at the proffered drink before accepting it. Although he rarely drank, the overseer did seem to be starting to enjoy the taste of the fiery liquid. Quin wondered whether he was a bad influence on the man, watching him take a modest sip, before urging Rupert to hand a glass to Mrs O'Sullivan as well.

Quite in contrast to Mr Dunne, the cook tossed back her whiskey as though it were water, making Rupert look at her with round eyes. He was soon distracted, though, by the appearance of a young boy, who was being ushered into the drawing room by the gangly form of Finnian, who in turn was studiously ignoring Rupert.

"Come, come, Benjamin." Mrs O'Sullivan put down her glass and waved a meaty arm toward the doorway, where the boy was hovering uncertainly. "I asked Finnian to bring him to ye, sir," she said to Quin before turning back toward the door. "Do come in, he won't bite." She grinned, revealing one or two missing teeth, which did nothing to erase the sceptical look adorning the boy's face. He allowed himself to be coaxed forward until he was standing in front of Quin's chair.

Quin got up and smiled at the skinny child. "Hello Benjamin," he said softly, trying to make himself as little intimidating as possible. "I hope you've been enjoying your time at Glaslearg?" He quirked an eyebrow and the boy nodded shyly, making Quin lean in a little closer. "Would you like to stay with us?"

The boy's eyes went wide at Quin's question, and he nodded again, this time eagerly. Alannah had written to Quin of Benjamin's arrival at the estate. A few discreet enquiries had led her to believe he likely had no home to return to and so Quin had quickly agreed to take the boy into the household, not willing to even contemplate sending him out to starve.

"Good," he said with a smile. "Then you shall be our new hall boy. And Finnian shall be promoted to...footman." He raised his brows at the two youngsters, trying not to blink. Although the roles sounded very formal, Glaslearg's staff had thus far been a rather informal arrangement, with the few people who were employed on the estate generally sharing duties as necessary.

Still, a little flattery never hurt.

Benjamin and Finnian evidently found their proposed new roles to their liking, both of them standing up straighter and puffing out skinny chests.

"Thank you, sir," Finnian said gravely, attempting a bow, while Benjamin only grinned from ear to ear.

"Now be off wi' ye." Mrs O'Sullivan made a shooing gesture with her hands. "There's biscuits waitin' in the kitchen."

Needing no further encouragement, the boys scuttled back into the hall, their shoes clattering on the floor as they went.

"Finish yer duties and ye can have some too," the cook informed Rupert, who was standing in the middle of the room, looking like he was deep in thought.

"Eh?" Coming out of his trance and seeing the stern look blooming on Mrs O'Sullivan's face, Rupert cleared his throat and turned toward Quin. "I'll unpack your things and prepare your room for bed, sir." His eyes darted briefly in Alannah's direction and his cheeks turned crimson as he dashed toward the door.

Quin chuckled softly, realising what his young valet must have been thinking about—the very thing he'd been contemplating himself just a short while ago, an activity that tended to be of immense interest to most young men.

"I'd best go see they don't eat tomorrow's breakfast as well."

Mrs O'Sullivan's voice interrupted Quin's wandering thoughts. He inclined his head to her as she stormed off to defend her territory, leaving Quin and Alannah alone with Mr Dunne. The overseer, too, looked to be deep in thought, staring into his whiskey as he swirled the amber liquid slowly around the glass, a melancholy expression on his face.

"Are you alright, Mr Dunne?"

The man's eyes snapped open at Quin's question. "Yes…I suppose…yes."

"You needn't worry about the fate of Glaslearg's tenants," Quin said. "We have enough food to see everyone fed until the next harvest. And I for one intend to use a good portion of our stores for just this purpose, even though the government has refused to stop exports."

Dunne nodded gravely. "It does ease my mind to know that, sir, although I fail to understand the government's lack of interest."

Quin sighed, having thought of little else over the last few weeks. "There are many who are equally shocked by parliament's handling of the crisis, while others have no such concerns." He clenched his jaws briefly, remembering the numerous meetings he'd attended and the opinions he'd heard expressed—some focused solely on seeking help for the poor, while others were more concerned with financial affairs. "Those with money are the ones in power…which frequently proves to be rather unfortunate for the poor. But at least some attempts are being made to increase the import of foreign grains to help feed the hungry."

"And what will the people have to pay for the imported grains?" Alannah asked with a puff of annoyance. "Already, the cost of potatoes has more than doubled and the price of grains has also shot up. Where are the poor to find the money to buy food?"

"Public works, I suppose," Quin responded, feeling suddenly dejected.

"Hmph." Alannah looked unconvinced. "And what about finding out what caused this blight in the first place? Has anyone managed that?"

"Many have tried," Quin began tentatively, earning himself a dark blue look, which he ignored. "From what I heard in Dublin, there are some differing theories as to the cause, as well as potential remedies."

"Remedies?"

"To stop the blight from consuming any more of the stored potatoes."

Alannah compressed her lips. "I'd as soon know that as well. The tenants live in daily fear of uncovering further spoilage."

"Unfortunately, as yet, there seems to be little consensus as to the best way of achieving that.—First came the insistence that above all else, stored potatoes must be kept dry, with the proposed pit ventilation scheme distributed via hundreds of pamphlets, followed but a week later by the suggestion that immersing affected potatoes in bogwater would halt the progress of the disease." Quin gave a humourless laugh. "The Freeman's Journal concluded that the commissioners have shown only that they know nothing whatsoever about either the cause of the potato blight, or a remedy therefore."

"That seems an apt conclusion," Alannah said with a frown.

Quin shrugged and glanced toward Mr Dunne, who had fallen silent and was looking rather glum. Alannah gave Quin a concerned look.

"Mr Dunne," she addressed the overseer gently, "are you sure you're alright?"

Dunne looked up in some startlement, his eyes flickering from Alannah to Quin and back again. "I...I am worried for someone," he admitted in a small voice.

"Is there anything we can do to help?" Alannah asked.

Dunne shook his head slowly. "I don't think so."

"Are you sure?" Alannah leaned toward him. "You needn't be afraid to ask."

Dunne sighed heavily. "I...I don't know where she is."

"Who is she?" Quin asked softly.

The overseer was silent for a long moment before speaking again. "Mr Thompson's daughter," he said at last, making Quin look at Alannah in surprise. Neither of them said anything, though, waiting for Dunne to continue. He was looking down into his lap, seeming to be weighing his words. "I had...quickly become acquainted with my former employer's character," he began hesitantly, still not looking at either of them. "I knew enough about Mr Thompson to realise it could never be, but"—he shrugged—"we fell in love."

"What happened?" Alannah's voice was filled with sympathy.

"We planned to marry.—She thought she could persuade her father it was a good match. I had a good position, with decent pay. She thought that would be enough for him, that her happiness would make him happy." Dunne took a sip of his whiskey. "She was wrong."

"What did he do?"

The overseer looked up at Quin's question, his eyes slightly bloodshot. "He forbade her from seeing me. I tried to talk to him but...well, I was dismissed before I could even cross the threshold. And then"—he clenched his jaws in remembrance—"then he told me he was sending her away."

"Sending her away?" Alannah furrowed her brows.

Dunne nodded slowly. "I haven't seen her since."

"Is that why you...?" Quin broke off the question he was about to ask, thinking it was perhaps a little indelicate.

"Is that why I hit the man?" Dunne gave a humourless laugh. "When he told me I'd never see his daughter again I thought I'd drown my sorrows. But after I'd consumed the better part of a whiskey bottle, I convinced myself he could still be persuaded that I would make a decent son-in-law after all.—So I set off to find him." He smirked before continuing. "As soon as he saw me, he yelled at me that it was too late, that she was already gone. And I...well..." He cleared his throat. "Vast quantities of liquor do not lead one to making good choices."

Quin watched the overseer slowly clench and unclench his fists. "I was pulled away as soon as the first blow landed. Of course, that's not how the story will be remembered..." He waved his arm dismissively.

From the beginning, Dunne had insisted he'd only dealt his former employer a single blow and that he had no idea how the man had acquired the multiple contusions that had seen the overseer arrested for drunken assault. Quin was about to ask if he was sure he didn't know anything else about that when Alannah forestalled him with her own question.

"Did you try to find her?"

Dunne gave a deep sigh. "I did. For several months." He glanced at Quin, who nodded, understanding at last what had kept the man from coming to

Glaslearg immediately after his release from gaol. "I found no trace of her. She could be anywhere.—I may never find out what happened to her. And now, with the blight..."

"I'm so sorry, Mr Dunne," Alannah said, reaching out a hand and placing it on his arm.

He patted her hand absently. "Ah well, such is life." He shook his head, no doubt wishing to rid himself of his memories. "At least I have found some happiness here." He gave a shy smile as he got up from his chair, before bidding Quin and Alannah good night and heading to the door.

The two of them were silent for a while after Dunne had left.

"Well, now we know the whole story," Quin said finally, rubbing a hand over his face. He glanced at the longcase clock, surprised to see it wasn't as late as he'd thought. But after the long ride back from Dublin, he was ready for bed.

"Poor man."

Quin nodded but got up and pulled Alannah into his arms. "At least we have each other," he murmured into her hair.

"Yes." She ran her hands up and down his back. "I don't know what I'd do without you." She pulled his head toward hers, kissing him urgently and pressing herself to him.

"I feel the same way," he said a little breathlessly a short while later. Running his hands slowly along the swell of her hips, he cocked an enquiring brow. "Might I have the pleasure of your company upstairs, Mrs Williams?"

Alannah's mouth turned up at the corners. "You may, Mr Williams," she breathed into his ear, making a pleasant shudder run down his spine. He lifted her into his arms and when their eyes met, he could see the memory of their wedding night flash across her face. He grinned, holding her tighter as he carried her to the stairs, determining to make this as memorable a night together as their first.

"DO YOU REMEMBER the day we wed?"

"Of course I do." I stroked Quin's cheek, the bristles of his growing beard rasping pleasantly under my fingers. "How could I forget?"

"You looked so beautiful in your gown." A slow grin spread across his face. "And even better without it."

I laughed, pulling him closer. His soft lips touched mine and I closed my eyes, savouring the memory of our wedding night as much as the present moment, relishing in having him beside me once more.

"I had never seen a naked man before that night," I murmured against his mouth.

"I trust I didn't disappoint you," he said, pushing himself up onto his hands so he was hovering over me. He raised one brow and flexed his torso for my appraisal, making me smile.

"Not at all. I thought you were beautiful.—I still do." I ran my hands slowly up his arms, tracing the hard muscles with my fingertips. His broad back blocked out much of the flickering candlelight, making me feel enveloped by his strength, safe and nurtured with his body covering mine—a feeling I had missed while he was away. I slid my palms over his shoulders and down his chest, pausing briefly as I encountered the rough patch of scar tissue on his right side, feeling my own chest tighten, as always, at the thought of its origins—shot in China while fighting with the British Army, Quin had been lucky to escape with his life.

I pushed the thought aside and held his eyes as I placed my arms around his back. "And I love you now as I loved you then," I said softly, running my hands slowly down to the swell of his buttocks. "Or perhaps more."

"And I love you," he said, one large hand stroking my hair, "more than I ever thought possible." He lowered himself gently onto my chest, making me tremble. I pressed him to me as a sudden, desperate longing overcame me.

The intrusion was both startlingly new and intimately familiar, making us both gasp.

"I missed you so," Quin whispered, his voice thick with emotion as we rocked together gently, his hand cupping my face.

"And I missed you." I felt my throat tighten, as the worry and uncertainty of the last few weeks flooded my mind, unbidden. I wrapped my arms around him, and he kissed me roughly, his own fears adding to my yearning as we sought to lose ourselves in each other's arms—so that each could make the other whole once more.

20.

WITH QUIN FINALLY back at home, I felt a lightening of my spirits—for whatever else was still in store for us, at least we'd be able to face it together.

"Benjamin," Mrs O'Sullivan's stern voice rang out as I entered the kitchen a few days after his return, "use yer spoon!"

I had come in search of a cup of afternoon tea—none of the servants seeming to be about—only to interrupt the cook's continued efforts to civilise the newest member of our household. Benjamin had revealed very little about himself in the time he'd spent with us, but it was quite clear he had not been a frequent visitor of fine dining establishments in the past.

Mrs O'Sullivan cuffed the boy lightly on the back of the head. "Ye don't eat a crumble wi' your fingers!"

"Yes, mum," came the muted reply. Benjamin dutifully picked up the spoon next to his bowl and used it to shovel the crumble into his mouth.

"That smells wonderful," I said, sniffing the air appreciatively. "Apple?"

"Aye." Mrs O'Sullivan deftly placed a generous portion into a second bowl and handed it to me. "Eat it while it's warm."

Finding no reasonable objection to these instructions I sat down opposite Benjamin, who eyed me a little suspiciously. I smiled at him, and he smiled back through a mouthful of crumble.

"This is delicious!" I said a moment later, making Mrs O'Sullivan beam with pride. "Don't you think so, Benjamin?" I cocked my head toward the boy.

He nodded shily. "It is," he assured me, before using the tip of his index finger to extract every last crumb from his bowl.

He suddenly hunched his shoulders and looked at Mrs O'Sullivan with big eyes, no doubt remembering her earlier instructions regarding the use of cutlery. Fortunately for him, the cook had her back turned toward us as she tended something by the fireplace. He looked nervously back at me, but I winked at him. His responding grin grew ever wider when I cleaned my own bowl in precisely the same fashion. I placed a finger across my lips, and he nodded eagerly, making me smile.

Sipping my tea in the drawing room a little later, I laughed once more at Benjamin's antics, finding I was growing quite fond of the child. Unfortunately, though, that thought inevitably led me to contemplate whether Quin's return home may yet come to signify an impending pregnancy and a child of my own.

Despite my best efforts I soon descended into a gloomy spiral, convinced no such thing would ever occur and that I was doomed to die childless—my future transmuted into a series of barren months interspersed with yet more early disappointments.

I sighed. Why was it that some women could have multiple babies while others struggled to bear even one?

Unable to come up with an answer to the question I was grateful to be distracted by Quin's appearance at the door. He was followed into the room by Rupert, who was slinking along looking rather glum himself.

"Will you be needing anything else, sir?" the valet asked.

"No, thank you, Rupert."

Rupert bowed his head and turned toward the door, his shoulders slumping as he left the room.

I looked after him in some surprise. "Is he alright?" I asked, turning toward Quin as he sat down next to me.

"Actually, I suspect he's rather miserable."

"And that doesn't worry you?" I frowned at his apparent disinterest, but he chuckled.

"I believe young Rupert is in love."

"Oh." I felt an answering smile growing on my own face. "Who is she?"

"One of the tenants' daughters," Quin said, a twinkle in his eyes.

"Did he tell you about her?"

Quin shook his head. "Oh no, he hasn't said a word.—But we happened to come across her when we rode out to the tenants' cottages this morning."

"I see." A thought suddenly occurred to me. "Is that why he's been accompanying you on your rounds of the estate since you've been back from Dublin?"

"I expect so." Quin grinned. "He tried to convince me he was suddenly interested in the estate's management, but having seen him mooning over Miss O'Hagan, I strongly suspect he has ulterior motives."

"Well," I said drily, "let us hope she returns his affections—and his alone."

Quin laughed. "I'm sure Rupert will do his utmost to keep all other young men away from the girl, particularly his arch-rival, Finnian. The two of them do seem to have the same taste when it comes to the fairer sex.—And we wouldn't want them to have another fistfight, much less kill each other in a duel."

I raised one brow. "Surely it wouldn't come to that.—Would it?"

"You never know. Some things are worth fighting for."

I gave an unladylike snort. "If a woman can't make up her own mind about who she's in love with, I doubt any man would do it for her by fighting a mindless duel."

"Perhaps it depends on the man," Quin suggested before breaking into a wide grin. "Or on the weapon he wields? I've always preferred a sword myself."

"Have you, then?"

"Indeed. Would you like me to show you mine? It's quite impressive, I assure you." He wriggled his eyebrows suggestively.

I patted his hand. "A little later perhaps."

His face drooped, and he gave an exaggerated sigh. "As you wish." Seeing my own face falter, he looked at me in some concern. "Are you alright?"

I nodded. "I've just been thinking…about…" I trailed off, waving a hand toward my abdomen.

He sat forward in his chair so he could grasp my hands. "We'll have a child of our own one day, I know it." He sounded so certain that I couldn't help but break into a lopsided smile.

"What makes you so sure?"

"Because I always get what I want," he declared, sticking his nose into the air.

"Is that so?"

"Of course. I convinced you to marry me, didn't I?—Although I dare say you weren't entirely averse to the suggestion," he added, cocking his head.

"No, I wasn't," I assured him.

"Good." He pulled me suddenly from my chair and settled me on his lap, patting me familiarly on my rump. "As for the other...I'm afraid there's nothing for it but to keep practising.—Every day if we must!"

I laughed. "I suppose we do have to make up for lost time," I said, leaning my forehead against his.

He smiled as his eyes flickered between mine, large and green—and determined. He searched for my hand with his, giving it a gentle squeeze. "You just have to have faith."

QUIN QUICKLY FELL back into his old routines at Glaslearg, which absorbed him as if he'd never been away. Reports and orders filled much of his time, as did the numerous other practicalities of running a large estate. And while Mr Dunne had capably taken the reins in his absence, Quin wanted to be involved, to know first-hand how Glaslearg and its people were faring.

He took joy in visiting his tenants and in seeing his staff happy, smiling as young Benjamin grew into his role in the household and at hearing of his penchant for all things sweet. He chuckled at Rupert and Finnian, who continued to do their best to ignore each other when they crossed paths in the hallway, one scowling and the other sticking his nose into the air, seeming to have come to an agreement on who would wear which expression which day.

Most of all, though, Quin delighted at seeing Alannah every day, even when it was only in passing as they rushed off on different errands; a brief touch of her hand here, a tender look there, the simple pleasure of hearing her voice and knowing she was there—small things he had missed over the past two months.

Like he did himself, Alannah regularly checked on the tenants' welfare, although she particularly made a point of spending time with the women. She also continued to teach the children twice a week, usually coming home beaming and filled with pride at her students' progress, sure they were well on their way to making a better life for themselves.

And perhaps they were—though their day-to-day existence hadn't changed much.

For despite the poor potato harvest, life on the estate continued much as before. Glaslearg's tenants fared better than many, it was true, but even those in Ireland who were less fortunate somehow made do, getting through the lean months as had been done countless times before—with the help of local relief efforts and the goodwill of others.

As the weeks went by, though, and winter slowly began to loosen its grip on the land, Quin started feeling a change, a soft ripple that would scuttle over his skin, giving him pause momentarily as he went about his day. It was subtle at first, as the nights started getting shorter and the days started getting warmer. But by the time tiny buds of greenery dotted the dreary landscape, he felt it distinctly. Along with the usual anticipation that came with the first signs of spring, a sense of anxiety was snaking its way across Glaslearg's fields.

The situation in Ireland remained dire and many thousands of people were teetering on the brink of disaster. Everything depended on the harvest gleaned from this year's spring planting.

Quin breathed in deeply, suddenly overcome with unease.

He tried to remind himself to take one day at a time. Besides, there was no reason to think the potato crop would fail again. In fact, a number of his own tenants and much of the Irish peasantry as a whole seemed not to share his concerns—the occasional bad harvest was normal, after all, even if it was substantial.

Struggling to shake off his apprehensions even so, he tried to distract himself by turning to his waiting mail. He frowned, though, when he picked up the thin correspondence bearing his father's seal.

"Hmph," he grumbled after a moment. "If this is your idea of a joke, you old codger, I'm going to…"

"You're going to what?"

"Oh…ah." Quin looked up at Alannah, who was sitting across from him at the desk, having momentarily forgotten she was there in the study with him. "I just…" He shrugged one shoulder and waved the sheet of paper he was holding. "Take a look at this!" He slapped his father's note—which the baron, no doubt, would dignify with the term *letter*—onto the tabletop in front of her and glared at it. "Well?" he demanded, having given Alannah the thirty seconds needed to read it.

"Do you think he's alright?" Alannah's eyes were creased with concern.

"Of course he's alright!" Quin responded without hesitation. "He's only trying to make me feel guilty for having *left him*, as he so eloquently put it in his last dozen so-called letters. Never mind that he was only too happy to see the back of me when it was the British Army I was leaving with!"

"But"—Alannah gestured feebly at the sheet of paper—"surely..."

Quin snatched up the single page once more. "*Quinton*," he started reading, before lowering the page and scowling at it. "You'd think he might have found a more affectionate term of address for his only son by now," he growled, before continuing his recital. "*Quinton, if my being in good health is not sufficient enticement for you to venture a return to England, perhaps the alternative will provide you with the necessary incentive. A little time remains to you yet. Yours. Wilfred Williams.*"

Quin snorted as he dropped the piece of paper. "Signed Wilfred Williams," he muttered irritably, "as if I were some vague acquaintance rather than his flesh and blood and only living heir!"

"Is that so unusual for your father?" Alannah asked, looking at him cautiously.

"Well...no," Quin admitted. "I don't recall him ever being any friendlier...including in his memorable missive informing me of my mother's death."

"Then it's the rest of the content we should concern ourselves with," Alannah said quickly, evidently trying to prevent Quin from fixating on that sorely lacking one-line correspondence.

"I still say it's a cry for attention, nothing more." Quin flipped his wrist in dismissal.

"And if it isn't? If he really is ill?"

"Hmph." Quin shrugged his shoulders noncommittally.

"And even if it is just a cry for attention," Alannah continued, clearly sensing him weaken, "is that so bad?" Quin opened his mouth to respond but before he could say anything Alannah had forged ahead. "Surely a father is entitled to miss his son...and to want to see him?"

"A father, yes," Quin agreed, "*mine*, though…"

Alannah laughed and leaned toward him over the desk, her eyes searching his.

"He is getting on in age, isn't he?"

"Well…yes, I suppose he is," Quin conceded grudgingly, finding it difficult to believe his father could ever be anything except tough as nails, both physically and in his conduct toward anyone he had ever met. "I suppose he is," Quin repeated more softly before sighing heavily. "And I suppose…once the spring planting has been completed…I suppose we could arrange a visit to London.—You'll be coming with me, of course?" he added hastily, slightly horrified at the thought of having to face his father on his own.

"Of course." Alannah smiled as Quin laughed at his own idiocy. "I very much look forward to meeting him!"

"I wouldn't if I were you," he responded drily. "He really is every bit as miserable as his letters suggest." He took a deep breath, which resulted in the delectable smell of their dinner drifting up his nose. He shook himself and rose from his seat. "Shall we?" He cocked his head toward his wife, who took his arm. "I suppose one good thing that may come from such a trip is that he might at last learn your name," he said mischievously as he led Alannah into the entry hall.

Her cheeks turned pink, and she pursed her lips, clearly remembering his father's vague references to his supposed wife—if he deigned to mention her at all—in his rage at Quin having married an Irishwoman without his father's consent.

"Well," she said as she lifted her head and squared her shoulders, "I don't really care about any of that, do I?" Her piercing blue eyes glared defiantly up at Quin.

"Of course, you don't," Quin responded gravely. "Nor should you!" He squeezed her hand and grinned. "Now come along, nameless woman who lives in this house…our dinner awaits."

THE BUSY WEEKS of spring that followed the baron's galling invitation kept Quin from obsessing about the upcoming reunion with his father.

Working long hours also kept him from worrying about the year's potato harvest—which was still some months away in any case. They had enough food at Glaslearg to see themselves and their tenants through the summer months, and Quin dedicated even more fields to the planting of grains than the year before. The tenants, of course, had little choice but to plant mostly potatoes, as they did every year, the normally prolific crop being well suited to feeding whole families occupying tiny plots of land.

Quin straightened up, his spine giving a series of small pops. "That's the last row," he said, wiping his brow. He had ridden to the tenants' land to see how they were faring with the planting, only to find himself rolling up his sleeves to help. Having watched the elderly Mr Fagan bent double as he laboriously dug the ridges into which the sprouting tubers were placed by his equally elderly wife, Quin had decided to intervene. Ignoring Mr Fagan's objections, he'd snatched the older man's spade and gotten to work. After a while, he'd been joined by a few strong young men who'd completed the planting on their own neighbouring fields, and between them, they'd soon had the Fagan's small plot arranged in the neat rows that made up the potatoes' lazy beds.

"They're all done, sir."

Quin turned toward the voice, which belonged to the stocky Mr Connell. Looking around, Quin saw the tired but pleased faces of numerous tenants who were milling about, wiping dirt-smeared hands on rags and chatting among themselves. Quin nodded in contentment, filled with hope. He felt a hand on his arm and looked down at the small figure of Mrs Fagan, who had appeared beside him holding a cup of buttermilk, which she urged on him with a wrinkly smile. He accepted with thanks, enjoying the fresh, creamy taste as the sun started dipping below the horizon.

A few torches were lit in the twilight, but he lifted his brows in surprise when Mr Fagan started hobbling along with a blazing brand in his hand, tracing the edge of his field as he went. Quin turned curiously toward Mr Connell, who was still standing beside him.

"It's for protection," the older man explained, "against fire, evil spells and...disease." He threw Quin a quick glance before turning back toward the Fagan's field and slowly waving one arm. "But you must walk in the direction of the sun," he informed Quin earnestly, "otherwise only bad luck will find you!"

"I see." As Quin watched, another man started walking purposefully around the neighbouring plot, taking careful steps with his burning torch held high. Others were dispersing with their brands, perhaps to repeat the ritual on their own newly planted fields.

Quin could hardly blame them. With the disastrous potato harvest of the previous season, those who relied heavily on the single crop were likely to try anything to prevent a repeat of the ruinous blight (no matter how confident in the harvest they may outwardly seem)—even if it was based on the pagan belief of witchcraft and curses.

And having seen the affected potatoes himself, Quin wasn't entirely convinced the blight had not, in fact, been a curse after all.

21.

"IT'S SAE LOVELY t' see ye, my dear."

I smiled at the elderly Mr Docherty as he affectionately patted my hand.

"It is," I agreed, gently extracting my fingers from his grasp.

Mr Docherty and his wife lived on a moderate estate not far from Glaslearg, and he had called on us for tea. With one thing and another it had been some time since we'd had a formal call, and I had to admit I was quite enjoying spending the afternoon with our visitor. With his soft Scottish accent and sprouting grey eyebrows, Mr Docherty always made me think of a doting grandfather.

"We must meet again after our return from London," Quin said, having earlier been obliged to recount in great detail his visit to Dublin and the Mansion House Meeting. "And I do hope your wife will be able to accompany you then."

"Och, I'm sure she will," Mr Docherty ensured us before giving a mournful sigh. "Poor Mrs Docherty, put out by the megrim.—I did ask would she wish t' join me still, but she waved me away from her bedroom." He waved his own hand weakly in illustration. "I did hesitate t' leave her so, her face covered wi' a cool cloth as it was, and the room darkened by the drawn curtains.—But she did bid me go and assured me her maid would take care of her."

He sighed once more but then suddenly brightened up. "But we'll see each other at the O'Malley wedding. I know Mrs Docherty doesna want t' miss that!"

"I'm afraid we're rather unlikely to attend," Quin said, making the older man's face droop. "We do want to stay in London for several weeks after all."

"Aye, I suppose ye're right," Mr Docherty conceded. "Still, is it no' something that the younger O'Malley brother will be marrying int' a far greater estate than he ever stood t' inherit from his father? The older brother is sure t' be turning green wi' envy"—he wriggled his bushy brows—"even if the estate's in Cork." He gave a hoarse laugh before continuing, "But the brothers lost their real chance some years ago when this young man here snapped ye up for 'imself, Mrs Williams." He inclined his head toward me while grinning up at Quin, who smiled back indulgently.

I kept the smile on my own face, although Mr Docherty's comment had given me something of a turn. For a time, Kieran had entertained the thought of seeing one of the O'Malley brothers married to me. A lot had happened since then, though, and I was quite content with my existing husband—whom I had married of my own free will.

"Even so," I said, "their father must be quite pleased. With one brother having gained a considerable dowry to add to the family holdings and the other taking over a large estate in Cork, they both seem very well settled."

"And I believe Sir Spencer, too, is quite well settled," Quin put in, making me look at him in some amusement. Although he was hardly prone to idle gossip, he did try to stay informed about what was happening around him. Clearly, he was taking the opportunity to reacquaint himself with his neighbours—as it were—even though only one of those neighbours was in fact present.

"Aye," Mr Docherty said with a nod, "he evicted the last of 'is tenants just a few months ago. T' turn his land t' pasture, as he'd planned"—he leaned conspiratorially toward me—"although I suspect he was glad t' be rid 'o them before they could fall too far behind on their rent."

I wrinkled my brows at the casual comment. After the poor potato harvest last season it was even more difficult for Ireland's peasants to scrape together enough money to pay their rent, without having to worry about the additional threat of being evicted by their landlords for the sole purpose of using the land for more lucrative agricultural practices involving livestock.

"Nay doubt it was no' a popular move wi' the tenants, but Sir Spencer is certainly makin' a good profit."

"Quite," Quin said in a level tone.

"I've not done the same on my own estate, bein' far too old t' abide change." Mr Docherty winked at me. "And it has o' course been rather a tryin' year for the tenants, forbye.—One can only hope this year's harvest will see things return t' normal."

I wondered if there would ever come a time when the pitiful existence of much of Ireland's populace would cease to be considered normal, but I let it go.

"The tenants on your old family farm seem t' be faring well enough, Mrs Williams," Mr Docherty observed, waving a hand in the direction of the neighbouring Talamh na Niall.

My heart gave a sudden lurch, but I nodded mechanically. After Herbert Andrews had blackmailed Kieran out of the O'Neill estate, he had leased the land to a local family. Of course, the details of the transfer of ownership were not common knowledge, with most people simply assuming Kieran had sold the farm.

"Yes," I said, "although it is natural that they should fare better than the smallholders and labourers, having far more land available to farm and not having to depend solely on the potato harvest.—The estate did sustain my own family for generations, after all."

I compressed my lips, being suddenly overcome with an overwhelming sense of sadness at Niall's loss. In a time when countless Irishmen had been dispossessed of their land by their English conquerors, my forefathers had managed to hold onto theirs, only for my brother to lose everything with the bad choices he had made. I suppressed a sigh. It was the loss of everything that had finally made Kieran see the error of his ways, allowing us to bridge the gap that had come between us and giving us a brief time of shared happiness before his death.

"Quite right, quite right." Mr Docherty's voice pulled me out of my revery. "But they do seem t' keep mostly t' themselves, no?" The older man looked from me to Quin with raised brows.

"They do," Quin confirmed with a shrug. "We met them only briefly when they first arrived at the estate and see them only now and then."

"Och well, no' everyone can be as sociable as we now, can they?" Mr Docherty grinned, revealing his yellowing teeth.

I rather thought the lack of social connection likely had something to do with the distance many perceived between those who owned their land and those who did not, but I didn't say anything. Fortunately, the remainder of the afternoon was spent in pleasant conversation of more light-hearted content, until Mr Docherty finally declared it was time for him to leave.

"I really must be on my way now," he said, getting up from his chair with a creaking of his aged knees. He bowed to me and then to Quin. "Mrs Williams, Mr Williams, I thank you most kindly for your hospitality today. I look forward t' hearing all about your stay in London when you return." He started walking toward the door but turned back with a twinkle in his eyes. "Do give my regards t' the Queen."

"WE'RE GOING TO London! We're going to London!"

"Do try to calm down, Rupert." Quin grinned at his valet, who was vibrating with excitement as he bustled around the sitting room outside Quin and Alannah's bedroom. "We're only leaving next week."

With the spring planting completed, they had at last been able to turn their attention to their impending trip. Rupert would be traveling to England with Quin and Alannah, but would be staying with his family, a prospect he could hardly wait for, it seemed. Not surprising, Quin thought, as Rupert hadn't seen his family since he'd come to Ireland with Quin a few years back.

"Do you think my mum'll find that I've changed?" Rupert stuck out his chin and puffed out his chest, turning this way and that for Quin's inspection.

"I think she'll find that you've grown into a fine young man," Quin assured him, making a soft pink blush creep across Rupert's round cheeks. While the roundness of his face was unlikely ever to change much, Rupert did now look more like the young man he was, rather than the large child he had resembled when Quin had first employed him about four years ago.

"And I wonder how my brothers are…and my sisters. My dad's bound to be exactly the same as he's always been, which means he won't have much to say at all, but my mum…"

Quin smiled as Rupert prattled on, remembering his own enthusiasm for his homecomings during his time with the army, looking forward to the perpetual normalcies of homelife. That was all an illusion, though, he thought with some regret, remembering the devastation of returning to a home that no longer included the comforting presence of his mother.

"And they won't believe the grand places I've lived!"

Quin chuckled. Glaslearg's manor house would hardly have been called grand when they'd first come to stay there, being rather neglected and in disrepair. Then again, even in its initial state the house would have far surpassed many a lodging in the poorer parts of London, the likes of which he knew Rupert to hail from.

"I'm sure your parents are very proud of you," Quin said sincerely, placing a hand on Rupert's shoulder.

His valet beamed. "I *am* the first in the family to work for a baron," he declared with a raised chin.

"I'm not a baron just yet."

"Still..." Rupert flipped a wrist at such trivialities. "One of my sisters is a gentleman's maid and one of my brothers drives the coach of a local solicitor, but to be valet to a baron..."

"A baron's son."

"A *future* baron!" Rupert grinned, making Quin laugh. "And to have a room all to myself. My brothers and sisters will die of envy!—But I must pack!" he suddenly exclaimed, a wild look appearing on his face.

"Er..." Quin was quite sure all of Rupert's portable belongings would fit comfortably into a moderate carpet bag. "We're not leaving for several days yet. There's still plenty of time..."

But Rupert was already off, no doubt heading to his small adjoining chamber, where he would presumably pack and repack the same few items until their departure. Quin watched him disappear through the doorway in amusement, glad the young man would have the chance to see the family for which he clearly held much affection.

Quin contemplated once more how he felt about seeing his own family, namely, his father. While he was in fact looking forward to visiting London and his family home—and indeed his father—whatever closeness there might have been between the two of them had been heavily besmirched in recent years. And without his mother's calming presence their reunion may well become a heated affair.

Not for the first time in his life Quin wished he had a sibling or two. While he'd always wanted a brother or sister to play with as a child, as he got older, he mostly wished he'd had a sibling who would take his father's attention away from him and his supposed flaws. Quin smiled wryly at the thought. He'd remained an only child, though, and whatever was in store for him upon his return to London, he would have to face on his own. Or not entirely on his own, Quin reminded himself fondly. Alannah would be by his side and however his father would react to him, or to her, at least they'd be together.

22.

"IT'S GOING TO be fine," Alannah said for at least the dozenth time as their carriage rattled along the cobblestone street on which stood The Baron Williams of Wadlow's modest London house. Modest only in relation to the sprawling mansion that was the baron's family seat, Wadlow Manor—situated on a vast ground in the countryside, the enormous building was large enough to house a good portion of the baron's beloved British Army, a use to which he probably would gladly have seen it put.

"You don't even know the man," Quin replied brusquely. Despite his best intentions, he'd managed to work himself into a distinctly bad temper the closer they got to London, as he replayed past arguments with his father in his head. And although he was weary of travelling, he was nevertheless sorely tempted to turn around and make his immediate way back to Ireland before they'd even reached their destination.

"And what will he think of us?" he growled. "The son of a baron traveling without a valet and his wife traveling without a lady's maid?"

Alannah narrowed her eyes at him. "I could hardly drag Margaret away from her baby, nor Mary away from her children to perform such duties for me, could I? And I'm sure he'd understand that Rupert would want to spend time with his family.—Besides," she continued before he could respond, "since when do you care what your father thinks?"

"Hmph," Quin grumbled, crossing his arms in front of him. "Still, if you think he's going to welcome me back with open arms, you're mistaken!—And he's unlikely to give you a better reception either."

He stared gloomily out the carriage window, remembering the last time he'd come home to his father after an extended absence. He had resigned his commission from the army and returned to London in disgrace—or so his father had made him believe, ranting and raging at every opportunity, accusing Quin of disloyalty, cowardice, selfishness and a good few other character traits that were none too flattering.

What was awaiting Quin now, he had no idea.

While there was a slight chance his father might have felt a sprinkling of gratitude toward his son for having travelled to Ireland to see to the running of the family's estate, any such goodwill would have been heavily tainted by Quin's decision to settle in Ireland and marry an Irish bride—a fact Quin had known would infuriate his Anglophilic father, even without the baron being so very willing to voice his displeasure during their subsequent correspondence (although he had at least deeded Quin the estate, as promised).

"I wasn't expecting him to."

Quin turned toward Alannah in some startlement, having almost forgotten she was there. She scowled at him now, which explained the clipped tones punctuating what she'd said.

"Is that so?" Quin was sure his foul mood was the cause of her annoyance but was unable to much improve it, even so.

"No, I wasn't!" Alannah responded with some heat. "You've told me often enough that your father is bad-tempered and self-righteous, not to mention that he dislikes anyone who isn't English.—And I have read his letters, after all." She looked at Quin through narrowed eyes. "Nevertheless, he *is* your father and I for one am looking forward to meeting him for that reason alone.—And if you were to put your mind to it, I'm sure you'd find some part of you is happy to see him too!" Alannah glared at him for a few moments longer, making him narrow his own eyes before finally breaking into a lopsided grin.

"I may have to admit you could possibly be right." Alannah's face took on an I-told-you-so expression. "But don't say I didn't warn you when he starts insulting us the minute we walk through the door!" Quin prophesied as the carriage pulled up in front of the sizeable house.

A butler in uniform materialised while Quin was handing Alannah down from the carriage, with two more servants in livery appearing to remove their heavy trunks with the help of the driver. "Welcome to Wadlow Cottage, sir," the butler said formally and bowed to Quin. "I am to escort you inside." Before Quin could so much as respond, he felt himself compelled to follow the man as he headed toward the stairs. He raised his brows but offered Alannah his arm and led her inside.

The entrance hall was just as he remembered it—sizeable and impressive, yes, but also rather cold and uninviting, lacking the softening touches his mother had provided before her death.

"In here, sir," the butler announced, having come to a stop in front of the reception room. He ushered Quin and Alannah inside, before retreating and closing the door on them.

"Well, we're here." Alannah's voice came from behind Quin as he stood with his arms crossed, scowling at the closed door.

"Yes," he agreed in clipped tones, feeling highly irritable, "and a less hearty welcome could scarcely be imagined." He turned toward Alannah and blew out his breath forcefully through his nose. "The nerve of him! To allow his servant to bustle us in here after barely acknowledging us—and ignoring *you* altogether!"

Alannah shrugged. "I suppose he had his instructions."

"And to have him send us in *here*," Quin went on, ignoring Alannah's comment as he turned back toward the door, "to await his appearance as if we were here to discuss business. And not even so much as the offer of some refreshment, when the man knows what a long journey we have behind us." Quin's irritation was rapidly turning into anger, and he clenched his hands into fists. Alannah came up behind him and wrapped her arms around his middle.

"It doesn't matter," she said softly, leaning her head against his back. "At least we're here together."

Quin turned in her arms to face her, feeling some of his anger recede. "Yes, we are." He brushed back a strand of hair that had fallen across her face. "I did warn you though." He raised one brow and cocked his head, but she shrugged.

"You did." She pulled his head down toward her so their foreheads were touching. Quin heard the door open behind him but didn't release his hold on her, instead pulling her closer and kissing her thoroughly. When he was good and ready, he let her go and turned toward the door, where the stern-looking form of The Baron Williams of Wadlow stood, his eyes narrowed in disapproval.

"Father," Quin said, raising his chin ever so slightly in defiance as he continued to hold his wife firmly around the waist. His father appeared healthy enough, he observed, looking him up and down.

"Quinton," the baron responded shortly, giving him a curt nod but making no move to come any closer, much less to embrace his only son, whom he hadn't seen in over three years.

Quin took a deep breath. Deciding that at least one of the men present ought to behave like an adult, he let go of Alannah's waist and, taking her by the hand, led her toward her father-in-law. "Father, I would like to present my wife, Mrs Alannah Williams, born Miss O'Neill of Talamh na Niall of the O'Neills of County Tyrone in the Province of Ulster, Ireland." Not that it was likely to make much difference to his father's disposition, but Quin thought he'd add a few formalities to his introduction of Alannah. He had, of course, related something of her heritage in his letters to the baron when the two of them had married, but that had made no difference to the man's discontent at being informed about the wedding after the fact—nor had it made him any happier Quin had chosen to marry an Irishwoman and to settle in Ireland in the first place.

"Mrs Williams," the baron greeted her stiffly, performing the briefest of bows in her direction, before straightening up like a ramrod.

Alannah smiled at him and curtsied elegantly. "I'm very pleased to meet you, Lord Wadlow," she said in her soft Irish lilt, which made the baron purse his lips.

"Quite." His father's rude response made Quin's eye twitch with the effort of not saying something nasty in turn. They'd only just arrived, though, and he wasn't particularly keen on immediately being thrown out. Give it a few days then, he thought with a snort. Alannah gave him a curious look and the baron frowned, clearly unimpressed with his manners. Quin wasn't overly fond of his father's manners either, though, and so he grinned back, making the baron give him a long look. Otherwise ignoring his son's antics, he addressed them rigidly, "I've had rooms prepared for you. Best get settled in. Haughley will show you the way.—I shall see you at supper at eight."

And with that, he turned on his heel and left, followed almost immediately by the entrance of the advertised Haughley, the butler who'd shown them to the reception room and must have been waiting outside the door.

Alannah glanced at Quin, but he shrugged and offered her his arm, before following Haughley up the wide staircase to their apartments. Quite unexpectedly, Quin started feeling a little nostalgic as the butler led them through the house, finally coming to a stop in front of the very rooms Quin had lived in for much of his life.

"Your rooms, sir," the butler announced, looking at Quin as he opened the door to the small sitting room. After a brief pause, he turned toward Alannah and added, "ma'am," inclining his head ever so slightly in her direction.

"Thank you," she responded, smiling at him.

Were the man's cheeks looking a little pink? Quin wondered as he offered his own thanks and sent him on his way. With a sigh of relief, he closed the door on the retreating butler and walked to the two armchairs in front of the fireplace. Alannah stood beside him as she surveyed her new surroundings. The room looked much like Quin remembered it. In addition to the armchairs, it contained a small couch and a few side tables, as well as a writing desk, which his tutor had seen him make good use of when he was younger.

Quin smiled at the memory, thinking with fondness of his childhood, and his mother. He sighed wistfully, wishing she were still with them and that she could have met his wife. Quin was sure his mother would have loved Alannah and accepted her wholeheartedly into the family, unlike his intractable father.

He scowled, as a sudden recollection of their last encounter in this very room flashed across his mind.

The baron had once again been badgering him relentlessly about his decision to leave the British Army, paying no heed to the reasons why he had done so, only seeing the very act itself as an insult—not only to Her Majesty the Queen, but to the army itself, as well as to him personally, being the retired major that he was. Having reached the limit of his endurance for listening to the sorts of things his father was accusing him of, Quin had declared in the midst of their dinner that he would be finding alternative lodgings, with immediate effect. He had stormed out of the dining room into his quarters and started throwing random items into a bag, his father hot on his heels.

Thinking his son might be persuaded to change his mind if he were insulted on top of being ridiculed, he had given it his all, not letting up until Quin had slammed the front door shut behind him. Spitting with rage but congratulating himself on the considerable restraint he'd shown by not punching his father squarely on the nose, Quin had walked away from his family home without a backward glance.

"Hmph," he grumbled to himself now.

After he'd stormed out of Wadlow Cottage that day and settled in his own apartments, the relationship with his father had in fact returned to normal—which wasn't saying all that much, truth be told, but at least their interactions had become slightly more civilised.

How would it be living under his father's roof again now, with an Irish wife by his side?

"At least the butler acknowledged my existence this time." Alannah's voice cut in on his thoughts. She had moved to the window and was looking out onto the small garden at the back of the house. "And so did your father, come to think of it." She turned around and lifted one sleek black brow, cocking her head.

He snorted. "If you equate that pitiful attempt at a welcome with an acknowledgement of your existence, then I suppose he did." He shrugged his shoulders.

"You never told me you resemble him so much," she said, neatly changing the subject.

"I do?" he asked in some surprise. A few people had made similar observations over the years but seeing his father as he had greeted them today, rigid and unapproachable, Quin rather hoped any resemblance between the two of them was slight. The thought made him scowl. He quickly rearranged his features, though, as he realised he was wearing precisely the sort of grim expression his father so often did.

Alannah laughed. "In appearance, not temperament."

"Ah, well I suppose I can live with that.—Do you really think so, though?" He stuck out his chin and stood a little straighter so she could better examine him, which made her laugh once more.

"Yes, you do. He's older of course, and your colouring is different, with his hair being grey.—Was it brown like yours when he was younger?" She raised an enquiring brow and Quin nodded. "You have the same green eyes," she went on, "and much the same features. If you were to grow a moustache and side whiskers, you'd look just the same!" She gave him a wide smile, making him chuckle.

He ran his hands over his cheeks, which were normally clean shaven but had not been receiving much attention from his razor during their travels. "If I wait a few more days, I *shall* have a moustache and side whiskers, not to mention a full, magnificent beard!"

Alannah came to stand in front of him and cocked her head, assessing him. "Now that I know what your father looks like, I can imagine it. Although I've seldom seen you looking anything less than perfectly groomed."

"Ah well, without my valet to hand, I'm afraid I shall be looking more and more disreputable each day."

They had bid Rupert farewell that afternoon. Quin had seen him deposited in a public coach with his small bag of belongings, on his way to visit his family while they'd continued on to Wadlow Cottage. Although Quin had offered to take Rupert wherever he wanted to go, his valet had insisted that his employer not go out of his way for him. Quin knew Rupert didn't come from much and suspected he didn't want the two of them to see his family home.

"But what do you say," Quin said, pushing the thought aside, "should I shave before going down for supper?"

"Not on my account." Alannah reached up a hand and ran it along his cheek. "Besides," she added with a glint in her eye. "I wouldn't want you to cut your throat."

"Very funny," Quin retorted drily. "I am in fact perfectly capable of grooming myself.—I didn't always have a valet you know."

"I know. And that's not what I meant." She batted her eyelashes at him in feigned innocence, making him laugh.

"I am not going to let my father drive me to *that*! Besides, I couldn't possibly deprive him of his favourite thing to complain about, namely, me." He grinned at her. "Now let's see what's become of our luggage. I'd at least like to put on a fresh shirt." He strode into the adjoining bedroom, where he spotted their travelling trunks next to the wardrobe. Nodding to himself he came to a stop in front of the bed, looking contemplatively down at the smooth coverlet.

"What are you thinking about?"

"Hm?" He turned toward Alannah, who had followed him into the room.

"I asked what you were thinking about. You have a very peculiar look on your face."

Quin chuckled and pulled her suddenly toward him, making her squeak in surprise. He murmured into her ear, "I was just remembering...all the agonising nights I spent here in my youth, contemplating naked women." Alannah laughed, the sound reverberating against his chest. "I never thought I'd be so lucky as to actually have one in this very room one day." He let his hands skim down her sides until they reached her buttocks, pulling her close.

"I'm not naked yet," Alannah pointed out wryly.

"We can change that." Quin lifted an enquiring brow.

"Perhaps later."

"Hmph." Quin dropped his hands, feigning disappointment.

"I'm sure there'll be plenty of time after supper," she went on cheerily.

"Time yes, but inclination...? I can make no promises as to the state of my mind after I've shared a meal with my father." Quin frowned, even more so when Alannah laughed.

"I'll take my chances," she quipped, reaching for one of the trunks. "Best get changed now. Your father will be waiting."

DINNER WITH THE baron was a peculiar affair indeed. Quin had told me enough about his father that I wasn't expecting much warmth from him, but I still found it surprising how stiff and formal he was being with a son whom he hadn't seen in several years.

"Any thoughts of rejoining the army?" the baron asked at some point during the evening, managing to make it sound more like a command than a question. I knew Quin had no intention of going back to the army, as he disagreed with a number of policies being employed in the Empire's vanquished lands, and I turned toward him with interest, awaiting his reaction.

"No," he responded shortly, giving me a long-suffering look.

"Hmph." The baron wrinkled his nose, making his grey moustache quiver. "I suppose things are quiet in any case.—Not like in my day." He looked at me and raised his brows meaningfully, which rather surprised me, as he'd been doing his best to ignore me for most of the evening. "We drove back those

Frenchmen, didn't we?" His eyes glowed briefly in remembered glory. "Forced old Bonaparte to surrender too." He looked into the distance, clearly reliving his time spent serving under the Duke of Wellington in the Napoleonic Wars, which Quin had told me about. A brief smile came to his lips, which quite transformed the usually harsh lines of his face, making him look even more like Quin.

"Politics," he proclaimed suddenly, startling me. Quin looked suspiciously at his father as he waved an admonitory finger at his son. "Politics," he repeated with a nod, "that's what you ought to be thinking about.—If you don't want to get your hands dirty, then the least you can do is to sit in parliament."

Quin's nostrils flared at the implied insult, and he shook his head as he took a deep breath, evidently trying to compose himself. "I have no interest in politics." The statement came out in clipped tones, and he raised his chin defiantly. "As for getting my hands dirty...I do so regularly while working on the estate—mucking out stables, planting and reaping crops and such." He gave me a wry look, one corner of his mouth turning up.

The baron pursed his lips, clearly not impressed at the thought of his son's grimy descent into a farmer's life. I held my breath, waiting for him to explode, but he simply finished the rest of his wine, before waving a hand to one of the servants to clear the table.

"I am glad to see you looking so well, father." Quin's observation made the baron give him a curious look. "In your last letter you implied that you were practically at death's door."

The older man waved a dismissive arm. "Nothing but a spot of the gout."

"I see," Quin said, raising his brows as he looked at me. He had doubted his father was seriously ill, and his suspicions had now been justified. I shrugged—we were here now after all.

"And how are things on Glasleer?" the baron asked into the silence.

"Glas-la-rug," Quin corrected him slowly, grinning at me.

When Quin and I had first met, I'd rather pretentiously informed him of the correct pronunciation of the name of his estate, Glaslearg, which meant green hillside in Gaelic.

The baron lifted his brows in surprise but turned toward me, evidently willing to give it a try. "Glaas-laa-rrrug." He cocked his head, waiting for my approval.

"Very good, Lord Wadlow." I nodded at him and smiled, making him look rather smug, which in turn made Quin emit a short laugh.

"Very good, father. We'll have my wife teach you a little Gaelic while we're here, shall we?" He looked expectantly at his father, who scowled at the suggestion.

"Speaking of your stay here," the baron said, briskly changing the subject, "I have a few things to discuss with you while you're here."

"Of course."

"Without your wife," the baron continued pointedly, raising his chin as he gave Quin a long look.

Quin clenched his jaws and narrowed his eyes, and I felt heat rising in my cheeks. Father and son would naturally have private matters to deal with, but the baron's rather rude dismissal of me had taken me utterly by surprise.

Subtlety was clearly not one of his strongpoints.

"Yes, father," Quin responded coldly as he pushed his chair back from the table. "Now if you will excuse us"—he offered me his arm and pulled me rather brusquely from my seat—"we shall retire for the night. It's been a long day." He inclined his head toward his father by the barest of margins before turning on his heel and stalking out of the room, towing me alongside.

"Good night, Lord Wadlow," I called as I was dragged past our host, giving up the customary curtsy in favour of staying on my feet in our speedy exodus.

Quin stormed up the stairs, his body practically vibrating with anger, not letting up until we had reached our rooms. He closed the door in what was almost a slam, before rounding on me.

"Infuriating man!" he hissed, frowning down at me.

I patted his arm consolingly. "It could have been worse."

"Hmph." He gave me a highly sceptical look.

"Your father is simply...a little tactless."

"Tactless, ha! Yes, he certainly is that!" He gave a brief snort. "I have been trying for years to teach my father manners," he muttered as he ran his hands vigorously through his hair, making it stand on end. "A bit of a lost cause I'm afraid…"

I laughed, making him narrow his eyes at me suspiciously, which made me laugh even more. After a moment, one corner of his mouth turned up reluctantly and he broke into a lopsided grin.

"Ah, well," he said with a sigh as the tension seemed to go out of him all at once, "that's my father. He's not going to change!"

I came to stand in front of him and smoothed down his hair. "Probably not," I agreed, running a hand along his cheek, feeling the soft bristles of his emerging beard under my fingertips. "But we're not going to let him ruin our stay in London, are we?" I lifted an enquiring brow.

"Certainly not." He shook his head, and I was glad to see his usual good humour return. He captured my hands in his and held them clasped between us. "Speaking of which…" He cocked his head toward the bedroom door, making me smile broadly.

"Oh. So your mood wasn't entirely ruined after all then?"

"Certainly not," he said once more, grinning down at me with a glint in his eye as he pulled me toward the door. "Come with me and I'll prove it to you."

23.

OVER THE NEXT few days Quin showed me around London. Despite some of the city's less pleasant aspects I frequently found myself gaping wide-eyed at some landmark or architectural wonder I'd only ever read about before. Coming from a moderate country estate as I did, the sheer size of the city astounded me, as did the thousands of people who inhabited it—even in comparison to Dublin, London was enormous. The level of activity alone was mind-boggling and often left me feeling exhausted at the end of the day.

I nevertheless enjoyed our excursions immensely, as they tended to be generously peppered with stories from Quin's youth. He could regale me for hours with his boyhood adventures and adolescent mishaps, making me laugh out loud in fine dining establishments, with disapproving glances thrown our way from the snooty clientele. I could see that Quin, too, was enjoying himself tremendously, particularly when he was out from under the baleful eye of his father.

Unfortunately, though, he couldn't ignore his father entirely while in London and so tonight, he was scheduled to attend the requested private meeting with the baron. I, on the other hand, would be seeing my former tutor, Mr Henderson, which I was very much looking forward to.

For reasons known only to him, Mr Henderson had lived in Ireland for several years, where he had ended up tutoring my brother and me on our family estate. Having grown very fond of him over the time he'd spent at Talamh na Niall, I had kept in contact with him even after he'd returned to London and had written to him of our intended visit. A note had been waiting for me upon our arrival at Wadlow Cottage, Mr Henderson expressing himself delighted at the prospect of seeing me again and insisting I visit him at his home. I was only too happy to take him up on the offer, both for his own sake and particularly after the baron's less than courteous insistence that I make myself scarce.

And so, I would be enjoying the evening with Mr Henderson at a small soiree he was throwing for me, while Quin had the pleasure of spending the evening in the dour company of his father.

"You're certainly getting the better end of this deal," Quin grumbled as he helped me button up my gown. I smiled smugly at him over my shoulder, having come to the same conclusion. "My father is sure to spend the evening reminding me what a laggard I am and how I've defiled the family name." He sniffed deprecatingly, before turning me around to face him.

"Perhaps he really does want to discuss business with you," I suggested. Although the baron had made the odd disparaging comment about Quin's decision to leave the army, he had—thus far—not badgered him about it, at least.

"Hmph."

I gave a short laugh at Quin's response. His non-verbal communication seemed to have increased ten-fold since we'd been at Wadlow Cottage. He grinned at me sheepishly.

"Perhaps," he conceded finally, before looking appreciatively at me in my new gown. I had seen it in a shop window and had been instantly drawn to it, with its rich blue colour and delicate golden stitching on the full skirt.

"You should always wear blue," he said softly, stroking my shoulders gently. "It brings out the colour of your eyes."

"That's why I often do." I smiled at him, feeling quite gratified at his obvious admiration. He pulled me close, running his hands over the smooth fabric.

"Mmm."

A soft knock at the door made me pull away regretfully.

"Your carriage awaits, ma'am," the butler announced from the sitting room after Quin had called him in.

"Thank you, Haughley," I responded from the bedroom, picking up my small purse. Quin accompanied me downstairs and handed me into the carriage, with strict instructions to the coachman to see me safely home at a reasonable hour. I scowled at him, determined to stay out for as long as I could stand upright. I laughed at the thought and Quin gave me a curious look.

The carriage started pulling away, rattling along the drive, and I waved demurely through the window. Once Quin had disappeared from sight I turned back to the front, eagerly anticipating the evening as we passed the mansions neighbouring Wadlow Cottage.

The baron's home was situated in a prosperous London neighbourhood, where the large houses of the upper classes sat on generous properties and the air was still reasonably fresh. This changed dramatically, though, as we made our way through the overcrowded city. Soon, a fetid miasma of horse dung and human excrement was snaking its way into the carriage, borne on the choking wings of a coal-fired fog. I coughed and pulled out a scented handkerchief I had brought along in the hopes of masking the stench. I found it to be only reasonably effective, but kept it in place anyway, trying to breathe shallowly through my mouth as I looked out at the bustling town.

The number of horse-drawn contrivances to be seen was astonishing, and the pedestrian activity reminded me of an ants' nest. It was early evening and by the looks of it, half the city's inhabitants were out on the streets, likely heading home after a day's work. As carriages rumbled along beside people rushing on foot, ragged children dashed out between horses' legs to sweep a path through the sludge-covered street for finely dressed ladies and gentlemen who wished to cross.

I squeezed my eyes shut and put a hand to my heart as a rake-thin urchin barely avoided being trampled, hoping the rich man whose shoes and trouser legs the boy had saved from being soiled would at least throw him a few coins.

When at last we arrived at Mr Henderson's modest house in a respectable neighbourhood, I was quite glad I didn't live in London myself. While there was certainly plenty of excitement and variety to be found here, the filthy narrow streets and tall surrounding buildings were starting to make me long for the open spaces and freedom of our estate in the Irish countryside, not to mention the fresh air!

Nevertheless, I was looking forward to spending an evening with my former tutor, reminiscing about his time with us in Ireland and meeting a few of his friends. As I walked up the steps to the house, the front door opened and Mr Henderson himself came out. He rushed toward me and before I could say a thing, had embraced me warmly.

"Oh, dear Alannah," he gushed, finally letting go of me and holding me at arms' length, "how good it is to see you."

"Mr Henderson," I replied, equally enthralled at seeing him again, "I am so pleased you invited me." I was smiling from ear to ear as I looked at him. He had always been a slight man, with a rather unruly head of auburn hair, and he looked much the same as I remembered him, although a little older of course.

"But come inside. We needn't spend the evening on my doorstep." He offered me his arm and we turned into the small entrance hall. I could hear a good deal of noise coming from behind one of the closed doors, but before I could comment, Mr Henderson suddenly stopped and turned toward me. "But my dear," he said with a pained expression on his face, "I must once more offer my condolences on the passing of your brother."

My heart gave a small lurch at his words, but I forced myself to smile. "Thank you, Mr Henderson." I patted his hand reassuringly. I had informed him of Kieran's death some months after the event and he'd sent me a heartfelt letter in return. But he had known Kieran as a child, and the fact that he still thought of him fondly meant much to me, especially after all the trouble Kieran had gotten himself into before his death.

"Sweet, curly-haired Kieran." Mr Henderson shook his head and sighed at the waste of it all, making me swallow a lump in my throat. "Not much of an academic," he added with a wink, "but a sweet boy, nonetheless."

"He was," I agreed, for my brother had once been a sweet and innocent boy, before disillusionment and resentment had gotten the better of him. Mr Henderson clasped my hands and we stood together for a moment in remembrance.

The noise level suddenly increased as one of the doors off the entrance hall flew open.

"Ah, there you are," a ruddy faced elderly man observed at sight of us. "Been wondering where you'd disappeared to." Eying me he asked, "The former pupil I assume?" He raised an enquiring brow and I nodded mechanically in response. "The pleasure is mine." He gave me a small bow before being distracted by a number of voices raised in raucous laughter. "Well do come join us," he urged before heading back the way he'd come.

Mr Henderson laughed as he offered me his arm once more, leading me to what I assumed to be the drawing room. "Mr Philips," he exclaimed, gesturing with his chin, "a proper gentleman I assure you, but not a stickler for all the pomp.—At least not at a friendly little soiree amongst friends."

"*This* is a friendly little soiree?" I looked in amazement at the number of people milling about the room. I had anticipated meeting four or five of Mr Henderson's acquaintances, not the thirty odd people who were in fact present.

"Well"—Mr Henderson waved a hand and shrugged his narrow shoulders—"I do like to entertain." He grinned and steered me into the room. "And knowing what fascination all things scientific hold for you, I invited a few like-minded friends."

"You did?" I asked eagerly, looking with even more interest at the assembly.

"Indeed, I did. Ah, and here comes one of them now…my good friend Mr Pennington, a most avid stargazer."

I turned toward the approaching man, who was not quite the size of a planet, but amply proportioned, nonetheless.

"My dear Henderson, you've outdone yourself yet again." Mr Pennington clapped Mr Henderson on the shoulder with one meaty hand. Looking at me, he asked, "And is this the young lady we're here to impress?" He laughed heartily, making his small button eyes all but disappear in his well-rounded cheeks as his large chest heaved with mirth.

I felt my own cheeks go red but smiled at Mr Pennington in turn.

"Yes, it is," Mr Henderson said with a nod, beaming. "My dear little Alannah…although not so little anymore, I'm afraid." He sighed nostalgically, having to look up a little to meet my eyes. "But where are my manners?" He shook his head. "Mr Pennington, I would like you to meet Miss O'Neill…oh no, wait, that's not right…it's Mrs Williams now, isn't it? Let's start again. Mr Pennington, I would like you to meet Mrs Williams, my former pupil—and a most inquisitive mind she has, too," he added with a smile.

"I am very pleased to meet you, Mrs Williams," Mr Pennington pronounced formally as he gave me a short bow. "Henderson's been telling us about you for years, extolling your virtues and all that. I think he wishes you'd been born a man." He chuckled to himself as he gave Mr Henderson a sideways look I couldn't quite read. Mr Henderson pursed his lips, evidently uncomfortable about something, before clearing his throat and turning back toward his friend.

"She'd have made an excellent scientist if she had," he said in clipped tones, his cheeks slightly pink. "In any case"—he flipped his wrist—"Mrs Williams and her husband have only recently arrived in London from Ireland."

"Ireland?" Mr Pennington exclaimed in sudden interest, leaning toward me. "But of course, I had forgotten.—But then you must know about the Leviathan! Have you seen it?" He leaned his bulk toward me eagerly, practically vibrating with excitement.

"The Leviathan?" I asked slowly, before understanding dawned. "Oh, you mean the telescope?"

"Yes! Yes, I do!" If his corpulent form hadn't been keeping him firmly anchored on solid ground, I thought the large man might have started bouncing with excitement at my statement. "The biggest and best telescope in the world!—Have you seen it?" he asked me again, nodding his head enthusiastically, willing me to answer in the affirmative.

"I'm afraid I haven't," I had to disappoint him. "I read of its construction last year, but I haven't been to County Offaly to see it."

Mr Pennington looked momentarily crestfallen but quickly perked up, excitement gleaming in his eyes. "The Leviathan of Parsonstown," he said dreamily, evidently intending to regale Mr Henderson and me with the wonders this construction entailed. "Seventy-two inches in diameter...imagine casting such a large mirror!" He nodded earnestly, waiting for his listeners to appreciate the enormity of the task achieved. I was suitably impressed—and had been when I'd first read about the telescope, its construction by William Parsons, third Earl of Rosse, and its early observations. "Sir James South himself conducted the first official viewing.—He's a famous English astronomer," Mr Pennington added as an aside to me.

"Was Sir James South not accompanied by an Irish astronomer on the first official viewing?" I batted my eyelashes innocently.

"Ah...why...why yes," the large man stammered, his cheeks going slightly pink, "indeed he was." He looked at me in some fascination for a moment before recovering his good humour and continuing with his lecture. "Dr

Romney Robinson, the director of the observatory in Armagh, accompanied Sir James."

"And what did they see?" Mr Henderson asked in interest, winking at me at his friend's enthusiasm.

"Just what they'd hoped for! Many bright nebulae from the catalogues of Charles Messier and John Herschel, not to mention the double star Castor in the Gemini constellation. What a success it was!—And now astronomers from around the world are flocking to Ireland to make use of the famous telescope."

"Well, old friend," Mr Henderson said, clapping Mr Pennington companionably on the shoulder, "perhaps you'll be one of them one day and make a few discoveries yourself."

"Ah," Mr Pennington exclaimed dreamily, "if only I could. Unfortunately, though, my physique prevents my achieving this greatest of pleasures."

"Your physique?" Mr Henderson gave me a quizzical look, but I shrugged.

"Yes," the large man sighed. "By all accounts, mounting the telescope in order to use it requires something akin to mountain climbing skills. And I'm afraid I'm not quite as agile as I once was. Although"—he chuckled and patted his ample midsection—"I suppose I'd be less likely to be blown off the contraption by a blustering wind."

The three of us laughed together until Mr Pennington was distracted by a passing tray of savouries. Giving his abdomen another pat, he followed the tray-bearing servant, inclining his head toward me in parting.

Mr Henderson grinned. "So, that would be Mr Pennington," he said light-heartedly. "An interesting character, as you can see." He looked affectionately after his friend but froze suddenly, a frown appearing on his face instead. "And what the devil are *you* doing here?" he asked with some irritation.

I turned in the direction he was looking and spotted a tall, handsome man approaching us. As he came closer, I could see his features were marred by thin lines of cruelty around his eyes and mouth, which made his middle-aged face less attractive on closer inspection.

"Henderson," the man said pleasantly, running his eyes up and down the shorter man, one eyebrow raised and an unpleasant smile on his face.

"Owen," Mr Henderson replied shortly, not smiling in the least. "I don't believe you received an invitation to this gathering." He lifted his chin and looked pointedly at his uninvited guest.

The other man shrugged. "Aren't we old friends?" He reached a hand toward Mr Henderson, who narrowed his eyes, making Owen drop his hand slowly before it had reached its goal. He pursed his lips briefly, before lifting one shoulder.

"What are you doing here?" Mr Henderson demanded rather rudely.

"Is this not a gathering of inquiring minds?"

"This is a gathering of *friends*, of which, you are no longer one!" The two men stared at each other for a long moment, during which something passed between them that I didn't understand. "Do you think you have the right to do as you please, just because you have a famous relation who fiddles about with old bones?" Mr Henderson glared up at Owen without blinking.

"Old bones?" Owen replied in clipped tones. "They're called *fossils*, as you well know. And my cousin's fiddling, as you put it, allowed him the unique pleasure of discovering an entirely new lifeform—the Dinosauria," he added for my benefit, nodding briefly in my direction.

I realised then who this man's cousin must be and felt excitement bubbling up inside of me, despite Mr Henderson's evident dislike for him. The term Dinosauria, which meant terrible lizard, had been coined by an English anatomist called Richard Owen a few years ago, after his examination of prehistoric bones made him believe they came from an entirely new kind of animal. Mr Henderson himself had written to me about Richard Owen's discoveries, and I was fascinated to find out now that he perhaps knew the man himself.

I had about a hundred questions I wanted to ask, but before I could voice even one of them, Richard Owen's cousin spoke again, his face taking on a look of disgust. "Not that he deserves any praises, the miserable git.—If anyone ought to be called terrible, it's him!" He laughed at his own wit, before snorting briefly through his nose and turning his attention back to Mr Henderson, inclining his head. "I shall take my leave," he announced shortly. "Mr Henderson, you've been a gracious host, as ever." Owen's voice was dripping with irony, but Mr Henderson didn't take the bait.

"Adieu," my former tutor said curtly, before tucking my arm firmly in the crook of his elbow and turning his back on his unwelcome visitor, pulling me along.

I reluctantly allowed myself to be towed away but had to ask at least one question before I should burst. "Is he really Richard Owen's cousin?" I blurted out, as Mr Henderson came to a stop in front of a table bearing assorted pies and pastries.

"Eh?" he asked, his thoughts clearly elsewhere. His eyes cleared as he looked at me and he nodded slowly. "Oh, yes...yes, he is. A second cousin, I believe, but yes. Cousin to the famous—or should I say infamous?—Richard Owen."

"Infamous?" I cocked my head in curiosity.

Mr Henderson flipped his wrist. "An extremely unlikable fellow, by all accounts—can't take criticism or acknowledge his mistakes and doesn't give credit where it's due." He paused and pursed his lips. "Family traits, I dare say," he added in a grumbling voice, his eyebrows drawn together in a frown.

I thought it best to distract him. "You haven't met him yourself?"

"Richard Owen?" Mr Henderson raised his brows. "No, I haven't had the pleasure. But his cousin Henry and I...well, let's just say that we used to be...particular friends. So I heard rather a lot about Richard Owen from him." He sighed. "Why I ever thought..." He shook his head before continuing, "As you will have noticed, the cousins are not particularly close. Professional jealousy perhaps?—No doubt that's where many of the stories about Richard Owen started in the first place. Who knows which of them are actually true?"

He shrugged, and I sensed it was time to change the subject. "Perhaps you could introduce me to a few more of your friends?" I suggested.

"Yes, of course, Alannah. I do apologise for my poor manners!—It's just that...well...hmph..." He waved a hand vaguely in the direction of the door, where Henry Owen had presumably disappeared.

Visibly perking up at the prospect of enjoying better company for the rest of the evening, Mr Henderson insisted I try a few of the pastries—which were crumbly and delicious, truth be told—and saw me equipped with a glass of syllabub, before leading me around the drawing room to meet his guests.

And what a fascinating mix of people it was, too, from well-known intellectuals in their field, to the remarkably well-read, some of whom seemed to know just about everything about every imaginable topic. One such individual was a crusty old gentleman named Sir Linklater, who sported a long pointy moustache with which he seemed likely to skewer anyone who came too close. I stayed at a safe distance, but found myself enjoying his company immensely, listening raptly as he regaled me with one astounding fact after another, interspersed with random bits of information he felt it necessary to add.

"My friend told me about some fellow in Georgia," he was saying, "I forget his name—he's always aboard some ship, you see, my friend that is, travelling far and wide. He comes back with the most fascinating stories, I tell you. In any case, this fellow in Georgia—that's in the United States of America, you know, which is quite some way from here, much further than Ireland—this fellow apparently uses the ether on his patients when he performs surgery on them. Can you believe it?"

"Ether?" I asked, making him bob his head.

"Yes," he replied eagerly, pointy moustache quivering. "A most fascinating substance, I tell you. But not the Devil's work, not at all! Just an intriguing chemical compound, you know! And apparently"—he leaned toward me conspiratorially, wiggling his bushy, grey eyebrows—"apparently, the ether makes the patient feel no pain...even when the doctor's knife slices into his flesh. Imagine that!"

"Really?" I was intrigued.

"Yes!" he ensured me, nodding madly. "Just imagine the possible applications! Removing an abscessed tooth or a most vile tumour...or even a gangrenous foot, all without pain." I could imagine it all too well and made a face. "And childbirth!" Sir Linklater exclaimed, making a few curious heads turn in our direction. "Childbirth without pain. What a wonder.—My wife did tell me after our first child was born that she'd rather die than go through *that* again. Ah well," he continued with a shrug, "she went on to have six more in any case."

My eyes bulged at the thought of giving birth to seven babies, remembering the pain Margaret had endured to bring little Quinnie into the world.

"Painless childbirth," I mused, fascinated. "That would be a marvel indeed! And a great gift to women from the *men* who get to make such marvellous discoveries in the first place," I added somewhat sarcastically.

"But there are also women in science"—Sir Linklater leaned toward me enthusiastically—"although they wouldn't necessarily be called scientists as such." I lifted my brows in some surprise. While I had heard of the odd historical figure who happened to be both female and a famous great thinker of some kind, I was reasonably sure the prospects for such an achievement were exceedingly limited—not least of all because most women didn't receive the appropriate schooling when they were children, couldn't go to university to hone their craft when they were older and were unable to join the male-only scientific societies that would allow their voices to be heard, or their opinions to be taken seriously.

"Oh, yes," my elderly companion said, nodding his head vigorously at my sceptical expression. "Not many, of course," he conceded with a shrug, "but there are some. Let me think now." He rubbed his chin and tapped a finger against his lips to aid his mental faculties. "Hm...let me think...let me think." He wrinkled his brow. "There have been a few Italians and Frenchies, of course," he said finally, "but Englishwomen?—Oh, but wait, you're not English, are you? I'm afraid I don't know of any Irishwomen who became scientists." He spread out his hands apologetically, making me laugh.

"That's quite all right," I assured him with a smile.

"Englishwomen, though...hm...hm...ah yes, there's Mary Anning, of course!" he declared, with some excitement at having remembered a name at last. "She's famed for the excavation of many fossil finds. In fact, I believe she's been credited with one of the most complete skeletons ever dug up. Now what was the creature called? Something with a P, I think. Ply..., Plo..., oh, I forget. Never mind"—he flipped a hand dismissively—"in any case, her discoveries had quite a few tongues wagging some years ago, I'll have you know."

I assumed this to be a relative observation—most people had probably never heard of Mary Anning, and never would. "Fossils again," I offered instead.

"Eh?" Sir Linklater leaned toward me, cocking his head.

"I was speaking to Mr Henderson about Richard Owen earlier. It seems fossils are quite a popular area of study."

"Oh, yes, indeed they are. And people are happy to pay to get their hands on them, too, apparently. I read somewhere that Miss Anning's family made much of their money selling fossils they dug up. Imagine that!"

"That is interesting," I agreed. Picturing Quin and me digging up old bones for our livelihood, I laughed, making Sir Linklater smile at me in turn.

"But you'll want to hear about other women scientists, won't you?" I nodded. "Hm...let me think. I'm fairly sure there are more"—he wrinkled his forehead—"in fact, I *know* there are. But...I can't seem to think of any just now." He sounded rather surprised, and a little irritated, at this admission. He leaned toward me, one sharp grey moustache end coming dangerously close to my face. "A most unfortunate consequence of aging," he informed me slowly, raising his eyebrows for emphasis, "is that the brain no longer works as well as it once did." He sighed. "Ah...but what is to be done about it?" He shrugged his shoulders, and I patted his arm reassuringly, thinking his brain must still be working quite well, judging by all he'd been able to tell me over the past half hour.

The old man took an absent sip of his sherry, perhaps to aid thought. If that had indeed been his aim, it seemed to have worked, as he suddenly exclaimed "Ada Lovelace" at high volume, making me jump and several panicked faces turn in our direction. Seeing nothing untoward, they soon returned to their own conversations, only to be thoroughly startled once more a moment later, as Sir Linklater yelled, "And Anna Atkins. Ha! Take *that*, old age!"

I laughed at the sight of the old man standing with a fist raised in triumph, grinning from ear to ear, and the bewildered faces that surrounded him.

"Ada Lovelace and Anna Atkins," he repeated, beaming, "how could I forget?" He slapped himself on the forehead. "Ada Lovelace—a countess you know and most gifted mathematician, by all accounts." He bobbed his head energetically, making me smile. "And Anna Atkins," he continued. "Oh, you would find her book so very fascinating, as did I. I have a friend you know—well, a friend of a friend, really—in any case, this friend is most frightfully interested in plants and such. And he managed to obtain a copy of Anna Atkin's book—not an easy feat, by any means, since there are so few available—and he showed it to me. And how very interesting it was too. Not because of all the algae themselves, oh no—Miss Atkins examined the different algae in the British Isles, you see—but because of the *pictures* contained in the book." He paused and raised his bushy brows.

"What were the pictures like?" I asked, riveted.

"Cyanotype impressions, they were," Sir Linklater pronounced slowly with an air of pride. "Now why can I remember *that*, but not the lady's *name*?" He looked at me in some bewilderment before flipping his wrist and continuing. "Photographs—pictures so very life-like that it seemed to me the specimens must be embedded in the paper itself!"

"Really?"

"Yes! My friend's friend told me the impressions are made by placing the specimen on a specially treated piece of paper and exposing it to light. And apparently there's a similar technique being developed to take such photographs of buildings, landscapes and even people, using special machinery.—Well, that does make sense now, doesn't it? One can hardly fit a mountain on a piece of paper! Haha!"

"How incredible," I said, smiling at Sir Linklater.

Fascinating though all of this was, my head was starting to spin with all the wondrous things I had learned this evening. Glancing unobtrusively at the longcase clock that stood in the corner of the room, I realised it was getting rather late. I should probably start heading back to Wadlow Cottage, I thought, wondering suddenly whether Quin and his father had concluded their business—or if they had not, whether Quin needed me to rescue him. I suppressed a laugh at the thought.

"Oh, but I've just remembered..." Sir Linklater's sudden outburst made me blink. "Have you heard of Dr Francis Rynd?" he demanded, leaning toward me eagerly, his eyebrows drawn up to his hairline.

My appetite whetted yet again, I shrugged. I supposed I could stay a little longer after all.

"AND HOW WAS your evening?" Alannah asked, suppressing a yawn. She had arrived back at Wadlow Cottage a short while ago, and she and Quin were getting ready for bed.

"Ah," Quin started tentatively, weighing his words, "most...interesting." He gathered her close for a moment before turning away and yanking viciously on the tight cravat that seemed about to suffocate him. She came to stand in front of him, giving him a quizzical look.

"What do you mean?" She gently started loosening the fabric wrapped tightly around his neck.

"Ah...well...we had some...visitors," he stammered, studiously avoiding her eye.

"Visitors?"

"Well...yes."

"I thought your father had meant to talk to you alone, about some business proposition, or some such.—Or to complain about me, perhaps?" She lifted one brow and cocked her head, making him emit a short laugh.

"He did that too—talk business, that is." He grinned. "However, unbeknownst to me, he also invited a few...friends, as it were."

"I see." She had loosened his cravat by now and slowly pulled the fabric away from his throat, making him sigh in relief. "And are you going to tell me who these visitors were?" She blinked up at him, waiting.

"Ah...yes...of course. Ah...well...it was Sarah Alford, her parents and her new husband," he finally blurted out. He stood still, waiting for Alannah's reaction.

"I see," she murmured after a moment, her face unreadable. "Sarah." Alannah wrinkled her brow as she said the name.

Quin could hardly blame her. Sarah Alford had turned up unexpectedly at Glaslearg a few months after their wedding, which had resulted in Quin having to confess to Alannah that Sarah was, in fact, his former paramour, who had been under the mistaken impression that Quin had wanted to marry her. He felt heat rising in his cheeks thinking about his ungentlemanly behaviour when he'd returned to London from his time fighting in China with the British Army. He and Sarah had parted amicably, though, when he'd made the decision to go to Ireland, which had made her appearance at Glaslearg all the more unexpected. Particularly so, since he hadn't been able to shake the feeling that she still thought of him as more than just a friend—not surprisingly, as she'd thrown herself amorously at Quin upon her arrival on the estate.

"I thought your father wasn't terribly fond of Sarah?" Alannah's voice cut in on his thoughts.

"Well...no," he began slowly, "but...it's complicated." He weighed his head from side to side, wondering where to begin. "Sarah's father saved my father's life, you see, during the Napoleonic wars. He was only a simple sergeant, though, and my father felt it was...unbecoming for a major such as himself to show too much gratitude to someone so low in rank." Quin wrinkled his brow at such pomposity. "My mother, though...well, she thought that was a load of nonsense, of course." He grinned at the thought, making Alannah smile in response. "She insisted they invite the Alfords to their social gatherings and include them in their circle of friends. I suppose my father went along with it to please my mother, but...in truth, the relationship between our two families is not as close as it may seem. I'm afraid my father has never stopped believing the Alfords are simply beneath him."

"So why would he invite them now?"

"Well, that's the question, isn't it? Why now, just when I'm visiting?"

"And you say Sarah's married?" Alannah let the question hover in the air.

"Yes," Quin responded absently, "to the son of a baronet. And a rather sullen-looking, inhospitable man he is, too." He pursed his lips, remembering the awkwardness that had pervaded the evening. Sarah's new husband hadn't seemed to care overly much for Quin, even though they'd never met before. He dismissed the thought, turning back toward Alannah. "I imagine Sarah's husband was the reason for the invite."

"Oh?"

"He's in politics. A Whig...with particularly conservative views, apparently."

Alannah cocked her head and studied him for a moment. "And your father is hoping you might be persuaded to become a politician yourself and come back to England...as he already hinted at on our first night here."

"That's what I had surmised myself."

"But why didn't he simply invite one of his own acquaintances to browbeat you into a life of politics? Why the Alfords?"

Quin laughed at her description. "Perhaps my father thought Theodore Foster was more likely to persuade me than one of his own acquaintances, being of a similar age as I. Unfortunately for him, though, the fellow didn't much warm up to me.—Although he did invite me to meet again tomorrow evening...for further intriguing conversation no doubt." And with his father having already agreed to the invitation on Quin's behalf, he was likely to have to go through with it, too.

Quin frowned, not sure what to make of the man.

A look of understanding suddenly settled on Alannah's face. "It's Sarah," she said, nodding to herself. "Your father thinks you might still have feelings for her, and he's hoping that if you see her you might decide to stay. That's why he invited the Alfords instead of someone of his own acquaintance."

Quin shrugged uncomfortably. "You know that's not true."

Alannah waved a hand in dismissal. "So maybe he did send her to Ireland to lure you back, after all." Sarah had told Quin something of the sort during her visit to Glaslearg, but he hadn't quite been able to believe it—his father and Sarah never having been anything more than the barest of acquaintances. The story was looking a little more likely now, though.

"What a devious old man!" Alannah exclaimed before looking sideways at Quin.

"He is that!"

"And she's married now, in any case.—And so are you! Not that the latter seems to present much of a hindrance in his eyes…"

"Hmph." Quin wrinkled his brow for a moment as he contemplated his father and their relationship. "I did warn you," he said finally, his good humour returning. "He's not a particularly pleasant man."

"I don't know about pleasant," Alannah said with a lopsided smile, "but he certainly is cunning."

"He is that! But enough about my father"—Quin flipped his wrist—"tell me about your intellectually stimulating evening."

Alannah's face lit up, her deep blue eyes sparkling. "Oh, it was wonderful," she exclaimed, her cheeks going pink, "I learned so many interesting things! About fossils, and women who collect them and do the most extraordinary things.—Women, imagine that!" She gave Quin a broad smile tinged with amazement at the thought of women managing such astonishing feats. "And about an Irishman in Dublin," she went on eagerly, "a Dr Francis Rynd, who somehow managed to make a hollow needle. Made of metal and sharpened at the tip, just like a sewing needle, but hollow." She nodded vigorously, urging him to understand her description. "How it's even possible to make such a needle, I don't know. But in any case, the doctor uses this hollow needle to administer morphine directly into the body to relieve pain. Can you believe it? And it works, too! Much better than using the morphine orally, apparently."

Quin smiled at her enthusiasm. "Oh," she continued, clapping her hands together, "and there's a doctor in America who's doing something similar, only he's discovered a way that he can even perform surgery and cut into people without causing any pain, using something called...oh what was it again? Oh, yes, ether, that was it!"

"That is remarkable," Quin agreed, thinking that being stitched up after his various adventures with the British Army and elsewhere would have been a lot more pleasant if he'd had some of these pain relief options at his disposal.

"Yes, it really is!" Alannah exclaimed, her face aglow with excitement.

"And so are you," Quin said softly, pulling her into his arms.

"Me?" She sounded surprised, moving her head back a little to look up at him. "I haven't done anything remarkable."

"Of course, you have," Quin countered, making her raise a questioning brow. "You've married me, haven't you?" He grinned at her.

"I suppose you're right," she said, and laughed. "That is an incredible feat indeed."

24.

"WILLIAMS!"

Quin groaned as he turned toward the voice coming from the taproom door. He thought he'd managed to avoid seeing Theodore Foster again, but there was Sarah's dour-looking husband, heading in his direction, his drooping countenance enhanced by his sagging moustache. After much deliberation, Quin had finally decided to come to the proposed meeting—mostly to appease his father—hoping to be able to keep things brief before returning to his wife. Sitting there waiting, though, he'd begun to hope the man wouldn't show up.

"Mr Foster," Quin said politely in greeting, getting up and extending his hand. Foster shook it, squeezing his fingers rather more firmly than strictly necessary, Quin felt. He squeezed back decisively for good measure.

"Do call me Theodore," Foster said in a rather pompous tone, making no excuse for his tardiness.

Quin inclined his head. "Thank you for the courtesy. In that case, please do call me Quin."

"Quin, yes…quite. I have heard that name mentioned rather a lot, haven't I?"

"Oh? From my father, I suppose?" Quin suggested, although he wasn't sure whether the man had even met his father before the ridiculous evening the night before.

"From him too, yes." Foster compressed his lips briefly. Teetering slightly, he turned toward the table Quin had been sitting at. "Shall we?" he asked, cocking his head.

"Ah…certainly." By the looks of him, Foster was already deep in his cups. Quin shrugged. He'd agreed to meet with the man, after all—although he sincerely hoped he wouldn't have to linger too long.

The two of them sat down on opposite sides of the small table, and Foster ordered brandy.

"I daresay my wife is rather taken with you," he said once they were alone.

"Ah...um...I see," Quin stammered, taken completely by surprise. He had expected the evening's conversation to be more of a political nature, rather than a personal one.

Foster wrinkled his brow. "She mentions you frequently," he said, sounding a little cross. He leaned over the table and Quin detected a waft of brandy fumes, confirming his suspicions that the man had already made something of a night of it.

"Um...well...we've known each other for rather a long time," Quin offered, spreading his hands in supplication. He had no idea what Foster was getting at, but this type of discussion was unlikely to do either one of them any good. It did seem to explain, though, why the man had taken such a dislike to Quin from the first instance—although it also left him wondering why Foster had wanted to meet with him now in private.

He was about to change the subject when their brandy arrived. Foster immediately took a good swill of his and ordered some more, while Quin merely sipped at his.

"It's a good thing the two of you didn't...you know..." Foster raised his brows suggestively and Quin inhaled a sizeable dose of brandy, making the other man thump him on the back as he sputtered helplessly.

"Ah..." Quin managed eventually, his eyes watering.

"I don't much object to a gentleman having a go at it before the wedding night, you understand"—Foster nodded seriously at Quin, who could only gape back idiotically—"but when it comes to your own wife...well, one wants a virgin in the marital bed, doesn't one?" He gave Quin a triumphant look, suggesting he had somehow won the day.

"Um...yes...quite so." Quin tried not to blink as he looked the man in the eye. *Had he come here to gloat?*

"Now that I've shown her the...pleasures of holy matrimony, she can hardly keep her hands off me." Foster laughed bawdily while Quin hoped to God the conversation would soon come to an end. He was not to be so fortunate, though. "If you'd already deflowered her," the wretched man went on to Quin's horror, "the two of us could never now be friends."

Fairly certain that the two of them were not now friends, nor were they ever likely to be, Quin mumbled "right you are" in response. His thoughts were running wild, though, and he hoped they didn't show on his face. For whatever Theodore Foster had been led to believe, his wife certainly had been no virgin on her wedding night and he, Quinton Fletcher Philbert Williams, had reason to know it. Clearly, she had deceived the man, pretending for his sake—and no doubt her own reputation—that she was, as yet, inexperienced in the arts of love.

"Hmph," Quin grumbled under his breath as Foster finished the last of his brandy, not sure how he felt about such deception. Should he be feeling pity for the man? Before he could come up with an answer, though, another thought struck him. When he and Sarah had been *having a go at it*—as Foster had so eloquently put it—after his return from the war in China, Quin had been under the impression that he had been her first. He inhaled deeply, suddenly remembering a conversation between the two of them. He'd been concerned their past indiscretions might pose difficulties for her in the future, but she'd ensured him flippantly there were ways to deceive a man. Clearly, her methods had worked on her husband but had Quin himself also been deceived?

"Quin!" Foster's forceful voice broke in on Quin's thoughts and he realised the man must have been trying to get his attention for some time.

"Um...?" Quin had quite given up trying to be eloquent under the circumstances, simply giving Foster an inquiring look instead.

"And where has your mind wandered then?" the man asked. "Ah...your own wedding night, no doubt!" He grinned and gave Quin a lewd look, his eyes looking slightly crossed.

"Well..." Quin let him think what he would—which was better than the truth in any case.

"I hear your wife is quite...becoming." Foster was slurring his words ever so slightly as he took hold of his second glass of brandy, which had just arrived. Quin was fairly sure the man had had quite enough, but he only shrugged, not feeling himself in a position to interfere.

"She is," he answered succinctly, offering no further details.

Foster looked at him speculatively for a moment. "For Sarah to admit even that much is quite the compliment." He gave a bark of a laugh. "But tell me," he continued while he started rooting around in his jacket pocket, "what about this potato blight in Ireland?" He withdrew his hand from the pocket, emerging with a folded piece of newspaper.

"The potato blight?" Quin blinked down at the tabletop, bewildered by the sudden change of topic.

Foster smoothed out the paper. "What do you say to that?" The corner of his mouth lifted in a cruel smile and Quin frowned, leaning over the illustration on the page. It was from Punch Magazine, dated 13 December 1845, and titled 'THE REAL POTATO BLIGHT OF IRELAND', showing a corpulent man in the shape of a potato with a face clearly meant to be that of Daniel O'Connell.

"That man truly is the real scourge of the land, isn't he? Harping on about the repeal of the union and such, and stirring up the Irish populace into seditious antics using this ridiculous blight as an excuse."

Quin's brows rose to his hairline but before he could respond, Foster leaned toward him, his eyes rather unfocused. "There are those who demanded a ban on grain exports from Ireland. All because of a few rotten potatoes. Can you believe it?"

Considering his evident intoxication, Quin was mildly impressed with Foster's continuing lucidity—although this did nothing to improve his growing dislike of Sarah's chosen husband, particularly as his last comment had been dripping with disdain. Remembering Sarah's own disparaging comments about the less fortunate, though, it seemed she had found her ideal match.

"Well...yes," he responded slowly, "in fact I can believe it." He was not about to humour such ludicrous notions, even from a man who was evidently quite drunk.

"You can?" Foster sputtered in surprise.

"Yes, indeed." Quin gave a curt nod. "Thousands of Irish people are heavily, or even entirely, dependent on potatoes for their very survival. With a large portion of the previous year's harvest ruined, what are they to eat?"

Foster flipped his wrist. "Reports of the damage were vastly exaggerated, everybody knows that."

Quin narrowed his eyes but made an attempt to remain civil. "Early assessments might have been exaggerated," he conceded. This was in fact true. In one of the earlier reports, the Doctors Playfair and Lindley had mistakenly concluded that at least half of Ireland's potato crop had been either destroyed or was unsuitable for human consumption. "Nevertheless," he continued, "subsequent assessments established that one-quarter to one-third of the crop was indeed ruined, which is still a considerable amount, particularly for the hardest hit who have nothing else to eat."

Foster seemed unperturbed. "The overall potato acreage was larger than ever before, and the year's oat yield was substantial, enough to cover any other losses."

Quin flared his nostrils in annoyance. Clearly, the man was just repeating what had been said in parliament by those who refused to stop Ireland's trade with England, choosing the aristocrats' pecuniary interests over helping those in need. Evidently, Theodore Foster was of the same ilk.

For the first time in his life, Quin actually saw some merit to entering into politics himself—to counteract the pompous, callous idiocy he was witnessing at this very moment.

"And what of those," he demanded, managing only with considerable effort not to yell, "who have no oats, who have no money, and whose potato harvest has been ruined? Should Ireland continue to export vast quantities of produce while letting such people starve?"

Foster shrugged. "Peel seems to have found a way to feed them all, hasn't he? And without putting a ban on exports."

Quin had to admit there was some truth to this statement, at least. Seeing the lack of governmental support for a ban on grain exports, the prime minister had purchased large quantities of Indian corn and meal from the United States, which were being distributed to the Irish relief committees to be sold at cost price. He had also overseen the establishment of public works across Ireland, to provide employment and the funds necessary for the poor to be able to purchase the imported grain; and had been campaigning for months for the repeal of the Corn Laws to lower local grain prices and allow more foreign corn to be brought into Ireland.

"And how ungrateful they are, too, referring to the corn meal as 'Peel's Brimstone' and all that." Foster gave a snort, his nose wrinkled up in distaste.

"They are simply unused to eating corn, and unused to preparing it properly to make a fine meal. They're likely to come around to the idea in time." Foster looked unconvinced but Quin continued, "Besides, even with the imported corn there are still plenty of people who are in dire need—as evidenced by the continuous unrest in Ireland, if nothing else." He shook his head. "And in any case, Peel's got his own political agenda in all of this, one that goes far beyond helping the Irish poor!" For it was widely known the prime minister viewed the current crisis as a providential means to reorder what in his mind was the backwardness of Irish society, namely, by permanently substituting the potato with cheap, imported maize and encouraging the poor to work as landless labourers on farms focusing on 'higher' produce, in order to improve Ireland's agricultural output.

Foster waved his hand flippantly. "At any rate, it's God's Will, should those people starve."

This callous comment gave Quin the immediate and overwhelming desire to throttle the vile man. His fingers tingled at the thought, and he quickly linked them together under the tabletop, so as not to disgrace himself in public by leaping at his throat.

"Is that so?" he managed between clenched teeth.

"Of course." Foster nodded, oblivious to Quin's growing anger. "God's Will be done, and all that? Why else would He send such a blight in the first place? It must be some kind of punishment, in any case.—You know there are those who say it's a sign from God that He's unhappy with Ireland's determination to remain largely Catholic. And if England should choose to help those very offenders? Well, then surely we should end up being punished as well." Quin was staring at Foster like a simpleton, so utterly disgusted was he. "I think there's some merit to this thinking, don't you agree?—Quin?"

Quin shook himself to attention, glaring at the man sitting opposite him, who was waiting for him to respond. "No," he began slowly as he gathered his thoughts, shaking his head from side to side. "No, I don't agree at all." He leaned forwards suddenly, anger bubbling up inside him until he was just about ready to burst. "And if you had ever interacted in any way with anyone less fortunate than yourself, you wouldn't agree either.—Oh, the bigotry of it, the arrogance, the very belief that you are better than others because you were born into more privileged circumstances."

Abruptly, Quin pushed his chair away from the table and got up, making Foster gawp at him in some surprise. He was so furious he felt he was in real danger of doing the man physical harm.

"You speak of God and His Will," he growled, his clenched fists shaking, "yet you have forgotten the very tenets of Christianity. Loving your neighbour and helping those in need cannot simply be dispensed with because you feel yourself above those in need!" Foster opened his mouth to speak but Quin cut him off with a vicious slash of his hand through the air. "God created all of mankind in His image, have you forgotten that? Thus *all* of us are equal, including those with whom you wish to have nothing in common." He took a deep breath and blew it out forcefully through his nose. "You," he hissed, pointing a finger at the other man, who was glaring at him with a look of extreme dislike, "and all those who are like you...*you* are what is wrong with the world!"

He turned on his heel, then, and left without a backward glance.

"WHY DO I keep having to have the same conversation?"

I stroked Quin's arm, feeling the tension that was still pulsing through him. He had come back about an hour ago, spitting with rage, pacing furiously up and down the room. I had been almost asleep before he'd stormed through the door, and he'd apologised profusely for disturbing me, before telling me of his encounter with Sarah's husband. Only a short while ago I'd finally been able to persuade him to come to bed.

"Over and over again," he went on, "I keep trying to convince the most pompous and selfish of people that there are others who deserve to have at least the most basic of amenities in life. And for what?" He gave a humourless laugh. "Not a single one of those people is ever going to start believing it, hiding as they are behind their so-called *God-given* superiority."

"I'm sorry Quin."

"You shouldn't have to apologise for other people's prejudices, particularly not since they're my own countrymen." He frowned but pulled me closer, so I nestled into his shoulder.

"It's not only Englishmen," I countered, laying a hand on his chest. "There are plenty of wealthy Irishmen who are just as uninterested in helping the poor Irish people in need."

"I suppose you're right.—The same conversation came up repeatedly around the time of the Mansion House meeting in Dublin." He gave a deep sigh and was quiet for a moment. "I'm sorry to have left you alone for two nights in a row."

"Don't be." I shook my head. "I had a wonderful time yesterday evening and I rather enjoyed the peace and quiet I found today. I'm not used to quite so much activity." I laughed, making a brief smile flash across his lips in response.

"It's all very different here, isn't it?" His face took on a pensive look. "People of high society flitting from one event to the next, each trying to outdo the other to show off their wealth, often completely unaware of what's happening around them, or a little further afield.—The rich concern themselves with politics, but to what end? They barely see the beggars lying practically on their very doorsteps, much less consider the welfare of a desperate people across the Irish Sea."

"It's easier to ignore something you've never seen with your own eyes."

Quin snorted. "Oh, to be blissfully ignorant!—If my mother hadn't concerned herself with the less fortunate, I might have turned out the same."

"But you're not the same," I said softly, stroking his cheek. "She did care, and so do you."

He compressed his lips before responding. "It might have been different if I'd never gone to Ireland. Like you said yourself, it's different to hear about something from afar and to actually see it. Most Londoners likely can't even imagine the abject poverty that prevails among the Irish peasants...I myself had thought I could and yet my imagination fell far short of the reality that confronted me. For those who live elsewhere in relative comfort, the desperate state of the Irish peasantry is impossible to grasp."

"And even those who have seen it often choose to ignore it." I sighed and Quin nodded, before gathering me to him once more.

He kissed me gently on the forehead. "We shall continue to do what we can. That will have to be enough."

25.

"WHAT THE DEVIL?"

Quin backtracked around the corner, not sure if he could believe his eyes. He cautiously took another peek.

"That's him alright," he muttered, making a passer-by give him a curious look. He leaned against the wall of the building as pedestrians rushed past and horse-drawn carriages rumbled along one of London's busy streets, speeding through the intersection at an alarming rate, barely avoiding collision.

Quin carefully edged to the corner once more.

There he was, flawlessly dressed as ever and coming toward him—Herbert Andrews, trailed by his hulking guard.

Growling deep in his throat at this unexpected—and decidedly unwanted—appearance, Quin contemplated his options. Should he follow Andrews and see what he was about? He rubbed his temple, remembering how things had ended the last time he'd tried that. Not that he'd be quite so careless again but still...

He stepped out onto the pavement, directly into Andrews' path.

Let the man see him, he decided.

Within a few heartbeats, Andrews had spotted him. A pleasant smile appeared on his face as he stopped in front of Quin. "Mr Williams, what a delightful surprise!"

Quin narrowed his eyes. "What are you doing here, Andrews?" he demanded rudely.

Andrews raised his brows. "What a peculiar question, sir. Should I have obtained your permission prior to my arrival?" He smirked, making Quin compress his lips in annoyance. "In answer, I travel to London frequently, as befits a *businessman* such as myself." He looked down his nose at Quin, whom he likely considered little more than a lowly farmer. "Why, in comparison to

London, Dublin is really just a rural village, isn't it?" He laughed and tapped his walking stick on the ground in amusement.

"Hmph." Quin eyed the older man with extreme dislike.

"Well, I must be on my way, Mr Williams," Andrews continued, sounding horridly cheerful, "I do hope you enjoy your stay."

He tipped his hat in Quin's direction before sauntering off, his guard following obediently in his wake. As the guard walked past Quin, he pulled back his lips in a toothy grimace, his eyes boring into Quin's with a look of undisguised hatred.

"The feeling's mutual."

The bull-like man was no doubt burning with the desire for vengeance after his clash with a wooden crate in the backstreets of Dublin the previous year. Quin grinned at the memory—although he had of course received a good knock on the head himself, as he'd just been recalling.

He stared after the receding pair for a few minutes before finally heading off, his thoughts running wild. Although Andrews probably did travel to London frequently to conduct business, the fact that he was here now at the same time as Quin struck him as highly suspicious—even more so that they'd actually run into each other in a large city of several thousand people!

Thinking about the unlikely encounter, he barely noticed where he was going, his feet taking him without conscious thought along once-familiar paths.

"Quin!"

He gave a start, dumbfounded for the second time that day by an unexpected appearance. Looking up, he realised he knew the modest house in front of which he stood.

"Sarah. Theodore," he said in cautious greeting. Sarah batted her eyelashes at him, while Theodore Foster gave him a grim look. Relations between the two men had *not* improved after their second encounter the week before.

"Have you come to see Mama and Papa?" Sarah asked, sticking out her hand. Quin kissed it automatically, all the while looking at Foster, who continued to scowl.

"Um…" Quin rubbed his chin, unsure how to explain his appearance at Sarah's parental home, when he was as bewildered as she to find himself standing in front of it.

"Well, do come in. We've just arrived for a visit ourselves. Our house is down the street." Sarah waved her arm down the narrow lane.

"I see. I...ah..." Before he could object, Sarah had linked her arm with his and was pulling him toward the entrance. "Um..." He looked back helplessly toward the street, catching Foster's hostile glare as he let Sarah lead him up the steps to the house.

The door opened as soon as they stood in front of it and Sarah's parents arrived hot on the heels of their servant, filling the foyer with exclamations of surprise and delight at Quin's appearance in their home. While Quin was feeling rather awkward, he couldn't suppress a self-satisfied smirk as Sarah's parents ignored their scowling son-in-law in favour of greeting Quin.

Not quite so popular with the in-laws perhaps, Quin wondered.

He was soon bustled into the drawing room, where he was seated in front of a selection of sweet and savoury treats and equipped with a watery cup of tea. Pretending to sip slowly at this beverage he wondered how best to extricate himself from the situation. While getting up and leaving when he'd just arrived would no doubt be considered rude, he had no intention of spending the rest of the day holed up with the Alfords. Besides the fact he could barely stand the sight of Theodore Foster after their previous meeting, he had told Alannah he was only going to town for a short errand and would be back at Wadlow Cottage that afternoon.

"Oh, Anna, do have a care!"

Quin looked up at Sarah, who was scowling at the maid as she briskly ran her hands across her skirt, which was sprinkled with crumbs. The maid quickly righted the plate of biscuits she'd been trying to place on the table, apologising in a low voice.

Quin frowned at the evident distress on the woman's face as she left the room. Catching Sarah's eye, he tried to rearrange his features, but she smirked at him.

"Oh dear," she said, placing a hand to her heart, "I do believe I've offended you, Quin."

Mr and Mrs Alford threw her a curious look, making Sarah lean toward them as if she were about to impart a great secret.

"Quinton and his wife would never talk thus to their servants, believing them all to be part of a big happy family."

Sarah tittered mockingly and Mr Alford's eyebrows rose in surprise.

"I simply believe in being courteous to those around me," Quin said. Glancing at Theodore Foster, he added, "As far as that is possible, at least.—Just because someone is born to a lower station in life does not mean they deserve to be treated unkindly."

"Still"—Sarah flipped her wrist and wrinkled her rounded nose—"inviting them all to your wedding, including your tenants? That is simply unnatural!"

Mrs Alford's eyes grew wide, but Quin shrugged. He had no intention of explaining himself, no matter how peculiar others might perceive his social habits to be.

Fortunately, nobody pressed the point, and they all drank their tea in silence for several minutes.

"Will you be returning to Ireland after your visit?"

Quin shook himself to attention, realising Mr Alford had been addressing him. "Indeed," he responded with a curt nod, hoping Sarah's father wasn't looking for another exhaustive discussion on Anglo-Irish politics. He'd had quite enough of that on the evening the Alfords had visited Wadlow Cottage—not to mention in conversation with every other acquaintance he'd met thus far during his stay in London!

"And your father is content with you living there?" the man asked instead.

This being another topic Quin had no desire to go into, he provided another brief answer. "Quite."

"What a pity that your dear mother is no longer with us." Quin looked toward Mrs Alford, a pale, frail-looking woman who always seemed to want to disappear, even now dropping her eyes before she could meet Quin's.

"It is, Mrs Alford," Quin said with feeling, eliciting the briefest of glances.

"She was always so very kind to us."

"Ah...if only things had turned out differently," Sarah's father put in. His eyes flickered to Quin and then to his daughter, where they lingered as his brows drew together.

Quin frowned. The Alfords, like many others in London society, had assumed Quin and Sarah would marry—and indeed, for a time, part of Quin had believed this himself. But while Mr Alford had likely been imagining himself boasting of his daughter's marriage to a future baron, Quin had come to the realisation that he simply didn't love Sarah, thus putting an end to their purported union. Although Quin and Sarah had never actually been engaged, the Alfords had no doubt felt slighted, presumably in large part because their daughter would not now rise to Quin's higher social rank.

Quin compressed his lips irritably. Despite what others might believe, Sarah had agreed their parting was for the best. Well, he thought, she caught herself the son of a baronet, didn't she? That ought to make her and her parents happy. Glancing at Theodore Foster, though, Quin wasn't so sure, contemplating how very different the two of them were.

Suddenly, the man himself stood up, barely pausing to mumble "excuse me" before storming out of the room, throwing Quin an angry look as he passed by his chair. Quin looked after him in a mixture of amusement and annoyance but was soon brought back to the present by the soft voice of Sarah's mother.

"Should we not go into the garden on such a lovely day?" She glanced toward her husband, ignoring her recently departed son-in-law.

"Yes, I suppose we might," Mr Alford responded absently, his face set in something of a scowl. He was soon herding them through the door, into the small garden at the back of the house, where the maid started preparing the table for their tea things, while throwing nervous glances at her employers.

"Your roses are looking lovely," Quin said politely to Mrs Alford, determining to make a few minutes of small talk before extricating himself from this unintended visit.

Her answer was interrupted by a low-voiced exclamation from Sarah, who was standing a short distance away with her father, the two of them seeming to be in the middle of a heated conversation. "I did nothing," she hissed. "He left of his own accord." Sarah's mother gave Quin a horrified look while her father grumbled something Quin couldn't catch. He did catch Sarah's response, though, which effectively ended the discussion. "I've never been good enough for you."

Quin wondered if the afternoon could get any worse, looking at the three Alfords, who were now standing dispersed around the small garden, ignoring each other like strangers, with Sarah's husband nowhere to be seen. With a suppressed sigh Quin walked up to Sarah, clearing his throat to announce his presence.

"Are you alright?"

She lifted one shoulder in a shrug as she turned around to face him, her mouth in a pout. "Why wouldn't I be?"

Quin made an effort to ignore her tone. "Your father…"

"Anything that displeases him must perforce be *my* fault." She gave an unladylike snort. "I never stood a chance, no matter what I did. He wanted a boy, and I was born a girl. I was doomed from the start."

"Was he…" Quin paused before slowly voicing his question. "Was he berating you about me?"

Sarah lowered angry blonde brows, making Quin wonder whether he had misread the situation. Her next statement confirmed his suspicions, though.

"He blames me that you left…and that we never married."

"But…"

"It doesn't even matter to him that *you* were the one who ended it with *me*." She glared at Quin, making him open his mouth to object. She cut him off with a sharp wave of her hand and a shake of her head that made a few blonde tendrils of hair swing around her face. Abruptly, she turned her back on Quin, lifting her small nose ever so slightly in defiance as she strode purposefully toward the newly laid table, her usual self-assured manner returning with each step.

Quin watched her go, feeling a sense of guilt creep over him.

In a society that prized the birth of sons and placed great value on affiliations and titles, being born the only girl could prove to be something of a burden. With no son to carry on the family name, it fell upon that girl to marry well. And with Sarah's father having made the acquaintance of a baron, whose son had become friendly with his daughter, it would have been a great disappointment for that friendship not to have blossomed into marriage—and the affiliations and titles this would have brought with it.

Although Sarah always came across as exceedingly confident, even arrogant, Quin was starting to believe Alannah had been right when she'd said it was all an act—an act to hide Sarah's deep-rooted need to seek others' approval and affection in replacement of her father's, perhaps. The thought made Quin wonder whether it was this need that had made her throw herself at Quin—and possibly other men.

Not sure how this made Quin feel about himself he turned toward the table, where Sarah and her parents were standing in grudging companionship, seemingly ignoring one another.

"Do come sit down," Mr Alford called to Quin as he took a seat himself.

Just then, Theodore Foster reappeared, stalking toward the small gathering, not looking at Quin.

"I thank you, Mr Alford, but I must be on my way." Sarah's father looked rather disappointed, but Quin quickly bade them all farewell before anyone could object, insisting he would see himself out.

When he finally found himself back on the street, he gave a sigh of relief. He started walking away but stopped when he heard someone calling his name behind him. Turning, he saw that Sarah was coming down the steps in front of the house.

"It would have been easier for me if you had just married me," she snapped without preliminaries, giving him an accusatory look.

Quin shrugged his shoulders uncomfortably. "I'm sorry, Sarah, I just…" Although he would never regret his decision to go to Ireland, he did regret how things had transpired between Sarah and him.

She sniffed. "You don't love me, I know that."

"Should I rather not have told you? And married you anyway?"

She pouted her lips before responding. "I suppose not."

"But you…you came to Ireland…"

"Just because you had no feelings for *me* doesn't mean I had no feelings for *you*."

His heart gave a lurch at her words—which confirmed what he had long since suspected. "I'm sorry," he said once more, having nothing else to offer.

"It is what it is." She waved a hand irritably. "I came to Ireland thinking…" She shook her head briefly before continuing, "When I saw you and Alannah together it was clear I could never take her place.—And poor, dear Kieran made me realise it too."

Quin raised his brows in surprise at the depth of feeling he could hear in her voice.

"He was…I was very fond of him." Sarah compressed her lips and blinked away tears, which made Quin have to swallow an unexpected lump in his throat.

Sarah and Kieran had become inordinately close during her brief stay in Ireland—and had very likely enjoyed a few less than virtuous encounters—but Quin had always assumed the attachment to be a superficial one, at least on Sarah's part. Hearing her talking about him now, though, made Quin wonder whether there hadn't been more to the relationship—two people with a troubled past finding solace in each other, perhaps? It also made him wonder whether he'd been sufficiently sympathetic in the letter he'd sent informing Sarah of Kieran's death. He'd thought he was simply being courteous to someone who had been acquainted with Alannah's brother for a short time but now…

Before he could further contemplate this new possibility, Sarah took a deep breath, getting herself under control once more.

"Of course, you staying with Alannah wasn't what your father might have hoped for.—Not that I was ever good enough for him before you ran off to Ireland."

"My father?" Quin asked, wanting to hear more about the baron's involvement in the affair.

She ignored his question, though. "And despite what anyone might believe I do *not* wish to be married to a man who doesn't love me."

Quin gave her a long look. "And Theodore?"

"He adores me."

"And do you love him?"

"Of course I do!" she snapped, quite back to her usual acerbic self.

Quin raised his brows sceptically, making her scowl. "My marriage is none of your business, Quin!"

"And yet you and my father stick your noses into mine," he retorted, unable to help himself.

Sarah's face flushed a soft pink. "I should go back inside," she said abruptly, turning toward the steps leading up to the house.

She had just reached the door when he called after her, making her look back over her shoulder at him.

"I do hope you find happiness," he said, holding her eyes.

She gave a curt nod before disappearing into the house. Quin looked after her for a long time before finally walking away.

26.

WHILE QUIN WAS, for the most part, able to put his confrontation with Sarah out of his mind (they had both made their choices, after all), his peculiar run-in with Herbert Andrews returned to him frequently over the next few days, bursting suddenly into his consciousness as he met with acquaintances, helped his father with some business dealings or showed Alannah around town. Each time he would assess and reject myriad possibilities, while something at the back of his mind would insist it had been no coincidence and that Andrews' presence in London had something to do with Quin himself. Self-centred though this conclusion no doubt was, Quin was nevertheless unable to fault it.

When he'd told Alannah of his unexpected encounter with the man, she had looked at him with big eyes, a flicker of fear flashing across her features. But besides her evident unease at the mere mention of the man's name, was her unerring conviction that Herbert Andrews was having them watched—and Quin was starting to believe it too. How else could it be explained that Andrews had shown no surprise at seeing Quin on a busy London Street, or of meeting Alannah at his Dublin Inn the previous year? Not to mention the private things he appeared to know about the two of them.

And if Andrews was indeed having them watched, he was probably waiting, waiting to see if they would stumble upon something too damning to ignore. Quin was sure a man like Herbert Andrews would let no-one threaten what he had built, not even someone from the aristocracy—when it came down to it, he would protect himself and his assets above all else.

If Quin stayed in line, he was safe, but if not...

He looked surreptitiously around him now. A man of average height and build in a dark suit glanced at him but dropped his eyes when Quin turned his head toward him. Had Quin seen the man before? He couldn't be sure. With the many people bustling around London daily, no single individual was likely to stand out, especially not an ordinary looking one such as that. But perhaps that was the very thing that kept Andrews' spies invisible? Their ability to blend into the background?

Quin got up from the bench he'd been sitting on and walked casually toward the shops on the other side of the street, where he browsed windows filled with the latest fashions and must-have items. He peered at a very tall, very shiny gentleman's top hat, taking the opportunity to study the passers-by reflected in the spotless window. Turning back a short while later he continued along the busy street, stopping here and there, all the while scanning his surroundings for anything suspicious.

By the time he went into an upscale tavern an hour later he was quite sure he was indeed being followed. Sitting at a table by the widow he glimpsed the man with the dark suit outside, as he had done on more than one occasion while making his way around town. Quin's cynical nature refused to believe the man's continued proximity was nothing but a coincidence.

"Quinton Williams!"

Startled out of his wandering thoughts, Quin turned toward the door, getting up automatically as a portly gentleman made his way into the tavern, the thin mouth beneath his generous moustache lifted in a smile.

"Why, I haven't seen you in years!" the man exclaimed, tucking his top hat under one arm and extending the other toward Quin as he looked him up and down.

"Commissioner Leventhorpe," Quin greeted him, shaking a pudgy hand.

"Oh, I thank you, my dear boy, but it's only *Assistant* Commissioner." Leventhorpe leaned toward Quin and winked.

"Even so, I haven't yet congratulated you on your appointment," Quin said with a smile, making the man incline his head toward him in a gratified manner. "My father mentioned it in one of his letters." The letter informing Quin of Leventhorpe's appointment as Assistant Commissioner of the London Metropolitan Police had reached him while he was with the army in China.

"I don't suppose I could...?" The Assistant Commissioner cocked his head and looked pointedly down at the table Quin had been sitting at.

"Of course." Quin waved his hand. Although even his father considered Leventhorpe little more than an acquaintance, he could hardly stop the man from joining him, alone as he was.

"I trust the baron is well?" Leventhorpe asked as he took a seat, depositing his hat on the table.

"Quite well, thank you. And how is your father?"

"Gone, I'm afraid."

"I'm so very sorry. My deepest condolences." Quin leaned toward the older man in sympathy.

"I thank you," he said before shrugging his shoulders. "My brother is quite enjoying the title now, I assure you."

Quin detected a hint of resentment in his tone but supposed he couldn't blame him. Like Sarah's vile husband, Leventhorpe was the son of a baronet, a rather lowly rank. And with two older brothers, his chances of ever inheriting his father's title and small estate were poor. Instead, Leventhorpe had made a career for himself in the military, before taking on the role of Assistant Police Commissioner a few years earlier.

The man waved over an attendant. "Some days demand a stiff drink," he confided in Quin before placing his order.

Quin smiled noncommittally and they lapsed into silence, waiting for their drinks. When these arrived, Leventhorpe took a large swallow, before sighing in contentment as he set the glass back onto the table.

"And what do you think of our new government?" he asked, lifting his brows and cocking his head, making him look rather like an overweight owl.

Quin pursed his lips before answering, gathering his thoughts. Just the day before, Sir Robert Peel had resigned as prime minister, shortly after the government had finally repealed the Corn Laws, for which he'd been campaigning so tirelessly. But with ongoing resistance from traditionalists, Peel had immediately thereafter been defeated on an Irish coercion bill he'd put forth to quell the continuing unrest in Ireland.

"I'd say it was rather convenient for the Whigs and the Tories who opposed Peel that he gave them an excuse to get rid of him so soon after the repeal of the Corn Laws."

"Are you suggesting the members of parliament voted against him for the sole purpose of forcing him to resign?" Leventhorpe looked affronted at the thought of such dirty politics, which made Quin suppress a snort.

"I daresay," he said with a shrug. "They knew he was unlikely to continue in the face of such stark opposition, including from within his own party. They left him little choice.—Besides, you know as well as I do that Peel's coercion bill would have been easily passed under any other circumstances. The British have hardly shied away from oppressing the Irish at every opportunity."

"Why...why that is..."

"Am I so wrong?" Quin interrupted. "There are plenty who believe that so much as discussing a repeal of the Act of Union of Ireland and Great Britain is a danger to the Empire."

"And so it is," Leventhorpe said with a scowl, which nevertheless made Quin smirk. Whether the man realised it or not, he had just strengthened Quin's argument that there were many in power who wouldn't hesitate to send in military forces to prevent an Irish uprising.

"But wait a moment," Leventhorpe burst out suddenly, eyes agog, "didn't I hear that you're *living* in Ireland these days?"

"I am, yes," Quin responded cheerfully, "and enjoying it immensely."

"But...but...do you not feel that..." With this, the man launched into the inevitable discussion of Irish politics, making Quin sigh in resignation. Quite familiar with the exercise by now, though, he took it stoically, until the conversation had at last run its course. By the time Leventhorpe declared he'd be on his way, it was near sunset. Leaving the tavern, Quin looked casually around. He didn't see the man in the dark suit anywhere but spotted several other suspicious-looking characters, who he imagined were watching his every move.

"Stop being so paranoid," he muttered under his breath.

No doubt he was imagining the whole thing. And even if Andrews did have his spies keeping an eye on Quin, he wasn't about to let that ruin the rest of his stay in London.

27.

"THIS IS THE place, sir."

"Thank you, Peters." Quin smiled at the driver as he got out of the carriage in the narrow street. They had come to a stop next to an even narrower alleyway, down which he'd been told stood Rupert's family home. As the carriage would barely be able to squeeze between the buildings on either side, the driver would wait here while Quin went to fetch his valet.

Having spent time with his family, Rupert was to come to Wadlow Cottage that day, there to remain with Quin until their return trip to Ireland the following week. Despite Rupert's insistence that he take a public coach, Quin had arranged for the baron's driver to fetch his valet. He hadn't told him, though, that he himself would be coming along too. He grinned in anticipation, patting his coat pocket to assure himself the small bag of coins was still present. He'd wanted to surprise Rupert and his family with a small gift but hoped his valet wouldn't be too disconcerted by his employer showing up at his home unannounced.

A few youngsters spilled out of a doorway as he passed, and he unobtrusively quickened his steps. Although this wasn't the very worst part of London, there may be those lurking about who would be only too eager to dispossess him of his valuables. He had purposefully dressed down for the occasion but was no doubt recognisable as a well-off man, nonetheless. He greeted a pair of apron-clad women, who gawped at him wide-eyed, confirming as much. He was suddenly grateful he'd arranged to fetch Rupert in broad daylight, having no desire to find himself in the alleyway after dark.

Not that the alley was particularly bright even now, mid-afternoon. What little sunlight there was on this cloudy day was further obstructed by the encroaching walls and overhanging roofs.

Quin continued along the dim path, trying not to look too closely at the filth smeared across the cobblestones. This seemed not to bother the locals in the slightest, with a group of children playing noisily amid the rubbish, noses and cheeks bearing streaks of dirt. At least they're happy, he thought as he reached another narrow alleyway intersecting the one he was on. He paused, looking closely at the buildings on either side of the small crossing.

He smiled as he spotted an incongruously bright set of yellow lace curtains adorning a ground floor window on the far side. Rupert had told him the curtains were his mother's prize possessions, his chest puffing out in pride at the fact that he himself had saved up the money to buy them for her.

Standing in front of the narrow door, Quin adjusted his waistcoat and took off his hat. His knock elicited a few bellows and a clattering of footsteps on the inside, followed by a shrill screech as the door was pulled halfway open.

"I keep tellin' meself I must be oilin' these hinges but I…"

The voice faded as its owner looked up at Quin, surprise blooming on his face.

"Good day, sir," Quin said politely and bowed.

Visibly flustered at Quin's formal bearing, the man returned the greeting before making an attempt to stand up straighter. His round cheeks wore a pink tinge, enhancing his resemblance to Rupert, who had appeared beside the man who must be his father, his eyes popping wide open at sight of Quin.

"Hello Rupert," Quin greeted his valet cheerfully over the sound of the excited voices coming from behind the two men.

"Mr Williams…sir…I…" Rupert looked in some bewilderment from Quin to his father and back again.

"This is Mr Williams?" The older man's bushy eyebrows rose halfway up his forehead and he lifted a hand to tuck the remaining tufts of his greying hair behind his ears. "The baron?"

"The baron's son," Quin corrected with a chuckle.

Rupert's father only blinked at him, clearly completely out of his depth at having to receive such noble personages at his home.

"Well do let the man in, Harold!"

The door gave another screech as it was pulled all the way open by a small older woman who Quin assumed to be Rupert's mother, revealing a host of curious faces in the narrow hallway at her back.

"It's an honour, sir," she said and gave Quin a creditable curtsey. She shot a quick glance behind her, making the rest of the assembly bow and curtsey in reaction, with varying levels of success. "Please come in." She waved her hand, making her offspring scatter away to make space, all except a young boy of about ten who stood at the base of the narrow staircase, observing Quin with a cocked head.

"I thank you, Mrs Jones, but I have no wish to intrude."

"Nonsense, nonsense! I insist!" Leading Quin into a small sitting room, she yelled, "Girls, prepare some tea for our disting'isht guest! And bring some biscuits. The good ones, mind you!"

As the girls hurried off to do their mother's bidding the others settled on the assorted furniture around the room.

"Is your father really a baron?"

Quin turned to the small boy who had materialised at his elbow. "He is," he answered with a smile.

"And does he live in a fine house? With servants and silver spoons and silk pillows?"

Quin laughed. "That sounds about right."

"And does he have a gold pocket watch and fancy clothes and a big, shiny shanticlear hangin' from the ceiling?" The boy's eyes were glowing with excitement. With the same rounded cheeks as his father and elder brother, Quin imagined he looked much like Rupert would have looked at that age.

"He does have a very fine pocket watch and a whole wardrobe of fancy clothing," Quin admitted, "and a chandelier that can hold two-hundred candles." The boy gasped, leaning eagerly forward. "But that's only very rarely lit," Quin added.

"Why?"

"Because it has to be very carefully lowered by its chain for the candles to be placed inside and lit, and then very carefully pulled back up without extinguishing the flames. It's a lot of effort and takes several strong men." Rupert's brother was listening raptly, his mouth hanging open. "It would of course be much more convenient to use if my father simply converted to gas lighting," Quin said under his breath. Although gas lighting had been brightening the streets of London for several years, many of the city's inhabitants remained sceptical of its use inside their homes. The baron was no different, insisting on ever-reliant candles and oil lamps to light his house, rather than depending on mistrustful innovations.

"Eh?" The young boy wrinkled his small nose in confusion.

"Never mind." Quin waved his hand. "In any case, because of the effort involved in lighting it the chandelier is only ever lit on special occasions."

"Like what?"

"A grand ball, perhaps. Or a special celebration such as a wedding."

"And why…"

"That's enough, Emmett!" Mrs Jones scolded, making the boy hunch his shoulders and look guiltily up at Quin.

"It's quite alright," Quin said. "I don't mind at all."

"When I'm big, I want to work for a baron, just like Rupert." Emmett lifted his small chin self-importantly before lowering his head and whispering, "He's my favourite brother, you know."

"Emmett!"

The boy squeaked and scuttled away from Quin, sitting down next to Rupert on the other side of the room. He grinned at Quin, who couldn't help smiling back as Rupert's sisters came into the room with the tea things. Throwing furtive glances at Quin, they served him his tea and biscuits, before turning to their family members in a far more casual manner. Once everyone had settled down, a few minutes of awkwardness ensued, broken finally by Quin commenting on what a fine valet and companion Rupert had become.

Mrs Jones took this statement as an excuse to launch into an exhaustive list of her son's many merits, with Mr Jones unable to do more than mutter "my dear" before being interrupted by yet another story his wife had just remembered. Throughout her recital, the object of her admiration was turning ever redder in the face, while his siblings sniggered and smirked at his discomfort.

Rupert gave a great sigh of relief when the conversation finally turned to other matters, looking awkwardly across at Quin and lifting his shoulders in an apologetic shrug. Quin smiled indulgently, finding that he was enjoying himself a good deal despite Rupert's obvious embarrassment. The family's casual chatter was a pleasant change from the stiff and formal interactions he had so often encountered in his father's circles.

Finally, though, it was time to bid the family farewell. "I thank you for your hospitality, Mr and Mrs Jones, but I'm afraid Rupert and I must be on our way."

"Aw, d'you have t' go, Rupert?" Emmett's face was crestfallen.

"Afraid so, mite." Rupert patted the boy on the head and got up. Emmett quickly followed suit, clinging to Rupert's arm.

"I'm goin' with you!" he declared, scowling in determination.

"Emmett!" Mrs Jones looked sternly at her youngest son, hands on her hips. Reluctantly, Emmett let go of Rupert's arm but stayed stubbornly by his side.

The matriarch turned toward Quin with a wide smile of yellowing teeth. Quin smiled back warmly and reached out a hand to hers.

"It's been a pleasure, sir," Mrs Jones cooed. Grasping Quin's hand, a look of surprise bloomed on her face. "What's this?" She looked down at her palm and the small bag that rested there, a metallic clinking sounding as she weighed its contents.

"A small token of my gratitude for lending me your son."

"But..." She made as if to give the bag back to Quin, but he firmly closed her fingers around the coins with both hands.

"I insist!"

"But..." She glanced at her husband, who gave a brief nod. "Thank you, sir." Clearly at a loss for words, she turned her attention toward Rupert, who had gone to fetch his bag and was standing in the doorway, Emmett close beside him. Several minutes of heartfelt leave-taking followed, with Quin finding himself being embraced and thumped on the back as if he too were a member of the family. When the front door finally closed behind them, Quin felt not a little bereft himself.

He glanced at Rupert, who was visibly trying to hold back tears.

"Come along, Rupert," Quin said, draping an arm over the youngster's shoulder. "We'd best try to make it to the carriage before the rain starts."

For what had been a dreary sky before had turned into a grey and brooding mass. If Quin hadn't had the benefit of his pocket watch, he'd have thought it was already past sunset, dark as it had become in the alleyway. And although it was in fact only late afternoon, the place seemed to be deserted. A sudden gust of wind whistled down the narrow lane, making Quin hunch his shoulders. He glanced toward a warped window, where a cheerful candle was burning, understanding why the inhabitants had chosen to secrete themselves behind closed doors this early in the day.

He pulled his coat closer around him and walked a little faster, Rupert by his side. They had just passed the spot where the children had been playing earlier when Rupert reached out a hand, grasping Quin firmly by the arm, bringing him to a stop. "Sir," he whispered, his voice sounding shaky as he pointed with his other hand.

Quin squinted into the darkness. A sudden flash of light illuminated the shape of a man standing in the middle of the alley, facing them with his hands clasped together and raised in front of him. There was a loud crack and Quin felt himself being shoved to the side as something whizzed past his head.

He crashed into the wall, Rupert ending up crouched beside him.

Momentarily winded, his thoughts were rapidly catching up with recent events. He pulled Rupert to his feet. "Someone shot at us!"

He looked down the alley but couldn't see anything. That didn't mean their assailant had gone, though, and they couldn't risk trying to reach the carriage if the man was hiding somewhere along the way. He glanced back toward the Jones' house.

"This way," Rupert hissed in his ear, grabbing him by the arm and propelling him toward a narrow path between two houses he hadn't noticed before. Quin wondered vaguely what had happened to Rupert's bag but dismissed the question in favour of staying on his feet as he skirted rubbish heaps and jumped over obstacles, losing all sense of direction in the warren of dim alleyways through which he was being led.

"We'll come out down the street where the carriage is waiting," Rupert panted as he splattered through a puddle of muck, making droplets fly in all directions. No sooner had he said this than they emerged on a wider alleyway that looked vaguely familiar to Quin. Stepping into the middle of the street, he spotted their mode of transport down to the right, experiencing a sense of relief at the sight.

"There it is!" he exclaimed and started running toward the carriage, Rupert's footsteps following along thunderously as they passed the few people present to witness their escapades.

The sounds of a scuffle and a piercing scream behind him made Quin come to a sudden stop. With a dreadful feeling of having experienced all this before, he turned, only to be greeted by the sight of Rupert slumped in a heap on the pavement. The onlookers were scattering far and wide, while the large figure looming over Rupert's supine form gave Quin a toothy grin.

"Been 'ere before 'aven't we?"

"Oh, I don't know," Quin responded flippantly as Herbert Andrews' guard started smacking his preferred weapon rhythmically against his palm, as seemed to be his habit. "For one thing, we're in London, not Dublin." Quin looked closely at Rupert, trying to see if he was still breathing, but couldn't be sure. "For another, it's broad daylight."

The large man scoffed, glancing up at the brooding sky.

"I suppose you have a point." Quin shrugged. "But you do recall how that incident ended for you, don't you? The head's quite recovered, has it?"

The guard scowled and took a step forward. Quin stood his ground though. Being taken unawares from behind was one thing but fighting the man face to face was quite another. As a trained soldier Quin knew how to defend himself; besides, he wasn't about to leave Rupert lying in the gutter. Although the club he'd been hit with was a formidable weapon, Quin hoped he'd only been knocked unconscious.

The guard's eyes flickered to something behind Quin. He was tempted to turn around but instead kept facing the man in front of him, thinking it might be a trick. A groan from the figure on the ground made Quin's heart leap.

"Rupert!" he exclaimed, not looking away from his adversary.

Rupert gave a mumbled reply that Quin couldn't decipher. Suddenly, though, he sat up, waving his hand feebly. "Sir, sir," he said urgently, pointing behind Quin. Quin looked back at the guard, whose scowl had transformed into a self-satisfied smirk.

With the small hairs on the back of his neck standing on end, Quin turned around.

A man was coming toward him, hands out in front of him. This time, Quin knew that he was carrying a gun.

He also knew that he had come to kill him.

Quin raised his hands, glancing sideways at Rupert's terrified face before looking back at his killer. The man smiled as he pressed the trigger.

"Greetings from Mr Andrews," he said as the shot rang out.

Quin tried to throw himself to the side, but it was too late. A searing pain hit him high in the chest and he was thrown to the ground, landing a few short feet away from his valet. The sound of Rupert's retching filled his ears as his eyes closed, with a distant memory of hoofbeats and pounding footsteps lingering in the back of his mind, until that, too, faded away and only darkness remained.

28.

FIRE WAS BURNING within him, radiating from his shoulder into his fingertips and to the top of his head.

He moaned.

A cool, wet cloth was placed on his brow, providing welcome relief.

"Mother." He opened his eyes to his mother's soft smile and her gentle hand on his cheek.

His vision blurred and her face faded, moving further and further away.

"Don't go," he cried, struggling to reach for her. "Don't go." He dropped heavy limbs, despair at her loss filling his soul as his body started shaking, his vision going dark.

"...wound's infected..."

"...nothing more we can do..."

Quin moved his head away from the intruding sounds and the bright flashes of light that hurt his eyes, willing it all to end.

A cup of water was held to his mouth, an insistent hand at the back of his head urging him to drink as the cool liquid dribbled past cracked lips until he fell back, spent.

A light touch on his temple made his eyes flutter. He turned his head slowly as the caress slid along his neck, down to his sound shoulder and along his arm, pulling away the thin blanket. Something soft tickled his face and he grasped at it feebly with one hand, his fingers slithering through a mass of dark hair and touching smooth, bare flesh. With a flash of white teeth, the coppery body started moving above him, his heart thudding in rhythm to its intimate touch until he gave a long sigh.

His head dropped back onto the pillow, and he drifted off into a deep sleep.

"QUIN?"

"Mmmm."

He felt someone take hold of his hand and opened his eyes a slit.

"Quin!" There was relief in the voice that reached him from a distance.

He looked around slowly, feeling disorientated.

"How do you feel?" A worried, dark-blue look accompanied the question and he blinked, trying to work out where he was.

"You're safe. You're in your father's house."

His father, the baron.

He moved his head from side to side, realisation dawning slowly. He was in London, in one of the guest bedrooms of Wadlow Cottage, not the army encampment that had been in his dreams. His eyes focused on the woman sitting at his bedside, who was not the Indian woman who had nursed him back to health in China, but his wife.

"Alannah." A relieved smile broke out on her face as he said her name.

"The doctor says you should make a full recovery."

He nodded slowly as his memory came back. A London alleyway, the barrel of a gun. He lifted his left hand to his right shoulder, feeling the thick padding high on his chest. He drew down his brows in confusion. Was he in China after all?

"You were shot," Alannah said, leaning over him, her face intent, "the same as before.—Well, not exactly the same. You were luckier this time, the bullet missed anything vital." She stopped talking abruptly, laying a hand gently on his chest.

The bullet missed anything vital.

Quin took a moment to work out what that meant. When he'd been with the army in China, the bullet that had hit him close to the collarbone had nicked a large blood vessel and he'd almost bled to death.

"You were shot lower down this time and the bullet went right through you. The physician says you were lucky, that it was a simple matter to patch you up." Alannah's voice cracked and she compressed her lips as she blinked away tears. "I was so afraid," she whispered as her face crumpled.

Quin squeezed her hand and drew her closer so he could stroke her cheek.

Her eyes searched his face. "What happened, Quin?"

He wrinkled his brows, trying to remember. His heart gave a sudden lurch when he did.

"It was Andrews...wasn't it?" Alannah's voice was flat, without emotions, but the look on her face betrayed her concern.

Quin nodded. They were silent for a minute, each occupied with their own thoughts. Finally, Quin took a deep breath, letting it out slowly.

"It will be alright," he said, stroking the back of Alannah's hand.

She pulled her hand away and shook her head. "That's what we've been telling ourselves this whole time...and now look at you!" She got up from the side of the bed and glared down at him.

"But I'll recover, you said so yourself."

She crossed her arms in front of her chest. "And the next time? Will you be so lucky then?"

"Alannah, we can't think like that."

"Then how should we think? Should we just continue as before, pretending this didn't happen?"

Quin reached a hand toward her, running it up and down her arm. "We cannot live our lives in fear," he said softly. "But we must see justice done."

Alannah pressed her lips together before nodding briefly. She gave a deep sigh and sat back down on the bed.

"I know you're right but..."

"I know."

They looked at each other for a long moment. Slowly, though, something else started niggling at the back of Quin's mind, something he knew was important but that he couldn't quite grasp.

He frowned, making Alannah give him a concerned look. "What is it?"

"Rupert!" he exclaimed suddenly, looking wildly around the room but not seeing his valet anywhere.

"He's asleep next door," Alannah said, and Quin exhaled in relief. "He's had quite a knock on the head. The doctor says he has a concussion and needs to stay in bed for several days, but he thinks he'll be alright."

"Thank heavens! But..." Quin waved a hand at his surroundings. "How did we get here?"

Alannah smiled weakly. "It seems Rupert's young brother followed you when you left his parents' house. When he saw you running away after somebody shot at you, he rushed to fetch his father and brothers."

"Emmett." Quin thought fondly of the small boy. "He saved our lives." For he had no doubt the assassins would have finished the job had they not been interrupted. "And he was following us, you say?"

Alannah nodded but lifted one shoulder in a shrug.

"He was probably hoping to stay with Rupert," Quin said with some amusement, before wrinkling his brow as another memory came to the surface of his mind. "But...I thought I also heard hoofbeats before I blacked out?"

"That was the carriage driver. When he heard the sound of a gunshot and saw you go to ground, he spurred on the horses and raced down the alley toward you.—With the help of Rupert's family he got you and Rupert into the carriage and brought you back here."

"It seems that our rescuers came from far and wide to save us."

"Awake, are you?"

Quin turned toward the opening door, where the baron was coming in, his usual stern expression on his face.

"Father," Quin greeted him cautiously, unsure whether to expect gruff dismissal, scathing ridicule or something in between.

The baron came to a stop at the bedside, looking down at his son with a frown. Quin braced himself.

"Feeling alright now?" he asked brusquely.

"Ah...as well as can be expected I suppose." Quin gave his father a curious look.

"Good." The baron nodded to himself, sitting down on the other side of the bed. "Then we can start getting to the bottom of all of this."

Quin's eyes popped open in surprise. He glanced at Alannah, but she gave a small shake of the head.

"So," Quin's father went on, oblivious to the exchange, "tell me what's going on.—I'd guess this was more than a random act of violence in one of London's back allies." He raised one brow and looked down his nose at Quin.

Feeling himself at a disadvantage, Quin tried to sit up in bed, grunting as a sharp pain shot through his chest and down his arm. Alannah propped up the pillows behind him and soon had him sitting up, sweat popping out on his brow with the effort.

"What makes you think this was no random act of violence?"

The baron gave a dismissive sniff. "Aside from the fact that most ruffians would likely have access to a knife, not a gun—not to mention that nothing was stolen off your person—it hasn't escaped my attention that you've been having some difficulties with a certain Anglo-Irish gentleman of dubious repute who has been spotted around London Town of late."

"Ah…" Quin nodded slowly, rather impressed with his father's quick wit. He had written to the baron following the events in Dublin the previous year, including a brief description of Herbert Andrews' involvement in Martin Doyle's release from gaol. He had barely acknowledged the tale in his reply but had evidently taken note of it, nonetheless.

"I had the misfortune of dealing with the man myself some years back," Quin's father went on, a look of distaste growing on his face, "when I acquired the estate in Ireland."

"Andrews said you bought Glaslearg out from under his nose," Alannah put in, before shutting her mouth abruptly, a soft blush creeping up her cheeks as she looked at her father-in-law through lowered lashes.

The baron snorted. "Hardly," he said and waved his hand. "He was the one who was trying to buy it out from under *my* nose."

"He was?" Quin leaned his head forward intently.

"At first he tried to convince me there was better real-estate to be found elsewhere. When that didn't stop me, he tried a few insults, and when I still refused to budge, he came at me with thinly veiled threats."

"Really?" Quin was fascinated. He had heard none of this before.

"I was determined to buy the place, though," Quin's father resumed his account. "With its ideal location, I had known it would provide a handsome income one day, which was to go toward your upkeep." He glanced at Quin and a small frown grew between his brows. Although his father had meant Glaslearg to be a source of income for Quin, he had never intended for his son to settle down there.

"And so it does," Quin assured him happily, grinning at Alannah, who gave a soft laugh.

The baron compressed his lips. "Yes, well, unfortunately, Herbert Andrews is not a good enemy to have." Quin wondered whether there was in fact such a thing as a good enemy but before he could ask his father continued, "The man has a vast fortune at his disposal and somehow manages to get away with just about anything. Attempts have been made to see him found guilty of *something* but so far, nothing's come of any of it."

"Oh?"

"It's not public knowledge, of course," his father assured him, "but there are those among the peerage who are convinced he's using crooked tactics—mostly those whom he seems to have swindled I suppose." The baron gave a bark of a laugh, startling Quin. There were not many occasions he could remember hearing his father laugh. "And with what he tried to do to me all those years ago, I've been privy to the ongoing enquiries."

"We've found out a few things about Andrews ourselves," Alannah offered tentatively, making the baron give her a quizzical look. "For one thing, it's highly likely he murdered his father to speed up his inheritance."

The baron nodded thoughtfully. "That story has been doing the rounds for years. Nobody's been able to prove it, though. And unfortunately, the Commissioner of Police is most unwilling to authorise a formal investigation into Andrews at all, being the influential man that he is." He wrinkled his brow. "There was one detective who had been looking into Andrews' affairs on the sly, working with those of us who wish to see him behind bars—a young fellow, eager to prove himself and willing to take risks. Last anyone heard of the man, he was sure he'd found something that could put Andrews away, but he disappeared into thin air while on another case some time back. Nobody's been able to find a trace of him, and nobody's gotten close to Andrews since then."

"The detective disappeared?" Quin cocked his head, an idea suddenly occurring to him. "And he was an Englishman?" The baron nodded. "Hm. I wonder..."

"What is it Quin?" Alannah asked, leaning toward him.

"Do you think..." He broke off, trying to gather his thoughts. "Might this detective have followed Andrews to Ireland, do you think?" he asked his father, squeezing Alannah's hand.

"Followed him to Ireland?" The baron pursed his lips. "If he was trailing Andrews, then I suppose it makes sense. The man does spend most of his time in Ireland, after all, although he's got frequent business dealings in London. But the detective was supposedly on another case—unless he only used that as an excuse to get out of town for several days."

"The missing Englishman in Dublin," Quin muttered to himself, making Alannah wrinkle her brow.

"What missing Englishman?" Quin's father asked.

Quin started slowly, trying to explain. "Archie and I had been looking into Andrews' involvement in Martin Doyle's release from Omagh gaol.—He's the man who murdered Alannah's brother." He glanced at Alannah. A brief look of pain flitted across her features. To Quin's surprise his father reached over the bed and squeezed her hand.

"I remember your letter, Quinton. I'm sorry about your brother...Alannah."

Alannah's eyes widened at the informal address. "Thank you...Wilfred." Somewhat hesitantly, the two of them smiled at each other, leaving Quin temporarily dumbfounded.

"Ah...right," he managed at last. "In any case, Andrews himself admitted to Alannah that he was the one who orchestrated Doyle's escape and the deceit of his hanging. Naturally, we wanted to find out who had been hanged in Doyle's stead but hadn't had much luck, with all leads seeming to be dead ends." The baron was listening intently, a small frown between his brows as Quin continued. "Some months ago, Archie found a report of an Englishman who went missing from an inn in Dublin a short time before the hanging." He glanced at Alannah, who was looking curiously at him. "I didn't mention it as not much was made of the man's disappearance. He had an unassuming name and there had been no signs of violence. It looked as though he'd simply left one day, not returning to settle his bill. The latter was the main reason the story made it into the newspaper at all, it seems."

"I see," Quin's father said slowly, "and you think this missing Englishman may have been the detective from the London Police?"

"It's plausible." Quin nodded. "It may have been arranged to look as though the man had simply run off without paying what he owed when in fact he had been abducted and dragged to Omagh gaol."

"There to face the hangman's noose," Alannah concluded.

They were all quiet for a moment, thinking about this new possibility. Finally, the baron spoke up. "It may just make sense. If the detective was indeed tailing Andrews because he thought he was about to uncover something damaging—which he presumably did, to risk being dismissed for disappearing off the force for several days—he would have had to do so in secret, whether here or in Ireland, as he didn't have permission to investigate the man. Not to mention to avoid being noticed by Andrews himself. So presumably, he would have told no-one who he was or what he was doing, or even given anyone his real name."

"Which would explain why his disappearance was barely noticed." Quin met his father's eyes, where he saw a glimmer of interest glinting in the background.

"But how would Andrews have done it?" The baron got up and started pacing the room. "He must have realised he was being followed, of course, but..."

"The idea probably came to him when he noticed the detective looked similar to Martin Doyle." Alannah folded her arms across her chest, a contemplative look on her face. "No doubt he had one of his associates spread the rumour about Doyle's attempt at a royal pardon, someone influential enough to give those in Omagh pause so they would delay the hanging, giving Andrews time to replace Doyle with the troublesome detective."

"And by having the man disappear in Dublin and hanged as Doyle in Omagh," the baron put in, a scowl on his face, "he ensured nobody would suspect a connection. Nor would anyone have realised that an unassuming Englishman who seemingly left a Dublin inn without paying was the missing detective from the London Police Force."

"Plus, the guards at Omagh gaol told me the man who was hanged had been babbling and incoherent on the day of his death," Quin observed. "No doubt the guard who was working for Andrews simply slipped the detective something to prevent him from revealing the truth."

"If this is true, Andrews must have been planning it all for weeks," Alannah murmured, clenching her fists. Quin and the baron gave her a quizzical look. "Think about it. Doyle's hanging was called off more than a month before it was rescheduled, and the detective was in Dublin for only a few days before his death. The rumour of the royal pardon probably coincides with Andrews first coming up with the idea of the false hanging after realising the detective was investigating him.—But he needed time to get the detective to Omagh for his plan to work."

"You're right," Quin agreed. "Which means he may even have lured the unsuspecting detective to Dublin, by leaving some false clues perhaps, knowing the man was likely to follow him if he thought it would ultimately lead to Andrews' arrest."

"Instead, it led to the man's death." Alannah compressed her lips into a tight line. "It would have all worked out for Andrews if Doyle hadn't come to Glaslearg."

Quin's heart gave a sudden lurch. If Doyle hadn't come to Glaslearg, nobody would have realised the wrong man had been hanged—and Kieran would still be alive. "But he did come." He reached out a hand to Alannah. "And no doubt Andrews hoped that he would, to exact his revenge on us for thwarting his plans of marrying you." The baron's brows lifted to his hairline. Evidently, Quin had neglected to tell his father about that particular detail. "And unfortunately for Andrews, Doyle left the two of us alive"—Alannah flinched, no doubt remembering how close the man had come to killing her too—"and we'll soon know enough about the affair to see him arrested."

"This"—Quin's father waved an arm toward Quin's thickly padded chest—"would suggest that Andrews believes you already do!"

"But..."

"You must have stumbled upon something that made him nervous, nervous enough to send someone to kill you."

Alannah's hand squeezed Quin's tightly at the baron's words. Quin stroked the back of her wrist with his thumb. "Well, I'm sure he's wishing now he'd gotten rid of Doyle when he had the chance, instead of setting him free, hoping for him to do his dirty work."

"But he didn't, did he?" The baron sniffed contemptuously before getting up off the bed. "We'll ponder this all a bit later. Right now, you rest," he commanded, looking down his nose at Quin, like he used to do when Quin was a little boy, "while I go and talk to a few of my friends."

Quin suppressed a smile at his father's unaccustomed concern for his welfare. "Yes, sir," he responded meekly and obediently closed his eyes.

QUIN DID IN fact fall asleep after his father left. Alannah helped make him comfortable, and he found he was exhausted, the events of the day draining his energy. It was not a restful sleep, though, the pain in his shoulder keeping him tossing and turning while his mind mulled over all that had happened. Repeatedly, he would feel himself drift off, only to be jostled back to wakefulness by brief stabs of remembrance—the feeling of being trapped in the narrow street, the look of hatred on the assassin's face, the sight of the barrel of the gun trained on him—all intertwined with long-suppressed memories of the war in China.

At some point in the night, he woke up with a start, drenched in sweat. He tried to get up, crying out as he jarred his shoulder painfully.

A hand on his chest pressed him back onto the mattress. "Lie still." He opened his eyes, meeting those of his father glaring down at him in the dim light. "Do you want to start bleeding again?"

He shook his head wordlessly, lifting a hand to gently probe his shoulder.

"How do you feel?" the baron asked gruffly.

"Better than the last time I was shot." Quin snorted, remembering how he'd hovered near death after that encounter, when the doctors had all but given up on him. He had been so far gone he'd hallucinated, seeing his dead mother. The thought made his heart give a painful thump and he turned his head away.

"But you'll be alright." It was a statement not a question, which made Quin give his father a curious look.

"I suppose." One never knew when a wound might fester, swelling and oozing, sapping the life out of some poor sod who thought he'd gotten away with a minor injury. Quin shook his head to rid himself of such morbid thoughts.

"Good." Quin turned back to his father, who was looking grim. "Your wife is too young to be widowed."

Quin's brows shot up in surprise. "So you do care." The comment had escaped his lips before he'd made a conscious effort to speak, and he quickly clamped his mouth shut.

The baron narrowed his eyes and pursed his lips. "Yes, Quinton, I do care."

"Well you have a curious way of showing it," Quin mumbled under his breath.

His father inhaled sharply through his nose. "No matter what our differences may be, you are my only son and heir."

"And I shall be sure to take good care of my inheritance when the day comes." Quin couldn't hide the scorn in his voice. For a brief moment he had thought his father actually cared about *him*, as a person, not just the heir to his barony.

"You are not just an heir to me...you are my *son*." His father emphasised the last word with a fierce scowl as he leaned over Quin.

Quin struggled to lift himself off the pillows, wanting to at least be seated during what looked to be developing into a confrontation that was some years overdue.

"If you cared so much about me as your son, as you say, you might have shown a little more support for my decision to stay in Ireland and marry the woman I love!" The baron opened his mouth to speak but Quin continued ruthlessly as all the injustices he had experienced at the hands of his father over the years came bubbling to the surface. "It was my decision to make, not yours! And the way you treated me when I came back from China"—Quin shook his head—"as if I had dishonoured generations of Williamses by leaving the blasted army."

The baron's nostrils flared. No doubt he was deeply offended at Quin's sacrilegious reference to the British Army. "I had expectations," he said in clipped tones, jerkily shrugging his shoulders.

"And I had expectations of how a father should treat his son!"

An oppressive silence descended upon the room as father and son glared at each other. Finally, Quin looked away.

"I was never going to be good enough for you..."

"You *are* good enough!" The baron started shaking Quin's shoulders but stopped abruptly. He looked down at Quin's chest and removed his hands, clasping them together on his lap. "You are good enough," he repeated in a calmer tone. "I just thought...I expected you to..."

"To follow in your footsteps and become a major in the army," Quin suggested with a raised brow. "Or better yet, a general." He snorted, thinking if anything could have satisfied his father, *that* would have been it.

"That would have been nice." One side of the baron's mouth twitched.

"It wasn't what I wanted."

"I know that now."

"Then why did you...?" Quin shook his head, remembering how his father had berated him day after day for resigning his commission.

A look of pain crossed the older man's face and he got up abruptly, turning away from the bed. "Your mother had died," he said softly.

"I know. Your note..."

"That note was appalling," his father cut him off as he turned back toward the bed. Quin raised his brows, surprised the baron would admit as much. The one-line correspondence he had sent informing Quin of his mother's death had nearly broken her son's heart.

"I'm not good with words, as you know." The baron sat down on the side of the bed once more. "Your mother was always better at that."

"Undoubtedly true, still..."

"I was grieving." Quin's father gave him a long look filled with despair. "I could scarcely force myself to write the little I did. Putting it into words made it all real. She was never coming back." Quin swallowed heavily, understanding for the first time what may have led his father to act as he had.

"And you were angry." The baron nodded, his eyes not meeting Quin's. "And you took it out on me."

His father's shoulders lifted in an awkward shrug, a look of regret flitting across his features. Ignoring the pain in his chest, Quin leaned forward and wrapped his arms around his father. For a moment, the baron sat frozen, taken by surprise, but slowly, he raised his own arms and the pressure of his embrace increased. Soon, though, he thumped Quin on the back and came away without looking at him, seeming embarrassed at the rare show of affection. He cleared his throat and started getting up. Quin stopped him with a hand on his arm.

"How did she die?" he asked, looking down at the clean white sheets.

"She died in her sleep. I told you."

Quin raised his eyes, but his father would not meet his. "I don't believe that!" He shook his head insistently, as confused now as he had been then at his mother's sudden loss. "She was still young, she was healthy."

The baron compressed his lips and studied his clasped hands. Finally, he sighed and looked up. "In the years before she died, your mother was not well.—A melancholy had overcome her."

Quin wrinkled his brow in confusion. "But..."

"She worried about you, away with the army—she knew well what war was like." His father gave him a long look. "And she started obsessing about all those she couldn't help. The orphans, the poor, all those in need..." The baron lifted one shoulder dejectedly.

Quin stared unseeing at the wall. "I never knew."

"She hid well what was on her heart."

Silence descended on the room as Quin contemplated what his father had told him. His mother had always seemed like a ray of sunshine to him—especially in contrast to her husband's gruff demeanour. It was difficult for Quin to reconcile the mother he had known with the image his father was describing.

"But..." Quin still didn't understand what this all meant.

The baron clasped Quin's hand, which gave him a turn at its unexpectedness. "Her thoughts started keeping her up at night," the baron said slowly. "She sought a sleeping draught to help her. But...one morning...she just didn't wake up."

Quin's heart leapt into his throat at his father's words, and he swallowed heavily as bile followed. "You mean..."

The baron nodded wordlessly. "I didn't want to tell you."

"And this started when I left to join the army?" Quin asked softly.

"You mustn't blame yourself."

"But..."

"No, Quinton"—his father shook his head—"if anyone should blame himself it should be me. If I had behaved differently...been a different man...a better husband..."

Quin lapsed into silence once more, stunned by his father's revelations. "Perhaps it wasn't anybody's fault," he finally said, squeezing his father's arm, making him look up.

"Perhaps you're right." The baron's features softened briefly, and he patted Quin's hand. "Your mother was too goodhearted for this cruel world. She couldn't bear to see anyone suffering. Knowing she couldn't help everyone broke her heart."

"As did knowing her son was off slaughtering men in a far-distant land."

"As did knowing her husband was part of a war that killed and maimed thousands."

The two of them looked at each other for a long moment, the thoughts that flickered across his father's face mirroring Quin's own as he contemplated his military career and the lives he had taken—justified or not. Finally, the baron sighed, looking toward the window. The curtains were drawn but Quin could hear the sound of raindrops spattering against the glass.

His father gave a snort. "Perhaps it was simply England's glorious weather.—That doesn't tend to do anyone's mood any good." He got up and put a hand on Quin's uninjured shoulder. "I shall send someone else to come and sit with you." He gave Quin a pat and turned toward the door.

"You were a good husband to her," Quin called after him. The baron stopped and turned back slowly, his jaws clenched. Quin's throat constricted seeing the tears that had sprung up in his father's eyes.

"Thank you, son." His mouth quirked into a brief smile before he left the room.

Quin looked after him for a long time, contemplating all he had learnt. On the one hand he felt some relief at finally having some answers about his mother's unexpected death. On the other, knowing what had killed her was difficult to bear. He wondered whether his father had hunted down the physician or herb woman who had given his mother the sleeping aid or whether he'd accepted her death as a tragic accident. The baron hadn't said anything about it and Quin was loathe to bring it up again—it had clearly been difficult enough for his father to talk about the matter at all.

Quin's heart constricted painfully at the thought, imagining himself watching Alannah slip ever deeper into despair, unable to help her. With a pang he realised that he didn't have to imagine it at all, he knew what it was like. After her brother had been murdered and she had barely escaped with her life after Martin Doyle's reappearance, Alannah had withdrawn from Quin, consumed every waking moment with thoughts of despondency and guilt over her own survival, unable to break away from her gloom. Quin had himself been plagued with remorse over his inability to protect her and Kieran, and only with great difficulty had they been able to find their way back to each other and she back to life.

He sighed, wishing his mother had been able to do the same.

29.

WHEN HE WOKE up the following day, Quin felt ravenously hungry. Assuming this to be a sign of his impending recovery, he carefully flexed his shoulder to take stock. The site of the bullet wound still hurt, of course, but the pain no longer radiated all the way into his fingertips, nor did he appear to have a fever. Moving very slowly, he managed to sit up and swing his legs out of bed. A small bell had been placed on the bedside table, but he was alone.

Remembering what Alannah had said about Rupert, Quin slowly got up, standing by the side of the bed for a moment before shuffling his way to the adjoining room. The room was dim, with the curtain's drawn and only a small lamp lit next to the bed, but as Quin walked through the door, Rupert's eyes popped open.

"Sir!" He looked around wildly before clutching his head.

"Don't fret, Rupert," Quin said, patting his valet on the arm. "I've just come to see how you are."

"How *I* am? But *you're* the one who's been *shot*!"

"And I'd seem to have gotten the better end of the deal," Quin responded drily, observing Rupert's slightly cross-eyed look. "How do you feel?"

"I...ah..." Quin lifted one brow, not interested in the sugar-coated version Rupert was clearly thinking of concocting. "Well, I do feel right strange, I do," the young man admitted at last. "My brain's a bit...foggy and I can't seem to recall what happened, only what I've been told."

Quin nodded sympathetically, which seemed to encourage his valet, for he went on. "And I can't stand the bleeding light!" He gestured toward the oil lamp. "I'd have blown out this one if I didn't need it to find the piss pot, wambly as I am. Not that I use it regular like. Getting up makes the room spin, and me want to puke. Ah...I mean..."

"That's quite alright, Rupert. You needn't be delicate on my account. Now, you are to stay in bed and rest."

"But..." Rupert waved a hand feebly at his employer.

"That's an order!" Quin said sternly before softening up. "Besides, I managed to take reasonably good care of myself while you were away."

Rupert looked Quin up and down, pursing his lips. Quin laughed. Clearly, his current state was not a good indicator of his abilities.

"I shall be very pleased to have you back to your usual duties once you are quite recovered," he said, making Rupert's eyes light up. "But the doctor will tell us when that time has arrived."

"There you are!"

Quin and Rupert looked toward Alannah, who had just come through the door, looking rather cross.

"Why didn't you call someone to help you?" she demanded, lifting her chin toward Quin.

"I'm quite all right," he assured her with a shrug of his sound shoulder.

"Yes, I can see that." She eyed him with the exact same sceptical look Rupert had just been bestowing upon him. Quin grinned, making a reluctant smile break out on her face.

"And how are you feeling?" she asked Rupert as she came to stand next to Quin by the bed. Quin sought her hand, giving it a light squeeze while the valet repeated what he'd told Quin—in a slightly more proper manner.

"There's some broth and freshly baked bread for the two of you, if you're feeling up to it," Alannah said once Rupert had finished his account.

Rupert went slightly green, pulling a face and shrinking back onto his pillows. Quin, on the other hand, felt his mouth watering at the mention of food. His stomach rumbled loudly, making Alannah laugh.

"I see I've come just in time."

They bid Rupert farewell and Alannah helped Quin return to his room, where she started leading him back toward the bed.

"I'm sure I'm well enough to dress and go down to the dining room," he objected, but she shook her head and gave him a stern look.

"I'll have one of the maids bring your supper up for you on a tray."

"Supper?" Quin goggled at her before glancing out the window. "How long have I been asleep?"

"After you finally settled down well after midnight you've been sleeping for most of the day."

"Huh." Although he was quite surprised to hear of it, Quin had to admit the lengthy rest had done him good. "That does explain why I'm so hungry," he said as his stomach gave another loud growl.

He gratefully accepted the tray that was brought up for him a few minutes later, hardly able to wait for the steaming broth to cool a little before devouring every last drop.

Finishing his third helping some time later, Quin sighed in contentment. Looking at Alannah, though, he saw that she was deep in thought.

"Are you alright?" he asked, reaching out a hand toward her.

She nodded. "I was just wondering...what all of this means for us and...how much longer we may have to stay here now."

"Ah." Quin wrinkled his brow. "Well, Andrews' intentions aside, I see no reason why we can't be on our way as soon as Rupert has recovered. I'll likely have to give a statement to the police in the next few days but beyond that...there's not much need for us to stay any longer." He shrugged. "My father said he'd make some enquiries of his own, but he certainly doesn't need my help to do so."

"It's not that I haven't enjoyed my stay here," Alannah assured him, making him smile and pat her hand. "But I do hope Rupert will soon be well enough to travel."

"Me too. The poor boy is in a sadder state than I am. But hopefully he'll have passed the worst of it by next week.—After all, we must be on our way soon if we still want to make it to the wedding," he added, the two of them having planned their return trip to coincide with the date of Ollie's nuptials.

"Oh yes! I'm very much looking forward to the wedding," Alannah said, "especially after all off this!—But I will admit I'm also very much looking forward to returning to Glaslearg. Not just to see how everyone is faring but...there's something comforting about being in one's own home. Don't you think?"

Quin reached out a hand to stroke her cheek. "There is, particularly with you in it!" He pulled her closer with his sound arm and kissed her on the mouth, stroking the nape of her neck. She fell against his chest, making him take in a sharp breath.

She pulled back immediately. "I'm sorry! I wasn't thinking!"

"Just help me lie down."

She looked cynically at him down her nose.

"Unless of course *you'd* rather be the one to lie down."

She burst out laughing, getting up and removing the pillows that were propped up behind him. "I see you're feeling better."

Once he was lying comfortably, she carefully lowered herself next to him, nestling her head on his good side. Quin gently ran his hand over her hair, and they were silent for several minutes.

"I'm very glad Andrews' man wasn't a better shot," Alannah said finally, a catch in her voice as she caressed his neck.

"So am I," he agreed with feeling, turning to place a kiss on her forehead.

His earlier ardour had cooled as tiredness overcame him once more, and he was quite content to lie there, holding Alannah close, ignoring—for the time being—all that troubled him.

"Stay with me tonight," he whispered as his eyes started closing.

Her soft response fluttered into his consciousness as he felt himself drift off to sleep.

"Always."

30.

"MRS JONES, EMMETT, how lovely to see you again."

Quin bowed, smiling broadly as the butler who'd admitted the pair stepped to one side, solemnly watching the scene.

It was four days after the attempt on Quin's life and he had finally been allowed downstairs. Alannah had been insisting that he confine his exercise to his sick room, making him spend the majority of his time in bed. With the baron of the same intractable opinion, Quin hadn't had much choice but to do as they said and was thrilled at the small amount of freedom he'd now been granted—despite the fact that said freedom had included the unpleasant task of giving his statement to the police. Quin's father had accompanied him to the interview in the reception room that morning, although Quin had otherwise not seen much of the baron since he'd spent the night at his bedside.

Soon after the detective had left, the baron had disappeared once more, looking preoccupied. He had, however, seen to it that Rupert's mother and young brother were brought to Wadlow Cottage that afternoon—by his own insistence, no less—and Quin and Alannah had come downstairs to greet them.

Mrs Jones curtsied, her cheeks pink with excitement, while Emmett looked around the entrance hall with big eyes.

"Emmett," his mother hissed out of the side of her mouth, before glancing at the stone-faced Haughley, who affected not to notice. Emmett hunched his shoulders and gave her a guilty look. She narrowed her eyes at him, and he quickly doffed his hat and bent into something resembling a bow.

"Welcome," Alannah said. "I am pleased to meet you, Mrs Jones, and I'm very pleased to be able to thank you in person for having saved my husband's life, Emmett." She smiled at the boy, who stood up straight and puffed out his chest.

" 'Twas nothin'," he replied with a modest shrug of one shoulder, although his brightly gleaming eyes gave away how deeply pleased he was at the praise.

"I do hope ye're quite recovered, sir?" Mrs Jones asked Quin anxiously, looking him up and down.

"I am, thank you," Quin assured her before returning to the reason for their visit. "Shall we go upstairs? I'm sure you'd like to see Rupert straightaway."

Mrs Jones nodded eagerly. "Oh, yes, sir!"

Quin led them toward the wide staircase, Emmett following close behind him.

"Is that the room with the shanticlear with two-hundred candles?" the boy asked in a loud whisper as they passed the double doors that led to the large hall off the foyer.

Mrs Jones threw her son a horrified look, but Quin smiled indulgently at him.

"It is," he said. "Would you like to see it?"

Emmett's head bobbed up and down madly. With a chuckle, Quin beckoned him into the room, followed by Alannah and Mrs Jones.

"There it is," he said, pointing toward the large chandelier suspended from the ceiling. "As you can see, it's not currently lit."

This seemed not to bother Emmett in the slightest and his mouth dropped open as he stared upwards, while his mother looked around the opulent hall wearing a similar expression of awe. The family's entire house would fit easily into this single room, and Quin doubted either of them had ever set foot in a mansion before.

Once Quin had shown Emmett the mechanism that allowed the footmen to lower and raise the chandelier when it was to be in use, the boy turned his attention toward the large fireplace.

"Who's that?" he asked, pointing at the sizeable portrait that hung above the mantel, showing a very stern-looking gentleman in military attire, sporting a short grey wig curled up at the sides.

"That, young Emmett, is my great grandfather, the first Baron of Wadlow."

"The *first*? You mean...there weren't one before 'im?" Emmett's eyes were wide as he studied the painting.

"That is correct," Quin said, smiling at Alannah and Mrs Jones, who had come to stand next to him and Emmett. "Great grandfather Williams was awarded the tile by King George for his service to His Majesty on the battlefield."

"Ooh!—But why's he called the Baron of Wadlow? I thought we was still in London." Emmett's small nose crinkled up in confusion as he looked at Quin.

"And so we are," Quin agreed, "although this house is called Wadlow Cottage.—And the Baron of Wadlow is so named because of the family seat, Wadlow Manor, which is situated in Surrey."

"Is Wadlow Manor as big as *this*?"

"Even bigger."

Emmett gave Quin a highly sceptical look. "Now ye're havin' me on, Mr Williams. If it was bigger 'an this it'd be...why it'd be a...a palace." The boy's eyes shone at the thought of such grandeur, making Quin laugh.

"That's enough, Emmett," Mrs Jones said before the boy could say anything else. "I'll 'ave ye thank Mr Williams for lettin' ye see his lovely home."

"Thank you, Mr Williams," Emmett repeated dutifully.

"You're quite welcome.—Now, shall we go upstairs to see Rupert?"

Both Joneses nodded eagerly and so Quin led his guests back toward the staircase and up to Rupert's room.

Mrs Jones gave a cry at sight of her son, rushing to his side and throwing her arms around him, while Emmett crawled onto the bed and nestled close to his brother's side. Rupert's face split into a wide grin, making him look better than he had for days—despite the fact that he was still rather green around the edges and tended to squint at bright lights.

"We'll give you some privacy," Quin said as Mrs Jones and Emmett launched into a barrage of questions for Rupert, having forgotten their hosts in their joy at being reunited.

He closed the door with a smile, turning toward Alannah.

"Shall we have some tea?" she suggested, one brow raised.

He nodded, and she soon had them comfortably seated beside a laden tea tray in the small drawing room, having seen to it that Rupert's room was similarly supplied. They spent a pleasant hour together before deciding to look back in on the Joneses.

Quin's knock was answered speedily, and he and Alannah were greeted happily by the family.

"I must be thankin' ye again for takin' such good care o' my Rupert," Mrs Jones gushed for the third time in as many minutes.

"Nonsense," Quick objected, waving a hand. "If he hadn't pushed me out of the way of the first gunshot, he'd never have been hit over the head himself and wouldn't now be lying here.—But of course, neither of us would be here at all if it weren't for the real hero of the day, young Emmett."

Quin smiled fondly at the boy, who grinned back impishly.

"A hero he may be, but he also snuck out o' the house wi'out permission." Mrs Jones gave her youngest a stern look. "He might 'a been killed 'imself!"

Emmett's face drooped at his mother's scolding, and he folded his hands in his lap. Rupert patted his brother on the back. "Aw, mum, Mr Williams is right, Emmett's a hero, he is. You should be glad he followed us!"

Mrs Jones sighed. "I suppose ye're right, Rupert." Turning toward Emmett, she gently stroked his head. "But ye did give me and yer dad a right fright, tearin' int' the house yellin' about guns and murderers when we'd thought ye safe upstairs wi' yer sisters."

"Why did you follow us?" Quin asked, although he thought he could guess.

Emmett blushed as everyone looked at him expectantly. "I...ah..." His mouth snapped shut and he glanced sideways at his mother.

"Out with it!" she commanded.

"Well, I wanted t'...I mean...I thought I could..." Mrs Jones narrowed her eyes. "I thought I could hide away and follow Mr Williams and Rupert t' Ireland," he burst out, looking down into his lap.

His mother's lower lip trembled. "And leave me? Wi'out even sayin' goodbye?"

"I'm that sorry, mum, it wasn't nothin' against ye." Looking crestfallen, Emmett came to stand in front of her. She pulled him into her arms and stroked his skinny back.

"It's always the little ones that worry ye the most," she said, not addressing anyone in particular. She sniffed a few times, before giving a great sigh.

A knock at the door made Emmett wriggle out of his mother's arms and stand next to her by the bed. The baron strode into the room, looking rather pleased with himself, making Quin wonder what he'd been up to all afternoon.

"Father, you're just in time to meet the hero of the hour, and his mother." Quin smiled, inclining his head toward the Joneses.

Mrs Jones gasped. "Sir, it's an honour t' meet ye, sir," she said breathily, dropping into a curtsy.

Emmett was looking at the baron with big eyes, seeming to have frozen to the spot. "Your majesty," he suddenly blurted out, folding at the waist until his forehead almost touched his knees.

The baron's lips twitched in amusement. "I thank you for your esteem, young man, but I am neither a continental king nor yet the Queen."

Emmett unfolded, his face and ears glowing bright red. He looked uncomfortably around the room, clearly wishing himself to be someplace else. His embarrassment abated as further introductions were made and the baron expressed his gratitude toward the Joneses for their role in saving Quin's life. As conversation continued between the adults, Emmett went to sit on the bed next to Rupert, still looking flustered.

"Oh, Rupert, I must be the biggest dolt in all the world," Quin overheard Emmett say in a low voice. "I know he ain't no king, but I couldn't think was there a special way t' greet a baron.—I panicked!"

"Don't worry yourself about it," Rupert responded. "The baron's a kindly fellow.—Don't let his grim face fool you!"

Quin smiled at the exchange, catching Alannah's eye. She gave him a curious look but soon turned back toward his father and Mrs Jones.

When it was time for Emmett and his mother to return to their home a little later, the baron pressed a small purse into Mrs Jones' hand.

"I can't take that, sir," she objected, trying to give it back. "Yer son 'as already been very generous."

"And my son wouldn't be here if it weren't for yours," the baron said, shaking his head. "It's the least I can do."

Mrs Jones looked uncertainly toward Quin, who nodded encouragingly.

"I thank ye, sir," she said with feeling before turning toward the bed to bid Rupert farewell.

Quin accompanied the rest of the party downstairs to see Mrs Jones and Emmett on their way. Waving after them as the baron's carriage rattled down the drive, he suddenly started feeling rather tired. Having been confined to his bed for some time, the day's activities had taken it out of him.

Back inside the house, his father disappeared into his study and Quin gratefully made his way to his former room—determined to spend the last few nights in London there with his wife. Alannah had seen to it that supper was brought up for the two of them and they shared a quiet meal in the sitting room. Quin chewed his food slowly, having to suppress a yawn every few minutes.

"Right, you're going to bed," Alannah declared once they'd finished eating.

"Yes, ma'am." Quin let her tow him into the adjoining room and help him change his clothes.

Having removed his shirt, Alannah gently ran a hand along the bandage around his chest. "How do you feel?" she asked, a slight frown on her face.

Quin flexed his arms and shoulders. "All in all, quite well." She raised one brow. "The pain is quite localised to the site of the gunshot wound by now so…I'd say I'm almost back to normal." He grinned, making her smile at him.

She handed him his nightshirt and soon had him tucked into bed while a maid bustled about, banking the fire and drawing the curtains.

Just then, the baron came in. He waited for the maid to leave, before sitting down at the foot of the bed. "I've been talking to some of my acquaintances over the last few days," he began without preliminaries, "and I just may have come to the bottom of all of this."

Quin's heart gave a lurch, his tiredness evaporating all at once.

"What do you mean?" he demanded as Alannah came to stand closer to him, a look of confusion on her face.

The baron wrinkled his brow. "You told me the other day that you crossed paths with Leventhorpe in town."

"Yes. What of it?"

"I happen to have discovered that the Assistant Police Commissioner finds it rather difficult living within his means, having grown up with a good deal more money than presently at his disposal.—And turning to gambling to drown his sorrows has only made matters worse."

"Oh?" While that was all very fascinating, Quin couldn't see what it had to do with his current predicament.

"I have reason to believe Andrews is paying him off."

"Of course," Quin exclaimed, everything suddenly making sense. "Andrews pays Leventhorpe to keep the police from investigating him."

"No doubt the Commissioner himself would have been better, but Andrews probably couldn't find any dirt on him. So the assistant had to do."

"I thought Leventhorpe has been Assistant Commissioner for only a few years," Alannah said. "But I imagine Andrews has been bribing and blackmailing all sorts of people for much longer."

"I'm quite sure of that," the baron said drily. "I very much doubt there was ever a time Herbert Andrews was entirely wholesome."

Quin snorted. "I would agree with that! But there may also be a particular reason for Andrews targeting the newly appointed Leventhorpe: the creation of the Detective Branch in '42."

The baron nodded. "My thinking precisely." He looked pleased with the fact that his son had managed to come to the same conclusion.

"I'm not sure I understand," Alannah said, looking from Quin to his father and back again.

"In 1842," Quin began, "the London Police brought into being the first division of police officers specifically tasked with solving serious crimes by tracking and gathering evidence against persons suspected of having committed such crimes."

"Although cases of murder, forgery and the like were solved before, of course," the baron took up the narrative, "the process has become far more efficient with the dedicated detectives at work."

"Which makes it all the more difficult for someone like Herbert Andrews to get away with his criminal activities," Alannah concluded.

"Exactly," Quin agreed, squeezing her hand.

"Which means," the baron put in, "that Andrews wanted to make sure he wouldn't be investigated in the first place."

Quin scowled. "And what better way to do that than by paying the Assistant Commissioner to prevent the detectives from getting the necessary permission to perform such an investigation?"

"Quite." The baron sniffed. "In any case, it is my assumption that Andrews concluded from your meeting with Leventhorpe that you knew of their arrangement, which led him to believe you had now become too great a threat to ignore."

Quin nodded. "I suppose for somebody watching the meeting from afar it might have appeared so."

"And you did say you believed Andrews was having you followed that day."

Quin's father raised his brows at Alannah's observation.

"We suspect his spies have had their eyes on us for quite some time," Quin explained, waving his hand.

"Hmph." The baron got up from the foot of the bed and came to stand on Quin's other side. "The thing to do now is to go after Leventhorpe and get him to crack. Once he does Andrews will be done for." Quin opened his mouth, but his father raised his hand. "Before you ask whether I think I can arrange that, the answer is yes, certainly. Not only do I personally know the Police Commissioner himself, but I am also acquainted with several judges and members of parliament, not to mention the numerous members of the gentry who have been waiting for just such an opportunity. With such an army at my back and with all you have told me of Andrews' dealings, not to mention your own statement to the police regarding the man's involvement in your shooting, it will be simplicity itself to tidy the man neatly away at last.—Now," he continued, "I shall retire. I suggest you do the same."

And with that, he turned on his heel and was gone.

Quin looked after him for a moment, deep in thought.

"So it all came down to bad luck."

"What?" Quin wrinkled his brows.

"If Leventhorpe hadn't happened to come across you at the tavern," Alannah said, "and Andrews' spy hadn't happened to see you, Andrews never would have sent one of his thugs to shoot you."

Quin shrugged his good shoulder. "He'd have done it sooner or later. Just because he had some qualms about snuffing out a baron's son doesn't mean he'd have tolerated me indefinitely." Alannah compressed her lips at his indelicate word choice, but he continued. "He knew we were asking questions about him. It was only a matter of time before we got too close—even if it was by accident." He patted Alannah's hand. "But with everything we know now, my father will see to it that the man is tidied away in no time, as he promised."

31.

"HERBERT ANDREWS HAS been arrested!"

"What?" I dropped the slice of toast I'd been holding, scattering crumbs across the breakfast table.

"So soon?" Quin turned toward his father, a look of surprise on his face. "It's only been two days!"

The baron puffed out his chest. "I told you it would be a simple matter." He sat down and poured himself a cup of tea, Quin and I watching him impatiently as we waited for further details. "As soon as I informed the Police Commissioner of my suspicions regarding Leventhorpe," he said at last, reaching for the toast, "the man was questioned. As I predicted, he was only too eager to cooperate once his dealings with Andrews became known—although he did reportedly weep pitifully at the uncovering of his treachery." He smirked as he briskly spread the toast with butter. "Naturally, Leventhorpe's career is at an end, but he may yet hope to escape the hangman's noose."

"And Andrews?" I asked, glancing at Quin. He squeezed my hand briefly before turning back toward his father.

"He was arrested in the early hours of this morning," the baron said, a self-satisfied look blooming on his face. "I'm told he was apprehended in the process of an attempted escape to Ireland.—Why he thought he would have evaded prosecution there I cannot say, but by all accounts, the man ranted and raged when the police came upon him at his residence, insisting he was far too important a person to be thus treated." He gave a bark of a laugh. "Despite his best efforts, he has been neatly deposited in prison to await trial."

Quin snorted. "Where is he being held?"

"The Queen's Prison," the baron answered between mouthfuls of toast.

"The Queen's Prison?" Quin frowned. "But that's a debtor's prison."

"I suppose Andrews paid someone to ensure he landed in the least wretched prison in London—at least for the time being."

"And no doubt he'll also be able to buy himself a fine private room and other niceties to make his stay more pleasant."

The baron waved his hand. "Such privileges aren't as easy to come by as they once were. Besides," he added dryly, "none of that will do the man any good. With all the evidence coming to light against him, Andrews is more than likely to stay locked up for the rest of his days.—Or to meet a premature end."

My heart gave a sudden lurch at the baron's words. As much as I wanted to see Herbert Andrews punished for all he'd done to us, the thought of him dangling from the end of a rope made me feel rather uneasy.

"How long until the trial?" Quin asked.

His father shrugged. "A few weeks I'd suppose.—The prosecution will want some time to prepare the case and Andrews will want time to buy himself an army of lawyers, being in the privileged position to be able to pay for his defence."

I wrinkled my forehead, looking from father to son. "Will Quin have to testify?"

The baron pursed his lips. "I find it doubtful. Although it was Andrews who sent his man after Quin, it wasn't Andrews himself who pulled the trigger. The prosecution will want witnesses who can directly attest to Andrews' misdeeds, such as Leventhorpe, and various other associates they are even now trying to turn against him." He nodded toward Quin. "Your statement to the police should be sufficient."

"So we can go home?" I asked, feeling a lightening of my spirits as I contemplated our return to Glaslearg—without the threat of Herbert Andrews hanging over our heads.

Quin nodded slowly, but with a distracted look on his face. "I think I'll pay Andrews a visit first," he said after a moment.

I frowned but was hardly surprised at Quin's declaration. With the man having sent someone to kill him, Quin no doubt had a few things to say to Herbert Andrews. He looked at me and raised one brow, but I shook my head. I had no desire to step foot in a filthy London prison, much less to lay eyes on Herbert Andrews ever again. I would trust the criminal justice system to see the man received his just deserts and get on with my life, finally able to close the door on Herbert Andrews and Martin Doyle once and for all.

THE ROOM QUIN was led to was small and grey, with a single narrow window high on the wall. Although the Queen's Prison was reportedly more spacious and better run than most others around London, the gloomy interior made it impossible to forget that it *was* a prison, nonetheless. And while inmates had once been able to enjoy amenities such as a coffeehouse, shops and even a marketplace, such luxuries had been dispensed with by parliament of late, in response to society's growing belief that the rising crime rates could only be countered by prisoner reform—this to be achieved through enforced isolation and silence, and otherwise harsh conditions for said prisoners.

Quin took off his hat and let out his breath slowly as he waited for Herbert Andrews to be brought in to see him, remembering suddenly how he and Alannah had waited in a similar room for her brother before his trial in Omagh. But while that meeting had been accompanied by distinctly mixed feelings, Quin felt nothing but satisfaction now as he thought of Andrews being confined to this dingy building for the rest of his life.

He wondered briefly whether such thinking made him cold-hearted or just but dismissed the thought when the door opened and the man himself came in. Quin eyed him warily as he sat down at the small table that stood in the centre of the room, placing his hat on the surface. Although Andrews carried himself as always, with his head held high and an arrogant set to his shoulders, his eyes were blood-shot and red-rimmed and he'd lost his cravat, with the rest of his clothing scuffed and grimy, indicating he'd had a rough few days. That his circumstances had changed was further revealed by the guard who walked close behind him, who was not his loyal servant but a prison officer. The man gave Quin a brief nod before shoving Andrews onto the chair opposite Quin and standing by the door with his arms crossed.

Andrews sniffed contemptuously as he adjusted his position on the chair, before looking across at Quin. "Have you come to gloat, Mr Williams?"

"I suppose I have, Mr Andrews," Quin said, unable to suppress the smile blooming on his face.

Andrews pursed his lips. "You needn't bother. I shan't be here much longer."

"Oh? Are you being transferred?"

"I am not," Andrews responded shortly, glaring at Quin. "I shall, however, soon be released when these ludicrous charges have been dropped."

Quin slowly shook his head. "I don't think so, Mr Andrews. I'm afraid you'll have to resign yourself to your new circumstances." He waved his hand around the small, dreary room and the guard standing watch.

"Ha!" Andrews leaned across the table toward Quin, pointing his finger at him for emphasis. "I shall do no such thing! Even if there were to be a trial, I have money…"

"And money rules the world, as you say," Quin interrupted, sitting back and crossing his arms. "Unfortunately for you, though, even your substantial fortune can't save you this time."

Andrews narrowed his eyes. "Of course it can!"

"And how will you talk your way out of all the evidence against you? If nothing else, have you forgotten you yourself admitted to my wife and me that you arranged the escape of a condemned murderer and traitor?"

Andrews' nostrils flared in anger, but Quin could see a rapid pulse beating at the base of the man's throat—beneath his outwardly bravado, there was a distinct sense of panic.

"I'll deny it and you can't prove it." Andrews lifted one shoulder in a jerk of dismissal. "Besides, nobody would believe you anyway should you start spouting such absurdities."

"Do you think so?" Quin cocked his head and wrinkled his brow. "The police officer whom I told of the matter was very interested to hear of it.—I dare say the son of a baron is granted some degree of credence based solely on his birth, no matter what another man's personal opinion of his character may be." Andrews' scowl made it clear what *his* personal opinion of Quin's character was. "And you've been quite aware of my noble birth from the start, haven't you?"

"That makes you no better than me!" Andrews snapped.

"Of course not," Quin agreed. "But it *was* something of an obstacle when trying to get rid of me, wasn't it?" He leaned toward Andrews, holding his eyes. "That was a mistake, you know."

"I'm sure I don't know what you're talking about," Andrews said, dropping his gaze.

"Is that so? Then you might find it interesting to learn that the assassin who came after me not too long ago was kind enough to give me *your* regards before shooting me."

Quin saw Andrews' eyes widen ever so slightly in response to this statement, although he didn't move otherwise. Clearly, he hadn't been aware of the man's parting words to Quin.

"Now if you hadn't tried to have me killed," Quin continued casually, "then my father never would have gotten involved, and we'd never have uncovered your various misdeeds as speedily as we did."

Based on the expression growing on Andrews' face, he was clearly wishing his attempt on Quin's life had been successful.

Quin smirked. "Of course, you could have avoided any interference from us in the first place simply by letting Martin Doyle hang for his crimes.—Didn't your father ever tell you not to stick your nose into other people's affairs?" Quin raised his brows, before touching his fingers to his forehead in an exaggerated gesture. "But I forget. I believe your father died when you were still a young man, perhaps before you'd quite understood the difference between right and wrong?"

"What do you know about my father?" Andrews snarled.

"Quite a lot actually." Quin gave him a long look, making the man's cheeks flush before dropping his eyes.

"You can't prove anything."

Quin shrugged. "While your father's murder might go unpunished, there's plenty of evidence for your other crimes, as I said. And even if members of the nobility should perchance be dismissed when taking the stand, the former Assistant Commissioner of Police is also singing like a bird, trying desperately to save himself.—So you see," Quin went on, experiencing a distinct sense of satisfaction at finally seeing Andrews unsettled, "there really is no way for you to escape the law this time round. You've committed one crime too many and now it's time for you to pay."

"I don't have to pay for anything! People like *me* don't end up in *prison*!"

"And yet, here you are." Quin waved his arm around the room. "I do wonder, though, why you allowed me to run into you in London. Did you not think I would become suspicious?" He cocked his head, waiting for an answer, but Andrews only continued to stare at him.

"Ah, I think I'm beginning to understand." Quin nodded slowly to himself. "It was arrogance, of course, just like you were arrogant enough to admit to Alannah what you'd done, thinking you'd never get caught even so. But after that little slip-up, you wanted me to know you were watching me, perhaps thinking that might scare me off any ideas I might have?" He lifted one brow, but Andrews ignored him, his jaws clenched tight. "And while you still refused to believe I would uncover anything truly damaging, *if* I did, you wanted me to know you'd make sure I'd pay for it." Quin chuckled. "If only you'd known I hadn't uncovered anything at all and wasn't even looking, you may not have ended up here—at least not yet."

"What do you mean?" Andrews demanded, beads of sweat breaking out on his forehead.

"I mean that my father only found out about your arrangement with Leventhorpe *after* you tried to have me killed...after Leventhorpe happened upon me by chance.—It was your own actions that made him suspicious."

"You lie!"

"Think what you will. It is rather unfortunate for you that I not only survived your assassination attempt but also managed to see you deposited behind bars for the rest of your life—which, incidentally, may yet prove to be rather short."

Andrews' face became suffused with hatred, and he growled deep in his throat. He leaned toward Quin, his lips pulled up in a snarl. When he spoke, the words hissed between his teeth, quite in contrast to his usual eloquence. "I should have had Martin Doyle burn the house beneath you and your whore of a wife as you slept in your beds!"

Quin breathed in heavily as he slowly pushed back his chair and stood up, his eyes all-the-while boring into Andrews'. Without warning he drew back his fist and smashed it into Andrews' face, feeling the bones of the man's nose shatter beneath his knuckles in a gratifying crunch. Such was the force of his blow that Andrews toppled back in his chair, landing on the floor with a heavy thump, his arms and legs sprawling and blood running down his face.

Quin flexed his fingers, ignoring the sharp pain that radiated down his arm from his injured shoulder. He walked around the table, glowering down onto the dishevelled form of his enemy. He felt a restraining hand on his arm and turned his head back in annoyance. He narrowed his eyes at the guard, who slowly removed his fingers but hovered next to Quin as he leaned over Andrews.

"It has been a pleasure conversing with you, Mr Andrews, as always. I do hope you will enjoy your new abode.—Although I suspect I shall not visit."

Andrews' eyes flashed murderously above his ruined nose, his hands pressed over his face as blood seeped between his fingers. Unchristian though it was, the sight filled Quin with a deep sense of satisfaction, and he felt one corner of his mouth lifting in a smile. "I wish you a pleasant day," he said as he replaced his hat on his head. Turning on his heel, he marched toward the door and strode out of the room without a backward glance.

"AND YOU'RE QUITE sure that you're able to travel, are you?"

Quin nodded patiently in response to his father's question.

"I am." He moved his shoulders experimentally but felt only the slight twinge that still accompanied movements on the injured side. The hefty blow he'd dealt Andrews two days earlier hadn't had any lasting effects. "And the doctor's assured us Rupert is well enough to do the same," he went on, remembering with fondness the sight of Andrews sprawled on the prison floor, "so we're all set."

"Hmph." The baron wrinkled his brows at the sight of Rupert coming down the stairs of the house.

Quin had to admit his valet didn't yet look entirely healthy. After more than a week spent in bed with little appetite, he was rather pale and scrawny, truth be told.

"He'll be his usual self within a day or two," he said as he spotted Alannah making her way along the drive. "Ready?" he asked her once she'd reached the carriage.

"Yes." She smiled at Quin before addressing his father. "I've left a letter for Mr Henderson on the table in the entrance hall. Could you see that it's sent?"

"Of course, my dear," the baron answered, inclining his head.

"Well, that's it then," Quin said as one of the footmen secured the last of their trunks. He turned to face his father, feeling suddenly awkward. Although they had grown closer over their stay in London, shows of affection still tended to be kept to a minimum.

The baron extended a hand, which Quin took, shaking it firmly. After a moment, though, he decided life was too short for such unnecessary restraints. Drawing the hand he was shaking closer, he embraced the baron with his other arm.

"It was good to see you, father," he said with feeling.

"It was good to see you, too, son." The baron thumped him vigorously on the back for several seconds before pulling away and avoiding his eye. He turned toward Alannah, who was watching the proceedings with a wide smile on her face.

"Wilfred," she said affectionately.

"Alannah." His usually gruff expression softened as he looked at her, replaced briefly by startlement as she embraced him heartily. When they finally separated, Quin observed with some amusement that his father's cheeks were flushed with pleasure. "Be sure to watch over that son of mine," he instructed his daughter-in-law, whose eyes were shiny with emotion.

She laughed. "I will."

"And try to stay out of trouble, Quinton." The baron gave him a long look down his nose.

"I'll do my best."

When they were finally settled in the carriage and it got underway, Quin looked out the window for a long time, watching Wadlow Cottage getting smaller and smaller, a peculiar feeling growing in his chest.

He sighed. "I never thought I'd find it this difficult to leave."

One corner of Alannah's mouth lifted in a knowing smile, making him narrow his eyes at her. "Are you about to tell me 'I told you so'?"

She laughed softly and shook her head. "I wouldn't dream of it."

32.

"HOME AT LAST," I said, sighing in contentment.

"It is good to be back," Quin agreed, smiling as he handed me a tumbler of whiskey.

We had arrived at Glaslearg a little earlier, to bustling excitement from the staff, tired but happy after our brief stay in Dublin following our return trip from England. Having washed the road dust off my face and hands and changed into a clean gown, I settled blissfully into one of the comfortable armchairs in the drawing room before supper.

Quin took a large sip of his whiskey, closing his eyes and leaning his head against the padded backrest of the chair next to mine. "Although I am happy we were able to witness Ollie tie the knot before heading home," he said, looking across at me.

I laughed at his word choice. "Was it such an unlikely prospect for your friend to get married?"

He grinned. "I suppose he just needed to find his match—although I must admit I never would have pictured someone like Miss Anne Cartwright as Ollie's bride."

I had thought as much myself when I'd first met the pair, the two of them being quite different not only in their physical appearance but also in their character. There was something else that had struck me at the wedding, though. "She seems nice enough…"

"But?"

I pursed my lips, wondering belatedly if I should rather have kept my thoughts to myself. "I'm not sure.—The wedding was certainly lovely, and Ollie looked as though he couldn't believe his luck…but she…"

Quin wrinkled his forehead. "You think...that she's playing him false in some way?"

I shrugged. "I don't know if I would say that, but he did seem far more enthusiastic than she—which I found rather peculiar for a bride who had chosen her groom of her own free will."

"I had assumed she was just nervous."

"Perhaps."

"You don't sound convinced."

"It's only that..." I paused, weighing my words. "I watched her a little after the ceremony and...well...she seemed...a little too friendly with other men for a bride on her wedding day."

Quin raised his brows.

"It was nothing overt, of course," I said, waving a hand, "just a few glances, standing a little closer than strictly necessary, that sort of thing. But no doubt I'm reading too much into it." I shook my head, feeling suddenly guilty for doubting the woman's intentions—I hardly knew her, after all.

"Hm. She did act rather familiar with me too," Quin admitted, glancing sideways at me. I had noticed this myself of course—which was perhaps why I had been watching her in the first place—but I didn't say anything. "I had assumed it was just her way," Quin went on. "It would be odd if her behaviour were anything but innocent. She had no need to marry Ollie after all—if she hadn't wanted to, I mean."

I nodded. Although Ollie came from a rich, upper-class family and would have been found desirable for that reason alone by some, the new Mrs Penhale herself hailed from the aristocracy and would no doubt have been able to have her pick of husband.

"Well, I do hope they'll be happy together," I said, meaning it. Despite the fact that I hadn't spent much time with Quin's friends, I had come to care a great deal about them.

"So do I," Quin said, reaching across the low table and squeezing my hand.

I smiled at him but suddenly had to stifle a yawn.

"Bored with farm life already?" Quin asked with a glint of humour in his eyes.

I laughed. "Who wouldn't be, after the adventures we've had over the last few weeks?"

"I for one am looking forward to a little boredom," he replied, rubbing a hand over his chest.

I frowned as I remembered in vivid detail the dread that had come over me when the baron's driver had stormed into Wadlow Cottage, yelling that Quin and Rupert had been injured, and the mayhem that had followed—not knowing whether my husband was dead or alive. "Quite," I said shortly.

Quin leaned toward me and took hold of my hand once more. "You needn't worry about Andrews. He's as good as convicted."

I pushed my memories aside and gave Quin a sceptical look. "Do you really think it'll be as easy for the courts to see him found guilty as your father says?" Having gotten to know the man rather a lot better than I'd ever wanted to, it hadn't escaped me that he was a very resourceful fellow when it came to protecting his own interests.

"I don't see how he can avoid the law this time round—as I said to the man himself. With Leventhorpe's little secret exposed he's already cooperating eagerly to minimise his own punishment, and with the police now likely to find more and more witnesses against him, the noose will tighten further." Quin shook his head as he continued. "Even if Andrews attempts to convince the courts all his accomplices acted of their own volition, there isn't much he could do to silence the numerous members of the gentry who wish to see him punished."

"He should have better chosen his victims," I said drily.

Quin chuckled. "Indeed, including myself. Unfortunately for Andrews, he realised a little too late that someone such as myself couldn't simply be brushed off, nor all too easily disposed of.—There really is no way for him to get out of it this time!"

"Someone such as yourself?" I raised my brows, making him grin.

"I'm a very important person, didn't you know?" He stuck his nose into the air in an exaggerated fashion. "The heir to a substantial barony shan't ever be ignored, least of all by an untitled Anglo-Irishman such as Herbert Andrews."

"I'd hardly call it ignoring you when the man tried to have you killed," I muttered.

A sudden gasp at the door made me look up. Benjamin was hovering at the threshold, his eyes huge with shock at what he'd obviously overheard.

"Is...is it true?" The boy looked from me to Quin. "Sir? Did someone try t'...t' kill ye?" He swallowed visibly, evidently in distress.

Quin took a deep breath before answering. We had agreed not to tell the household staff about the incident, not wanting to alarm them, but clearly, they would soon know all about it anyway.

"I'm afraid so," he said gently, which nevertheless caused Benjamin to turn a few shades paler.

"Sir...I..." the boy stammered, wringing his hands.

Quin got up and came to stand in front of him, placing a hand gently on one small shoulder. "I thank you for your concern, Benjamin, but I'm quite all right. No harm done, as you can see." He spread his arms in indication of his vibrant health.

"But..."

"The man responsible has been locked away, likely for a very long time."

"Locked away? Mr...Mr Andrews?" Benjamin whispered the name, making Quin compress his lips.

"The very same. But you needn't concern yourself with him. Once he's been convicted, you'll never have to hear the name Herbert Andrews in this household again!"

Quin smiled down at Benjamin encouragingly. "Now, what is it you came to tell us?"

"Tell ye?" Benjamin looked at Quin blankly for a moment before giving himself a shake. "Oh...uh...Mrs O'Sullivan sent me...t'...t' tell ye that supper is waitin' for ye in the dining room."

"Ah, I thank you, Benjamin." He came back to where I was sitting and offered me his hand. "Would you like to join us?" he asked Benjamin, who was still hovering by the door.

The boy shook his head. "I already ate," he said quickly and turned on his heel. He was gone before we'd made it to the threshold.

"Poor child," I said, looking after him in some concern.

Quin shrugged. "He'll get over it in a day or two."

"I suppose."

After a quiet supper we returned to the drawing room, but I soon found myself nodding off, despite the fact that the sun hadn't yet set on this late summer's day.

"I'm calling it a night," I said to Quin, suppressing a yawn.

He looked up from the paper he'd been reading and smiled. "I'll come to bed shortly."

I nodded and got up, glancing outside the window as I did so, catching sight of movement near the terrace. Benjamin was stomping toward the hedgerow, scowling and covered in streaks of mud. I watched in amazement as he disappeared around the corner of the house. Quin was still immersed in his paper and clearly hadn't seen the boy. I contemplated for a moment whether I should go after him but eventually decided against it.

I would give him a little time and speak to him the following day.

QUIN AND I spent the better part of the next day catching up with the estate's affairs. As before, though, Mr Dunne had managed everything very competently in our absence, including the staff and tenants, all of whom were faring well. And so it was mostly for our own interest that we were perusing some ledgers in the afternoon when a great deal of shouting reached us from the entrance hall. Quin gave me curious look before getting up to investigate.

I followed him to the door, which, once opened, revealed the unexpected sight of Benjamin and Conor yelling at each other while standing nose to nose. I wrinkled my brow. Conor being a frequent visitor to the manor house, he and Benjamin had become fast friends after the latter's arrival at the estate, with the two of them usually inseparable—so much so that Quin had had to have a word with them after Conor's parents complained he was neglecting his duties at home because he was spending all his time with Benjamin.

Assuming the neglect of their household duties was not, in fact, what they were fighting about, I wondered what had gotten into them—or rather, into Benjamin, I amended, realising he was the one who was doing most of the yelling. Ignoring Quin's attempts to get the boys' attention, Benjamin soon progressed to finger-pointing, followed in short order by a quick jab to Conor's midsection. Conor yowled and gave Benjamin a look of disgust, raising his arms defensively as Benjamin came at him once more, this time with both fists raised.

"That's quite enough," Quin thundered, grasping Benjamin around the middle and jerking him off the floor, away from his adversary. The boy wriggled in a mad attempt at escape while Conor threw one look at Quin and fled with speed out the front door.

With a few long strides Quin reached the study, where he dumped Benjamin unceremoniously onto one of the chairs in front of the desk.

"Well?" Quin demanded, hands on his hips.

"I didn't do nothin'!" came Benjamin's response, as if shot from a canon.

Quin growled deep in his throat and leaned menacingly over the small figure, whose face remained set in a petulant scowl.

I laid a hand on Quin's arm and gently pushed him back. He frowned at me, but I ignored him, thinking I had an idea of what was going on.

"I know you're upset, Benjamin," I said, stooping down next to his chair so I could look him in the eyes. "But hitting your friend is no way of dealing with your concern for Mr Williams. And it won't change what happened."

"You don't know nothin'," Benjamin grumbled, not looking at me.

He clenched his hands into fists, making Quin take a step closer. I waved him away irritably.

"I know you're concerned about what you overheard yesterday," I prodded, but Benjamin only stared into his lap. I tried again. "Mr Williams is no longer in any danger," I said, hoping it was the truth, "so you needn't worry yourself any further.—Although your concern is admirable."

I smiled at Benjamin, but he clenched his jaws stubbornly, still not looking at me. I glanced at Quin, who shrugged. Next to me, Benjamin suddenly muttered something I didn't understand.

"I beg your pardon?" Looking back at the boy I was surprised to see that his lower lip was trembling.

"It's all my fault." Benjamin's voice was low and filled with despair.

"What's your fault?" I asked in some bewilderment.

"Mr Williams." The words came out in a whisper and Benjamin clapped his hands over his face, his thin frame shaking as he burst into tears.

"Mr Williams?"

"He could 've died!"

I patted his bony shoulder as he continued to sob. "That had nothing to do with…"

"It was my fault!" The boy pulled away from me, his face splitting into a grimace of despair as tears and snot ran down his cheeks and chin. "I told 'im."

"You told who what?" I shook my head in confusion. "Here, use my handkerchief to blow your nose and then tell me everything from the beginning." I pressed the fabric firmly into his hand, but he just held it limply.

I shrugged. "Right," I said, gently squeezing his arm, "tell me what you think you've done."

"I told 'im," he said once more, speaking so softly I had to lean closer to hear him.

"Who did you tell?"

Benjamin threw me a sideways glance, his lips quivering once more. I breathed in heavily, trying not to get annoyed.

"Benjamin," I said firmly, "tell me what's going on."

He opened his mouth to respond but snapped it shut, sniffing briefly before trying again. "He sent me here," he whispered at last.

A prickling sensation crept down my back and I swallowed heavily. "Who sent you here?"

"Andrews."

Benjamin's eyes flew wide open, flickering to Quin, who I had momentarily forgotten was standing behind me.

"Andrews," Quin repeated, nodding slowly to himself as he sat on the edge of the desk. "He sent you here to spy on us, didn't he?"

Benjamin fidgeted with his hands and looked down onto his lap. Quin leaned toward him, making the boy hunch into himself before giving a quick nod.

I gasped and Quin compressed his lips briefly before pulling out the other chair for me. I sat down gratefully as he returned to his perch on the desk.

He gently laid a hand on Benjamin's shoulder. "Tell me," he said softly.

Benjamin lifted his tear-streaked face and I nodded encouragingly at him.

"Mr Andrews," he began hesitantly, "he…he found me in Dublin. I was alone, livin' on the streets. He gave me money t'…t' do things for 'im."

"What kinds of things?" Quin asked.

Benjamin sniffed, still holding my handkerchief absently in one hand. "To find things out. Where somebody was goin', who they was talkin' to and the like."

"You were never caught?"

"Never! Mr Andrews said that...that people don't notice someone like me."

I thought back to the first time I'd seen Benjamin and concluded that Herbert Andrews had been right. Dirty and wearing ragged clothing, the boy had looked like just another street urchin, who would at most be taken for a pickpocket, if he was seen at all.

"And Mr Andrews told you to come here?"

Benjamin nodded silently in response to Quin's question, before giving a sudden sob. "He promised me money but...but...I didn't know ye'd all be so...so wonderful!"

Quin gently squeezed his arm. "He's a heartless man who took advantage of a poor and lonely boy."

"But I told 'im ye were goin' t' London! And ye could've been killed...ye could've been killed because o' me."

Quin gave a deep sigh, rubbing a hand over his face. "If you hadn't told him he would have found out from somebody else. And if it hadn't been London, it would have been someplace else. There's a history between us, one that's got nothing to do with you."

"But..."

"I don't blame you, Benjamin. He has to have had other spies in England to have found me there—in fact, I'm quite sure I saw at least one of them. You, on the other hand, were here at Glaslearg the whole time, weren't you?"

"Well, yes, but..."

"Do you still wish to stay here?" Quin asked abruptly.

Benjamin nodded, silent tears running down his face. "More than anythin'."

"Then promise me to have nothing more to do with Herbert Andrews and it is done."

"Truly, sir?"

"Truly."

The boy's skinny shoulders started shaking in relief and I felt tears stinging my own eyes.

"Now run along into the kitchen and let Mrs O'Sullivan give you something to eat," Quin said. "We'll talk again later."

Benjamin scrambled off the chair. Noticing the handkerchief he still held, he gave his face a quick wipe before heading toward the door, his mouth splitting into a disbelieving grin as he disappeared into the hallway.

SOME TIME LATER, fortified by Mrs O'Sullivan's excellent fare and assured once more he was in no danger of being thrown out, Benjamin's story came bubbling out of him.

He told us Andrews had first approached him when he was ten years old, one of a throng of orphans trying to eke out a life for themselves on the back streets of Dublin. Having grown up begging and snatching what food he could find, Benjamin had recently progressed to pickpocketing, finding this to be a surer way of being able to feed himself—although not without its dangers, as he discovered when the hand he'd been stealthily extracting from a gentleman's coat pocket was grasped firmly by a mountain of a man.

Sure the mountain was soon to mete out a brutal punishment, Benjamin had been terrified when the elderly gentleman he'd been trying to rob instructed the man to take the boy with them. His fears had grown as he was dragged through the streets, ending up in a neighbourhood that seemed to Benjamin to be more suited to himself than his finely dressed captor.

"And so, I closed me eyes and prayed he would be quick about it," Benjamin told us, squeezing his eyes shut in illustration. "But when I felt no fist on me face or knife in me back, I peeked about. The gentleman—Mr Andrews—he was lookin' at me strangely and then he started talkin' to me in a very fine way, like I'd never been talked to before. He said he had a proposition"—he carefully enunciated each syllable—"for me."

"I can just imagine it," Quin said drily, before waving a hand for him to continue.

"He said I wouldn't 'ave to steal nothin' no more if I would work for 'im. He would pay me." Benjamin looked back and forth between Quin and me.

"Did he take you into his household?" I asked.

"Oh no." Benjamin shook his head. "It was all to be a secret."

"So he would meet with you in a dark alleyway to get the information he wanted?"

"Not 'imself. Another man that worked for 'im, looked like a rat. He would tell me what Mr Andrews wanted t' know and give me a coin or two when I'd found out." Benjamin looked rather smug at this, but I wasn't so impressed.

"But you were still living on the streets. Did you still have to steal?"

"Sometimes." He shrugged. "But mostly I got by without."

"And how did you come to be here?" Quin asked, bringing the conversation to order.

Benjamin explained that the man who worked for Andrews had told him one day that he was required to catch a coach to Ballygawley, from whence he should make his way to Glaslearg, there to inveigle himself into the household in order to spy on the inhabitants and provide what information he could—all in exchange for a generous sum, of course.

"And he knew ye'd take me in too," Benjamin informed Quin and me, sounding rather impressed with his previous employer.

I scowled but Quin snorted. "He knows what sorts of people we are," he said, giving me a wry smile. "Although he would of course call such kind-hearted actions weakness."

"Never mind," I muttered crossly. "You did have us all fooled when you arrived here, Benjamin."

"That wasn't no act, mum." The boy's eyes were wide as he leaned toward me. "I really was starvin' when I came 'ere. It was a long walk t' get here, took me days."

My heart gave a sudden lurch at Benjamin's words, remembering Kieran's homecoming after his release from gaol. He, too, had taken days to walk back—not because he didn't know the way from Omagh but because he kept turning back, unsure whether he would be welcomed. I took a deep breath and pushed the thought aside.

"Of course," I said, patting Benjamin's hand. His gauntness upon his arrival at the estate had certainly been no act. Even with some of Andrews' coin, he had clearly been struggling to survive.

"To whom did you pass on the information you gathered?" Quin asked.

Benjamin wrinkled up his small nose. "A nasty little man that came t' find me. Just as Mr Andrews' man in Dublin said 'e would. He did give me a right fright when 'e came on me the first time."

"Where did the two of you meet?" I demanded with some heat, imagining a horde of malevolent strangers descending on my home.

"Here and there," Benjamin responded with a flip of the wrist. "He said not t' always meet at the same place or at the same time, so as t' keep it a secret." He nodded eagerly, having clearly enjoyed his clandestine activities. I gave him a stern look, making him fluster. "I mean...ah...well, 'e did tell me when t' be where for our next meeting, that's all." I raised one brow. "Once at the bend in the river at nightfall," he hurried to explain, "once behind the barn before the sun was up...or no, that was twice. Then there was the time I went t' the market at Ballygawley and and..." His eyes flitted from me to Quin and back again, his cheeks turning pink.

"I think we're starting to get the general idea," Quin said. Wrinkling his brow, he tapped a finger against his chin in thought. "When were you next meant to meet with the man?"

Benjamin shrugged. "I dunno, sir. He said he'd find me when ye got back from London."

"Well, we're back now, aren't we? And I doubt he'll know yet Andrews has been arrested." Quin gave Benjamin a wry smile. "Do let me know if he calls."

THE NEWS OF Quin's close encounter with a loaded gun (and Rupert's equally close encounter with a blunt object) quite shook up the household—which was precisely why we hadn't wanted to tell the staff about the incident in the first place.

Mrs O'Sullivan fussed over Quin and Rupert constantly. While he knew it was kindly meant, Quin had informed me privately that her ministrations were slowly driving him mad—unlike his valet, who was thoroughly enjoying the cook's devoted attentions.

Fortunately for Quin, he found some distraction a few days after our return to Glaslearg, with the appearance of Andrews' associate at the estate. It being an unannounced visit, so to speak, Quin had been unable to attend, but

Benjamin, eager to appease his master and prove his newfound devotion to us, ran to find Quin as soon as the man had left.

"He came, sir!" the boy burst out breathlessly as he stormed into the drawing room shortly after sunset.

Quin lowered his book. "That was quick," he remarked, cocking one brow.

Benjamin nodded vigorously. "I was cleanin' up the muck in the barn after helpin' old Bryan move some hay. He was there when I came out. Hidin' in the shadows, like, callin' to me."

"And?"

Benjamin puffed out his thin chest. "I told him right t' his face that I wouldn't tell 'im nothin'!"

"You did?" I gasped, simultaneously amused and a little horrified—the man was likely an unsavoury character, to say the least.

"That's right! I said that ye was nice folks and that I would 'ave nothing t' do with nobody wantin' t' harm ye! I said that I wasn't working for Mr Andrews no more and that he'd been arrested besides."

"What did he say to that?" I asked, wrinkling my brow.

"He didn't say nothin'," Benjamin continued, looking very pleased with himself, "but his eyes bulged like, and 'is face went all red like he thought I was lyin'. He tried to grab me by me shirt but I ran away right quick, yellin' at 'im t' go and join 'is master in hell!" Benjamin's own eyes bulged as he threw me a guilty look. "Ah…beggin' your pardon mum."

I waved a hand in dismissal. "Never mind that. But do you think…?" I glanced at Quin.

He, evidently, had decided on amusement as an appropriate reaction, but now cleared his throat, his face taking on a more serious expression.

"Did anyone else see you?" he asked his charge.

Benjamin shook his head, making a thick sheaf of his red hair flop from side to side. "No, sir. All the other outdoor servants 'ad already done for the day. Any case, I was much too quick t' dash out and away from the outbuildings. I knew he'd not follow me down 'ere." He grinned at Quin, who smiled back briefly.

"Well, I do thank you for your loyalty, young Benjamin," he said in a grave voice. "But I hope you'll consider resolving similar situations in the future with a little more...delicacy?" He arched one brow before leaning toward the boy. "Lest your adversaries wish to seek revenge for the insult."

Benjamin gulped. "Ye mean...d'ye think...is he going to...? D'ye think the man's gonna come kill me?" he finally blurted out, his cheeks going pink with the effort.

Looking at his glowing face I narrowed my eyes suspiciously, sure I could detect a hint of excitement in his demeanour—evidently, he found the thought of being the target of an assassination attempt quite thrilling.

I didn't find it nearly so thrilling myself.

I opened my mouth to berate him, but Quin forestalled me. "I shouldn't think so," he said, shaking his head. "He'll likely be needing new employment soon when he receives confirmation of Andrews' arrest. And I doubt he'd find it worth the effort to pursue you in the meantime."

Benjamin scowled at the dismissal of his own importance, which made me want to laugh.

"Still," Quin went on with his lecture, "it's best not to provoke these things."

That did make me laugh, thinking about Quin's various misadventures of a similar nature. He gave me a sheepish look, before lifting one shoulder in a shrug. "At least not until you've learnt how to defend yourself," he amended with a grin. "Speaking of which, perhaps I'll give you boys a few lessons. Might come in handy, after all."

"Oh yes, sir!" Benjamin nodded, clenching his fists and waving them madly in the air as he bounced back and forth. He jabbed at an imagined enemy, losing his balance and almost tripping over his own feet in the process.

"I see I've got my work cut out for me," Quin said wryly before sending the boy on his way with a pat on the back.

"And you're quite sure this man is not going to come back to harm Benjamin?" I asked as soon as he was out of earshot.

Quin compressed his lips before responding. "One can never be entirely sure, of course. I have been wrong before..."

"That wasn't your fault," I countered immediately, reaching toward him. "Nobody knew Martin Doyle was still alive."

"Perhaps." Quin sighed and patted my hand. "Still, in this case, I'm reasonably sure the man won't come back. He was presumably getting his orders for his various…activities from Andrews. And with no further monetary recompense likely to come from that quarter, the man is unlikely to bother with Benjamin of his own volition.—As for Andrews himself," he added with a gleam in his eyes, "he'll have his hands quite full fending off accusations from people who are far more likely to be taken seriously than a street urchin. Benjamin will be the least of his troubles!"

33.

"INCOMING!"

Quin stopped at the warning shout as a gust of foamy water cascaded onto the path in front of him, droplets splattering his shoes.

"What in the world?"

A gasp from the open doorway made him look up.

"Sir!" Rupert's eyes were round as saucers as he gaped at Quin, empty basin in hand.

Quin raised one brow, making his valet sputter an apology. "Sir, I'd never have thought…I mean…" Rupert raised a hand and waved it at the doorway. Clearly, he hadn't expected to come upon his master at the servants' entrance at the side of the house.

Quin shrugged. He normally wouldn't have been there either, if it hadn't been for the fact that Mr Dunne had told him the servants' door likely needed to be replaced—just one of the numerous practicalities brought to Quin's attention within the two weeks or so he'd been back at the estate. "No harm done," he said, his usual good humour returning. "Thank you for the warning though."

"Oh…ah…" To Quin's surprise, Rupert's cheeks turned bright red. "I…um…"

"The warnin' wasn't for you, sir." Finnian's face appeared over Rupert's shoulder, making the valet narrow his eyes as he threw him a quick glance. Quin was happy to see, though, that the deep scowls that tended to accompany encounters between the two young men were largely absent.

"Well," he said, "naturally, Rupert wouldn't have expected me in particular to be here but…"

"No, sir, ye misunderstand." Finnian shook his head. "The warnin' wasn't meant for any people at all. It was meant for the hill folk."

"The hill folk?" Quin wrinkled his brow before a vague memory of something Alannah had once said surfaced. "You mean...fairies?" he asked, finding it difficult to hide the incredulity in his voice.

"Ye shouldn't call them that," Finnian admonished him while Rupert avoided Quin's eye, "they'll hear ye! Ah...but yes, sir," Finnian added, looking a little embarrassed at his outburst, "that is who I mean. And ye must always warn the hill folk before throwing water out o' the door!"

"I see." Quin cleared his throat. "Um...and what happens should one not call a warning in time?"

Finnian's eyes went wide. "If one o' them be passing by and get wet, it would get very annoyed!"

"And then it would...?"

"Oh, anything could happen, sir...*anything*!" Finnian nodded vigorously. "The little people are known for all sorts o' mischief, from turnin' the milk sour to causing serious injury and even...even death." He whispered the last word, his eyes flickering rapidly between Quin and Rupert. "And sometimes," Finnian continued in hushed tones, "one of 'em will steal a newborn babe and replace it with one o' their own folk, leavin' a sickly or deformed child behind."

Despite himself, Quin felt the hairs on the back of his neck rise at Finnian's description. He glanced at Rupert, whose shoulders were hunched and eyes wide. Clearly, his valet had been completely taken in by the stories he was hearing from the local staff. And who could blame him? Quin was quite sure there was no such thing as fairies—Irish or otherwise—and yet he felt the sudden need to do all things possible to protect his house against their wrath.

"And besides warning them of an impending shower, what is the correct protocol for appeasing the...um...little people?" Quin felt ridiculous asking such a thing but tried not to blink.

Finnian, though, took the question very seriously. "Hm, well there's the iron over the door o' course," he began, wrinkling his brow in thought. "And wearin' a red ribbon can protect ye, some say. Me granda also always made sure t' keep the first glass o' freshly brewed *poitín* for the hill folk." Finnian glanced sideways at his employer, but Quin made no comment about the family's illegal practice of brewing homemade spirits. "Oh, there's pissin' on the doorposts o' course..." Finnian stopped abruptly, his eyes going wide. "Ah...um...I mean..."

Quin waved a hand. "Go on."

Finnian cleared his skinny throat. "Yes, sir. Um…" He looked around for inspiration before suddenly declaring, "Whatever ye do, ye must *never* disturb one o' their forts!" He waved a menacing finger, lest Quin be about to do such a thing.

"A fairy fort?" Rupert asked, making Finnian give him the sort of dark look Quin had gotten accustomed to seeing on his face when the valet was around. "Ah…the hill folk build forts?" Rupert amended quickly.

"Oh yes," Finnian assured him, smoothing out his features, "only they're underground and all connected wi' tunnels, and wi' secret entrances."

"And how does one recognise a fai…um…a hill folk fort?" Quin caught himself just in time, blinking innocently.

Luckily, Finnian seemed not to have noticed. "Ye can't miss them, sir," he said. "They're perfectly round, sometimes just a hill where everythin' else is flat. Or sometimes a patch o' greenery surrounded wi' a circle o' stone, or maybe just trees or shrubs."

"You mean like…? Isn't there something just like that near the river not far from here?" Quin looked into the distance, seeing the place in his mind's eye. He had often noticed the strange hill—slightly elevated with a ring of bushes at its base—but had never thought to ask anyone about it. The people on the estate did seem to avoid it, though, and nobody had ever suggested farming it—although it lay right on the edge of a field and constituted a sizeable area that may well yield a decent crop.

"Yes, sir," Finnian confirmed eagerly, "and that's a big fort too.—There must be loads o' little people that live there!"

"Mmh." Quin nodded absently. He couldn't quite believe the hill was in fact home to dozens of supernatural creatures, but he did wonder about its origins. Was it the result of some strange geological phenomenon or the remnants of a long-lost civilisation, perhaps?

"I beg your pardon?" Quin turned toward Finnian, having missed what he'd said.

"I was just sayin', sir, as I wouldn't want t' be cursed for interferin' wi' that fort!"

"No, I suppose not.—We'd best leave it be then." Quin smiled at Rupert, who had a rather haunted look on his face, making him think it was time to change the subject. "Hill folk or not, though," he said, raising a brow at his valet, "is it your usual practice to dispose of my shaving water by flinging it out the door?"

"Ah...um..." Rupert's cheeks turned pink as he continued to stammer.

"Perhaps you'd consider at least throwing it into the bushes instead of muddying the entrance." Quin pointed at the path to the servants' door. Although it looked like it had once been covered in gravel, most of it had been carried off, leaving little more than dirt behind.

"Yes, sir." Rupert threw a guilty look down at his feet, where the thick mat that lay on the threshold sported several muddy footprints.

"But that's from the rain, sir," Finnian came to Rupert's defence, to the evident surprise of Rupert himself. He nodded willingly enough, though.

"You have a point," Quin conceded. "This path really ought to be paved." When it rained as much as it did in Ireland, any unpaved surface had the potential to turn into a quagmire. Glancing at the door, Quin saw further evidence of the island's damp climate—had he needed any. The wooden frame was swollen with moisture, while the door itself was cracked at the base, no doubt making it difficult to close, as Mr Dunne had said.

"We'll have all of this neatened up over the next few weeks," he said, waving a hand at the door and the muddy entrance. "We wouldn't want to upset any of the hill folk with our unseemly ways, now, would we?"

LATER THAT DAY, Quin was sitting at his desk compiling a list of materials he needed to order when there was a soft knock at the door.

"Come in," he called absently, his mind still busy with calculations.

Glancing up, he saw that Finnian had come into the study, looking a little nervous. Perhaps he was still preoccupied with thoughts of malevolent fairies, Quin mused.

"Hello Finnian. What can I do for you?" he greeted the youngster.

"Sir, I...I wanted t' ask"—Finnian paused, wringing his hands—"t' ask if I could be excused from me duties for a few days. Ye see, my sister's had a baby and..."

"And you'd like to meet your nephew or niece," Quin concluded with a smile, pleased to be dealing with earthly concerns at least.

"Yes, sir."

"Of course. That can be arranged. When would you like to leave?"

"Um..." Finnian looked down at his shoes.

"As soon as possible," Quin guessed, making the footman nod vigorously. "I don't see why not. Rupert and Benjamin can take over some of your duties while you're gone."

"Thank you, sir!" Finnian beamed at him, making Quin feel a little ashamed he hadn't been aware of Finnian's impending unclehood beforehand.

"Did your sister have a boy or a girl?" he asked, deciding he would make a little more effort to get to know the people who worked for him.

"A boy," Finnian said, "and she named him after me.—Well, his second name in any case." Second name or not, the pride was evident in his voice and his upright posture, gangly limbs notwithstanding.

"How wonderful! And do you have any other nephews or nieces?"

Finnian shook his head. "No, sir. Agnes is the oldest and me other two sisters are only eleven and twelve."

"I see.—I do hope you find your time here with us tolerable, having to be away from your family."

"Oh, yes, sir! I like it here very much!" Finnian assured him with all evidence of sincerity.

"Even when you and Rupert are having words?" Quin asked, unable to help himself. He cocked his head, making Finnian break out in a bright blush. "But the two of you do seem to be getting along a little better these days. Isn't that so?"

"Ah...yes, I suppose so. I mean after he was almost...that is, when he was in England and...hmph..."

Quin raised one brow. "You were concerned for his safety."

Finnian scowled, compressing his lips for a moment. "Well, I suppose I was," he finally blurted out, looking none too pleased about it.

Quin suppressed a laugh. "I think that's very admirable of you, trying to put aside your differences—especially when you're living under the same roof." His thoughts flickered briefly to his relationship with his father, which had suffered from very similar difficulties in the past.

"Hmph."

This time, Quin did laugh. A truce of sorts may have been reached between them, but clearly, the two young men were far from being fast friends.

"You may find the two of you have more in common than you think," he said before changing the topic, to Finnian's evident relief.

Having arranged for his departure the following morning, Finnian left the study a few minutes later, his excitement about the impending week-long trip palpable.

Quin had just turned back to the paperwork on his desk when another knock sounded at the door. He sighed, wondering if he'd manage to finish what he'd set out to do that day, but called for his visitor to enter.

"Some letters, sir," Denis, the elderly butler, announced, carrying a small tray bearing the advertised mail. Tottering toward the desk he presented Quin with his correspondence before giving him a shaky bow and shuffling back out the door.

Watching his halting retreat, Quin smiled. Although the man was well past the age of retirement he absolutely refused to stop working—even though Quin had assured him he would suffer no financial detriments and that he could stay on at the estate for as long as he liked.

Just a few days ago when the topic had come up, Denis had proclaimed to Alannah in Gaelic that being a butler was all he knew how to do, that he would sooner die than suffer the boredom of forced retirement, and—swearing on the Virgin Mother and a host of other Catholic saints—that he was still entirely capable of doing all that was required of a butler (and more). He had attempted to prove the latter by proficiently pouring and serving Quin and Alannah a generous quantity of whiskey—and downing a healthy portion himself without demur at Quin's insistence.

Laughing whole-heartedly, Quin had assured the old man he could stay on for as long as his legs would hold him upright, which had caused Denis to give him a wide smile, revealing that he was likely to sooner be without teeth than without an occupation.

Chuckling in remembrance Quin sorted through the letters Denis had brought. Seeing one from his father he extracted it from the pile, stacking the remaining ones neatly on the desk before reaching for the letter opener. Looking at his father's crest made the corner of Quin's mouth curl up in amusement. Before their trip to London, Quin had groaned inwardly at sight of his father's seal, not infrequently putting off reading his missives until he could find no further excuses to do so. Now, though, he found he was looking forward to the baron's correspondence, feeling closer to his father than he had in years after they'd hashed out some of their differences.

Wondering whether that might change again in the future Quin opened the letter, expecting the usual few gruff words his father tended to write.

Dear Quinton, he read and paused, raising one brow in surprise at the term of affection adorning the top of the page—and the sheer length of the letter he was holding. Feeling a sense of warmth spreading through his middle he started again.

Dear Quinton,

I trust you and your wife have returned safely to your estate, and that your valet has quite recovered his health.

I write to inform you that the sentence against Herbert Andrews has been handed down, after a brisk trial. Only hours ago, he was found guilty of perverting justice, extortion and blackmail, which are at least some of the crimes he is in fact guilty of. The few witnesses required by the prosecution to seal his fate painted such a vivid picture of the man's vile character that none in the courtroom could have thought any less of him had you been called to testify against him yourself.

Grim evidence was provided by a creature named Parker, whom the police seem to have extricated from the cesspool of civilisation for the purpose. He told the court he had been employed by Andrews to perform all manner of heinous acts and confessed that he was the man who attempted to kill you on Andrews' orders. As you might imagine, it took considerable effort on my part not to strangle the misbegotten cur right there in the courtroom upon hearing this declaration. Fortunately for him, Parker is likely to evade my vengeance by being transported for his crimes, unless perchance he yet meets his maker on a London gibbet.

His former employer shall fare little better than he, having met with the full force of the law, the judge in the matter being a fine gentleman of my own acquaintance. While Andrews likely never before considered the fact that extortion is a crime punishable by transportation for life, that is precisely the sentence he has now been dealt. Although I am told there is some doubt he will ever actually be transported, in the interim, he will be biding his time in a holding cell in Newgate, which I suspect will not please him in the least. The man will of course make every attempt at a pardon, but I trust that our fine Criminal Justice System and The Queen herself will pay no heed to any such vulgarity.

Thus the news from London, which I am confident will meet with your approval.

As for myself, matters progress at Wadlow Cottage much as usual, albeit somewhat quieter following your departure.

Do give my regards to Alannah.

Yours,

Wilfred Williams

Quin smiled as he reached the end of the letter. This was the first time the baron had mentioned Alannah by name, his previous correspondence having barely acknowledged her existence at all. He suddenly felt a deep sense of gratitude that his father and his wife had gotten to know each other in London. Despite the rocky start to their relationship, there was now clearly a degree of affection between the two of them, which made a very pleasant change—to the baron's attitude in particular.

Quin's smile became broader as he turned his attention to the rest of the letter's content. Ungentlemanly though it may be, he felt a deep sense of satisfaction thinking about Herbert Andrews' continuing misfortune. In his opinion, Andrews was getting exactly what he deserved, and he sincerely hoped the man would indeed spend the rest of his life on the other side of the world—or at least behind bars—no matter how much he tried to appeal the verdict.

"That's the end for Herbert Andrews," Quin said firmly out loud. He hadn't quite doubted his father's promise of impending justice but was nevertheless pleased matters had proceeded so quickly following their departure from London.

He was equally pleased the police had managed to capture the man who had attempted to take Quin's life. Knowing this Parker would be punished for what he'd done was reassuring—and would be particularly so for Alannah. Of course, even if the man had not been apprehended, his dealings with Andrews would certainly be at an end. In fact, Quin considered, a good number of less than savoury characters presumably now found themselves without employment. And not only those in London, but elsewhere, including Benjamin's erstwhile acquaintance from Ballygawley and the man Morrison, whom Archie and Quin had espied in one of Dublin's backstreets—not to mention Andrews' hulking guard who had followed the man everywhere.

Quin wondered whether more of Andrews' associates would be apprehended in the wake of his own arrest or whether they would simply slink back into obscurity, waiting for the next man with a heavy purse to lure them into an ongoing life of crime.

Either way, though, none of those individuals were likely to want anything further to do with him or his family—they would presumably be safe enough. He looked over the letter once more, before folding it and depositing it in one of the desk's pigeonholes.

Another knock sounded at the door, making Quin emit a short laugh. He felt as though he were sitting in a clerk's office this afternoon.

"Come in," he called for the third time in the space of thirty minutes.

Alannah stuck her head into the study, and he smiled, beckoning her toward him. She gave him a curious look but sat down on the other side of the desk. Her eyes grew wide as he told her about his father's letter and Andrews' sentencing.

"I can't believe it," she said when he had finished. "After all these months and after everything..." She trailed off, waving at Quin's chest.

He rubbed a hand over the site of the bullet wound. "As I said before, trying to eliminate me was a mistake. And Andrews knew it, too.—Now if he'd succeeded..." He shrugged, although he was reasonably sure Andrews would have been caught even so. "He used one dirty trick too many," he said, pushing away the thought of his own demise. "As I said before, it was only a matter of time before it would all come crashing down around him."

"Well, I'm glad it finally has!"

Quin nodded and got up from his chair. "So am I." He came around the desk and pulled Alannah into his arms. "Now, let us never utter the name of Herbert Andrews again!"

34.

AS THAT YEAR'S summer came to an end, Quin felt a deep sense of satisfaction. The estate's bountiful grain harvest had been collected and Glaslearg was thriving. Even the previous season's failed potato crop seemed like nothing but a bad memory, especially in light of the vibrant, healthy plants once more covering the tenants' fields.

Quin was more than content with the life he and Alannah had built for themselves and was confident their dream of having a child would also soon be realised. His enemies had been vanquished and he felt like nothing could stand in the way of their happiness. He woke up with a smile on his face each day, feeling that the future held endless, wonderful possibilities he only needed to grasp to make them a reality.

All of that changed in early autumn.

QUIN SPURRED ON Gambit, hardly able to comprehend what he was seeing.

Left and right, his tenants' fields were spread out, neatly demarcated by low stone walls and arranged in their lazy beds, tendrils of smoke rising peacefully into the air from cottage chimneys all around.

But what had been luxuriant potato vines just the day before had been decimated, replaced by masses of putrefying vegetation.

Quin had been feeling so confident about this year's harvest that the sight struck him like a cannonball to the chest. He clenched his jaws hard, pain radiating down his neck as he pulled on the reins, thundering on to the adjoining estates.

Their neighbours had fared no better. Everywhere he looked were signs of destruction, with some fields entirely ruined.

Quin passed a group of peasants leaning against a fence, staring vacantly into the distance. He swallowed heavily at sight of the blank faces turned toward the fields they had so carefully tended. A wail cut through the air, making him look around. Several women were sitting on the ground weeping, wringing their hands over and over again as their children clung to their skirts. Quin felt his own eyes fill with tears at their despair, knowing he could not help them all.

Everywhere he rode he was greeted by similar scenes until finally, he turned back to Glaslearg with a heavy heart—there to try and comfort the men, women and children who lived on his land, whose livelihoods had been destroyed yet again.

"HOW CAN THIS happen? Two years in a row..."

Quin shook his head silently, feeling himself too much in shock to respond to Alannah's question. She put a hand on his arm, and he grasped it firmly. He squeezed his eyes shut, trying to dispel the images he'd seen that day. But try as he might, he could not rid himself of the looks of fear and despair on the faces of the people who depended on that rotting harvest for their survival.

"How will they live?" Alannah's soft voice made him look down at her.

"I don't know," he admitted, swallowing heavily as bile rose in his throat. "The situation was reasonably under control last year but now..." He shrugged. "One can hope the local landlords will provide more assistance but..." He trailed off once more, knowing full well that many landlords would again offer no real help to their suffering tenants, waiting for the government to respond instead.

And was England likely now to sacrifice a considerable portion of her own resources to save Irish peasants? Peasants whose situation was already far worse than the year before—not only because of the second consecutive failed harvest but also because many had sacrificed their pigs the previous season, eating the few available potatoes themselves instead of feeding the animals usually used to pay their rent. Now, without the livestock they depended on and once again facing the partial or complete ruination of the single crop that sustained whole families, how were they to find food to eat, much less pay the rent their landlords would nevertheless come collecting?

A sliver of dread ran down Quin's back as he realised the full extent of the calamity before them. Tenants being evicted by uncaring landlords, and hunger, starvation, disease and pestilence sweeping through the land, with no bar to hold back the torment.

He pulled Alannah to him roughly, crushing her to his chest. She reached her arms around him and held him just as tightly.

When his heart finally stopped pounding, he loosened his hold on Alannah and they looked at each other for a long moment. Finally, she lifted a hand and gently ran it over his head.

They would do all they could to see everyone at Glaslearg fed and to see them all safe—but what truly awaited them remained to be seen.

A TENDER TOUCH woke me, a soft stroke of the cheek. I opened my eyes and met a troubled gaze in the moonlight.

"I'm sorry to wake you. I just needed to look at you."

"You didn't need to wake me up for that." I turned my head away, irritated at the intrusion in the middle of the night.

"I'm sorry," he said once more. "I dreamt you were lost.—I was looking for you, calling your name over and over, but you didn't come. I couldn't find you."

"It was just a dream." I turned back toward him, stroking his arm.

"No!" The single word was filled with violence. "This was more than a dream. It was...it felt like...I can't explain it, but this felt *real*, it *was* real."

"It was just a dream," I repeated, but with a sense of foreboding that caused the skin on the back of my neck to prickle in fear.

He looked at me for a long moment.

"Yes, I'm sure you're right," he finally said. "I was just dreaming. I'm sure it's nothing to worry about." He sounded like he was trying to convince himself as much as me.

I edged closer to him, wrapping myself around him to provide what comfort I could, feeling the tense set of his shoulders and the rigid way he held himself. He suddenly turned toward me and pulled me to him with such force he squeezed the breath out of me.

"I couldn't bear to lose you, Alannah!" he said hoarsely.

"You won't!" I assured him with what conviction I could muster, trying to suppress the sense of doom creeping into my heart.

"You are my life. I couldn't go on without you."

"You won't have to. I'm not going anywhere," I whispered.

We turned to each other in unison, then, to repel the dreadful reality surrounding us and find what solace we could in each other's arms.

35.

IN A NIGHTMARISH echo of the year before, the newspapers were filled with reports of ruined potato crops coming in from far and wide. Already hampered by a reduction in the acreage planted, due to the scarcity of seed potatoes the previous spring, the losses were disastrous. Once more, no county in Ireland had been spared, as the blight spread across the land from the western shores, driven by the prevailing winds, reaping destruction everywhere it went. Even in Ulster Province, which had again been less severely affected, massive losses of the harvest were nevertheless reported.

Some estimated three-quarters of Ireland's total potato crop had been ruined, while others believed it to be even more.

Whatever the exact numbers, that a harrowing year lay ahead for the Irish people was clear—made all the more so by the refusal of those in power to stop the export of Irish grains. Although a larger than usual portion of the season's oat harvest was being retained for Irish use, this was not nearly enough to make up for the enormous quantity of lost potatoes. And while the government promised to again provide maize from America to fill the gap, there was a deadly flaw in this plan: by the time these imports were expected to arrive, thousands would likely already have starved.

But parliament, merchants and landowners refused to budge, insisting that a ban on exports would lead to discouragement and feelings of insecurity in those depending on Irish trade, and hamper the nation as a whole. And so, precious life-saving grain kept leaving Irish shores, reaping bitterness and hatred among the populace. Before long, food convoys had to be accompanied by military detachments to guard the bulging wagons from the desperately hungry poor.

The news that reached us daily oppressed me like nothing I had ever experienced before, dragging me into despair.

I knew, though, that somehow, we dared not give up and that life must go on. And so, those of us who called the estate of Glaslearg our home continued with our daily existence as best we could, in the midst of the turmoil surrounding us.

With the foresight we'd had the previous season to plant large quantities of grain, Glaslearg's tenants would not go hungry—even those who hadn't been able to reap a single healthy potato. For Quin and me, there was no question of lamenting the loss of income our distributing the normally exported crops entailed—it was a matter of saving the lives of the people we cared for.

At times, even this aid we offered seemed pitiful, and thinking about the hundreds of thousands of peasants across Ireland we could not help, made me feel hopeless. I tried to focus on the people around me, pushing the thought of all others out of my mind, but as soon as I picked up a newspaper or went to the market in Ballygawley, their suffering was there—there was no place in Ireland the famine did not reach.

"We can't save everyone."

I looked up from the paper I had been reading, meeting Quin's green gaze across the dining table. My mouth quirked into a reluctant smile. "It seems you can read my mind."

He reached a hand across the table to grasp mine. "You've been thinking of little else."

I shrugged one shoulder. It was undoubtedly true.

"Perhaps you need a distraction," he suggested with a raised brow.

"What kind of distraction?" It would have to be something fairly monumental to take my mind off *this*, I thought, looking back down at the article I'd been reading.

"Christmas is coming up. We might hold more of a celebration than we normally do."

"Well..."

"We could invite the servants and the tenants. God knows they need a distraction too!"

"I suppose…" The idea did hold its attractions. I enjoyed a good celebration after all. Although…

"We shan't let any food go to waste.—Naturally."

I laughed. "It seems you really can read my mind."

"Perhaps I can," Quin agreed with a grin. "Or perhaps I just know you."

I smiled and squeezed his hand. Even before the potato harvest had failed for the first time, I had been very much aware of the peasants' limited resources and had never agreed with the wastefulness of many of the rich.

But Quin was right. Sharing our blessings with the people on the estate and celebrating that for which we could all still be thankful might be just what we needed in these dark and desperate times.

"WHAT IS THAT?"

Quin turned away from the window, where he had been contemplating a dark and brooding sky.

"It's a tree," he said with a grin as he came toward me.

"I can see that." I stopped in front of the tree in question, cocking my head as I inspected it. It was a small spruce standing in dark soil in a large clay pot, occupying one corner of the drawing room.

"It's a Christmas tree," Quin announced, his voice containing a distinct note of pride.

"A Christmas tree?"

Quin nodded enthusiastically. "It's all the rage in London, or so my father informed me when we visited. All the aristocrats are rushing out to get one for Christmas since it became known that Queen Victoria and Prince Albert have one every year."

"I see." I looked at the tree with renewed interest as I imagined an enormous spruce adorning a royal palace. "I am of course familiar with placing sprigs of evergreen around the house at Christmastime, but I'd never have thought to bring in an entire tree."

"This is the larger, more modern version," Quin said with a laugh. "It'll be decorated too."

"Oh?"

"Yes! With candles, small sugar ornaments and anything else Mrs O'Sullivan can think of. She's very enthusiastic!"

"I can imagine."

Just then, the sound of giggling reached us from the hall, followed in short order by the entrance of two pairs of legs poking out from under two enormous mounds of holly.

"Benjamin?" I looked at the foliage a little more closely. "And Conor?"

"Yes, mum," came the sound of Benjamin's voice from behind the green leaves. These started swaying precariously as the boys came closer until, with a sudden cry, one mound slid to the floor, revealing the surprised-looking face of Conor. He looked down at the strewn holly sprays, then up at me and down again, his eyes large and his mouth formed into a perfect 'O'.

I burst out laughing at the sight, making a soft red blush creep up his cheeks.

"What is all this?" I asked, waving a hand.

"It's holly, for the Christmas feast," Benjamin answered from behind the bushels he still held.

"For all of Glaslearg?"

"No, mum, for the house! It must look nice, no?"

"I suppose so.—Do put those down, Benjamin."

Not one to be asked twice, Benjamin dropped his burden, the twigs scattering all over the carpet.

"Ah..."

"Where were you planning on putting all of that?" Quin asked with some amusement, coming to stand next to me and surveying the mess in the drawing room.

"On the tables," Benjamin piped up.

"And over the fireplaces," Conor added.

"And we thought t' hang some on the doors..."

"...if we can find how t' hang them."

"And there must be some on the windowsills!"

"Aye, Ben, but we must be sure to leave space for the candles." Conor nodded gravely at his friend. Although Benjamin was a year or so older, Conor was the taller of the two.

"Candles!" Benjamin exclaimed, slapping himself on the forehead. "Course there must be candles in the widows!—But the holly can go 'round. That'll look right bonny!"

"Just do me the one favour," Quin interrupted the boys' chattering. "Don't set the house on fire!"

"Oh no, sir, we'd never!"

"Not a chance, sir!"

The boys' expostulations collided in their eagerness to appease their master, and I laughed at their earnest expressions.

"And do remember to clean up after yourselves," I said, waving a hand at the holly strewn floor.

"Otherwise, Mrs O'Sullivan will leather your backsides for you," Quin added, making the boys' eyes pop wide open. Although Quin was smiling, it wasn't quite an idle threat. As was the tradition in Ireland in the days leading up to Christmas, Mrs O'Sullivan and the other staff members had been hard at work scrubbing every last corner of the house until it gleamed. At the other end of the estate, the tenants had been doing the same, with the men taking on the additional task of whitewashing the walls of their cottages.

Nobody wanted all that hard work besmirched quite so soon.

Benjamin and Conor threw Quin identical sideways glances before quickly gathering the holly into one large mound. Having carefully collected every last stray leaf and twig, they set off to distribute the holly around the house, their laughter trailing behind them.

"They're certainly enjoying themselves!"

Quin came to stand in front of me. "And are you?"

"Well..." Being distracted by preparations for the Christmas celebrations did help keep my mind off Ireland's troubles, but it also left me feeling terribly guilty at times, as I thought of all those who were suffering.

"Enjoying yourself is not a sin."

I gaped at Quin for having read my thoughts yet again, making him grin. He pulled me into his arms and kissed the top of my head.

"I want you to enjoy yourself."

I sighed, making him put me away from him so he could look me in the eyes. "Promise me you'll try," he said, giving me a stern look down his nose.

I gave a short laugh at his expression. "I promise you, I'll try."

AS IT TURNED out, I did manage to enjoy myself after all, quite to my own surprise. Whether it was the sense of joy and peace that naturally accompanied the Christmas celebrations, or the exuberance of the staff and tenants, I felt my own spirits lift as the manor house was transformed around me—although feelings of guilt still tended to accost me throughout the day.

True to their word, Benjamin and Conor had covered every available surface of the house in holly and had contrived to hang more of the green sprigs from the doors and windows. Where they were getting the vast quantities of foliage, I had no idea, but their efforts were clear to see.

I laughed at the sight of Denis, who tottered past me sporting a small leafy spray behind his ear. The old butler gave me a toothless grin and returned to the task of placing candles in the windows. I smiled after him before making my way to the kitchen, my mouth watering at the delectable smell of freshly baked biscuits.

Mrs O'Sullivan's face was red-cheeked and gleaming as she placed a tray of piping hot biscuits onto the counter. She greeted me courteously before turning her attention to the dough rolled out on the tabletop. I watched in fascination as she used small tin cutters to shape the dough into horses, stars and even people.

"What's that for?" I asked as she began making small holes at the top of each shape.

"For the ribbon," she said, wiping her brow with the back of her hand. "These are for hangin' on the tree."

I nodded, remembering what Quin had told me. "Is there anything I can do to help?"

"Hm." Mrs O'Sullivan squinted around the room and the different foods in various stages of preparation. "If you've a mind t' help with the decorations, there's some over there that are needin' a ribbon." She inclined her head toward a bulging tray covered with a tea towel.

I peeked under the fabric, my eyes growing wide at the treasures hidden beneath—small bits of confectionary, dried and candied fruit, and nuts.

"There's ribbon in the basket on the side."

With tray and basket placed in front of me at the table I set to work, soon finding myself immersed in the process.

I picked up a sugar plum, breathing in its sweet fragrance as I carefully attached a red ribbon. "The whole house smells wonderful," I said. "We'll scarcely be able to walk from one room to the next without thinking about eating."

Mrs O'Sullivan chuckled. "And I haven't even prepared all o' the Christmas feast."

"I'd never have thought of holding such an extravagant celebration for Christmas. It's always been such a simple day."

"Aye," Mrs O'Sullivan said before breaking into a wide grin, "but I will say this 'ere is much more fun. Especially now…" Her face drooped and I sighed.

We were both silent for several minutes, each absorbed in our thoughts. Shaking off the sense of doom that seemed never too far away, I carefully tied together a cluster of dried berries and walnuts. Pleased with the result I turned my attention to a delicate ball of spun sugar, imagining the edible ornaments swinging gently between the spruce's branches, just waiting to be plucked.

As if drawn by the thought, Benjamin poked his head into the kitchen, scanning the quantities of sweetmeats scattered around the room. He licked his lips, before giving me a brief smile. When he turned to Mrs O'Sullivan with big eyes, the cook looked at him suspiciously.

"Will ye be needin' anything, Benjamin?"

The boy shrugged his shoulders, darting a quick glance toward the tray of biscuits on the countertop.

"Um…"

"Ye've only just had your dinner," Mrs O'Sullivan said, waving her wooden spoon. "Ye can't possibly be hungry."

"Well…" Benjamin looked down, shuffling his feet, and Mrs O'Sullivan gave me a conspiratorial wink.

"I would give ye one of the biscuits, lad, but these are meant for tomorrow's festivities."

Benjamin nodded and started turning away dejectedly, making the cook chuckle.

"Oh, go on then, here's a plate o' broken ones."

Benjamin's eyes lit up as he reached for the offering. Mrs O'Sullivan lifted one brow, holding the plate away from him.

"Thank ye, Mrs O'Sullivan," he chimed dutifully before sitting down and stuffing a handful of crumbs into his mouth.

I suppressed a laugh at the sight. In the time he'd been with us at Glaslearg, it had emerged that Benjamin had a particular fondness for all things sweet, capable of devouring huge quantities of biscuits, cakes and puddings without pausing for breath. Having probably eaten little such fare in his previous life, he was evidently making up for lost time.

He'd filled out since he'd landed on our doorstep half starved but was by no means fat—nor was he likely to become so over the next few years. I did, however, worry about his teeth.

I smiled, remembering how I'd tried to impress upon Benjamin the importance of cleaning his teeth at the end of each day. He'd stared at me for a moment before looking down at the object I'd pressed into his hand. Clearly, he'd never seen a toothbrush before in his life, nor had any idea how to use it. I'd explained it to him in detail, showing him how to make sure he removed every last particle of food stuck to his teeth. He had seemed to grasp the concept easily enough but had nevertheless given me a sceptical look, particularly so when I'd told him eating too much sugar resulted in tooth decay.

Since a good number of scientists did in fact believe this, though, I had insisted he use the brush daily. Whether or not he was actually following my advice, I couldn't say, but sincerely hoped so—else he would soon be sporting the meagre dentition displayed by the elderly Denis, who was currently hobbling into the kitchen, the sprig of holly still stuck behind his ear.

The butler smiled as Mrs O'Sullivan offered him a biscuit, revealing the largely empty gums I had just been contemplating. Not deterred by his lack of teeth, he popped the biscuit into his mouth, his jaws working industriously until he'd finally mashed the treat into a consistency he could swallow.

Having enjoyed a biscuit myself, I ran my tongue over my own complete set of teeth, feeling the sudden urge to clean them.

They would likely endure until evening, though, I decided. So instead, I turned my attention back to the remaining ornaments awaiting their ribbons, including the cooled biscuits Mrs O'Sullivan had baked earlier. Once everything was beribboned, I could hardly wait to start decorating the tree.

"Ye're welcome to it," Mrs O'Sullivan said when I asked if she had wanted to hang the decorations herself. "I've not got nearly enough food t' feed everyone yet." She waved a hand at the enormous pile of root vegetables waiting to be prepared. "This'll keep me busy enough!"

Seeing the work that still awaited the cook, I wondered if she would even get to her bed that night. Leaving the kitchen, though, I ran into Margaret and Mary, who were rushing to her aid.

"Where's Quinnie?" I asked Margaret as she tied on an apron.

"Young Bridget is looking after him," she said, nodding toward Mary, whose eyes softened at mention of her eldest daughter.

"She's had the care of her brother and sisters for some time. Quinnie will be quite safe."

"Of course," I said. "Bridget is a very sensible girl."

Mary beamed at me, and I inclined my head in farewell before crossing the entrance hall and going into the drawing room. In my absence, it had acquired even more greenery, being now also bedecked with long garlands made of evergreen sprigs hung across the windows and mantelpiece.

I placed the tray of ornaments on one of the low tables and admired the room, understanding why even the ancient pagans had used evergreens to celebrate winter festivals. Seeing the bright colours, I couldn't help but think of the springtime, when fresh greenery would emerge on every hill. It was a promise—a promise that the darkness of winter would come to an end.

Feeling my spirits soar I started decorating the tree, humming softly under my breath.

"That will look wonderful with the candles lit."

I looked at Quin, who was carrying a box of candles and a small canvas bag that clinked metallically as he came toward me.

"What's that?" I asked, pointing at the bag.

He removed a thin piece of metal and handed it to me. "For attaching the candles."

I turned the piece over in my hand. It was about one and a half inches long, with a sharp end on one side and a loop on the other. "This looks like a nail that's been bent at one end," I said, raising one brow.

"That's precisely what it is." Quin grinned. "John and I had to be a little creative."

"And you think the candles are going to hold?" I placed the loop on the tip of my little finger, looking at it sceptically.

Quin shrugged. "I suppose we'll see."

"What do they use in London?" I asked.

"My father said people have tried various methods—needles or string or adhering the candles with melted wax. No one technique seems to be entirely fool proof, though."

"I see." I had a sudden vision of the candles drooping and the tree going up in flames—followed in short order by the house.

"We'll be careful," Quin assured me, taking the piece of metal back from me. He lit a large candle standing on the mantelpiece and held the sharp end of the nail into the flame, before driving it into the base of one of the thinner candles meant for the tree. Looking pleased with the result he then carefully slid the loop over one of the branches, folding down the needles as best he could, until the candle was wedged firmly in place.

"See?" He cocked his head and raised his brows, waiting for my admiration.

I stood in front of him and patted his arm. "Well done." He frowned, looking suspicious. "I mean it," I said quickly, "this is wonderful." I waved an arm at the tree. "But not just the Christmas tree, all of it. It was a wonderful idea."

He smiled and kissed me briefly on the forehead before turning his attention to the remaining candles, while I hung the rest of the ornaments. We worked companionable side by side until we both stepped back to examine our efforts.

Never having seen a Christmas tree before, I had no idea whether ours looked like those standing in halls across the Irish Sea. I did know, though, that I absolutely loved the way ours had turned out and would insist on having one every year from now on!

"I like how you attached that large star-shaped biscuit to the top of the tree," Quin said, nodding approvingly. "It's a nice touch."

"We must thank Mrs O'Sullivan for all her hard work. I doubt I would have come up with half as many baubles on my own."

"Let's go then." He offered me his arm. Inhaling deeply as the scent of something rich and meaty drifted into the room, he added, "Perhaps we'll even be lucky enough to sample some of the feast before tomorrow."

WHEN TOMORROW CAME, the excitement around the house was palpable. As everyone bustled about with the final preparations, Benjamin was practically bouncing off the walls, so demented with anticipation was he.

"Why were ye not at midnight mass, mum?" he demanded in the middle of a mad dash across the entrance hall as I descended the stairs.

Denis, who had just come out of the drawing room, gave him a stern look, but I waved away his rebuke as I came to stand in front of the boy.

"The service you attended was Catholic," I explained patiently, "but Mr Williams and I are Protestant."

Benjamin wrinkled his brow.

"We went to a different service," I assured him, "at a different church."

"But *everyone* was at midnight mass," he insisted, giving me a suspicious look.

"Not *quite* everyone." This distinction clearly meant very little to Benjamin, as just about everyone he knew would in fact have attended the Catholic mass, including all of Glaslearg's servants and tenants. Indeed, the majority of the Irish populace remained Catholic, despite England's best efforts to convert the locals to Protestantism.

So determined had the English Crown been during the sixteenth and seventeenth centuries that many Irish Catholic landowners had been replaced with Protestant imports who were more likely to act in the best interests of the British—not to mention control and civilise the native inhabitants by spreading English beliefs and customs. My many times great grandfather, Cathal O'Neil, had narrowly avoided losing his own land (and possibly his life) by converting to Protestantism and declaring his loyalty to King James.

I wondered briefly whether my ancestors hadn't been particularly devout, to have continued the deception throughout the ensuing centuries, but soon dismissed the thought. They had done what they'd had to in order to survive.

"Both Protestants and Catholics belong to the Christian faith," I said to Benjamin, thinking it may have been this simple knowledge that had eased my ancestors' choice. "And both worship the same God, albeit a little differently." Although these differences had been reason enough for the persecution of thousands throughout history, I had not been brought up to believe such persecution justified—not least of all because my own mother had come from a Catholic home.

"And whichever way we celebrate Christmas, it is a time of joy as we honour our Saviour's birth; a time of being grateful for those we care for and taking pleasure in all our blessings." I smiled at Benjamin and cocked my head. "I hope you have experienced something of the sort over the past few days?"

"Oh yes, mum!" he said, his previous excitement returning in full force. "I've never seen nothin' like this before. I never once celebrated Christmas when I lived in Dublin, or ever before this."

"No, I wouldn't suppose so." The poor boy would hardly have had the opportunity to celebrate Christmas while living on the streets. And with the shock of the first failed potato harvest and Quin's lengthy stay in Dublin, we had barely acknowledged the festive season the year before. We were fortunate to be able to make up for it now—although there were many across Ireland who would find even less joy this Christmas than the last. Taking a deep breath, I firmly shook off the thought. "I'm glad you can do so now," I said, placing a hand on Benjamin's arm. "What has been your favourite part so far?"

His eyes went wide at the question. "Oh, I couldn't possibly say, mum. But maybe..." He skipped toward the staircase and pointed at the greenery adorning the banister. "Makin' everythin' look nice, I think!" He nodded madly before being distracted by the delicious smell of roasting meat. "Or maybe the food." He smacked his lips and took a few quick steps in the direction of the kitchen. "Yes, the food, definitely the food!"

Following his nose across the entrance hall, he passed a small table set in an alcove, which sported a miniature nativity scene made of straw and wood, surrounded by candles of varying sizes. "Oh, but the candles," he exclaimed, dashing back toward me with gleaming eyes. "I never saw nothin' like it. All the candles in the windows on the way t' mass. It was like all the stars had fallen from the sky." His face was filled with wonder in remembrance, making me smile.

It had been a sight to behold, indeed. With most poorer households relying on turf fires for light and warmth, the Irish countryside was usually black as pitch on a winter's night. But with candles burning in every window on Christmas Eve, the scenery was transformed into something magical. Benjamin was not the only one to have been enchanted as he made his way to the church in the dark.

"And did ye know all the candles are lit by a girl called Mary?" he asked, wriggling his brows as he bounced up and down. "Mrs O'Sullivan told me so. Only if there's no Mary, the youngest child gets t' light them.—But there's usually a Mary," he assured me in a tone echoing exactly that of our cook.

I laughed. "It is a very common name."

"D'ye think it's because o' the Blessed Virgin Mary?"

"I expect so."

He nodded gravely. "And will we get a Mary t' light these later?" he asked, rushing back to the small table and waving a hand over the unlit candles, almost causing one to topple.

He gave me a guilty look, making me lift one brow. "We might," I said, "unless you would like to light them for us?—Carefully, of course."

He puffed out his chest. "Could I really?" Not waiting for an answer, he darted toward the door to the drawing room, which sported an evergreen garland hanging across the top of the frame. "Then I can tell everyone I lit the candles and made this..." He touched the garland, causing it to swing lightly. "And did this..." He raced up the stairs to a decorated table on the landing. "And this..." He flew back down to a tall pottery vase containing spruce sprigs hung with ornaments. "And...argh..."

In his excitement he had bumped into the vase, barely managing to catch it before it shattered on the floor. Several ornaments flew across the entrance hall, scattering biscuit crumbs and berries across the tiles.

Still holding the vase at an angle, Benjamin stared at the mess with wide eyes, his mouth hanging open. Seeing me looking at him, his cheeks went bright red, and he quickly righted the vase and dropped to all fours.

"You might do better to fetch a dustpan."

I turned toward Quin, who had come out of the library at the noise and was observing Benjamin's efforts to scrape together the scattered fragments with his bare hands.

"Yes, sir," Benjamin said with a sideways glance toward his employer.

He was about to race off when Quin added, "If you have no further duties when you're done here, see to it that you find some entertainment *outside* of the house until the festivities begin."

Benjamin hunched his shoulders but gave a brief nod as he rushed off. Quin and I laughed after his receding form before each returning to our earlier pursuits.

When everything was in readiness a little later Benjamin returned to the manor house with Conor's family. He was still vibrating with excitement but took a wide berth of any potential hazards as he proudly showed off the decorations to the arriving tenants. He and Conor pointed out each item they had personally collected and distributed, earning themselves a few congratulatory pats on the back. Beaming alongside Benjamin and Conor, the tenants were equally impressed with their surroundings, wandering around the house with big eyes, sampling the small savouries Finnian and Rupert were distributing.

The feast would soon be awaiting us in the dining room, and my mouth watered in anticipation. There were too many of us to sit around the table, of course, but the ground floor provided plenty of space for everyone to spread out, eating morsels here and there—not to mention picking them off the Christmas tree.

"Let go, Quinnie!"

I turned toward Margaret's voice and smiled as she snatched her son away from the decorated spruce for the dozenth time. He wasn't quite walking yet but was eager to explore, pulling himself up to stand wherever he could, looking for hidden treasures. The ornaments dangling from the branches in front of his nose were proving to be far too tempting to ignore, and he was returning again and again, determined to collect his prize.

He clamped a pudgy hand over his mouth, the end of a green ribbon dangling between his fingers as his cheeks bulged and his jaws began to work.

"You little rascal," Margaret scolded good-naturedly as she attempted to prise open his fist. "You can't eat the ribbon!"

Quinnie seemed determined to try, though, scowling and shaking his head as his mother continued to accost him. Eventually, she managed to get hold of the end of the ribbon, pulling it out of his mouth when the biscuit had dissolved sufficiently to set it free.

Quinnie grinned with a mouthful of crumbs, making us both laugh.

"Don't think ye'll be stuffing yourself with biscuits all day long," Margaret informed him. Quinnie smacked his lips together, clearly of a different opinion.

"Oh, go on, it's Christmas Day after all."

Margaret nodded at Mr Dunne, who looked indulgently at the small boy as he sought his next adventure.

"So it is, Mr Dunne," Margaret agreed, running a hand over Quinnie's silky hair. "But I do hope he doesn't dismantle the whole house!" she added as Quinnie dropped to all fours and crawled away at speed. Margaret followed at a distance and was soon joined by John, who offered her a steaming cup before plucking his son off the ground and swinging him into the air, making the small boy squeal in delight as Margaret looked on with a smile.

When Denis announced a short time later that the food was ready, Quin beckoned me toward him in the entrance hall, where the majority of the guests was congregated.

"We are here today to celebrate the birth of our lord and saviour," Quin said once a degree of silence had descended, "and to share in our good fortune in these trying times. But while we count our blessings this day, let us not forget the many who are not as fortunate, for whom a hard road lies ahead." He paused for a moment, catching an eye here and there as the faces turned solemn. "Let us help those in need where we can—while remembering to live our own lives to the fullest." He squeezed my hand briefly, making me swallow a lump in my throat. "And so, let us enjoy ourselves this day as we celebrate with family and friends. *Nollaig shona duit!*"

Similar Christmas greetings echoed around the hall and Quin had to raise his voice to be heard above the din. "The feast awaits," he said, waving an arm toward the dining room.

"*Nollaig faoi shéan is faoi shaonas duit, máistreás.*"

"A happy and prosperous Christmas to you too, Mrs Moore," I said, smiling at the small, timid tenant as she passed me on her way to the heavily laden dining table. Her two teenage sons followed behind her, throwing me shy glances, but puffing out their chests in importance when Quin greeted them both by name before shaking hands with their father.

With most of the tenants wanting to greet us personally, it was some time before Quin and I found ourselves in the dining room. There was still plenty to eat, though, and my stomach grumbled as I contemplated the numerous dishes before me, wondering where I should start. Reaching for a slice of roast goose with buttery bread stuffing, my mouth watered at the sight of the crispy skin. Next to me, Quin was piling his plate with spiced beef. Seeing me watching him he grinned, before adding a few winter vegetables, raising his brows for my approval. I laughed as I took some vegetables myself. After helping myself to a slice of boiled ham, I turned away from the table, looking for a spot to sit and eat.

In the end, Quin and I simply stood in the entrance hall with the tenants, holding our plates and biting off chunks of food that we speared with our forks.

"My father would be horrified at such an unorthodox dinner party," Quin said between mouthfuls.

"Oh, I don't know. He did seem a lot more tolerant when we left." I skewered the last piece of turnip. The softly cooked vegetable dissolved on my tongue, and I closed my eyes briefly in bliss.

"It's one thing to accept an Irish daughter-in-law," Quin continued. "It's quite another to eat a grand feast whilst standing in the hallway surrounded by one's tenants."

"Perhaps we'll persuade him to join us next year."

Quin laughed. "Perhaps."

"It's snowing!" Quin and I turned toward the excited voice as a squealing mass of children stampeded past us and headed toward the drawing room.

Looking into the room from the doorway, I was just able to make out the soft flakes floating past the windows in the fading light. Several children were pressed up to the large double doors leading out onto the terrace, emitting loud "oohs" and "aahs" at regular intervals, enchanted by the sight.

Finnian appeared at my elbow to take my plate and I thanked him before making my way into the drawing room. I felt not a little enchanted myself, with the small flames of the numerous candles reflected in the darkening windows, while the snowfall started coming down in a steady white blanket. Cocooned in the warmth of the drawing room I looked out onto the demesne with Quin beside me, feeling as though the rest of the world had disappeared.

He took my hand, squeezing it lightly and I leaned my head against his shoulder, at peace for the first time in weeks. We stood companionably side by side for several minutes as the lawn and surrounding shrubs became dusted with snow, transforming the landscape into something magical.

The enchantment was broken a short time later by a sudden shriek that made my heart leap into my throat. I turned toward the noise, only for it to develop into a rolling wail, punctuated by a woman's anxious voice. I spotted Margaret holding a tear-streaked Quinnie and hurried toward her.

"What happened?" I asked but could immediately see the reason for Quinnie's distress. One of his hands was covered in angry red welts.

"I looked away for only a second," Margaret said, close to tears herself. "He went for the candle in the window and…" She broke off, waving feebly at her son's injuries.

"Here, *a muirnín*. This'll make ye feel better."

John appeared by Margaret's side, his head and shoulders dusted with small white flecks. He was holding a small dish of snow he must have scraped together outside. He reached for Quinnie's hand, but the little boy pulled it back, giving his father an accusatory look and snuggling closer to his mother.

"Come *leanbh mic*." Margaret gently extended his arm so John could apply snow to the burn. Quinnie's bottom lip quivered but instead of crying again, he stuck the thumb of his other hand firmly into his mouth.

"There now," Margaret soothed him, stroking his head.

"What's happened t' little Quinnie?" Benjamin appeared next to me, his brows wrinkled in concern. Behind him, Conor and a few other boys were craning their necks to see what the commotion was about.

"He reached for one o' the candles in the window and got hot wax all over his hand," Margaret explained.

"One o' *my* candles?" Benjamin exclaimed, his eyes going round as they darted from Margaret to Quinnie to me, and back again.

I placed a hand on Benjamin's shoulder. "It's not your fault. It was an accident."

Benjamin looked dubious but John gave him a smile. "He'll be alright.— See?" John dangled a biscuit on a ribbon in front of Quinnie's face, making the little boy take his thumb out of his mouth and reach for the treat with both hands. The rest of the snow slid off his skin, revealing several red patches that were no doubt painful but not blistered or cracked. "He'll be back t' his usual mischief in a day or two." John broke the biscuit in half, removing the ribbon and handing a piece to Quinnie, who instantly crammed it into his mouth, making us all laugh in relief.

"I suppose ye *will* be stuffing your face with biscuits all day long after all," Margaret said, hugging Quinnie to her as he chewed energetically, seeming to have forgotten all about his recent troubles. He bounced on Margaret's arm, craning his neck to see past her shoulder, his attention drawn by something in the corner.

I spotted Mary among a group of tenants standing in a circle singing an old Irish Christmas song, the soft notes reaching me above the surrounding chatter. As the singers' voices rose in the familiar refrain, more and more people joined in—some shyly, others boisterously—until the house was filled with the jubilant melody.

The first song was followed by another and another, and I soon found myself lifting my voice with the others, feeling my spirits soar. Quin hummed along to the unfamiliar Gaelic music, until someone started on an English song he knew. He joined in at full volume, making me laugh.

When at last people began drifting off, leaving only a small group of tireless singers behind, Quin and I made our way through the house, exchanging a few words here and there. Walking past the dining room I peeked inside, licking my lips at sight of the enormous quantities of Christmas cake that had made their appearance. I took the few steps to the table and reached for a large slice, only to have to take evasive action as a small boy dashed in front of me and snatched some cake for himself. He grinned at me and ran off, trailing crumbs. These were soon crushed underfoot as others came in search of the delicious treat. I quickly took the piece I'd been eying before it should all disappear and retreated toward the wall.

Taking my first bite, I sighed in contentment, savouring the fruity taste on my tongue. Currants and raisins combined with bursts of flavour from candied citrus peel, all within the spiced dough baked to perfection and drizzled with a generous portion of whiskey.

"This contains enough alcohol to fell a horse," Quin observed next to me, eying the cake in his hand in some amusement.

"*Bhí siad ólta ar císte Nollag,*" I intoned, making him give me a curious look. "They got drunk on Christmas cake," I translated, before devouring the rest of my cake, wondering if I should have a second portion.

Quin laughed and took a large bite himself, nodding as he chewed. "That is a distinct possibility." He inclined his head toward the table, where several youngsters were stuffing themselves with the well-drenched cake.

I was about to comment when the elderly Mr Fagan stomped past, throwing the group an accusatory look. "*Féasta anocht agus gorta amárach,*" he muttered, leaving the dining room in a huff.

Quin wrinkled his brows as he looked after him. "What did he say?"

I compressed my lips, my appetite suddenly gone. "A feast tonight and a famine tomorrow." I caught Quin's eye and he reached for my hand, squeezing it lightly.

"Mistress, Conor says the Christmas celebrations go on for two weeks. Is that true?"

I turned away from Quin and looked at Benjamin, who had appeared at my elbow yet again. He had been pestering Quin and me with questions all day, it being his first official Christmas celebration. He was staring at me expectantly now, along with several other children, and I forced a smile to my face.

"Almost," I said, pushing aside thoughts of Mr Fagan's ominous observation. "Twelve days to be exact."

"See!" Conor stuck his nose into the air and puffed out his chest.

"Ye were wrong, weren't ye?" Benjamin countered, pointing his finger at Conor, making him scowl. Conor opened his mouth, but Benjamin forestalled him. Turning back to me he asked, "What happens over the *twelve days*?" He emphasised the latter, clearly wishing to impress upon Conor the vast difference between twelve days and two weeks.

"Well," I said, suppressing a laugh at the boys' antics, "tomorrow is St. Stephen's Day and…"

"On St. Stephen's Day we wearing straw and asking fo' money."

I smiled at little Alfie Garvey, who had offered up this wisdom in his broken English. While most of the children I'd been teaching weren't quite fluent yet, all of them could understand almost everything that was said and could communicate readily enough.

"You're more likely to get something to eat or drink," I assured him. "And you have to work for it," I added, looking at Benjamin.

"Work for it?" Benjamin looked appalled.

"Indeed. You have to provide entertainment at the houses you visit by singing and playing music or dancing."

"Hm, and what comes after St. Stephen's Day?"

"Things slow down a bit after that," I admitted. "Leftovers will be eaten over the next few days, maintaining something of a festive air, but normal farm and household work will also resume—at least until we celebrate the coming of the new year."

"Ooh! How d'we do that?"

"We stay up until midnight and leave all the doors open," Mary's daughter Bridget declared. With her mother also able to speak English, Bridget's was almost perfect.

"But it's winter!" Benjamin objected, looking at Bridget in disgust. "What's the point o' leavin' the doors open anyway?"

Bridget rolled her eyes. "To let the air from the old year out and from the new year in, of course."

"Oh, o' course." Benjamin stuck out his tongue but gave me a guilty look when he saw me watching him. Quin lifted one menacing brow, making

Benjamin's eyes pop wide open. "And is that the end o' the Christmas celebrations then?" he asked quickly, throwing Quin a sideways glance.

"That's not twelve days yet, *amadán*!" Cormac Fitzgerald pointed out, a sneer on his face.

Benjamin turned toward Cormac with a scowl. Evidently, he'd heard the Gaelic word for fool before and didn't appreciate being called one. The boys glared at each other, Benjamin baring his teeth and Cormac clenching his hands into fists. Before either could make a move, though, Quin raised a hand, waving his index finger from side to side, accompanied by a slow shaking of his head as he gave each boy a meaningful look.

Benjamin cleared his throat, his cheeks going pink. "What happens after the new year celebration?" he asked meekly, batting his reddish lashes.

"After that comes the best day o' the year!"

I laughed, turning toward the stout Mrs Fitzgerald as she came to stand next to her son. Cormac threw her a guilty look, clearly wondering whether she'd heard his less than polite exchange with Benjamin just moments ago. She smiled, though, and he relaxed.

"What's that?" Benjamin asked Mrs Fitzgerald, looking intrigued.

"*Nollaig na mBan*," she announced slowly, a dreamy look on her face.

"It's the Women's Christmas," young Bridget explained a little haughtily, seeing Benjamin's confused look, "when the men do all the work around the house and the women take tea and cake."

"The men do the work around the house?" Benjamin scoffed, clearly finding the thought absurd. Around him, a few of the other children giggled.

Bridget raised her brows. "You think the men won't manage?"

"Not manage? Pah!"

"Ye're right, Benjamin, it's naught but easy work." Benjamin hunched his shoulders at the sound of Mrs O'Sullivan's voice. She had come up behind him, having laid aside her apron. "There's only the milkin', the cookin' and the cleanin' o' the house t' worry about, and the feedin' o' the livestock. All easy work it is."

Mrs Fitzgerald nodded. "And the children really aren't much trouble either. The small ones may need a fresh clout of a time, but else it's only a matter o' feedin' them really."

"Quite so, Mrs Fitzgerald. O' course there may be a spot o' spinning or mending or even laundry t' be done, but any man would have such work finished in no time at all."

Benjamin's eyes flickered between the two women, a rather haunted look appearing on his face. "Ah…"

"Now, tendin' the fields is quite familiar work to the menfolk," the cook continued, unperturbed, "so t'would naturally be no trouble at all t' take over the women's portion o' that task as well.—But o' course there's not much in the way o' field work t' be done in the winter months so ye needn't worry about that now."

Mrs O'Sullivan gave Benjamin a broad smile, making his lips twitch in nervous response. "Um…"

"So ye see tis really hardly an effort for the men t' take over the women's work on the one day." Mrs O'Sullivan flipped her wrist.

"But we do enjoy it all the same," Mrs Fitzgerald concluded, patting Cormac on the head.

The boys glanced at each other, silent understanding passing between them. "O' course Mrs O'Sullivan" and "Yes, *máthair*" they murmured quickly before dashing off, followed by the other children.

Quin and I joined in the women's laughter as we watched their retreat, which was being held up by a group of departing tenants—to their obvious annoyance.

"And what's gotten into them?" Margaret asked, coming up to the rest of us with Quinnie balanced on her hip.

"They're having to rethink their opinions on the roles of the sexes," Quin said in some amusement, wiggling his fingers in front of Quinnie, making him giggle.

As Quin turned his attention to several men who were leaving, I explained to Margaret the gist of the recent conversation. She smiled wistfully. "I will say that I'm quite looking forward to *Nollaig na mBan* myself. Not that I don't enjoy taking care o' this little one"—she looked at Quinnie, who was fidgeting in her arms—"but it will be nice not t' have t' run after him all day for once." She sighed as the little boy immediately sped off when she placed him on the floor.

"How's his hand?" I asked, following Margaret as she kept pace with Quinnie. Although I could see some areas of skin were still red, it didn't seem to be bothering him.

"He's quite forgotten about it," Margaret confirmed. "Although he is avoiding going near any more candles." She shrugged. "That's a good thing I suppose.—Not that there isn't enough for him to get into even so." She removed Quinnie's grasping fingers as he tried to pull down a wreath from one of the small tables. Unbothered, he set off again, this time toward the Christmas tree.

I hung back, admiring the tree from afar, unencumbered by the many people who had been milling about earlier. Several of the tenants had already left and the whole house was less crowded, the day's celebrations coming to an end.

The lower branches of the tree had been picked bare, mostly by the children—although I'd also seen some of the adults make off with a sweet treat. Higher up, a few decorations still swayed gently, catching the light of the numerous candles. While these had burned down a great deal, the fasteners Quin and John had contrived were holding and we'd had no fiery incidents.

"We should blow out the candles."

Quin came up behind me, laying his hands lightly on my shoulders.

"Soon," I said, smiling back at him. "Let me enjoy them a little longer."

The day had been wonderful, a magical distraction from the world around us. But I had the uneasy feeling that extinguishing the candles would extinguish the day's joy, leaving us facing the harshness of our reality once more.

Quin wrapped his arms around my middle and pulled me gently against him, laying his head against mine. I looked surreptitiously around the room, but the few people who were still there weren't paying attention.

Besides, I realised, *I didn't care.*

I leaned back against Quin's chest, and we stood silently for several minutes, watching the flickering candlelight and the softly falling snowflakes outside the window.

The room slowly emptied around us, and still we stood there, frozen in this moment of peace.

When at last the candles had burned down to little more than stubs, Quin stepped in front of the Christmas tree and took a deep breath. Letting it out slowly, he blew out the first flame and then the next and the next until, with a final blast, the last of the twinkling lights was snuffed out, throwing the tree into darkness.

36.

"ARE YOU SURE you want to come with me, Margaret?"

"Aye, mistress! I've had little enough chance to go anywhere these past months."

I smiled at the small maid, who was bristling with excitement, although we were only going to Ballygawley's weekly market, where she'd been countless times before. With Finnian and Mary busy elsewhere, Margaret had hastily offered to accompany me.

"Well, alright, if you're sure," I said as she wrapped Quinnie in his carrying cloth.

"I'm sure!" she insisted. "Besides, little Quinnie needs to see something of the world, doesn't he?" She grinned, making me laugh. "Not that he'll be seeing much now," she added, stroking her son's downy brown hair as he rubbed his eyes with small fists.

Margaret pulled a woollen cap over Quinnie's head and tied a neat ribbon under his chin to keep him warm. It was only a week into the new year, and there was a distinct winter chill in the air. She adjusted the carrying cloth so the little boy lay snugly against her chest and started rocking him and cooing under her breath. Lulled by his mother's movements, Quinnie's eyes started closing, until he was fast asleep.

Margaret and I smiled at each other as his small pink lips parted slightly in absolute contentment.

"You'll have one of your own one day," Margaret said to me. "Perhaps soon." She reached out and gently squeezed my arm.

"Perhaps." I shrugged. "Um...shall we?" I asked to change the subject, heading toward the door.

On our way to the market, we chatted of this and that, until Margaret suddenly exclaimed, "Over there, mistress!"

We had reached the outskirts of Ballygawley, and I followed the direction of her gaze to see a sorry looking group of people begging at the roadside. A dirt-streaked man was sitting on the ground, his leg twisted awkwardly, perhaps badly broken sometime in the past, making him unable to work. He held his hat in his hands, his deep-set eyes pleading as he looked at us. A woman was kneeling next to him, staring at us with large, sad eyes as the wagon came to a stop next to her. Her hand was resting on the head of a young girl lying on the ground at her feet, who looked to be asleep, her long red pigtails dishevelled.

I sighed, putting down the reins and reaching for the cloth bag I'd stashed in the wagon for just such an encounter. Although poverty and misery had long been a staple component of Irish society, the second poor potato harvest in as many years had resulted in even more destitute souls wandering the countryside.

I jumped off the wagon seat and withdrew two loaves of bread from the bag, handing one to Margaret before giving the other to the man, whose lined and haggard face reflected the lifetime of hardships he'd endured. Margaret was kneeling in front of the woman and child, supporting Quinnie in his carrying cloth with one hand as she handed the woman the bread with the other. The woman murmured her thanks before looking back down at the child, who was stirring, sitting up groggily. The girl's face was a little flushed and her eyes looked slightly glazed, but she smiled as she looked at Margaret and the toddler. She leaned in close, studying the small face just in front of her own.

"*Tá sé beag bídeach!*" she murmured in a hoarse-sounding voice, her smile widening. *He's so tiny!*

"*Is ea, ach lá éigin, déarfaimid rinne sé fear brae,*" Margaret responded with a smile of her own. *He is, but one day we'll say he grew into a fine man.*

The little girl gazed at Quinnie a while longer before slowly turning her attention to her mother, who had torn off a piece of bread and was offering it to her. The girl took the bread but only held it in her hand while her parents started eating.

Margaret stood up, waving goodbye as she turned back toward the wagon.

"*Go dté sibh slán*," I murmured in farewell as I turned back myself, my heart feeling heavy as I looked at the family's threadbare clothes. Although they had something to fill their bellies for now, what would happen to them tomorrow or the next day? They depended entirely on the goodwill of others for their survival, as did many more. And while the government had vowed to provide imports from America to help ease the strain, as had been done the year before, the promised grains had not yet arrived—little comfort to those in desperate need, who watched with hungry eyes as local produce continued to leave Irish shores in droves.

I breathed in heavily as I climbed back onto the wagon seat, wishing I could do more. I should have brought blankets, I berated myself, or old clothes. But what spare material possessions we had were already being shared with our tenants.

"You're doing what you can, mistress," came Margaret's soft voice and I smiled at her, having read my thoughts.

I shrugged. "It's never enough."

"No," she responded, shaking her head, "it never is."

"WHAT'S WRONG?" I whispered in the dark, groggily awakening from a deep sleep.

"It's the baby," came Mrs O'Sullivan's shaky voice in response.

"The baby?" I sat up in a rush of bedclothes, causing Quin to leap up in turn, landing on his feet, crouched defensively next to the bed. Although he looked quite comical, I didn't feel like laughing. "Quinnie?"

"Yes, mistress, come quick!"

It was the middle of the night, and I quickly pulled my dressing gown over my nightdress as Mrs O'Sullivan picked up the lamp she'd placed on the floor. I fumbled for my shoes.

"What's going on?" Quin asked, coming around to my side of the bed, his hair sticking up wildly in all directions.

"Margaret's baby is ill," Mrs O'Sullivan answered. "John came to fetch me. He..." She stopped talking, lowering and shaking her head, making my heart leap into my throat in fear. "Come quick," she said again in a shaky voice.

"I'm coming." I hurried after her, not sure though what I could possibly do to help. We rushed down the stairs and into the cold night, the winter air biting through the thin cloth of my gown. I pulled it closer around me but ran after Mrs O'Sullivan as she hastened across the grounds, moving surprisingly quickly considering her ample proportions.

When we finally arrived at Margaret and John's cottage, the door burst open, and a haggard-looking John emerged.

"Aoife, mistress...the baby...he..." John gave up with a sob and shook his head, beckoning us with a weak wave of the hand to follow him into the cottage's dim interior. My heart was pounding, and my throat constricted as I crossed the threshold, making my way to the small sleeping chamber off the side of the main living quarters.

There I found Margaret huddled on the bed, wrapped protectively around little Quinnie. When I'd last seen him the previous afternoon after our return from the market, the little boy had looked at me with bright eyes, babbling happily, toddling around and inspecting everything in sight. He now lay limp on his mother's lap, his eyes glazed and sunken, his skin red and dry, lips cracked.

A prickling sensation crept from my scalp down to the base of my spine at the sight. *"Anbhás ag teacht,"* an old woman had warned on Margaret's wedding day, pointing a gnarled finger at her growing belly.

Death is coming.

Bile rose in my throat, and I swallowed heavily as Margaret tried to put Quinnie to her breast. Unresponsive, he just lay there without moving, not even turning his head away from the proffered nipple as droplets of milk started dripping ever more frequently, landing on his burning cheek.

"Margaret," I said softly as I made my way to the bed.

"He was fussing last night," she whispered, her voice thick with emotion and fear, "but then...then he wouldn't wake...and he won't drink..." She pulled the tiny body closer to her, wrapping her arms around him, heedless of the milk still dripping from one exposed breast. "He won't drink," she repeated so softly that I could barely hear her.

I clenched my jaws painfully, feeling utterly helpless. I gently patted Margaret's shoulder before reaching out a hand to stroke Quinnie's arm. I almost recoiled in shock; his skin was hot to the touch. I carefully ran my fingers over the small limb. The skin was dry and leathery, like coarse fabric, nothing like the soft and yielding flesh I had touched only hours before.

"I've sent Finnian to fetch the doctor." Quin's voice reached me from the other room as my throat constricted in dread. I turned my head toward him and saw John nod mechanically in response, but without any visible relief on his features. Quin threw a worried glance in our direction, our eyes meeting briefly, and I had to blink away tears.

The nearest doctor was in Ballygawley. By the time he got here it would probably be too late.

"I'll make up a cup of fever tea, that's what I'll do," Mrs O'Sullivan declared, briskly nodding her head as she bustled back out the door. I watched her leave with a sinking feeling. While she could very ably deal with all manner of common ailments and minor afflictions, I was afraid even her indomitable resolve would not be of help on this dreadful night.

A sob from Margaret made me turn back toward her. Quinnie's mouth was open, a dribble of undrunk milk running down his chin, his glazed eyes staring unseeing at the ceiling. With his mother huddling over him he gave a little gasp, like an angel's breath, followed by a thunderous silence that reverberated in my skull with the certainty of its finality.

"No!" Margaret's cry cut through me, the desolation in her voice so acute that I knew there was no way back for her from here, as Quinnie's body shook off its earthly torments, leaving behind a doll-like shell. Margaret clung to the small bundle, rocking back and forth as tears streamed down her face, wailing with the utter desolation of a mother who no longer has a child. I felt hot tears running down my own cheeks and leaned over her, wrapping my arms around her. Our tears mingled and pattered softly onto the little boy who had burrowed his way deep into our hearts, only to be ripped out violently just a few short months after his birth.

I heard footsteps behind me and felt Quin's gentle hand on my back. His eyes were filled with tears, while next to him, John's homely face was so contorted in agony I could barely look at him. I staggered to my feet and John dropped to his knees next to Margaret, who was still clinging to her child's lifeless form, rocking him and keening softly. John held the ruins of his family in his arms, a mournful moan escaping his lips as his own tears joined the deluge that had already been shed but been unable to wash away the devastation and the pain.

I turned into Quin's arms with a sob. He held me tightly while he himself shook with emotion.

The cottage door opened suddenly, letting in a blast of cold air and a panting Mrs O'Sullivan, who was holding a steaming teapot. She froze in front of the bedroom. "No!" she cried, trying to deny the reality that was all too apparent. "No!" She dropped the teapot, which shattered on the stone floor, pottery shards scattering around the room and hot tea splattering the walls.

I shook my head at her as a fresh onslaught of tears streaked down my face, her own face splitting into a grimace of despair. I turned back to Quin, and we clung to each other, our mournful sobbing interrupted only by the piercing cries coming from Margaret and John.

"Here, Margaret."

Mrs O'Sullivan's gentle voice brought me back to myself and I lifted my head from Quin's shoulder. My eyes felt swollen and painful as I looked toward the bed. John was slumped on the floor, keening to himself, while Margaret was still sitting on the coverlet, holding her lifeless son in her arms, rocking back and forth and crooning under her breath. Mrs O'Sullivan slowly reached out her arms, trying to take the little boy from her, but Margaret hugged him closer to her, shaking her head. Her eyes were red-rimmed and puffy, and her nose was running, but she buried her face in the small bundle she held, humming softly to herself, shutting out the world around her.

My heart bled for her and the pain she must be feeling.

And suddenly, I was glad I had no children of my own, children who could be snatched away so viciously, leaving utter desolation in their wake.

And I hoped I never had any.

"Come Margaret," Mrs O'Sullivan said softly, gently stroking Margaret's head. "You have to let him go."

"I won't," Margaret whispered, shaking her head, her eyes staring and dry. "I won't."

"You must," Mrs O'Sullivan urged gently.

Margaret shook her head once more as fresh tears ran down her blotched cheeks, but slowly, slowly, she loosened her grip, until at last she surrendered the small body with a gut-wrenching moan. She slumped in on herself, wrapping her arms around her knees, unmoving in silent despair. John came to sit next to her, taking her in his arms as he let his own tears fall unashamedly.

Margaret stared into space, unmoving—as if she had turned to stone.

WE BURIED QUINNIE'S small body several days later. He went into the ground lying in the arms of his mother, who had followed him into death.

Unresponsive and listless, Margaret had started burning with fever just a few short hours after her son had left her. It seemed almost as if she'd willed it to happen, wanting to be reunited with him. Toward the end her body had convulsed in protest, struggling to stay alive, but Margaret had taken it stoically, eyes closed and looking inwards, welcoming an end to her despair.

"Don't leave me too," John had whispered, kneeling at the side of the bed, holding Margaret's hand, his face etched with grief.

Margaret had opened her swollen eyes and slowly lifted her hand to touch John's cheek with her fingertips. She'd smiled at him, looking almost dreamy, even as her eyes glazed over and she exhaled for the last time, finally finding peace.

"This is all my fault," I said quietly now, sitting on the bed with my hands in my lap, feeling the burden of guilt rest heavily on my shoulders.

"Your fault?" Quin's voice was incredulous as he looked at me, in the process of removing his jacket. He'd been consoling John after the funeral, not wanting him to be alone. It was past midnight now, but I had been unable to sleep, oppressed by the events of the last few days.

Quin carelessly threw his jacket to the side and came to stand in front of me. He gently lifted my head with his hand, stroking my cheek and looking into my eyes. "This is not your fault," he said firmly, shaking his head.

"It is." I dropped my eyes as they filled with tears. "I took Margaret to the market."

"What does that have to do with anything?" he asked in bewilderment.

"The beggars. The girl...I think the girl was sick." I looked back up at Quin as tears started to overflow. "I saw the signs...I must have known..." I shook my head as I continued rambling. "I...I should have said...I should have warned Margaret to stay away."

"No Alannah." Quin tried to pull me against him, but I resisted, looking down and sniffing as my nose started to run.

"I saw the girl," I insisted, tears and mucus streaming freely down my face in my despair. "Her cheeks, her eyes...she even sounded sick." I wiped my hand carelessly across my face. "What was I thinking?" I whispered. "What have I done?"

"You haven't done this," Quin said gently, sitting next to me and wrapping his arms around me. "It's not your fault."

"For God will bring every deed into judgment," I quoted the biblical line, shaking my head in self-loathing as my tears continued to fall.

Quin stiffened and loosened his hold on me. "There is no God." His voice was cold, making me gasp. He looked down at me, his jaws clenched, eyebrows drawn together in an angry scowl.

"You don't mean that," I countered breathily, my eyes going wide. While I didn't agree with all of the Church's teachings, I had never questioned God's existence and was rather shocked Quin would do so now.

"Yes, I do!" He jumped up suddenly and started pacing in front of the bed. "If I didn't know it before, I know it now!"

"But..."

"An all-powerful, loving God?" Quin asked with some scorn, his nostrils flaring in anger as I continued to stare at him in shock. "Where is God when men slaughter each other on the battlefield?" he demanded, his hands clenched into fists at his side. "Where is He when wretched peasants dig up the sludge that was meant to feed them? And where is He"—his voice cracked and he continued in a whisper—"when a tiny, innocent life is snuffed out? And the mother who birthed him follows him to the grave in her grief."

"I..." I stopped speaking, realising I had nothing to say.

"If He is all-powerful, why does He not act?" Quin sat back down next to me, his shoulders slumped. "If He is all-loving, why does He allow evil to exist and lives to be ruined?"

"Nobody knows," I offered quietly, unhelpfully, reaching out a hand to Quin. He took it and grasped it tightly, not looking at me.

"If it had been you...and our child..." He trailed off, his face crumpling as a few tears trickled down his cheeks. He pulled me to him roughly and crushed me against his chest, swallowing heavily. I tightened my own arms around him, and we held each other in our despair.

"We have to believe that God has a plan for us," I murmured when Quin at last loosened his grip. He looked at me briefly, his eyes red-rimmed and filled with desolation. He dropped his gaze, his faith lost. "I think you're right," I continued quietly, feeling unutterably sad. "These things...these things just happen. There's nothing either of us could have done."

Even as my guilt over Margaret and Quinnie eased a little as I said the words, I felt another heavy weight settle on my shoulders, remembering a similar conversation Quin and I had had. It was about two years ago, shortly after Kieran had been killed. Quin had blamed himself for Kieran's death and his killer's attack on me, feeling that he should have been able to protect us from harm.

"You're thinking of Kieran, aren't you?" Quin asked softly, his voice thick with emotion. He knew my brother was often on my mind at this time of year. I nodded, unable to speak. Quin was quiet for a moment before gently putting me away from him so he could look at me. "Whether there is a God or not"—I was about to object, but he slowly shook his head—"that wasn't my fault, and this wasn't yours." He tried to hold my eyes, but I looked away. Quin gently lifted my chin. "You couldn't have known Margaret and Quinnie would get sick," he insisted. "It's not your fault."

I took a deep breath, suddenly feeling unspeakably tired. Quin pulled me gently into his arms. His chest rose and fell steadily next to mine, and I tightened my grip on him.

"Rest now," he murmured into the top of my head. "We all need to get some sleep."

37.

TWO DAYS AFTER the funeral I still felt dreadfully tired. Time was passing in a haze as everyone at Glaslearg tried to come to terms with Margaret and Quinnie's death. The little maid had been a constant feature on the estate and had made many friends, both among the servants and the tenants. She had been a friend to me too, and to Quin, and we felt her loss acutely, so much a part of our daily lives had she been. Thinking about little Quinnie was almost unbearable, a life snatched away so soon, when he'd barely begun to live.

I worried about John and made a point of checking on him throughout the day as I dragged myself from one chore to the next. We had told him to take as much time as he needed, but he'd thrown himself into his duties and hadn't looked back, clearly trying to keep himself busy. He assured me he was fine, and I had no choice but to believe him.

I sighed and turned to the sideboard, trying to shake off my gloom as I made myself a cup of tea.

"I'll be going to the Connells later to check on them," I said to Quin, who was sitting at the dining table behind me. Mr Connell was usually a regular visitor up at the manor house, keeping Quin and me informed about anything of importance to do with the tenants. He hadn't visited in the past week, though, and when I'd seen him at the funeral, he'd looked tired and listless—hardly surprising under the circumstances but I wanted to ensure myself of his welfare, nonetheless.

"You'll be doing no such thing!"

"Excuse me?" I whirled away from the sideboard at Quin's harsh tone. My sudden movement upset the teacup in my hand, making dark brown droplets splatter down the front of my dress. I swiped at them viciously as I turned to face Quin. "What do you mean?"

"It's no longer safe for you to visit the tenants." I gaped at him, blinking stupidly. "With this sickness…" he continued but I cut him off.

"And you're suggesting that I should simply abandon them to their fate?"

"I'm not suggesting you abandon them…"

"But you won't let me visit them?"

"Alannah, please be reasonable."

"Reasonable?" I sputtered, at a loss for words.

His eyes narrowed before he spoke again in a stern voice. "If you won't look after yourself, then I'll do it for you."

"What is *that* supposed to mean?" I demanded through clenched teeth. His eyes dropped briefly to my midsection, and I inhaled sharply through my nose. "Are you suggesting," I hissed, "that *I* am to blame for not giving you any children?" I glared at him before turning away, so angry I thought I might strike him if I looked at him.

"Of course not!" His voice came from behind me, and I felt his hand on my shoulder.

"Don't touch me!" I whirled back around, fists clenched at my sides.

"Alannah…"

"How dare you!" I was still fuming with rage and listening to another word he had to say was the furthest thing from my mind.

"I said no such thing…"

"It's always the woman's fault, isn't it?"

"What?"

"Because the woman carries the child it must therefore be her fault if there is no child to bear. Is that it?"

"No!" He grabbed me by the upper arms. I tried to turn away, but he forced me to look at him. "Alannah, that is neither what I said, nor what I meant! But if you must know, at this moment I sincerely hope you never give me a child at all!"

"How can you…?"

"Can you blame me?" he growled, his face right in front of mine, his eyes flickering back and forth between my own. In their green depths I could see the grief they bore, and the terrible fear.

My throat constricted as I thought of Margaret and Quinnie for the thousandth time. "I suppose not," I relented with a sigh, remembering how I'd had the same thought after Quinnie's death. "But the Connells…"

"Alannah…" Quin looked down briefly and swallowed heavily. When he looked up again his eyes were shiny with tears, making my heart give a sudden lurch. "I am afraid for you," he said softly in a shaky voice, extending a hand to cup my cheek, "afraid for all of us."

I felt my own eyes fill with tears and laid my hand over his. "I know you are. And so am I. But…" I shook my head and took a deep breath. "I can't stop caring for the people who live here, people who have become my friends.—They need me."

"I need you."

"I know," I said once more, gripping Quin's hands. We looked at each other for a long moment.

"Go," he said finally, inclining his head toward the door. "I know you're right, it's just…" He clenched his jaws, unable to go on.

"I know," I said for the third time, before stepping into his arms.

He crushed me to him, and I clung to him as a wave of fear swept through me. Fear for me and for us, and any children we might have, fear for our tenants and for Ireland's poor as they faced another season of desperate need. I closed my eyes, leaning against his chest, his heart thumping steadily beneath my ear.

When he at last let me go, he sighed. "You'll be careful, won't you?"

"I will," I promised.

He glanced through the open door before turning back to me. "Shall I go with you?"

I shook my head; I knew he had work to do. "Go." I nudged him gently toward the study as he continued to hover near me uncertainly. "I'll just finish my tea before heading out."

He compressed his lips briefly but nodded. I watched him cross the entrance hall and disappear into the study, receiving a lopsided smile as he turned to close the door. I walked slowly back to the sideboard, where I stood staring unseeing at the tea things, tiredness and worry dragging at me like a heavy weight. I shook my head to clear the fuzziness and took a deep breath. I poured some more tea into my cup, taking a spoon and stirring mechanically, watching the swirling motion as if in a trance. I stopped, realising I hadn't added any sugar, and didn't usually do so.

Taking a dollop of cream instead, I sat down at the table, holding the warm cup between my hands.

"Mistress?"

I turned toward Mrs O'Sullivan, who was standing in the doorway. I gave her a small smile and raised a questioning brow.

"Finnian and I will be going to the market…"

She trailed off and my heart gave a painful thump. I had forgotten it was Friday. Exactly one week ago, Margaret and I had gone to the same market, expecting to return with no more than a few essential items for the estate.

Instead, Margaret and Quinnie had returned with a deadly disease.

"It'll be alright." Mrs O'Sullivan came to stand next to me and laid her hand on my shoulder. I looked into her lined face, reaching up to place my hand over hers. She stood for a moment, her solid presence giving me comfort. "You should get some rest."

I nodded absently.

"We'll be back soon."

I waved after her as she disappeared.

She was probably right. I felt drained and tired; so tired—I couldn't remember when I'd last had a good night's sleep. Probably not since the harvest, I reflected. Exhaustion pulled at me, wanting to drag me under, and my head ached with the constant worry that filled my days and the deep sorrow of the last week.

I shook myself, reminding myself I wasn't alone. While I sat here wallowing in my own misery, there were many others who had far greater concerns. Across Ireland, thousands of people were facing the very real danger of starvation or succumbing to disease—disease such as that which had already claimed two of our own.

I thought of Mr Connell's sickly face at the funeral and braced my arms on the table, wanting to get up. I must go check on him, I thought, refusing to think about the possibility of losing anyone else. I pushed myself up from my chair, feeling terribly weak. My arms trembled with the effort, and I sat back down with a thump. Perhaps I would rest for a while, after all, close my eyes for a few minutes to regain a little strength. Feeling like I was underwater, I folded my arms on the tabletop and lowered my throbbing head onto them, before falling into oblivion.

QUIN RAN A hand roughly over his face, trying to rid himself of the recurring images of Quinnie and Margaret as they took their last breaths, images that had been haunting him ever since that dreadful night. He clenched his jaws as Margaret's face was replaced by Alannah's, holding their unborn child dead in her arms. He shook his head violently, trying to dispel the looming nightmare, his heart thumping painfully at the thought of losing her.

He inhaled sharply and looked back down onto the column of numbers in front of him, trying to distract himself by contemplating for the thousandth time how to help those in need. By sharing the estate's bounty of oats and wheat, he could at least assist the tenants on his own estate, but he felt there was more he should do to help the countless others who were suffering.

The sense of responsibility weighed heavily on him, shrouding him in helplessness. He stared at the vista outside the window, a beautiful green hillside—perhaps the one that had given the estate its name—with an unseasonable, idyllic blue sky above, dotted with picturesque clouds. The scene was imminently peaceful, in complete contrast to the turmoil within him.

With thousands and thousands of peasants going hungry, even giving away all of Glaslearg's surplus produce would not be enough. And it would leave them without an income from that produce, an income that was being further depleted by the diminished rent coming in from the struggling tenants. Quin had assured his tenants they would not be evicted if they were unable to pay and he'd meant it, but the lack of income from more than one source was slowly cutting into the estate's capital.

He sighed and closed the ledger, before looking outside the window once more. Taking strength from the beauty that could be found even in the depths of despair, he squared his shoulders, thinking about Alannah's fierce and selfless desire to care for the people on the estate.

Somehow, they would all get through this famine, he and Alannah would make sure of it.

Feeling sudden remorse for the harsh words he'd uttered to her earlier, when she'd only been trying to help those in need, he got up and headed to the dining room to see if she was still there.

As soon as he opened the door, he knew something was terribly wrong.

Alannah was slumped over the table, limbs hanging awry. Quin was beside her in a moment.

"Alannah," he shouted, without any effort to hide the terror in his voice at being confronted with the very image he had just been trying to repel. "Alannah!" He reached out to shake her and almost recoiled—she was burning with fever, her skin unfathomably hot and dry to the touch.

"Alannah wake up!" he cried desperately, his heart pounding. She moaned and her eyes fluttered as she looked briefly at him. She tried to lift her head but soon collapsed back onto the tabletop, her breath coming shallow and rasping, her face pale as a shroud under the fever's touch.

Quin picked her up and carried her up the stairs, shouting for help on his way. Rupert stuck his head into the passage, eyes going wide with shock, while Mary appeared beside Quin clutching a cleaning rag, mob cap askew. At sight of her mistress, she started weeping, wailing about Alannah's imminent demise. Thinking this really wasn't the sort of response required under the circumstances, Quin sent her out with stern instructions to fetch a bucketful of cold water, several cloths and all manner of febrifuges she could find—along with a firm word that she'd best get herself under control before returning, the latter said without the least bit of tact. Mary scuttled away, sniffing, while Rupert hovered anxiously in the doorway to the bedroom, unsure what to do.

Ignoring his valet, Quin laid Alannah carefully on the bed and knelt down beside her, holding her hand with one of his own and stroking her hot cheek with the other.

"Alannah, if you can hear me, I'm here with you. I'm going to take care of you." He was almost shouting, and her eyes opened for a moment, a weak smile forming on her lips. "Everything is going to be alright!" he insisted as she lost consciousness once more.

When Mary returned, face blotchy but no longer crying, he gently stripped Alannah down to her chemise and plied her with cloths dipped in cool water, while Mary busied herself with preparing what medicaments were on hand.

Quin was horrified at how quickly Alannah's condition had deteriorated. Only an hour earlier she had been vehemently arguing with him. Now she lay before him, still and helpless, her body shrunken and burning with fever. As he stared at her in utter shock, she started shivering, despite the fact that she was hot to the touch. Quin shook himself, desperately trying to keep his panic at bay. The vivid memory of little Quinnie burning with fever and dying in his mother's arms flashed once more across his mind. Quin's throat constricted with a paralysing fear as he thought of Margaret following her infant son to the grave, although she too had been healthy and vibrant only hours before.

Clenching his fists, he shouted at Alannah's supine form, urgently wanting to do something but feeling utterly helpless. "You are not going to die!"

Mary came up behind him and gently moved him away from the bed so she could administer the concoction she had prepared; Willow bark, by the looks of it. She dribbled the liquid into Alannah's mouth and Quin hoped some of it would find its way into her stomach.

"I've sent Rupert for the doctor," Mary said quietly. Quin was about to thank her when she added, "but he might not get here in time…"

Quin turned toward her in sudden fury. "Do not utter those words in my presence again!"

Mary lowered her head and hunched her shoulders. "But…"

Quin grabbed her by the arms and started shaking her, making her teeth clack together. "Alannah is going to be fine!" he roared. "Do you hear me?"

"Master, please…please stop!"

He let go abruptly and stared at Mary as she cowered against the wall, clearly terrified of him. "I'm sorry, Mary, please forgive me. I am not myself. I don't know what…"

"It's alright, sir, you are afraid. After what happened to Margaret…" She stopped talking abruptly, gauging his reaction from the corner of her eye. "I will do what I can," she promised, before quickly heading toward the door, where Benjamin's anxious face peeked in briefly before disappearing back into the passage.

"Thank you, Mary," Quin managed to call after her, feeling absolutely wretched. He took a chair and sat beside the bed, staring forlornly at his wife. Mary came and went, trying to ply Alannah with more willow bark and methodically straightening sheets and pillows. All the while Alannah tossed and turned, only sporadically gaining consciousness, her eyes flying briefly open before closing just as quickly, with Quin unable to do anything except look on in growing hopelessness.

After a time, Mrs O'Sullivan burst into the room, startling him.

"Finnian and I just returned from Ballygawley," she said breathlessly. "We met Rupert along the way, and he told us..." She trailed off and glanced at Quin. He nodded curtly at her, and she started bustling around the room, muttering to herself.

After she left, Quin took hold of Alannah's hand. It was still blazingly hot. Quin stifled a sob and fell down on his knees beside her. He put his head on her breast and clung to her.

"Please, Alannah, please...I can't lose you."

Tears rolled down his face, landing softly on the wet fabric of her chemise. He could see the dark areolas beneath as her chest lifted slowly and shallowly for each laborious breath. He stroked her burning cheek, his throat tight, feeling as though he could barely draw breath himself.

He heard a noise behind him but made no effort to get up. Out of the corner of his eye he saw it was Mary, returning with a fresh bucket of water and some more herbs, while Denis looked on anxiously.

"My grandmother swore by the meadow-wort to fight the fever," she said as she dipped the heated cloths into the fresh water to cool and apply them yet again. "I don't know if it will help but..."

Quin stared at Mary, unseeing, feeling the overwhelming urge to give up. Finally, he forced himself to lift his head. "Thank you, Mary," he murmured, making himself stand up and lift one corner of his mouth in an attempted smile. "We must try anything you can think of. Anything I can think of." Mary nodded earnestly, but Quin doubted there was in fact a single thing he knew about fighting disease; bandits, outlaws and all manner of enemy, yes, but something he couldn't grasp? Something he couldn't even see?

"Is there any news on the arrival of Dr Ayers?" he asked, wanting to turn his attention to something more tangible.

"Rupert hasn't returned yet..." Mary looked briefly at Quin before averting her gaze. "Dr Ayers has been busy..."

Quin knew the doctor had been busy of late. All around them, people were suffering, their malnourished bodies falling prey to diseases that were spreading like wildfire through settlements. And of the many who had fallen ill, a good few had died—not only the starving poor but also those trying to help them.

Quin felt panic rising within him once more but suppressed it.

"I'm sure the good doctor will be with us shortly and that he will have Mrs Williams on her feet again in no time at all," he said with as much confidence as he could manage. Judging by Mary's downcast look, the effort, which was a poor one in any case, was largely wasted.

Waiting for the doctor, Quin and Mary did what they could for Alannah, who was now moaning and flailing her arms weakly, while periodically experiencing shaking and shivering fits. Her breath was laboured and rasping, interspersed with hoarse coughs.

Another cry escaped her lips and her face bore a grimace that clearly reflected the pain she felt, even semi-conscious as she was. Quin's throat felt tight at the sight. He brushed her cheek, disconsolate that their efforts had made no inroads into reducing the fever. The entire bed was wet, and the matrass likely ruined, but Alannah blazed as she had been doing since Quin had found her hours ago.

Quin stared at her forlornly.

Soaked through, with her sodden hair plastered to her face and neck, her limbs splaying from underneath the transparent fabric of her chemise, it came to him that she looked like a drowned corpse. The thought infuriated him, and he abruptly got up, upsetting the stool he'd been sitting on. Raging with fear, anger and frustration, he headed toward the large armoire and drove his fist into the solid oak panelling. Again. And again. And again.

Fixated on the temporary relief his violent outburst could offer, he didn't hear the door open, nor footsteps approaching. When he felt a hand on his shoulder, he spun around with the blood roaring in his ears, ready to defend himself from this new threat. His fist was about to make contact with the menace before him, when his senses suddenly returned, and he realised there was no threat at all—just Mary, cowering in front of him, begging him to stop for the second time that day.

He abruptly averted his murderous swing, nevertheless dealing Mary a glancing blow on the cheek.

"I am so sorry!" he cried, appalled. "Dear God, Mary, please forgive me. I...I am so terribly sorry. Such execrable behaviour.—Are you alright?"

"I'm alright, sir," Mary responded quietly, looking down and holding her cheek. "It's nothing...really...I'm used to much worse." She emitted a startled shriek and clapped her hands over her mouth. Startled himself, Quin simply gaped at her, unable to come up with a reasonable response.

"Er...um..." he began finally, but Mary had regained her composure.

"I came to tell you that the doctor has arrived, sir."

"Well why are we still standing here? Call him in at once!"

Mary hurried off but only needed to go as far as the door, the proclaimed doctor having arrived at the threshold of his own accord, Mrs O'Sullivan hovering behind him. Quin rushed forward to greet him, feeling hopeful for the first time since finding Alannah in the dining room that morning.

"Dr Ayers, thank you for coming." He extended a courteous bow toward the diminutive figure before him, hoping his stature was not a reflection of his medical capacity. For Dr Ayers was extremely short, his head—with the addition of the obligatory gentleman's top hat—perhaps reaching the level of Quin's shoulder. Wearing a pristine black suit, complete with a tailed coat, he did not look dressed for dealing with blood and guts, and the saving of lives. Instead, he looked like he was seeking entertainment at a gentleman's club.

"Good day, Mr Williams," the doctor said in a surprisingly deep voice for such a small man, giving Quin a brief bow, before heading toward the bed where Alannah lay. "My apologies for my late arrival." He turned his head toward Quin, who was keeping step with him. "I was held up with another patient, several actually. While the current state of affairs is no doubt good for business such as mine, I'm afraid it is rather depressing to the soul. There is often very little I can do." He sighed. Catching sight of Quin's face out of the corner of his eye, he coughed apologetically and quickly got down to the business of examining Alannah, murmuring to himself under his breath.

"Hm...yes...I'm afraid...well, I shall be honest with you, sir, and tell you it doesn't look too good."

Quin emitted a growl and narrowed his eyes at the doctor, who jumped back a step at the sight of the towering, scowling form before him.

"I assure you, Mr Williams, I shall do everything I can to treat your wife, but...I'm afraid she is far gone in her illness and may not respond to my treatment." His voice dwindled at the last, but he put a hand on Quin's arm, surprising him, and looked him in the eyes. "I meant it when I said I would do all that I can. One must always have hope."

THE HOURS THAT followed were the worst in Quin's memory. At the first, his spirits were lifted when Alannah finally opened her eyes for more than a brief moment. She looked straight at Quin and smiled, seeming to really see him for the first time and trying to lift her hand to stroke his cheek. He lifted it for her and cried out in joy at seeing her awake once more. But even as tears of relief started trickling down his cheeks, she suddenly convulsed, her eyes rolling up in her head and her burning limbs flailing as she began to shake uncontrollably.

Quin tried to still her movements in his embrace, calling her name over and over, until at last she stopped shaking and lay slumped against him. Quin held her tightly, tears running freely down his cheeks, fearing her stillness was not a sign of returning health but one of permanent separation.

"Sir...sir...I must insist you let go of Mrs Williams so I can attend to her!"

The persistent voice filtered into Quin's inner being and he realised the doctor must have been trying to extricate him from Alannah since her fit started. He slowly lowered her back onto the bed, his own arms trembling in reaction, and saw with tremendous relief that a pulse still beat in her neck—light and barely visible, but present.

Dr Ayers gave him an accusatory look and pushed him aside so he could stand next to the bed.

"A purge is what is needed," he declared, wrinkling his brow as he glanced at Mary, who was quietly sobbing in the corner, being consoled by Mrs O'Sullivan. "We must rid the body of the contagion within."

With this he withdrew a small bottle from the large pocket at the front of the apron he had donned over his fine suit and proceeded to decant several drops of the foul-smelling liquid into Alannah's unresisting mouth.

Within a few heartbeats Alannah convulsed again, bringing up the odorous liquid, before falling back limply onto the bed. Quin wasn't sure whether this was the desired effect of the ominous-sounding purge or the entirely natural reaction of someone made to swallowing something so vile.

Apparently, it was the latter.

"No. No. No," Dr Ayers muttered, mumbling something about having to clear out the bowels—which was evidently only achievable if the concoction could reach said bowels.

"Perhaps some syrup of poppy to calm the patient's nervous disposition and make her more receptive to treatment?" he murmured, clearly not addressing anyone in particular. "That will help with the discomfort as well," he added with a sideways glance at Quin, who would hardly have used the term 'discomfort' to describe the agony Alannah was clearly experiencing. The lines of pain were stamped hard on her face, even in her unconscious state.

These did appear to lessen after the doctor administered the syrup, and Quin experienced some relief—at least until Dr Ayers tried the purge again. As before, Alannah could not keep it down and the repeated heaving left her trembling and looking ghastly pale. She emitted a wail so filled with torment that it nearly broke Quin's heart.

He watched in growing anguish as Dr Ayers plied Alannah with odorous ointments and tried to get her to swallow one revolting concoction after another. All to no avail. Quin clenched his fists and could feel his throat getting tight as he watched the woman he loved fading away before his eyes. He felt utterly helpless.

With all the strength he possessed, he could do nothing to save her.

Dr Ayers looked up and his eyes locked with Quin's. The expression he saw there made Quin rage with anger and denial.

"No!" he shouted. "No! You said you would save her!"

"I said I would try."

"That isn't good enough!"

"There's nothing more I can do."

"Then leave!" Quin yelled, giving the doctor a shove toward the door. "If you can't be of any use here, then you're no longer welcome in this house!"

Dr Ayers opened his mouth to argue but evidently realised it was futile and slumped his shoulders.

"I'm sorry," he said as he peeled off the filthy apron and picked up his discarded top hat and walking stick. Mary, who had started sobbing uncontrollably, followed him to the door, seeming to want to escape herself.

Quin went back to the bed, picked up the frail body that had been his wife and sat down with her on his lap. Just so he had held her on their wedding night, promising to keep her safe, to protect her from any harm that might threaten her.

And now he could do nothing.

He held her to him, feeling the life ebb out of her, the last glimmer of hope fading with it, as he cradled her head against his shoulder and wept unashamedly, wishing he could trade places with her, that she could go on instead of him. Because he feared he did not have the strength to face this life without her, could not bear the thought of never seeing her beautiful smile again.

"Alannah. Oh, Alannah," he whispered, cradling her against him, burning with her, even as her flame was extinguishing.

He lay down with her and held her close, just as he had done on countless nights before, wanting to feel her next to him one last time.

ALANNAH WAS STROKING his face, her long hair tickling his ear lobe as she leaned over him. She kissed his mouth, and he could feel her smile as his body responded to her touch. He pulled her on top of him. She came willingly, eagerly, and he lost all sense of his surroundings, until he lay spent, with Alannah nestled close to him, gently stroking his neck.

QUIN OPENED HIS eyes with a start, realising he must have fallen asleep. Alannah was lying next to him, intertwined with him, as she had been in his dream. But she was still, lifeless. An unbearable pain cut through his heart at the knowledge that she would never stroke him so again. He could still feel the dream of her touch on his skin and grasped the hand lying on his neck.

Alannah gave a soft wail. Barely audible and filled with pain, but a sign of life.

"Alannah!" Quin gasped and rolled over to look at her face.

Her eyes opened a slit, in what seemed like a terrible effort, before closing again.

"Quin." It was barely a whisper, but Quin felt his spirits soar at hearing her voice at all.

"Mary," he yelled. "Mary, Mrs O'Sullivan, come quickly!"

The two women burst through the door within moments. They must have been in the sitting room—waiting for the instruction to prepare Alannah's body for burial, no doubt. Mrs O'Sullivan looked grim, while Mary's face was blotched with tears, her eyes swollen, expecting the worst.

"She's alive. Alannah's alive!"

Mary and Mrs O'Sullivan wore identical looks of doubt as they peered at the still form on the bed. Mary was about to protest when Alannah's eyelids flickered and her breath came out in a sigh. "Mary."

Mary's eyes popped open, and she turned toward Quin, who grinned back at her. Mrs O'Sullivan clapped her hands together.

"She is still very ill, master," Mary said softly.

Quin compressed his lips. He looked at each of the women in turn, nodding slowly.

"We must have hope."

BUT HOPE ALONE was not enough. By evening, Alannah was burning once more.

Despite his sinking spirits, Quin was nevertheless reluctant to call back Dr Ayers. While he didn't know exactly what his treatments had entailed, it seemed to Quin that Alannah's condition had worsened, not improved, during his visit.

"But you must call the doctor, sir," Mrs O'Sullivan protested at Quin's announcement that they would care for Alannah themselves. Mary nodded in agreement.

"Listen to me," Quin said, giving the women a stern look. "Have you not both spent your lives caring for others and treating all manner of ailments?"

Mrs O'Sullivan nodded reluctantly. "Well, yes sir, of course. It's what's expected of simple women, to deal with everyday complaints. But settling an upset stomach or tending a blistered hand is a simple matter. This…" She waved at the soiled sheets and the corpse-like figure upon them. "This is far beyond anything I would know how to treat." Under her breath she added, "Just like with Quinnie and Margaret…"

Quin reached for her hand and grasped it firmly, feeling the callouses of years working in the kitchen beneath his fingertips. "You did everything you could for them, that wasn't your fault." Mrs O'Sullivan briefly met his eye. "All we can do is try.—And we must!"

"But…sir," Mary objected, giving Quin an anxious look, "Mrs Williams is a lady. A lady needs a doctor!"

Quin was starting to get a little annoyed with this conversation. Standing around and talking was not likely to do Alannah any good. He turned a baleful eye on the women, stemming his hands onto his hips. "Is it not true that Dr Ayers' attentions left Alannah retching and trembling, and even weaker than before his arrival?"

"A coincidence?" Mary suggested but started looking doubtful.

"Be that as it may, he clearly did nothing to actually help her!" Quin scowled as he continued, "Now, we shall do exactly what we did before the honourable doctor arrived, and more. You"—he pointed a finger at Mary, who looked at him with big eyes—"will brew some more of your grandmother's herbs and Mrs O'Sullivan and I shall ply Alannah with cold water and wait on her hand and foot until she damned well gets better!"

With that, Quin marched toward the bed, expecting no protest from Mary or Mrs O'Sullivan, who did in fact obediently follow without another word, setting themselves to the task.

DESPITE HER INITIAL objections, Mary proved to be far more knowledgeable than she would admit—even Mrs O'Sullivan was impressed. Not only did Mary know which herbs to use for fever, she knew how to treat pain and what to do for a variety of respiratory ailments, all of which applied to her current patient.

"It's nothing, sir," she said when Quin remarked on her apparent expertise. "Nought but old wives' tales."

Old wives' tales or not, it was all they had. Quin took the slightest improvement in Alannah's condition as evidence of their success, but as the fever continued to rage, Alannah became incoherent, even delusional, calling out to her father and mother, who had been dead these many years.

In between, she had moments of absolute clarity, where she looked at Quin with the dark blue eyes of the woman he'd fallen in love with, recognising him and trying to talk to him. But she was dreadfully weak, and the fever would not let go its grip on her frail body.

"She won't be able to hold on much longer," Mary said quietly, looking down at Alannah's face as the sun peeked over the horizon with a new dawn.

Quin stared at his wife for a long moment.

Abruptly, he bent down and picked her up, making her cry out. He carried her down the stairs and into the drawing room, out the double doors onto the portico and down the lightening garden path toward the stream. The wintry morning chill bit through his thin shirt but he gave it no heed as he continued on stubbornly. Without taking off his shoes he walked into the icy water, carrying Alannah into its cold, embracing depths. The shock of it made him gasp and Alannah moaned, but he held her tightly while the freezing water swirled around them, as likely to kill them both as bring her back to life.

For the first time in a long time, he began to pray, cradling her head in one hand and pressing his forehead against hers, refusing to let her go.

Suddenly, she opened her eyes and looked straight at him, recognition dawning on her face. Quin's heart leapt at the sight.

"You are not going to die!" he commanded, making her lift one side of her mouth in an exhausted smile. She gave an almost imperceptible nod and Quin crushed her to him as his throat constricted.

They emerged from the stream a short time later, shivering in the cold air. Ignoring their dripping clothes, Quin marched back into the house with Alannah in his arms, up the stairs and into the bedroom, careless of the mess he left behind. He stripped her of the soaked chemise and wrapped her in a thick towel, then deposited her in the bed that had been freshly made in their absence. He tucked her in under the blankets and tore off his own wet clothes, glancing frequently back at the bed, waiting to see whether his prayers would be answered.

"MASTER...SIR...MR Williams, it's a miracle. The fever has broken!"

Quin jerked upright on the chair and came awake with a start. He had nodded off at Alannah's bedside. Suddenly, what Mary had said made sense to him and he jumped up and leaned over the bed. Mary was right. Alannah's skin was bathed in sweat but cool to the touch.

"God be praised," Mrs O'Sullivan exclaimed and bustled off, presumably to tell the rest of the household of her mistress' miraculous recovery.

Quin's knees gave way in relief, and he abruptly knelt down beside the bed. He stroked Alannah's damp brow and her eyes opened, dark blue pools in the soft wintery light.

"Quin," she said in a cracked voice.

"Alannah." He smiled at her but then his face crumbled. The hours of anguish overcame him, and his eyes filled with tears. He lay his head on her breast and wept, shaking in reaction to the relief of feeling her chest rise and fall underneath his ear.

"I thought I'd lost you," he whispered at last, with a fist clenching his heart at the thought of how close he'd come.

"I'm sorry," she croaked, making him lift his head and look down at her.

He laughed at the remorseful expression on her face. "You're at death's door and you're apologising to me?" His voice was filled with disbelief. "Dear God in heaven, Alannah, you are an extraordinary woman!"

She smiled in response but closed her eyes. "I'm rather tired."

He gently stroked her cheek and kissed her forehead. "Sleep. I'll watch over you, keep you safe."

She had already drifted off before he'd finished speaking and he spent a long time just looking at her, hardly able to believe she was alive. She was very pale and looked so frail he thought he'd break her if he touched her. But underneath the pallor lay a hint of blooming colour and her breath, although still rasping at times, came regular and strong. And her eyes had been clear, no longer filmed with a feverous glaze—she had been alert and responsive, the Alannah he loved more than his own life.

"Thank you, Lord," he whispered, experiencing an unexpected spark of belief that a merciful God just may exist after all.

38.

I OPENED MY eyes and stared at the ceiling, trying to recall how to move my limbs. The thought alone exhausted me, and I closed my eyes once more.

"Are you thirsty?"

An anxious face appeared before me, green eyes startling in their intensity, captivating my drifting mind.

"I never left your side," Quin murmured when I offered no response to his question.

"How long..."

"You've been sleeping for most of the day."

"Oh," was all I could manage, and I suddenly realised I was thirsty indeed, very much so.

"Water," I croaked.

Quin gently lifted my head and held a cup to my lips. When I had drunk my fill, he lowered me back down.

"Thank you."

"How do you feel?"

"I feel like...like I've awoken from an enchantment." I looked up at Quin and wrinkled my brow. "I've woken up confused and unsure who I am." I feebly twitched my fingers. "And I've woken up a weak and limp ragdoll with not the strength to lift my arm."

"I'm grateful you've woken up at all."

Quin clasped my hand, and the sound of his voice gave me an inkling of the despair he must have felt as I hovered close to death. I knew myself how close I'd come to the abyss. Only the knowledge that he needed me had given me the strength to claw my way back.

"As for the rest"—he leaned over me, face only inches from mine—"you are my wife and I love you. That's all you need to know for now." He grinned and kissed my forehead. "We can work on the rest."

OVER THE NEXT few days, Alannah slowly regained her strength. At first, she could barely hold a cup of water by herself, so weak had she become. But with her persistence and Quin's encouragement, she got a little better every day, until she finally felt strong enough to leave the bed. Not convinced she was ready yet, Quin held her firmly by the waist as she attempted to stand up, having already exhausted herself by simply manoeuvring to a sitting position at the side of the bed. He narrowed his eyes at her but didn't say anything.

"I'm ready," she said.

She tried to push herself off the bed but was still so weak that Quin had to help her to her feet. She leaned against him, breathing heavily, and he took a firmer grip on her waist. She slowly extended one foot, sliding it across the floor, unable to lift it. As she leaned into the extended foot, her knee gave way, and she would have fallen had Quin not been holding her up. He would have scolded her for idiocy, but she smiled at him, and he couldn't help smiling back at her, revelling in the simple joy she felt at being alive and able to move at all—a joy he shared wholeheartedly.

They made their laborious way around the room, stopping every few minutes for Alannah to catch her breath. By the time she declared she'd had enough exercise, her cheeks were flushed, and she was gasping for air like a landed fish. Quin picked her up and carried her back to bed, where he tucked her in and gave her strict instructions not to move another muscle for the rest of the day.

She'd fallen asleep again before he reached the door.

I WOKE UP feeling better than I had for days. And ravenously hungry.

"Is there any more of this?" I asked Mary as I used the last of the bread to mop up the remaining dribble of beef stew she'd brought me.

"Yes, mistress, a little."

She hurried off and returned with another bowlful of stew and a small loaf, before rushing to her next errand. I ate the second helping as voraciously as I had the first. I was just finishing off the last bite when Quin came through the door, grinning at sight of me.

"How are you feeling?" he asked, kissing me on the forehead before sitting down on the edge of the bed.

"Better," I said, smiling at him.

"I'm glad." He held my eyes for a moment, until a strange expression started blooming on his face, one I couldn't quite read.

"I have news," he said at last, placing a hand on my arm, making me raise a questioning brow. "Herbert Andrews is dead."

My heart lurched. "Dead?"

He nodded briefly. "Killed in prison."

"What...how...?"

"He was being held at Newgate while awaiting transportation." Quin compressed his lips. "My father wrote from London.—Andrews had just made another attempt to appeal his sentence when he met with a knife in the heart instead."

My eyes flew open. "Who...?"

"Perhaps a fellow inmate who had a grudge against him...or one of the guards..."

"One of the guards?"

Quin shrugged. "Andrews made many enemies over the years. If someone saw an opportunity..."

"I suppose." My heart had resumed its normal, steady beating by now, but I couldn't help feeling a little uneasy.

"We may never find out who did it, but I can't say I'm sorry." Quin's voice was cold. "He got what was coming to him."

I frowned as I thought about everything that had happened to us because of Herbert Andrews—Martin Doyle's attempted kidnapping of me, his release from gaol and Kieran's murder, the more recent attempt on Quin's life. And suddenly, I was overcome with a deep sense of satisfaction that the man would never be able to harm us again.

"Of course," I said, even as the feeling was replaced with guilt. Andrews was dead, after all. "Still, it's difficult to imagine...and his last days..."

"They wouldn't have been too pleasant, I expect. By all accounts, prisoners at Newgate are treated harshly, isolated from one another for weeks on end or made to perform menial and laborious tasks in complete silence.—With no reprieve in sight after six months, even Andrews himself may have welcomed an end." Quin squeezed my arm. "But don't trouble yourself with such thoughts. Even his memory isn't worth it."

I nodded and we were silent for several minutes. Finally, Quin looked at the tray still sitting on my lap.

"I see you've regained your appetite."

I started to smile at him but sobered up quickly when thoughts of all the people still starving around us flooded my mind.

"Don't worry yourself about that now," Quin said. He lifted my chin and looked into my eyes. "You focus on regaining your strength. We will deal with everything else after that."

Everything else—the famine and the sickness sweeping through the nation, and the British crown's pitiful attempts at helping its Irish people, even while being urged to greater action by an ailing Daniel O'Connell and a handful of parliamentarians. I felt tears prickling the corners of my eyes as I thought of the catastrophe surrounding us, which may have been averted by a willingness of the government to take heroic measures. With no such measures forthcoming, a frustrated O'Connell had denounced Whig policies as hopelessly inadequate—and it was a sentiment I shared.

I pushed the tray away and Quin put it aside before turning back to me and pulling me toward him. I came willingly into his warm embrace, feeling safe in his arms. I closed my eyes and leaned into him, letting go of the pretence of strength I tried to hold onto in the presence of others, feeling able to be entirely myself, bearing my weaknesses for him to see.

"My father urged us to come to England," he said after a moment, "in his letter." He loosened his hold on me so he could look at me once more. "He said we would be safer there, safer than we are here."

I took a deep breath as a flood of emotions came over me.

Quin stroked my cheek. "We'll go if you want to." His eyes flickered between mine, a look of determination on his face. He meant it—he would do as I asked.

He had given me the same choice once before. As I had done then, I contemplated my options. The baron was right, of course, we would be safer in England, away from the famine and the misery it brought with it. But as before, the choice was a simple one.

"We'll stay," I said softly. I had to swallow a sudden lump in my throat before continuing. "We are needed here."

One corner of Quin's mouth twitched in response, and we looked at each other for a long moment, our hands clasped across my lap. At last, I closed my eyes, trying not to think too far ahead.

Quin pulled me into his arms once more. "It will be alright," he whispered into my hair, stroking my back.

I tightened my arms around him but couldn't utter the same words. While I couldn't abandon the people who depended on me, the future for all of us could very well be bleak.

I searched his face, suddenly overcome with a desperate need for him. He saw it in my eyes and kissed me, deeply, crushing me to him. I responded in kind and pulled him down to the bed with me.

"Alannah, we can't do this. You're still too weak."

"I need you, Quin. Please!"

"But..." He glanced at the unlocked door, but I pulled his mouth back to mine, urging him to continue.

Finally, I felt his resolve weaken as he slowly ran his hands over me. He touched me carefully, gently, cradling my body with his, afraid to hurt me. When he looked at me, his eyes reflected the desperate fear he had felt over the last few days—and the fear he held still, that my recovery was only a temporary reprieve from our doomed fate.

"Alannah, my love, my life."

He cried out and I felt tears prickle at the corners of my eyes at my own release, at the frantic need that drove us to join in the only way we could, in a world threatening to tear us apart.

39.

"MR MURPHY."

"Eh?" The burly man in front of Quin turned toward him, his stern face changing little in appearance when he saw who had addressed him, although he did at least pull off his cap. He eyed Quin with thinly veiled impatience. Quin had come upon Mr Murphy piling turf outside his cabin, and he clearly wanted to get back to work.

"I see you've got a good store for the rest of the winter," Quin observed, pointing with his chin.

Murphy nodded, still looking grim.

"I do hope your children are well. We see Mrs Murphy up at the house of course."

"Children good," the man responded in broken English. Although his wife, Mary, could speak very good English by now, Mr Murphy was clearly content with the limited vocabulary necessary to discuss his most basic needs with his landlord.

Quin pursed his lips, contemplating how best to broach the subject that had led him to seek out Murphy at his home. Quin had told Alannah of Mary Murphy's comment regarding her husband's pugilistic habits. She had urged him to have a word with the man out of concern for Mary, but Quin had been reluctant to interfere. Although he didn't approve of such physical assault, the reality was that a man could effectively do as he liked with his wife—if Mr Murphy chose to take out his anger on Mary, there was nothing Quin could do about it. The only reason he was here at all was because Alannah had finally convinced him to think of the children, who—she had informed him with pleading eyes—may yet become victims of their father's violence, if they hadn't already.

With a suppressed sigh, Quin steeled himself.

"I sincerely hope they remain that way," he said with raised brows, giving Murphy a long look.

The man grunted as a dark flush crept up his thick neck. Although he didn't speak much English, Murphy had clearly understood what Quin was hinting at—a fact that made Quin think Alannah had been right in sending him here.

"We very much appreciate Mrs Murphy's work up at the manor," he continued, eyes still boring into Murphy's, although his tone remained pleasant. "We'd never manage without her. It would be a shame if she or one of the children should fall ill"—he took a casual step forward—"or suffer an accident."

Although Murphy was a beefy sort, he didn't come close to matching Quin in height. Having his sizeable landlord standing nose to nose with him clearly made the man uncomfortable. He took a step back, coming up against the whitewashed rubble wall of his cabin.

Quin leaned forward and placed a hand against the wall, next to Murphy's head. "How lucky your family is to have you to take care of them." He smiled, making one side of the man's upper lip twitch reflexively, in stark contrast to the murderous gleam in his eyes. He looked down and Quin stepped back.

"Well, I must be on my way, Mr Murphy," he said casually and doffed his hat. "I wish you a pleasant day."

QUIN RAN HIS hands vigorously through his hair. He'd thought confronting Robert Murphy that morning would be the most unpleasant thing he'd have to face that day, but he had been wrong.

Returning to the manor, a pile of letters had been waiting for him—none of them bearing cheerful news.

Quin's mind flitted briefly to his father and his insistence that he and Alannah leave Ireland and come to stay with him at Wadlow Cottage in London. Exceedingly tempting though the offer was, Quin had known immediately what Alannah's answer would be. But much as he agreed with her, he would give anything to change their circumstances.

He clenched his jaws as his eyes fell on the scattering of newspaper clippings Archie had sent.

Quin had felt the effects of the famine on his own land and in his own home. But Glaslearg was a country estate situated in county Tyrone in Ulster Province, a comparatively prosperous region that had been spared the worst. Elsewhere though...

The newspapers spoke of a demand for relief employment that far outstripped what was being provided, the futility of the work being done, and the insufficient and often delayed wages paid to those who did find work; of the unattainable prices commanded by merchants as the demand for food increased and supplies dwindled; of riots as those desperate for food attacked shops and governmental depots and overran towns, cities and workhouses looking for help.

There were ludicrous quotes from politicians, blaming Irish peasants for having brought the famine upon themselves by their supposed laziness, and downplaying the seriousness of the situation. The famine was described as *merciful providence*, with the head of London's Treasury, Charles Trevelyan, insisting the Irish poor needed to learn to be self-sufficient instead of relying on handouts from the government, which were to be retained only for those in direst need.

That the people in Ireland were already in dire need seemed not to have occurred to him—despite the fact that above all else, the newspapers spoke of death.

In all corners of Ireland, her people were dying, in some places in droves.

Quin picked up the letter from Mr Docherty, the elderly Ulster Scot who owned an estate not far from Glaslearg. While he had assured Quin his own situation was reasonably tolerable (which made Quin think the man hadn't entirely escaped the ravages of the famine, either), he also bore far more disturbing news, in the form of a copy of a letter from the younger Mr O'Malley, who had moved with his new bride to her family's estate in county Cork not long before.

O'Malley had described to Docherty the dreadful state of the small Cork town of Skibbereen, whose people were succumbing by the dozens to starvation and disease. With so many dying, bodies were dumped without funerals or wakes into mass graves in the churchyard, the wails of the town's remaining inhabitants following the dead into the cold ground.

Quin swallowed heavily at the images O'Malley's letter evoked, before being suddenly seized by a glowing anger at Mr Docherty for having sent it—it hadn't been meant for Quin's eyes after all! He crumpled up the sheet of paper, wishing this simple act could erase the truth of the words written upon it.

Dropping the ruined letter onto the desk, he sighed heavily, his anger evaporating as quickly as it had come, leaving him only with a lingering feeling of despair. Had he not seen O'Malley's letter, he would have seen another, written by someone else's hand, describing a different town.

There was no escaping the nightmare they found themselves in, a nightmare that had already taken tens of thousands of lives in Belgium and the Netherlands and was on the same path in Ireland.

Quin closed his eyes, wishing for a sense of peace to descend upon him, trying desperately to cling to the knowledge that there were some who were willing to help those in need—the landowners who thought as he did, who provided their tenants with food and employment, and reduced their rent; the Quakers from the Society of Friends who were providing aid especially in areas where no other relief measures were available, without attempting to convert those whom they assisted; and the aristocrats, bankers and merchants who supported the recently established British Relief Association that had started distributing funds and donations of food throughout Ireland, with contributions coming in from even the furthest reaches of the British Empire.

But while it was comforting to know he and Alannah were part of a greater effort to fight this terrible battle, Quin was morosely aware that even all of this charity was unlikely to be enough to save the doomed Irish people.

A knock at the door made Quin open his eyes and shake his head vigorously before answering.

"Come in."

The door opened and Mr Dunne came in, wearing a determined expression.

"Mr Dunne," Quin greeted him and waved him to a seat, attempting to push aside his lingering despair. "What can I do for you?"

"Sir, I..." The overseer paused, fidgeting with his hands before continuing. "I would like to express my sincere gratitude for having been allowed to work here. It has been a great privilege."

Quin was about to dismiss Dunne's compliments when he suddenly realised what the man had actually said. "What do you mean *it has been*? You're not...? Are you thinking of leaving?"

"I'm afraid I must, sir." Dunne looked briefly down at his lap. When he lifted his eyes, they were filled with eagerness, tempered with something that looked like dread. "I...I think...I think I've found her."

"You've found...you mean Miss Thompson?" Quin goggled at the overseer. "Where is she?"

"In America, sir."

"America?" Quin ran a hand tiredly over his face. With everything else going on he didn't want to have to contemplate being left without an overseer—particularly not one as competent as Mr Dunne. "You do realise it will take you weeks aboard ship to get there?"

Dunne nodded, his mouse-like face looking earnest.

"And you also realise," Quin continued in a gentle tone, "that you have no idea what you might find when you do?"

The small man inhaled deeply before responding. "I must try, sir. I...I love her still." He looked down, making Quin reach across the desk to squeeze his shoulder.

"Then you must go. Lord knows there are plenty of ships that can take you." Quin compressed his lips. Many of the struggling peasants were opting to take their chances with the dangers of a voyage across the Atlantic rather than resigning themselves to near-certain starvation on their native shores. "When will you leave?"

"As soon as I can arrange passage.—With your permission, of course, sir."

"Of course." Quin waved a hand. "How did you find her?"

"Through the new overseer at the Thompson estate." Dunne gave Quin a sideways look. "He...ah...found some of Mr Thompson's correspondence, which led me to make a few enquiries."

"Oh, you had him spy for you?" Quin asked in some amusement, experiencing a welcome lifting of his spirits at the thought of the unassuming Mr Dunne as the instigator of such surreptitious activities.

"He was only too happy to help," Dunne responded with a shrug, "having discovered for himself what a brute Thompson is." He cleared his throat, seeming to realise suddenly how blunt he was being with his employer. "I've known the man for years and, well, when I found out he was working there, and he found out what had happened between me and the Thompsons..."

"I see.—Well, I do wish you good luck Mr Dunne." Quin rose from his chair behind the desk, making the overseer rise from his. "I hope you find her...and that she is as you remember her."

"Thank you, sir. And I mean it, it has been a great honour to work for you." He grasped Quin's outstretched hand and shook it firmly.

They stood still for a moment, hands clasped but unmoving, the thoughts reflected on Dunne's face mirroring Quin's own. Mr Dunne was embarking on a journey to find the woman he loved—but both men knew the chances of him ever returning were slim.

40.

WE BADE MR Dunne farewell in early spring.

As Quin had expected, he'd had no problems booking himself passage on one of the numerous ships taking throngs of desperate Irish people across the ocean. It did, however, take a little longer to put his affairs in order before his departure—in the likely event his leave-taking would prove to be permanent. I was sad to see the overseer go but wished him well. He promised he would write, and I hoped we would soon learn he and Miss Thompson had been reunited.

I smiled at the thought, holding onto the joy it evoked, as I knew I must in the terrible times we found ourselves in—if we couldn't find joy in the little things, we would be lost.

With the smile still on my lips, I opened the door to the unused room adjoining our bedroom. Dust motes swirled in the shafts of sunlight coming in through the uncovered windows. There was no furniture, just bare walls and open space—and possibility.

I ran a hand down the front of my dress, a feeling of warmth spreading from my middle. I stood still, looking inwards, listening for the tiny heartbeat that accompanied my own.

"Alannah?"

I opened my eyes at Quin's voice. I turned and walked slowly toward him, holding his gaze, drawing him to me. Our lips met in a tender kiss, alive with untold promises.

"What are you doing here?" he asked softly, his breath tickling my ear.

"Imagining our future."

He leaned his head back to look down at me, wrinkling his brow in confusion. The corners of my mouth lifted, and his eyes suddenly widened.

"You mean...?" He glanced at my midsection and then back at my face. "I had thought...and hoped...but...oh, Alannah, is it really true?"

I nodded, tears stinging my eyes. He lifted me in his arms, swinging me around, making both of us laugh. When he put me down again his face was aglow with emotion.

He placed a hand gently on my abdomen. "I hadn't dared to believe..."

"I know."

I placed my own hand over his. Neither of us had mentioned it over the last few weeks but we had both been silently waiting, not daring to put into words the yearning that bound us—for fear of it being snatched away from us once more.

"How long...?" he asked, a smile lingering on his lips.

"About three months, I think."

Quin's smile widened into a broad grin, and he pulled me into his arms once more. He held me for a long time before stepping back. "Anything you want is yours," he declared, looking around the stark space. He suddenly stopped, though, a slightly anxious look blooming on his face. "What does one need for a baby? Have you any idea?"

I laughed and patted him on the arm. "Not much, I think. A cot for him—or her—to sleep in. A nursing chair, some shelves." I shrugged. "Some curtains wouldn't come amiss."

I started pacing the room, envisaging a nursery taking shape. As I passed by the window, a movement on the far side of the courtyard caught my eye. The small figure of a boy was walking toward the house, and I looked curiously at him, thinking he seemed familiar. It wasn't Benjamin, though, nor yet one of the tenants' children. As the boy came closer, I suddenly gasped.

"Emmett!"

Quin came to stand next to me, his brows rising high on his forehead when he, too, recognised the boy.

"What is he doing here?" he exclaimed, before turning away from the window and heading toward the door. "Rupert," he called out as he made his way to the stairs.

The valet stuck his head out of his small closet. "Sir?"

"Your brother is in the courtyard."

"My brother?" Rupert froze on the landing, his face blank as he stared after Quin.

"Emmett," I specified the brother in question, coming up next to the valet.

Based on his expression, Rupert was trying to remember whether he had any brothers at all. "Emmett?" he repeated, blinking idiotically. "My brother Emmett is here? In *Ireland*?"

I laughed and grabbed him by the hand. "Let's go see." I pulled him after me, reaching the bottom of the staircase as Quin was opening the front door, not waiting on the ceremony of Denis doing it for him. Mrs O'Sullivan and Mary poked curious heads out of the kitchen as Rupert and I clattered past.

In the courtyard, the small figure I had seen from the window above was hurrying toward the house, a wide grin on his face.

"Mr Williams," he panted, having reached Quin's side.

"Emmett, it *is* you!" Quin squeezed the boy's shoulders in greeting.

Emmett nodded. "Yes, sir. I wasn't sure if I 'ad the right place, but then I saw ye comin' out o' the house..." He trailed off, looking up in awe. Spotting Rupert and me behind Quin, he beamed, dropped the small bag he'd been carrying and hurled himself at his brother. "Rupert!"

"Oof." Rupert staggered under the onslaught but was soon grinning as much as Emmett as the two of them clung to each other.

"What are you doing here, mite?" Rupert asked when Emmett finally let go of him.

"I've come t' stay wi' you." Looking adoringly at his brother, he suddenly paused, glancing sideways at Quin. "Um...ah...if ye'll let me...sir?"

"Well...certainly, although..."

"What about mum and dad?" Rupert interrupted, clearly a little flustered by his brother's unannounced arrival. He stemmed his hands on his hips and looked down at Emmett.

"They know I'm 'ere!" Emmett insisted, nodding vigorously.

Rupert narrowed his eyes and Quin raised one brow, probably remembering—as I was—Emmett's attempted escape from London the previous summer.

"But, but...how? Why...? How did you...?" Rupert took a deep breath and opened his mouth to try again, making Emmett square his shoulders in preparation for the onslaught of questions. Much to his evident relief, the boy was rescued from the impending inquisition by the appearance of Mrs O'Sullivan and Mary, who started clucking over our visitor like a pair of mother hens.

Emmett was soon being towed into the house, the cook commenting on his uncanny resemblance to Rupert—a fact that was no doubt contributing to her taking him immediately under her wing, being unable to resist his rosy cheeks.

I looked at Quin in some amusement. He shrugged and offered me his arm. Rupert followed us inside and by mutual agreement we turned toward the kitchen.

"I'm Emmett," Rupert's brother was saying as we entered.

He stood up straighter and lifted his chin, sticking out a hand to Benjamin, who was sitting at the table in front of an enormous piece of cake—which explained why he hadn't followed Mrs O'Sullivan and Mary outside.

Emmett eyed the piece of cake and licked his lips, making Mrs O'Sullivan hasten to serve him an equally generous portion. He sat down at the table and took a bite, his eyes closing in bliss as he swallowed.

I suddenly had to swallow heavily myself as I felt bile rise in my throat. I rushed past the bewildered butler, out of the kitchen and across the entrance hall, making it outside just in time.

Wiping my mouth a moment later, I leaned against the wall.

"Are you alright?"

I turned toward Quin and smiled weakly.

"I'm fine. I'm sure it's just..." I placed a hand on my abdomen, making the concerned look on Quin's face give way to unashamed delight.

"Mistress...is it true?" Mary's beaming face appeared next to Quin, her eyes on my midsection, where my hand still rested. "Could it be, after all this time?"

I smiled. "Yes, Mary, it's true.—I'm with child."

Her excited exclamation made the rest of the staff rush outside for the second time that afternoon, only to erupt into a cascade of well-wishes after hearing the news.

Laughing, with tears of joy rolling down my face, I caught Quin's eyes. He took my hand and squeezed it lightly.

Whatever else the future may hold for us, we had something to look forward to—and that was enough.

THE END

Thank you for reading *Beneath the Darkening Clouds*!
If you enjoyed this book, please consider posting a short review on Amazon or Goodreads. It takes me about two years to write one of these books and a little encouragement from my readers goes a long way toward keeping me motivated! Reviews and telling your friends about the book also help to get the word out. For an independent author, this is vital to the book's success.
Thank you for your help!

The gripping prequel to
Beneath the Darkening Clouds

Under the Emerald Sky

He's come to Ireland to escape his past. She's trying to run from her future.

Ireland, 1843. Irishwoman Alannah O'Neill is feeling trapped. Under the thumb of her controlling brother she finds herself contemplating the meaninglessness of her existence. When the Englishman Quinton Williams arrives on the neighbouring estate, Alannah feels drawn to him. Knowing that her brother hates the English for their role in Ireland's bloody history, Alannah keeps her growing relationship with Quin a secret. But it's a secret that can't be kept for long from those who dream of ridding Ireland of her English oppressors.

Among the stark contrasts that separate the rich few from the plentiful poor, Under the Emerald Sky is a tale of love and betrayal in a land teetering on the brink of disaster – the Great Famine that would forever change the course of Ireland's history.

"*Under the Emerald Sky* reaches another level in storytelling, the kind where the characters remain with you long after you have closed the book"
THE HISTORICAL FICTION COMPANY

"Intelligently plotted and atmospheric"
READERS' FAVORITE

Book Three in the *Irish Fortune Series*

Amid the Oncoming Storm

As the nation starves and resentment grows, can the people on their land be trusted?

It's the spring of 1847 and there's much for Quin and Alannah to look forward to. And yet, the previous years' hardships have left their mark. The famine that's had Ireland in its grasp for the past two seasons continues to rage unabated, with hunger and disease sweeping across the land. As thousands lie dying, dissension spreads among the Irish people, the British government's carelessness and their landlords' ruthlessness breeding hatred in the poor and the oppressed.

With suffering all around them Quin and Alannah hold onto what happiness they're able to. But can they trust the people living on their estate?

Set amongst the anguish of Ireland's most devastating time in history, Amid the Oncoming Storm is a story of hope and resilience in a land struggling to rise from the depths of despair.

Author's notes

HISTORICAL DETAILS INCLUDED in this book are based on extensive research and are portrayed as accurately as such a thing is possible when obtaining information from historical records, scientific papers, expert opinions and the like. Political figures and historical events, as well as existing scientific knowledge mentioned are based on this research. I have made every attempt to provide a balanced view wherever possible; for example, while it is well known that the British government made the decision not to stop food exports from Ireland during the Famine and that this was supported by many wealthy people on either side of the Irish Sea, it is perhaps a lesser-known fact that there were also many individuals and organisations who did try to help where they could, sometimes to their own detriment. The political situation leading up to and during the Great Famine is a complex one, and naturally not all aspects thereof can be included in a single novel, or even a series, which is meant foremost to entertain (although I do hope it also informs). For a succinct look at the situation in Ireland during the Famine I can recommend:

Gray, Peter. The Irish Famine (New Horizons). Thames & Hudson Ltd, London, 1995.

Acknowledgments

THE AUTHOR WOULD like to thank:

Members of the Historical Fiction Club for their vast knowledge of all things historical fiction and for their ongoing encouragement, not just of me but many other writers wanting to get their stories out there; Dee Marley at White Rabbit Arts for the stunning cover and unending enthusiasm for my book; my parents and extended family, as well as friends far and wide, for their unerring support of my writing; my dearest friend, Nikola Staab, for the endless discussions, useful suggestions and feedback, and for saying 'I want to know what happens next?!' after finishing the book; my children, for always believing in me; and my husband, for his unfailing support and encouragement, even when having to listen to me harp on about the same thing for the dozenth time when he really doesn't like repetition (!); I couldn't have finished this book without you.

About the author

JULIANE WEBER IS a scientist turned historical fiction writer, and author of the Irish Fortune Series. Her stories take readers on action-packed romantic adventures amid the captivating scenery and folklore of 19th century Ireland. The first book in the series, *Under the Emerald Sky*, was awarded bronze medals in The Coffee Pot Book Club 2022 Book of the Year Contest and The Historical Fiction Company 2021 Book of the Year Contest. The second book in the series, *Beneath the Darkening Clouds*, was selected as an Editors' Choice title by the Historical Novel Society and was awarded a bronze medal in The Historical Fiction Company 2022 Book the Year Contest.

Juliane spent most of her life in South Africa, but now lives with her husband and two sons in Hamelin, Germany, the town made famous by the story of the Pied Piper.

www.julianeweber.com

https://www.facebook.com/JulianeWeberAuthor

https://x.com/Writer_JW

Printed in Great Britain
by Amazon